DOPE, INC.,
Britain's Opium War
Against the World

by the Editors of
Executive Intelligence Review

Dope, Inc.:
Britain's Opium War Against the World

Fourth Edition, Revised and Updated
© 2010 by Executive Intelligence Review
Print on Demand edition, February 2021
Published by ProgressivePress.com,
info@progressivepress.com

ISBN: 1-61577-285-5, EAN: 978-1-61577-285-8

Length 130,000 words on 328 pages

TOPICS: Lyndon LaRouche's war on drugs; British Empire role in the drug trade, since the Opium Wars on China: the HongShang Bank, the Bronfmans and Prohibition, and the rise of Organized Crime in the U.S.
Financial derivatives; drug-money laundering; decriminalization; George Soros's funding of drugs; the Afghan opium trade; the Colombian drug cartel; the relationship between drugs and terrorism. Wall St. and the drug trade; medical marijuana; the East India company; IMF toleration of drugs; Russia targeted by Dope, Inc.; the increases in the cocaine, heroin, amphetamine, and marijuana trades to over $600 billion a year.

Library of Congress
Cataloging in Publication Information for the Third edition
LC Control No.: 91078004
Main Title: Dope, Inc.: the book that drove Henry Kissinger crazy /
    by the editors of Executive intelligence review.
Published/Created: Washington, D.C.: EIR, 1992.
Related Titles: Executive intelligence review
Description: xiii, 697 p.: ill., maps; 21 cm.
ISBN: 0943235022
Subjects: Drug traffic, Drug control, Drug abuse and crime, Conspiracies.
LC Classification: HV5801.D544 1992
Dewey Class No.: 64.1/77/0941 20

To Stop Terrorism- Shut Down Dope, Inc.

December 2001

A Special Report, including reprints from the Third Edition of the underground bestseller **Dope, Inc.,** and from **Executive Intelligence Review** magazine, as well as updated material on the scope and size of the international illegal drug-trafficking empire known as 'Dope, Inc.'

Photo Credits: Cover (New York Stock Exchange head Richard Grasso embracing narcoterrorist FARC 'moneyman' Raúl Reyes) Colombian government; Lyndon LaRouche: EIRNS/Stuart Lewis; Marijuana eradication in Virginia: Virginia State Police; Henry Kissinger: EIRNS/Stuart Lewis; HongShang Bank: EIRNS/Stuart Lewis; Chase Manhattan: EIRNS/Stuart Lewis; Resorts International: EIRNS; William Weld: EIRNS/Stuart Lewis; McGeorge Bundy: EIRNS/Stuart Lewis; Lee Harvey Oswald: Courtesy New Orleans District Attorney; Big Ben in London: EIRNS/Ian Levit; George Soros: EIRNS/Stuart Lewis.

The following individuals contributed to this report; Jeffrey Steinberg, Dennis Small, Valerie Rush, Joseph Brewda, Richard Freeman, Roger Moore and Christine Bierre.

Contents

Introduction

- Today's Opium War -

The LaRouche political movement literally "wrote the book" on the British imperial policy of the Opium War, a policy which led to the death of at least 20 million Chinese in the 19th Century, when the Empire imposed its policy of free trade in deadly drugs on China, through force of arms. As the underground bestseller {Dope, Inc.} laid out, despite treaty arrangements in the early 1920s, which allegedly banned trade in dangerous narcotic drugs like opium and heroin, major British banking networks, linked to the monarchy, have maintained their deadly trade to the present day.

Equally importantly, LaRouche laid out a war strategy against these death merchants that would work.

More than 30 years have now passed since the first edition of Dope, Inc. was published, and the tragic truth is that the global drug behemoth is winning their war. Every nation in the world is under threat from the drug trade, and its associated terror and organized crime networks. Civilization itself hangs in the balance, as it did in the Chinese opium wars, but this time on a global scale.

There could not be a more important time to reprint the core story of {Dope, Inc.}, which is what you have in your hands.

There are three reasons why the war against Britain's dope trade lies at the heart of the world strategic situation today.

First, the British-controlled dope trade plays the decisive role in providing the financing for the world's leading terrorist entities. From Afghanistan's Taliban, to the Chechen rebels, to the genocidal FARC guerrillas of Colombia--just to name a few--the illicit drug trade buys the weapons, the officials, and the other needed material to facilitate the wars against sovereign nation-states. It has been consistently documented that these drug networks have more resources at their disposal than the targetted governments themselves.

There is no way to defeat terrorist groups, without eliminating their source of income: the highly lucrative drug trade.

Second, the British-controlled drug-money flows represent the most significant support for the bankrupt world financial system. According to the most recent estimates available from the United Nations Office on Drugs and Crime, in 2008, the proceeds from the illicit drug trade amounted to at least $800 billion--nigh onto a trillion. This is an income stream based on putting huge amounts of drugs on a growing market.

Much of these drug-money flows operate "offshore," in locations such as the Cayman Islands, Isle of Man, and other unregulated (largely British protectorate) centers. There they enter a world financial system which, through usury, gambling, and other kinds of speculation, turns them into trillions more in financial obligations, now sucking the blood out of the dwindling real physical economy. Today, the top anti-drug officer of the United Nations has warned that the only source of free capital in the global banking system is the proceeds of the illegal drug trade.

To bankrupt the oppressive British imperial monetary system--a prerequisite for putting a credit system for economic reconstruction into place--eliminating the drug trade is a number one priority.

But it is the third reason for wiping out the British Empire's illicit drug trade which speaks directly to the needs of humanity at this time in history: the urgent task of reasserting the identity of mankind, as the creative species responsible for developing our universe for the future.

The British Empire never justified its assertion of its "right" to trade in mind-destroying drugs simply because it was a means of making money, or even of maintaining power. The real reason behind their drug-pushing was to {degrade} the human race to the level of animals that can be herded, and culled; to literally rob human beings of their minds, and of futures worthy of an ennobled mankind. They have done the same by taking over our education systems with positivism, and by turning our economy into a degraded "service" sector. But none of this works, unless they destroy the human quality of mind.

Just as the British East India company used opium as a means of breaking the will of the Chinese people to resist British neo-colonial looting, the goal of today's Dope, Inc. barons is to sap all nation states, emphatically including the United States, of the will to resist the horrors of a New Dark Age, which are the pending lawful result of the collapse of today's hopelessly bankrupt financial system.

Consider the following candid remarks, speaking for London's Dope, Inc. delivered by the late Aldous Huxley, at a lecture at the California Medical School in San Francisco, in the early 1960s, and then think carefully about the book you are about to read.

"There will be in the next generation or so a pharmacological method of making people love their servitude and producing dictatorship without tears, so to speak. Producing a kind of painless concentration camp for entire societies, so that people will, in fact, have their liberties taken away from them but will rather enjoy it, because they will be distracted from any desire to rebel--by propaganda, or brainwashing, or brainwashing enhanced by pharmacological methods. And this seems to be the final revolution."

--The Editors
www.larouchepub.com
April 6, 2010

Preface

Whatever the world really thinks about that culprit known as Osama bin Laden, the real threat to civilization is chiefly a product of the way in which leading and other governments, including the government of the U.S.A., promoted and used terrorism, political assassinations, and other expressions of "special" or "irregular" warfare during the age of nuclear weapons. To understand the importance of shutting down international money-laundering can be summed up in three points, as follows.

1. The ability to deploy, but deny the relevant government's role in deploying such methods of special warfare, has depended to an increasing degree on various forms of "money-laundering." A major role has been played by trafficking in drugs, such as marijuana, cocaine, and opium, and in the proceeds of illegal or quasi-legal weapons-trafficking.

2. The launching of such forms of state-directed irregular warfare, by Zbigniew Brzezinski, during the late 1970s, is an outstanding example of large-scale warfare fought with emphasis on funding through drug/weapons-trafficking. The softness of elements of the U.S. government toward operations such as those of "drug legalizer" George Soros, has been a crucial part of the support given to international terrorism through use of dirty-money channels.

3. The third essential element in the logistics of international terrorism, is the use of exotic financial channels, such as the notorious Cayman Islands conduit, junk-bond and related sorts of corporate takeovers and mergers, and the biggest money-laundering channel of them all, the international financial-derivatives racket.

Democratic Presidential pre-candidate Lyndon H.LaRouche, Jr.

If all three of those type of operations are shut down, the ability to deploy forms of irregular warfare such as international terrorism, will be greatly crippled. Without shutting down all three of these types of channels, no effective blocking of international terrorism were possible.

This report summarizes both our investigations of this side of the money-laundering racket over recent decades, and important updates on recent developments which you should be taking into account in our effort to shut this thing down.

-Lyndon H. LaRouche, Jr.

November 26, 2001

1. LaRouche's War Plan Against the Drug Traffic

The Drug Traffic for the Western Hemisphere

This speech by Lyndon H. LaRouche, Jr. was read at an antidrug conference in Mexico City, on March 9, 1985. In it, LaRouche presented his now-famous 15-point warplan for a War on Drugs.

Distinguished members of this conference! I take this opportunity to communicate my great respect for the President of Mexico, and to acknowledge the debt we all owe to those hundreds of soldiers of the Republic who have already lost their lives fighting against the international drug traffickers.

Not long after his first inauguration in 1981, President Ronald Reagan adopted the kind of policy which my associates and I had been recommending since 1978, a War on Drugs. Since the President's second inauguration, this past January, he has escalated his commitment to fighting and winning that War against Drugs. Naturally, some influential persons and institutions inside the United States, are not in sympathy with the President's War on Drugs; but, the President is stubbornly determined to win the War on Drugs, and there are many in our government who are in enthusiastic support of the President's policy.

It is clear to the governments fighting the international drug traffickers, that the drug traffic could never be defeated if each of our nations tried to fight this evil independently of the other nations of this Hemisphere. If the drug traffickers' laboratories are shut down in Colombia, new laboratories open up in Brazil. If the route into Florida and Georgia is attacked heavily enough, the drug traffickers reopen routes into California, through Belize and Mexico. If Mexico shuts down drug routes through its territory, the drug traffickers will use Pacific routes into the U.S. States of Washington and Oregon, through the marijuana traffickers of Hawaii.

The greatest political threat to democracy in Venezuela, Colombia, Peru, and other countries, is the use of the billions of revenues held by the drug traffickers to fund terrorist armies, and to bring corrupted military officers into right-wing coup plots directed by former officials of the Nazi regime of Germany. The ability of governments to resist these bloody threats is undermined by the increase of the number of officials of governments, political parties, and private institutions, who are bribed by the drug traffickers. It is impossible to break the ominously increasing political power of the drug traffickers in Mexico, Colombia, Venezuela, and other countries, without capturing the billions of dollars of drug revenues run through corrupt banking institutions.

Without help of closer cooperation between the United States, Mexico, Colombia, Venezuela, and other nations of this Hemisphere, neither the United

States nor any of the other republics could defeat the monstrously powerful complex of criminal, financial, and political forces who are behind the international drug traffic. The purpose of my remarks today, is to outline to you a proposed warplan, for cooperative action against the international drug traffickers, by the governments of this Hemisphere committed to that action.

Before I outline that proposed warplan itself, it is useful, and perhaps necessary, that I identify briefly my qualifications in this connection.

Since 1975, I have become an increasingly controversial public figure internationally. I became controversial, originally, because of a campaign I launched in April 1975, for reforms of the international monetary system consistent with high rates of capital-goods exports from industrialized nations essential to economic progress among the developing nations. As one of the most powerful bankers in Europe said a little over a year ago, "LaRouche's plan for monetary reform would work, but we don't like it much." Since spring 1982, I have come under increasingly violent attack by the Soviet government for my part in proposing the Strategic Defense Initiative which President Reagan announced on March 23, 1983. The most violent attacks upon me have been launched since May 1978, because of my demand that a War on Drugs be launched by all civilized nations, and because of the work of my associates in exposing the powerful financial interests of Europe, Asia, and the Americas who were collecting the major portion of the hundreds of billions of dollars gained by the international drug traffic.

My part in the War against Drugs began during the summer of 1977, as an indirect result of my being on the same Baader-Meinhof assassination list with two West Germany figures, Juergen Ponto of the Dresdner Bank and Hanns-Martin Schleyer of the Mercedes-Benz interests. To keep me alive, my associates retained the expert services of Colonel Mitchell WerBell; the specialists associated with me in our publishing activities consulted with Colonel WerBell and other specialists on the nature of the three-way connection among the drug traffic, international terrorism, and certain wicked and politically powerful financial interests. With indispensable help from law enforcement officials of many nations, my associates in 1978 produced the famous textbook on the War against Drugs, *Dope, Inc.*

It was the publication of *Dope, Inc.* which caused the beginning of violent attacks upon me by the Heritage Foundation and by business associates of Robert Vesco, in May 1978. Most of the attacks upon me and my associates in the U.S., European, and Caribbean television and news media, from 1978 to the most recent weeks, are directed by persons and agencies which are proven members or political allies of the international drug traffickers, or simply corrupt elements of political parties and governments under the control of the drug-trafficking interests.

At the same time that the drug traffickers attack me and my associates so violently, the law enforcement and other agencies of governments and private institutions, have recognized that the publications with which I am associated will publish the truth about the drug problem when even most of the major news media not controlled by the drug lobby are afraid to do so. With assistance of information reported to us by law enforcement and other agencies of concerned governments in many parts of the world, the specialists associated with my publication, the

Executive Intelligence Review, have become leading experts in the investigation of the international drug-trafficking and its connections to finance and terrorism. Also, over the past seven years, experience has shown that investigation of the source of the lies published against me and my activities, in various parts of the world, is usually a part or a political ally of the drug traffic. Investigation of the sources of such attacks, has uncovered information concerning the drug traffic and international terrorism, which has proven helpful to law enforcement agencies in various governments.

Also, through my own work, and that of my collaborators, in designing a proposed strategic ballistic missile defense, my attention has been drawn to existing kinds of military capabilities which represent exactly the kinds of technology we need for detecting and destroying the production, processing and transportation of marijuana, cocaine, and opiates. The republics of the Americas possess the technology needed to locate and to confirm sites used for growing and processing these crops, to monitor routes used for transport of these drugs, and to destroy quickly and mercilessly the vulnerable major elements of these facilities and activities.

That indicates the nature of my expert qualifications in this subject. Now, I outline to you my proposed warplan for our war against drugs.

1. What we are fighting, is not only the effects of the use of these drugs on their victims. The international drug traffic has become an evil and powerful government in its own right. It represents today a financial, political, and military power greater than that of entire nations within the Americas. It is a government which is making war against civilized nations, a government upon which we must declare war, a war which we must fight with the weapons of war, and a war which we must win in the same spirit the United States fought for the unconditional defeat of Nazism between 1941 and 1945. Law enforcement methods, by themselves, will fail; even joint law enforcement efforts by the nations bordering the Caribbean would fail. The nations Central and South America will each and all either fall under bloody, Nazi-like dictatorships, or will be destroyed through more or less perpetual civil war, unless the international drug traffic's invasion of this Hemisphere is crushed by the methods and weapons of war.

2. Law enforcement methods must support the military side of the war on drugs. The mandate given to law enforcement forces deployed in support of this war, must be the principle that collaboration with the drug traffic or with the financier or political forces of the international drug traffickers, is treason in time of war.

3. (a)   Any person caught in trafficking of drugs, is to be classed as either a traitor in time of war, or as the foreign spy of an enemy power.

    (b)   Any person purchasing unlawful substances, or advocating the legalization of traffic in such substances, or advocating leniency in anti-drug military or law enforcement policy toward the production or trafficking in drugs, is guilty of the crime of giving aid and comfort to the enemy in time of war.

A treaty of alliance for conduct of war, should be established between the United States and the governments of Ibero-American states which join the War on Drugs alliance to which the President of Mexico has subscribed. Other states should be encouraged to join that military alliance.

4. Under the auspices of this treaty, provisions for actions of a joint military command should be elaborated. These provisions should define principles of common action, to the effect that necessary forms of joint military and law enforcement action do not subvert the national sovereignty of any of the allied nations on whose territory military operations are conducted. These provisions should include the following:

(a) The establishment of bilateral military task forces, pairwise, among the allied nations.

(b) The establishment of a Common Command, assigned to provide specified classes of assistance, as such may be requested by designated agencies of either any of the member states, or of the bilateral command of any two states.

(c) Under the Common Command, there should be established a central anti-drug intelligence agency, operating in the mode of the intelligence and planning function of a military general staff, and providing the functions of a combat warroom.

(d) Rules governing the activities of foreign nationals assigned to provide technical advice and services on the sovereign territory of members of the alliance.

5. In general, insofar as each member nation has the means to do so, military and related actions of warfare against targets of the War on Drugs, should be conducted by assigned forces of the nation on whose territory the action occurs. It were preferred, where practicable, to provide the member nation essential supplementary equipment and support personnel, rather than have foreign technical-assistance personnel engaged in combat-functions. Insofar as possible:

(a) Combat military-type functions of foreign personnel supplied should be restricted to operation of detection systems, and to operation of certain types of aircraft and antiaircraft systems provided to supplement the capabilities of national forces; and

(b) Reasonable extension of intelligence technical advice and services supplied as allied personnel to appropriate elements of field-operations.

6. Technologies appropriate to detection and confirmation of growing, processing, and transport of drugs, including satellite-based and aircraft-based systems of detection, should be supplied with assistance of the United States. As soon as the growing of a relevant crop is confirmed for any area, military airborne assault should be deployed immediately for the destruction of that crop, and military groundforces with close air-support deployed to inspect the same area and to conduct such supplementary operations as may be required. The object is to eliminate every field of marijuana, opium, and cocaine, in the Americas, excepting those fields properly licensed by governments.

7. With aid of the same technologies, processing centers must be detected and confirmed, and each destroyed promptly in the same manner as fields growing relevant crops.

8. Borders among the allied nations, and borders with other nations, must be virtually hermetically sealed against drug traffic across borders. All unlogged aircraft flying across borders or across the Caribbean waters, which fail to land according to instructions, are to be shot down by military action. A thorough search of all sea, truck, rail, and other transport, including inbound container traffic, is to be effected at all borders and other points of customs inspection. Massive concentration with aid of military forces must be made in border-crossing areas, and along relevant arteries of internal highway and water-borne transport.

9. A system of total regulation of financial institutions, to the effect of detecting deposits, outbound transfers, and inbound transfers of funds, which might be reasonably suspected of being funds secured from drug-trafficking, must be established and maintained.

10 All real estate, business enterprises, financial institutions, and personal funds, shown to be employed in the growing, processing, transport, or sale of unlawful drugs, should be taken into military custody immediately, and confiscated in the manner of military actions in time of war. All businsss and ownership records of entities used by the drug traffickers, and all persons associated with operations and ownership of such entities should be classed either as suspects or material witnesses.

11. The primary objective of the War on Drugs, is military in nature: to destroy the enemy quasi-state, the international drug-trafficking interest, by destroying or confiscating that quasi-state's economic and financial resources, by disbanding business and political associations associated with the drug-trafficking interest, by confiscating the wealth accumulated through complicity with the drug trafficker's operations, and by detaining, as "prisoners of war" or as traitors or spies, all persons aiding the drug-trafficking interest.

12. Special attention should be concentrated on those banks, insurance enterprises, and other business institutions which are in fact elements of an international financial cartel coordinating the flow of hundreds of billions annually of revenues from the international drug traffic. Such entities should be classed as outlaws according to the "crimes against humanity" doctrine elaborated at the postwar Nuremberg Tribunal, and all business relations with such entities should be prohibited according to the terms of prohibition against trading with the enemy in time of war.

13. The conduct of the War on Drugs within the Americas has two general phases. The first object is to eradicate all unlicensed growing of marijuana, opium, and cocaine within the Americas, and to destroy at the same time all principal conduits within the Hemisphere for import and distribution of drugs from major drugproducing regions of other parts of the world. These other areas are, in present order of rank:

(a)   The Southeast Asia Golden Triangle, still the major and growing source of opium and its derivatives;
(b)   The Golden Crescent, which is a much-smaller producer than the Golden Triangle, but which has growing importance as a channel for conduiting Golden Triangle opium into the Mediterranean drug-conduits;
(c)   The recently rapid revival of opium production in southern India and Sri Lanka, a revival of the old British East India Company opium production;
(d)   The increase of production of drugs in parts of Africa. Once all significant production of drugs in the Americas is exterminated, the War on Drugs enters a second phase, in which the War concentrates on combatting the conduiting of drugs from sources outside the Hemisphere.

14. One of the worst problems we continue to face in combatting drug-trafficking, especially since political developments of the 1977 -1981 period, is the increasing corruption of governmental agencies and personnel, as well as influential political factions, by politically powerful financial interests associated with either the drug-trafficking as such, or powerful financial and business interests associated with conduiting the revenues of the drug-trafficking. For this and related reasons, ordinary law enforcement methods of combatting the drug traffic fail. In addition to corruption of governmental agencies, the drug traffickers are protected by the growing of powerful groups which advocate either legalization of the drug traffic, or which campaign more or less efficiently to prevent effective forms of enforcement of laws against the usage and trafficking in drugs. Investigation has shown that the associations engaged in such advocacy are political arms of the financial interests associated with the conduiting of revenues from the drug traffic, and that they are therefore to be treated in the manner Nazi sympathizer operations were treated in the United States during World War II.

15. The War on Drugs should include agreed provisions for allotment of confiscated billions of dollars of assets of the drug-trafficking interests to beneficial purposes of economic development, in basic economic infrastructure, agriculture, and goods-producing industry. These measures should apply the right of sovereign states to taking title of the foreign as well as domestic holdings of their nationals, respecting the lawful obligations of those nationals to the state. The fact that ill-gotten gains are transferred to accounts in foreign banks, or real estate holdings in foreign nations, does not place those holdings beyond reach of recovery by the state of that national.

On the issue of the international drug traffic, all honorable governments of Central and South America share a common purpose and avowed common interest with the government of the United States. By fighting this necessary war, as allies, we may reasonably hope to improve greatly the cooperation among the allies, in many important matters beyond the immediate issue of this war itself. Whenever allies join, as comrades-in-arms, to fight a great evil, this often proves itself the best way to promote a sense of common interest and common purpose in other matters. Many difficulties among the states of this hemisphere, which have resisted cooperative efforts at solution, should begin to become solvable, as we experience the comradeship of the War on Drugs.

2. Britain's Dope, Inc.: Marker for Humanity's New Dark Age

Britain's Dope, Inc.: Marker for Humanity's New Dark Age

Before you start reading this report, I would like you to look closely, again, at the photograph printed on the cover of this magazine. It is a haunting picture of a young Peruvian girl, chewing coca leaves—hungry, exhausted, frightened, with no hope for the future, yet crying out to the heavens for justice. There are millions like her all around the world—from Peru and Bolivia, to Afghanistan and Nigeria, to the inner city streets and the suburbs of the United States—all victims of Dope, Inc., the international drug cartel headquartered in London, as it has been for over a century.

This young girl is the face of the New Dark Age towards which humanity is careening, should we fail to enact Lyndon LaRouche's policies to dismantle Dope, Inc., and to place the current global financial system, which created it, into bankruptcy reorganization. And if that battle is lost, then those haunting images of millions will become, literally, *billions*.

There are a number of pressing reasons why *EIR* decided to research and publish this in-depth study of Dope, Inc. *now*, in the first weeks of the new Obama Administration in Washington, nearly 13 years after our last systematic report on the subject: "Britain's Dope, Inc. Grows to a $521 Billion Business" (*EIR*, July 26, 1996).

One reason is the fact that the global financial system is imploding under its own cancerous weight, and Dope, Inc. is moving in to take over the entire world economy. On Jan. 28, Lyndon LaRouche warned: "This is Doomsday Time. The world's available money supply is tied largely to the attempted bailout of financial institutions, and you've got a shortage of money, of any kind of credit, building up rapidly into catastrophic levels in every other area. Now, the argument is that you have to be good to the drug pushers, because they are the only ones who are supplying the loose cash with this situation presently, in which the world money supply is collapsing and the drug supply of money is increasing."

A second reason is that the British drive for drug legalization is rapidly accelerating, spearheaded by the Nazi-trained mega-speculator George Soros. Soros and his legions are beating the drums for "decriminalization," "medical marijuana," and so-called "harm reduction strategies," in the United States, South America, and around the world. They have placed particular focus on the upcoming special ten-year review by the United Nations Commission on Narcotic Drugs, which will meet in Vienna, Austria, March 11-20, 2009, where London's legalizers hope to induce the world community to take steps towards legalization by discussing "medical marijuana," by endorsing the "harm reduction" sophistry as an alternative to actually stopping drugs, and even by removing coca from the list of prohibited substances. Their basic argument is that the war on drugs simply can't be won, so we should admit defeat and throw in the towel.

**This Peruvian girl was featured on
the cover of EIR's, Feb. 27, 2009 issue.**

To which LaRouche responded on Jan. 19: "The only reason we have a drug problem is because governments don't want to take it away. People say, 'Well, you can't solve the problem.' What do you mean you can't solve the problem?! We have the technological means to detect everything in fine detail, to find all of this stuff; we know how to develop methods for solving the problem. They choose not to do it! That's the reason—it's the *only* reason. Because you have a *system* which is doing it. You have to shut down the *system*."

A third urgent consideration for publishing this study now, is the fact that the United States is in danger of stumbling into a blunder of strategic proportions, by sending tens of thousands of additional troops to Afghanistan to "fight the insurgency," a fool's errand concocted in London. "There is no hope for Afghanistan or Pakistan, so long as the drug trade is allowed to flourish," LaRouche stated on Jan. 19. "The most direct way to shut down that trade, and establish the necessary conditions for a viable policy for South and Central Asia, is to first eliminate George Soros. Shut down his offshore operations, remove him from any access to the American political process. Cart him off to jail. Then, come and talk to me about an appropriate strategy for bringing stability and prosperity to Afghanistan and Pakistan.

"George Soros is so pivotal to the British opium war operations," LaRouche added, "whether in Afghanistan/Pakistan, or in Mexico and other parts of the Western Hemisphere, that no victory is possible in either of these areas, so long as Soros is allowed to operate."

But behind each of these considerations, there is a single underlying reality: *That the drug trade is the marker of humanity's descent into a New Dark Age.* The British Empire is wielding Dope, Inc., today, just as it waged its Opium War against China in the 19th Century, with an eye towards menticide and the bestialization of the entire planet's population.

That coming Dark Age can already be seen in the shocking way Afghanistan has been transformed into a giant opium- and heroin-producing machine, with production soaring 280% over the last four years—a dynamic not seen, according to one frightening UN report, since the Opium War.

It can be seen in the horrific violence which the drug gangs have unleashed in Mexico, including more than 5,000 people murdered in 2008, and countless cases of bestial beheadings and ritual torture of competing narcos and of anti-drug police chiefs and army generals alike.

It can be seen in the fact that millions of peasants in drug-producing countries, such as Afghanistan or Bolivia, have become de facto work slaves of the cartels, since the collapsing world economy provides them and their families no source of simple survival, other than the drug economy.

It can be seen in the uncharted, huge rise of global consumption of high-potency, highly addictive marijuana, including in hapless Africa—most of which is starving, and yet today produces a fifth of the planet's marijuana.

And it can be seen, again, in the face of our young Peruvian girl.

Dope, Inc. in the 21st Century

The widely cited United Nations Office on Drugs and Crime (UNODC) asserted in its 2008 *World Drug Report* that there has been "long-term stabilization" in drug markets, and that "there is every indication that all four drug markets [opiates; marijuana; cocaine; and ATS (Amphetamine-Type Stimulants)] have been contained over the long term."

Alas, would that it were so.

A systematic review of the published literature—including the UNODC reports as well as numerous official U.S. sources—cross-checked with law enforcement and other experts in the field, in the United States and other nations, shows that between 2000 and 2007, the international drug trade has grown in tonnage of production available for sale by about 43%, with marijuana leading the way (see Table 1). The total street value of those drugs—i.e., Dope, Inc.'s potential annual "take"—rose from about $550 billion in 2000, to over $800 billion in 2007, according to *EIR*'s conservative estimate (Figure 1). In fact, it is quite possible that the actual total is closer to $1 trillion.

Qualified American intelligence professionals concur: They tell *EIR* that the figure for world drug sales most often bandied about by international agencies, $320 billion, probably underestimates the problem *by a factor of three.*

TABLE 1: Growth of Potential Sales, 2000-2007		
	Quantity	Value
Opiates	21%	59%
Marijuana	83%	128%
Cocaine	66%	-25%
ATS*	0%	12%
TOTAL	43%	46%

* amphetamine-type stimulants
Sources: INCSR; UNODC; NDIC; ONDCP; Interpol; European Monitoring Centre for Drugs and Drug Additction; EIR

That same process is reflected in the statistics of prevalence of drug use which the UNODC itself, and others, report. Although the accuracy of these statistics, like all consumption-based analysis of the drug trade, is highly questionable (see "Methodology" box, p.19), they nonetheless are indicative of the trend. At the turn of the century, the annual prevalence of drug use across all categories was reportedly some 180 million people. By 2007-08, that number had risen to about 210 million—a 17% rise, or 30 million new drug users.

Thirty million!

And this only purports to measure the total number of regular users, not the quantities that they consumed.

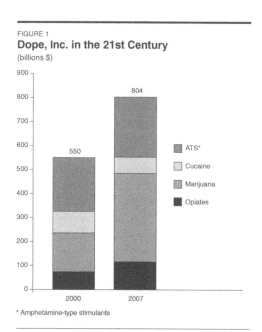

FIGURE 1
Dope, Inc. in the 21st Century
(billions $)

* Amphetamine-type stimulants

Sources: INCSR; UNODC; NDIC; ONDCP; Interpol; European Monitoring Centre for Drugs and Drug Addiction; *EIR*.

In part, the increased physical production of drugs may not be translating entirely into increased consumption. There are indications that some narcotics, especially heroin, are being "commoditized" and used in barter arrangements for the purchase of weapons for terrorists and others, gold, and even other speculative commodities.

As can be seen in Figure 2, the 21st-Century growth in potential drug sales occurred in all the major categories of drugs except cocaine, and it came after a period of relative stagnation in the late 1990s. But already, in our 1996 study, we had warned against being misled by this apparent subsidence: "It would be a serious mistake to conclude from this that the drug problem is somehow levelling off. Rather, what is going on is a period of relative consolidation, preparatory to a new take-off stage in production, consumption, and the value of total sales In other words, what we are seeing is a classic 'S-shaped' function, whose stage of relatively slower growth has already ended, as the curve accelerates back upwards."

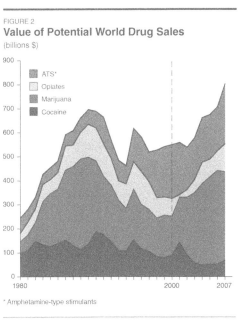

FIGURE 2
Value of Potential World Drug Sales
(billions $)

* Amphetamine-type stimulants

Sources: INCSR; UNODC; NDIC; ONDCP; Interpol; European Monitoring Centre for Drugs and Drug Addiction; *EIR*.

We were right—unfortunately.

In part, this is a result of a deliberate—and successful—marketing strategy employed by Dope, Inc., taken straight from the pages of a Harvard Business School manual: slash prices of your "product" in order to increase the volume of purchases by an even greater proportion. How well this worked for heroin, cocaine, and marijuana can be seen in Figures 3, 4 and 5, respectively, which cover the period 1980-2007. Heroin prices were cut by a factor of 5.5 over that period, while the quantity produced increased 17-fold. In the case of cocaine, prices were cut by a factor of 5.1, while production rose 5.5-fold. And for marijuana, when prices are adjusted to take into consideration the rapidly rising THC content of street sales, a similar process is evident from 1990 forward.

The idea that drug prices are somehow set by "market supply and demand" is utterly ludicrous. Dope, Inc. is a cartel, which establishes "fiat prices," in the words of one U.S. intelligence specialist consulted by *EIR*. This also points to the idiocy of the argument that drug legalization will get rid of the nasty criminals, supposedly because lower prices will make drug trafficking "less profitable." Lowering prices is exactly what Dope, Inc. itself has been doing for decades, with a resulting vast expansion of its market—and profits!

You can almost hear George Soros sneering: "You're threatening to lower drug prices by legalizing? Make my day!"

None of this need have happened. Lyndon LaRouche laid out the strategy for conducting a successful war on drugs as far back as his 1985 15-point plan, and he has reiterated and refined it over the years. Most recently, he has urged that high-technology measures be adopted, with a minimum of lethal force, to identify, eradicate, and seize the physical drugs and their required precursor chemicals, and especially, that drug money laundering be brought to a grinding halt as part of a global bankruptcy reorganization of the world financial system. This must be done, LaRouche has insisted, with cooperative agreements among nations which fully respect the national sovereignty of the affected states, and by placing special emphasis on great economic development projects to help free the millions of captive producers and consumers from their enslavement to Dope, Inc.—much as the Allied armies liberated the world from the grip of Fascism during World War II.

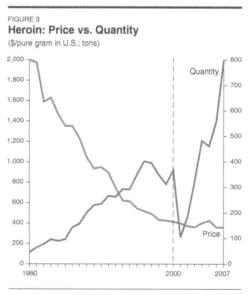

FIGURE 3
Heroin: Price vs. Quantity
($/pure gram in U.S.; tons)

Sources: INCSR; UNODC; NDIC; ONDCP; *EIR*.

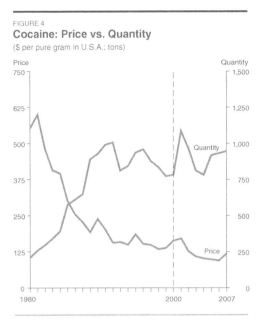

FIGURE 4
Cocaine: Price vs. Quantity
($ per pure gram in U.S.A.; tons)

Sources: INCSR; UNODC; NDIC; ONDCP; European Monitoring Centre for Drugs and Drug Addiction; *EIR.*

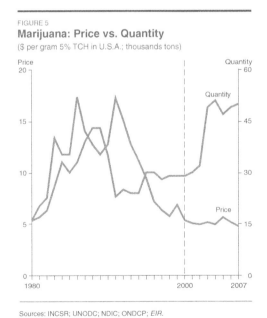

FIGURE 5
Marijuana: Price vs. Quantity
($ per gram 5% TCH in U.S.A.; thousands tons)

Sources: INCSR; UNODC; NDIC; ONDCP; *EIR.*

"Destroy the bastards! Shut them down. There's no reason to put up with this crap. Civilization is at stake," LaRouche stated bluntly Jan. 28.

Opiates: Where in the World Is All the Heroin Going?
Opium and heroin production today is completely out of control. This fact may
not be immediately apparent, if you look only at the trend of the area under poppy
cultivation internationally (Figure 6). From 2000 to the present, there were yearly
ups and downs, but the total area cultivated rose only slightly. About 14% of that
was eradicated in 2007, leaving about 225,000 hectares harvested—well below the
peak of 313,000 hectares in 1993.

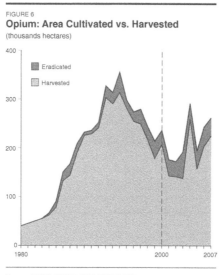

FIGURE 6
Opium: Area Cultivated vs. Harvested
(thousands hectares)

Sources: INCSR; UNODC; NDIC; ONDCP; *EIR*.

But there is something else going on. In the late 1990s, Myanmar, which had
historically been the world's leading opium producer, cracked down and reduced
production by almost 90%, from a high of 2,575 tons in 1993, down to 270 tons
in 2007. Dope, Inc. did not look kindly on what Myanmar had done, but quickly
shifted its base of opium production to Afghanistan—where the per hectare poppy
yields are *three times greater* than in Myanmar (48.5 kg/ha vs. 15 kg/ha), because
of the variety of poppy plant used, better irrigation, and so on. This explains the
phenomenon of a relatively constant total world area under poppy cultivation, at
the same time that world production has been skyrocketing.

The results can be seen in Figure 7. No lasting significance should be ascribed
to the visibly dramatic plunge in Afghan production in 2001, when the orthodox
Islamist "old" Taliban decided to crack down heavily on drugs, bringing production
down to a mere 74 tons in that one year. Some experts say that this was merely a
supply-control decision made by Dope, Inc., to use up a significant portion of
the stockpiles of heroin which had been accumulating. In any event, production
zoomed in subsequent years, under the watchful and approving eye of British and
allied NATO troops deployed in the country. In 2003, Afghanistan produced 2,865
tons of opium, an amount that rose 280% to 8,000 tons over the next four years.
The country's share of world production leapt from 75% to 94% in the same period.

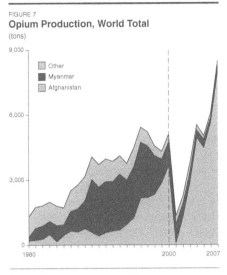

FIGURE 7
Opium Production, World Total
(tons)

Sources: INCSR; UNODC; NDIC; ONDCP; *EIR.*

The vast majority of Afghan opium is converted into heroin and morphine, in labs both inside Afghanistan and in neighboring Pakistan. In this stage of the process, too, Afghanistan has become something of an opiate superpower, because the efficiency of conversion of opium into heroin—which has historically been calculated at a ratio of 10:1, for all countries—improved significantly in Afghanistan, beginning in 2002, where it now takes only 8.5 kg of opium to produce 1 kg of pure heroin, a 15% increase in efficiency.

FIGURE 8
Opiate Trafficking Routes

Source: DEA, EIR

The opium boom of the last five years has meant that supply now far outstrips demand from consumption. According to the UNODC's 2008 *World Drug Report,* "vast amounts of opium, heroin and morphine (thousands of tons) have been withheld from the market." The report correctly notes, "These stockpiles are a time bomb for public health and global security." Further, the report states that nobody knows where the stockpiles are, except that they are not in the hands of the poppy farmers. We have to "find the missing opium," the UNODC says urgently. "As a priority, intelligence services need to examine who holds this surplus, where it may go, and for what purposes."

The UNODC could start by calling in George Soros for questioning.

Part of the answer may lie in the commoditization of heroin we mentioned above. Another significant factor is the vast increase in heroin use in nations along the overland trafficking routes from Afghanistan to Europe, especially Iran and Russia, which are known to be especially hard hit by skyrocketing addiction rates.

In 2008, according to the UNODC, Afghan opium production fell slightly to 7,700 tons, in part due to a drought in the north of the country. But opium cultivation in the British-controlled Helmand Province in the south *grew* from 102,800 hectares in 2007 to 103,600 in 2008. The vast majority of the world's opium comes from Afghanistan, and the vast majority of that is grown in Helmand Province; in 2007, Helmand's opium was 53% of the national total, but in 2008 it skyrocketed to two-thirds of the total. Between 2002 and 2008, cultivation in Helmand Province more than tripled.

The northern provinces may be shifting out of opium, but they are shifting *into* marijuana. Marijuana production has risen dramatically in Afghanistan, to the point that today the hectares cultivated are one-third the total dedicated to opium. Furthermore, the UNODC notes, "This is happening in some of the provinces that are opium free (for example in the north)," and marijuana cultivation actually "generates even greater *net* income (because of opium's high labor costs)."

Afghanistan may be the epicenter of the heroin holocaust, but it is not the world's only producer of opiates. There are three distinct production regions, which supply three distinct markets (Figure 8).

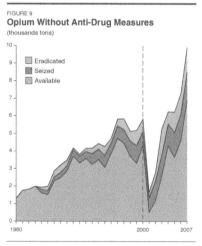

FIGURE 9
Opium Without Anti-Drug Measures
(thousands tons)

Sources: INCSR; UNODC; NDIC; ONDCP; *EIR*.

1) **Mexico and Colombia:** Their entire opium crop is converted into heroin, and most of it is shipped to the United States, where it supplies about 95% of the U.S. market; Afghanistan provides only 3% of the total consumed in the United States. The Mexican share has increasingly taken over from the Colombians, including in the east coast urban market which had long been Colombian turf. Mexican heroin production increased 105% from 1999 (8.8 tons) to 2007 (18 tons), while Colombian production decreased 47% in that same period, going from 8.7 to 4.6 tons.

2) **South East Asia:** Myanmar remains the largest producer in the region, and supplies the area, notably China and Australia.

3) **South West Asia,** i.e., Afghanistan, which supplies the "traditional" European market, and the newer and rapidly growing addict populations of Russia, Iran, and other victim countries along the trafficking routes. The growing preponderance of the south of Afghanistan in national opium production, has meant a corresponding shift in routes. Most opiates are now trafficked from southern Afghanistan via the Balkan routes into Europe, with the northern Silk Route declining in relative terms.

For example, the UNODC estimates that 53% of all opiates left Afghanistan via Iran, 33% via Pakistan, and 14% via Central Asia (mainly Tajikistan). If only heroin and morphine are considered, 51% exited via Pakistan, 30% via Iran, and 20% via Central Asia (Figure 8).

Intelligence sources consulted by *EIR* have also emphasized the growing importance of a sea route, where heroin is transported by land to Pakistani ports on the Arabian Sea, shipped to Dubai in the United Arab Emirates, and from there on to Europe.

How much of its opiate line of "products" does Dope, Inc. lose along the way? Only a small percentage of the opium crop is eradicated, as noted above. The key precursor chemical for producing heroin—acetic anhydride—is not produced at all in Afghanistan, but is smuggled in principally from China, India, and Germany, through neighboring countries. Seizures of acetic anhydride almost never occur.

As for seizures of the opiate drugs themselves, the global rate rose from 13% in 1996, to 23% in 2006. For opium, Iran seized 81% of the total world seizures; for heroin, Iran seized 19% of the total, followed by Turkey (18%), and China (10%).

The net result of both eradication and seizures can be seen in Figure 9. As unimpressive as the results have been, the fact is that, instead of the 6,900 tons of opiates that were available for sale in 2007, there would have been nearly 10,000 tons, had it not been for the half-hearted anti-drug efforts undertaken.

Imagine what the world could do if we decided to get serious.

Marijuana: No One Even Knows How Much Is Grown

Marijuana is the most widespread narcotic drug trafficked by Dope, Inc., and is well established as its entry-level product line for expanding the cartel's deadly grip on captive producing and consuming populations. For example, in the United States, marijuana has by far the highest abuse rate of any drug—five times that of cocaine.

There were about 520,000 hectares under cannabis cultivation in 2006, according to the UNODC—or perhaps it was actually three times that amount. As the UNODC itself admitted in its 2008 *World Drug Report*, it is "difficult, for most countries, to introduce scientifically reliable crop monitoring systems" for marijuana, since there are lots of small plots, hidden indoor hydroponic cultivation, and so on. "If all cannabis growing wild was included in the area estimates, the global surface covered by cannabis could be two to three times larger."

Yield estimates also vary widely, from 5 kg/ha (wild cannabis) to 40,000 kg/ha for hydroponic cultivation. So the total cannabis produced worldwide in 2007 may have been about 50,000 tons (as we estimate in Figure 10), or it could well have been double that amount! For example, in the United States, arguably the world's largest consumer and producer of marijuana, no one really has the faintest idea of how much is produced or imported into the country. As the Department of Justice's 2008 National Drug Threat Assessment (NDTA) stated frankly: "No reliable estimates are available regarding the amount of domestically cultivated or processed marijuana. The amount of marijuana available—including marijuana produced both domestically and internationally—in the U.S. is unknown."

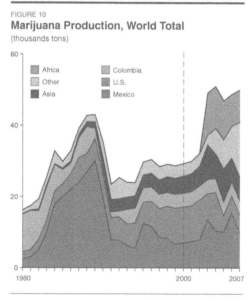

FIGURE 10
Marijuana Production, World Total
(thousands tons)

Sources: INCSR; UNODC; NDIC; ONDCP; *EIR*.

As for the number of consumers, the UNODC puts the figure at 166 million worldwide, but that also is more of a guess than anything else, since it derives its consumption estimates from "expert perceptions reported by States Members"— whoever they are, and whatever that means. Furthermore, these consumption-based estimates give wildly different numbers than most production-based estimates, which led the UNODC to admit in its 2004 report: "It should be noted that the current production estimates do not tally with consumption estimates for individual countries. Supply-side estimates for the U.S.A., for instance, see a cannabis herb market (including exports) of close to 18,000 tons for 2001-02. Consumption based estimates see a cannabis herb market of around 1,000 tons for the U.S.A. Thus far, this discrepancy [an 18-fold "discrepancy"!-ed.] has not been resolved."

Some intelligence professionals consulted by *EIR* have simply thrown up their hands, arguing that U.S. marijuana production is "intrinsically unmeasurable," since so much of it is grown: a) indoors in high-tech hydroponic environments; b) on public lands and parks, under double-canopied forests which make it largely undetectable from the air, even if U.S. intelligence services were allowed to engage in satellite imaging of the U.S. (as they do of other countries), which they are not, since it is prohibited by law; and c) in individual plots cultivated by millions of aging Baby-Boomer consumers.

Official estimates of the extent of domestic cultivation in the U.S. thus vary by more than a factor of six.

What *is* known, is that worldwide production and consumption of marijuana is rising rapidly, and that the THC content in the United States is double what it was a decade ago (Figure 11), producing a highly addictive effect on the consumer. In part, the zooming potency is due to the shift from outdoor to indoor cultivation, since "controlled growing conditions generally yield higher-potency marijuana," according to the 2008 NDTA. "Additionally, indoor cannabis cultivators are able to cultivate year-round with four to six harvests a year," they note, "compared to one or two harvests a year typical of outdoor cultivation."

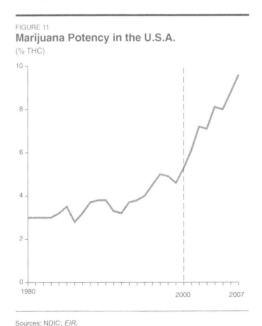

FIGURE 11
Marijuana Potency in the U.S.A.
(% THC)

Sources: NDIC; *EIR.*

Indoor cultivation occurs mainly in California, Oregon, and Washington state, "largely because of the exploitation of medical marijuana laws in some states," the NDTA notes. The case of Mendocino County, California, was recently made notorious by a CNBC documentary appropriately titled *Marijuana, Inc.*.

What is also known, is that there has been a huge explosion of production, consumption, and trafficking of cannabis in Africa. According to UNODC statistics, Africa today produces about 10,000 out of the 50,000 tons produced worldwide. The UNODC didn't even start reporting African production regularly until 2003, nor are there statistics available from other sources for earlier years. This accounts for the anomalous Africa "bump" in Figure 10, although the reality of the matter is that substantial African marijuana cultivation was surely going on prior to 2003, albeit under the radar of most international agencies. South Africa, Nigeria, and Lesotho are among the continent's major producers, but almost every country produces for its own consumption, especially by the poor, who use it to be able to work longer and harder—much as occurs with coca leaves among South America's Andean peasants.

We also know that cannabis cultivation in Afghanistan has risen dramatically in the last few years. In 2007, the UNODC reports, "the area under cannabis cultivation in Afghanistan was equivalent to over a third of the area under opium poppy cultivation. If production truly takes hold in Afghanistan there could be a rebound in consumption in West and Central Europe and an expansion in Eastern Europe." Much of the Afghan marijuana may be being converted into hashish, whose largest producer is currently Morocco.

It is also known that Mexico is the world's leading eradicator of marijuana; Mexican authorities reported that in 2006, they wiped out about 75%, or 31,000 out of a total of 40,000 hectares cultivated—although the State Department's INCSR thinks that the remaining amount available is higher than the Mexicans report. Very little marijuana is seized in the distribution chain, as can be seen in Figure 12. The combined impact of eradication and seizures in 2007 meant that the tons available for sale were cut in half, down to "only" 45,000 tons.

The net result is that cannabis (marijuana and hashish) has become the single largest component of the value of all potential drug sales, accounting for some $368 billion in potential sales in 2007 (Figure 13).

In 2006, the UNODC issued an alarming special study of marijuana as part of its annual report, headlined: "Cannabis: Why we should care." In it, the UNODC warns: "Cannabis has been allowed to fall into a grey area. Technically illegal but widely de-prioritized, the drug has grown in popularity at a rate outpacing all others. A global blind spot has developed around cannabis, and in this murk the plant itself has been transformed into something far more potent than in the past."

This brings into clear focus the sheer criminality of the Soros-led drive for "medical marijuana." Soros et al. are pushing it with a precise understanding that it is a foot-in-the-door for the unfettered expansion of Dope, Inc., and the drugging of virtually the entire planet's population.

FIGURE 12
Marijuana Without Anti-Drug Measures
(thousands tons)

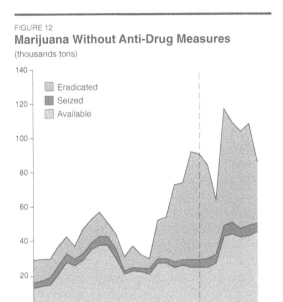

Sources: INCSR; UNODC; NDIC; ONDCP; *EIR*.

FIGURE 13
Marijuana and Hashish: Value of Production vs. Sales
(billions $)

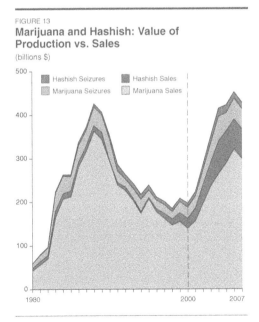

Sources: INCSR; UNODC; NDIC; ONDCP; *EIR*.

Cocaine: Eradication Works. . . If You Do It

Of the four major drug groups, cocaine is the only one which has remained pretty much flat from 1990 to the present, both in terms of area harvested as well as amount produced—although there has been an internal shift among the world's three producers, with Colombia taking over first place from Peru in the late 1990s. In the case of opium, total production (before seizures) increased by 122% between 1990 and 2007, from 3,816 to 8,484 tons. Marijuana likewise more than doubled in the same period. But cocaine production was 920 tons in 1990, and 940 tons in 2007—albeit with yearly ups and downs in between (Figure 14).

The reason? Eradication of over half of all coca plantations, principally in Colombia. If there had been no coca eradication, all 471,000 hectares cultivated would have been harvested, as opposed to the 233,000 that was the case in 2007 (Figure 15). Production would have been 1,903 tons, more than double the 940 tons that actually were produced. And the curve of rising cocaine production from 1995-2007 would have looked like a close copy of the curves for opium and marijuana production.

Achieving this success—partial though it may be—has come as the result of a decades-long political and military battle, both in the Andean region and in the United States. Drug legalizers and environmentalists have screamed bloody murder at aerial spraying of the (totally safe) herbicide glyphosate; Wall Street brazenly rallied to the defense of the Colombian narco-terrorist FARC cartel, as enshrined in the infamous *Grasso Abrazo* photograph of June 1999; and countless patriotic Colombian soldiers, policemen, judges, politicians and even Presidential candidates gave their lives to stop Dope, Inc.

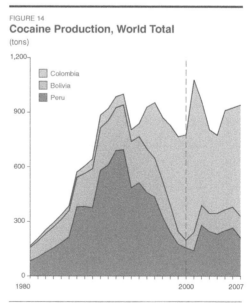

FIGURE 14
Cocaine Production, World Total
(tons)

Sources: INCSR; UNODC; NDIC; ONDCP; *EIR.*

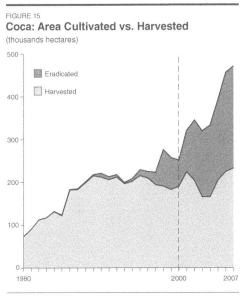

FIGURE 15
Coca: Area Cultivated vs. Harvested
(thousands hectares)

Sources: INCSR; UNODC; NDIC; ONDCP; *EIR*.

But eradication alone is hardly sufficient. To be successful, crop eradication must be deployed as part of a total anti-drug strategy. Especially under today's circumstances, you cannot simply wipe out the coca or poppy crop in a country and walk away, when the livelihood of millions depends on it, as with the captive populations of Afghanistan or Bolivia today. Those populations first have to be freed from their slavery to Dope, Inc.'s drug lords, and won over through a policy of serious economic development of their nations. At the same time, the drug-processing laboratories, and the drug-trafficking routes, and the international drug-money laundering financial interests especially, must be put out of business. As LaRouche has repeatedly stressed, this should be done with an emphasis on high-technology capabilities, employing only a minimum of lethal force, as needed to get the job done.

The cocaine case also raises another fundamental question that goes to the heart of the nature of Dope, Inc.

There are two possible interpretations of the picture presented in Figure 15. The first argues that there is an existing market demand for cocaine, and over the years the narco-traffickers cultivated enough coca to keep final production, after eradication, at the level needed to meet that market demand. This is the standard, "free market" axiomatics to which the legalizers and others always revert.

The second view is that demand for drugs is not a "market" phenomenon, but is created by Dope, Inc., in the same way that the British created a "market" for opium in China in the 19th Century—by shoving it down peoples' throats, with war if need be. This view argues that Dope, Inc. always tries to figure out a way to sell as much cocaine as could be produced without eradication, as it has with all drugs.

This second view is, of course, correct—for reasons we explain more fully in the "Methodology" box. Dope, Inc. is a drug cartel run by the world's most powerful financial interests intent on bringing on a New Dark Age, not a market competitor with a product line to sell wherever it finds "effective demand."

In June 1999, as the government of Colombia was successfully eradicating hundreds of thousands of hectares of coca, Wall Street, in the person of Richard Grasso (shown here in the infamous "Grasso Abrazo" embrace of narcoterrorist Raúl Reyes), came to the FARC cartel's rescue.

All of the world's coca and cocaine is produced in Bolivia, Peru, and Colombia, and the United States is the world's leading consumer market. A full 90% of the amount entering the United States now goes through Mexico (Figure 16). The 2009 National Drug Threat Assessment issued by the Department of Justice specifies that 69% goes through what they call the "Eastern Pacific Vector," travelling up to Mexico's Pacific coast by "go-fast" boats and fishing boats. The cartels are also increasingly using "Self-Propelled Semisubmersible-Low Profile Vessels (SPSS-LPV)"—i.e., mini submarines—on this route. An additional 21% is sent via the "Western Caribbean Vector," again with "go-fast" boats and private airplanes.

The second major market is Europe, where "cocaine use and cocaine-related problems have increased markedly since the mid-1990s," according to the European Monitoring Centre for Drugs and Drug Addiction, an EU body set up in 1993. It expresses special concern that, although the UNODC reports stable cocaine production for the last decade, "in Europe, overall cocaine seizures have tripled during this period," rising from 8% of the world total in 2000, to 14% in

2005, and 17% in 2006. This indicates that use in Europe has increased while prices have declined. The UNODC freely admits that "there is a lack of information on how much cocaine European markets may be consuming."

FIGURE 16
Cocaine Trafficking Routes

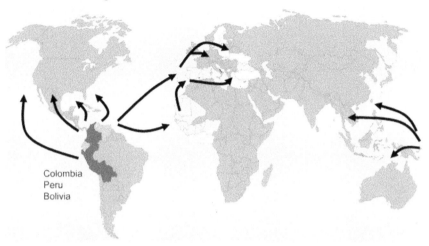

Colombia
Peru
Bolivia

Source: DEA, EIR.

The European Monitoring Centre identifies three main smuggling routes from South America:
1) The Northern route, from South America to Europe via the Caribbean, which brings in an estimated 40% of European cocaine, using "rapid and difficult to detect 'go-fast' boats, but also pleasure boats, cargo freighters and container ships. Aircraft are also used for dropping cocaine bundles in international waters to awaiting pick-up vessels."
2) The Central route, from South America to the Iberian Peninsula, with possible transits in Cape Verde, the Azores, or the Canary Islands.
3) The African route, to West Africa by large cargo ships or by fishing boats. The drugs are then taken to the west coast of the Iberian Peninsula.
   With these trafficking patterns, not surprisingly Spain and Portugal are the two main ports of entry for cocaine in Europe. The UNODC reported in 2007 that new trends include consumer markets in central and eastern Europe, and the "incorporation of cocaine into the range of products offered by traditional heroin trafficking groups operating along the Balkan route."
   Worldwide, a significant and rising amount of cocaine is being intercepted en route: In 2007 it was some 400 out of the 940 tons produced, or 42% of the total (Figure 17)—a substantially higher rate than for either opiates or marijuana. South America's share of global seizures has been increasing, from 31% in 1996 to 45% in 2006. The bulk of these seizures (181 tons) was carried out by Colombia.

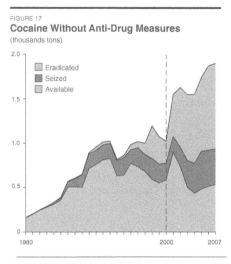

FIGURE 17
Cocaine Without Anti-Drug Measures
(thousands tons)

Sources: INCSR; UNODC; NDIC; ONDCP; European Monitoring Centre for
Drugs and Drug Addiction; *EIR*.

Taken together, eradication of coca and seizures of cocaine knocked out nearly 75% of the drug in 2007—which is good, but not nearly good enough. It is *EIR*'s contention, based on a review of the historical evidence and consultation with experts in the field, that a serious war on drugs, employing high-technology detection and combat capabilities, could lead to the eradication of about 90% of each of the major drug crops—poppy, cannabis, and coca—and seizure of some 75% of the remaining 10% that is produced. That would leave only 2-3% of the initial total that gets through.

The third leg of the stool, along with eradication and seizures, is to completely shut down the laundering of drug money—the most crucial step of all, and one which has to be carried out as a concerted, international campaign. As we said in our 1996 study: "The drug trade has to be fought simultaneously, in a coordinated fashion, on a global scale. Since Dope, Inc. is a multinational enterprise with operations in dozens of nations, it does little good to shut it down in one country only: It will simply move its operations to a more favorable environment."

ATS: A Quarter Trillion Dollar Business
Unlike the other three main drug groups, where one can physically measure crops and yields as a starting point for estimating total production and availability, Amphetamine-Type Stimulants, or ATS, can only be estimated indirectly, based on seizures of drugs and precursor chemicals, consumption studies, and so on. With that caveat, the available statistics indicate that total tonnage produced increased dramatically over the course of the 1990s, and has then grown more slowly from 2000 to 2007 (Figure 18). Today, some 550 tons of ATS are produced, of which a mere 10% is seized, bringing the total available to about 500 tons per year. The estimated total street value of those ATS is a cool quarter-trillion dollars.

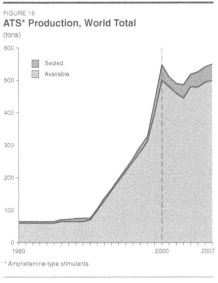

FIGURE 18
ATS* Production, World Total
(tons)

* Amphetamine-type stimulants

Sources: INCSR; UNODC; NDIC; ONDCP; Interpol; *EIR*.

The ATS category of drugs has two major groups: 1) the amphetamine group (which includes both methamphetamines and amphetamines); and 2) the ecstasy group (which includes MDMA, MDA, etc.). In 2007, out of a total 496 tons available, methamphetamines accounted for 267 tons (54%), amphetamines were 126 tons (25%), and ecstasy was 103 tons (21%). Judging by the pattern of seizures, methamphetamines are the dominant ATS drug in the U.S. market; amphetamines predominate in Europe and the Near East; and South East Asia has a large and growing methamphetamine problem.

As for ecstasy, Europe's role as the main manufacturer is declining. In July 2008, the Drug Enforcement Administration reported that "Asian Organized Crime groups play an important role in the global MDMA trade." Overall, the DEA reported, "synthetic drugs are the primary threat in South East Asia." And consumption of ATS in Africa and South West Asia is also on the rise.

In the United States, methamphetamines are the major ATS problem. In 2006, the 6,832 U.S. laboratories busted accounted for 88% of all dismantled methamphetamine laboratories worldwide. In the last few years, U.S. domestic manufacture of meth has been declining, but it has been more than offset by a shift of manufacturing to Mexico and Canada, with the product then smuggled into the United States. The DEA estimates that 65% of the meth available in the U.S. is produced in Mexico, with precursor chemicals coming into Mexico through Central America.

The NDTA's December 2008 report admits that a major part of the problem is "the limitations placed on customs inspectors by Free Trade Zone mandates" in various countries. As *EIR* has asserted for years, the provisions of NAFTA have not only been an economic disaster for both the United States and Mexico, but they have also helped open the doors wide for drugs to flow freely.

Highly centralized distribution networks of ATS are thought to be replacing independent dealers in the United States, which goes along with a shift from smaller labs to super and mega-laboratories. "Organized criminal groups in Mexico have expanded their methamphetamine distribution networks and they have also introduced highly addictive crystal methamphetamine into these markets," according to a DEA report.

As for Europe, the dubious distinction of being the leading producer of ATS falls to the Czech Republic; in 2006, 88% of all European laboratories detected were found there.

By Way of a Postscript

George Soros and his troop of legalizers are fond of arguing that consuming drugs is a "victimless crime," so why not legalize it? This is as offensive to the human mind as Soros's continuing defense of his collaboration with Hitler's Waffen SS in Nazi-occupied Hungary, against his own fellow Jews.

There is scarcely a family in the United States today that has not been scarred in one way or another by drugs—a brother, a daughter, a cousin, a father who were casualties of this modern Opium War. Nor is there a nation on the planet where the policies of Dope, Inc. have not wrought havoc.

Now return, if you would, to the picture of the young Peruvian girl with which we began this account. There is more to the story. That photograph was taken in Peru by Mark Sonnenblick, a founding member of the LaRouche organization who passed away in 2004, and who dedicated his life to being the voice and mentor of the uncounted millions who, like that little Peruvian girl, cry out for justice.

When I first saw that picture, probably taken in 1967, I thought immediately of Lyndon LaRouche's trip to Peru in 1987, 20 years later, where he talked about Peru's children—about that same girl. On that visit, LaRouche delivered an address commemorating the 20th anniversary of Pope Paul VI's encyclical, "Populorum Progressio," where he said:

"Where others see only poverty, I see potential. It was 41 years ago, in India, that I first committed myself to economic justice for what we today call the developing sector. The children and grandchildren of some of today's poorest rural families of Peru, will land on Mars. Some will stay as colonists; others will return, perhaps to share their experiences with some of you, who are here today in this hall."

LaRouche stressed: "Never accept the spectacle of human misery; human misery is unnecessary. Never accept the idea that some nations are rich, and others are poor. Never think of yourselves as people from a poor country."

And he concluded: "I've asked you to turn your eyes to the stars to see, with pride and with confidence, that which the mind makes you capable of achieving. In dreaming that dream, lies the potential of your nation; the potential of your nation is its future reality. What your nation will be in the future, is what it begins to do today."

And today, we should add that we *will* get that little Peruvian girl to Mars yet—and Dope, Inc.'s New Dark Age be damned!

A Note on EIR's Methodology

Over the past three decades, *EIR* has conducted a number of in-depth investigations of the size of the international drug trade. Each of these has addressed the matter from the same vantage point: that Dope, Inc. functions as a single, unified, multinational corporation, whose various production, processing, transportation, distribution, sales, consumption, and money-laundering phases are centrally coordinated to a single purpose.

We therefore discard as misleading, and inaccurate, all "demand"- or "consumption"-based approaches, whose implicit assumption is that the "aggregate demand" for drugs by a collection of autonomous individuals, "causes" drugs to be produced, presumably by a collection of equally autonomous producers who only associate, after the fact, into various criminal cartels. In this view, money laundering is merely an epiphenomenon, and drug bankers are only the occasional bad apples who are corrupted by the producer cartels.

Even the most thorough of such "consumption"-driven approaches inherently underestimate the actual scope of the drug problem, and vastly so, probably by a full order of magnitude. No amount of sophisticated mathematics and complex regression analyses can make up for flawed assumptions and methodology: It only makes the problem worse by convincing the gullible layman that it is somehow "scientific."

As a result of its very illegal nature, Dope, Inc.'s size and activities are not directly reported. However, one can obtain a far more accurate—if still not precise—reading, by analyzing the *physical economy* of the drug production process, and estimating what the annual value of the total physical output of the drugs would be, were they fully marketed at retail street prices. In using this approach, *EIR* has made use of official data provided by numerous governments and international agencies, as verified and corrected by direct *EIR* consultation with knowledgeable sources in various countries. We are convinced that our findings about the global dimensions of Dope, Inc. err on the conservative side.

There are two principal sources of publicly available comprehensive data on drugs: the U.S. State Department's annual *International Narcotics Control Strategy Report* (INCSR), which pulls together data from other U.S. agencies, including the White House Office of National Drug Control Policy (ONDCP), the Department of Justice National Drug Intelligence Center (NDIC), the DEA and others. The second, is the United Nations Office on Drugs and Crime (UNODC), which issues an annual *World Drug Report*.

The U.S. and UN numbers, by and large, indicate the same broad trends, although specific numbers vary from year to year. Exceptions to that rule include significant variations of coca area cultivated in Colombia, marijuana yields in Mexico, and so on.

Overall, we have chosen to use the U.S.-generated numbers as we have for our previous studies, for a number of reasons. The main one is that the UN numbers aggregate individual country reports, as supplied by each member state of the UN, so they reflect varying national methodologies;

whereas the U.S. numbers apply the same methodology to all countries. This latter is preferable, since what we are looking for are trends, not absolute numbers—which are inexact in any event. Exceptions include our use of UNODC figures for European street prices for drugs, as well as most data on drug seizures.

—Dennis Small

Message from Afghanistan: Get Rid of Opium or Perish

U.S. President Barack Obama is in the process of formulating a policy, implementation of which would apparently lead to the end of militancy in Afghanistan and peace in the region, we have been told. From the noises made by the media, and the talking heads of Washington, a number of old formulations, put in a new bottle, are about to be peddled as solutions. However, the new President must recognize that the only way Afghanistan can be stabilized, thus bringing peace to the region, is by ridding it of the menace of opium once and for all. As long as policymakers ignore this reality, the security environment in and around Afghanistan will continue to deteriorate, leading to a regional blow-up.

What is to be understood at the outset, is that the vast amount of opium produced annually in Afghanistan, and converted into lethal heroin, is not only funding the terrorists who are killing U.S. and other troops there, but is also financing operations aimed at breaking Pakistan apart, and causing violence and chaos within India and further West.

Rise of Opium-Funded Terrorists

In the north of Afghanistan, the Central Asian states, which were part of the erstwhile Soviet Union until 1991, have been devastated by drug-money-financed terrorist movements, acting in the garb of the orthodox Wahhabi Islamic tenet. Located south and west of Afghanistan, Iran has been inundated by opium and heroin, which are destroying a generation of Iranians.

This region has been systematically handed over to the terrorists since the United States and its allies launched the "War on Terror," ostensibly to eliminate violence and terrorism in Afghanistan. In 2001, the year U.S. invaded Afghanistan to oust the Taliban, which harbored the infamous enemy of the United States, al-Qaeda, Afghanistan produced less than 100 tons of opium. This occurred under the reign of an orthodox Islamic group, the Taliban, four years after that Islamic militia took power in Afghanistan with the help of the Pakistani military. Since the U.S. took over Afghanistan in the Winter of 2001, when NATO and a few non-NATO nations joined to fight America's war, opium production took off vertically (see graphs in lead article, this section). It is surreal to hear experts on Afghanistan expressing their surprise to find that the Taliban, which was routed in 2001, has made a comeback. What has made this possible, is opium. It's been happening right in front of their eyes.

In 2007, according to the United Nations Office on Drugs and Crime (UNODC), Afghanistan's opium production was 8,240 tons—U.S. official agencies report an equivalent amount of 8,000 tons—which is about twice as much as the Taliban ever produced during its five-year reign, and at least eight times the quantity Afghanistan ever produced before the Soviet Army invaded in 1979. This year, the production has been "reduced" through a "successful campaign," to 7,700 tons. This amount of opium, converted into heroin, generates about $4 billion to those Afghans who control the business, while the street value in Europe of that heroin is some $132 billion, more than 30 times as much (Table 1).

Even a fraction of that $4 billion in cash generated annually can recruit, train, arm, and maintain thousands of mercenaries, or jihadis, who then can be deployed in the region to develop "hot spots," encircling the foreign invaders, and multiplying the crisis. And, this is exactly what has happened, but Washington, advised by its pundits and experts, chose to ignore all that.

Remember again, the dastardly Taliban, who were recognized by only three countries—Saudi Arabia, Pakistan, and the United Arab Emirates—had cut down Afghanistan's opium production in the year 2000, to 100 tons. The question that crops up in many people's minds is: Did we go to war against the Taliban to jack up opium production again, or to get rid of the terrorists? Seven years later, the answer to that question seems to be that we indeed hugely succeeded in jacking up opium production in Afghanistan, and, in the process, spawned thousands of terrorists, who are now armed better than ever before, and are operating in a much-wider circle.

TABLE 1: Afghanistan Opiates: From the Farm to the Street		
	2006	2007
Prices ($/kg)		
Opium, farmgate	140	122
Opium, export to neighbors	560	500
Heroin on street, Europe	140,000	140,000
Value (billions $)		
Opium, farmgate	0.8	1.0
Opium, export to neighbors	3.2	4.0
Heroin on street, Europe	93	132

Sources: UNODC, ONDCP, EIR.

What went wrong? Did our experts miss the boat, in the same way Sir Alan Greenspan "missed" his, while cooking up toxic assets in the financial market, and assuring us that the fundamentals of our economy were sound? Did we really want opium production to rise dramatically in order to finance the based-on-fraud financial "boom" during the Bush Administration days? It is evident from the unraveling of the Madoff fraud that a large sum of money was coming from "unaccounted" for sources, a.k.a. drug money.

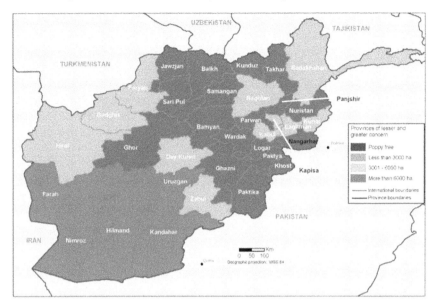

Five southern provinces—Helmand, Nimroz, Farah, Uruzgan, and Kandahar—produce 80% of Afghanistan's opium, and are patrolled by more than 8,300 British troops, who ensure that the drug lords remain in control of the poppy fields.

Or, did we allow the opium explosion, and illegal cash generation to recruit, arm, train, and maintain terrorists, to destabilize a region where three large nations—Russia, China, and India—meet? Did the Bush Administration wittingly, or unwittingly, get sucked into the old colonial Great Game of remaining "powerful" through weakening of other nations? In fact, by jacking up the opium production, nothing was achieved. It does not take an expert to fathom that if the opium production in Afghanistan is not shut down, it will not only engulf the region in flames, burning down many U.S. friends in the region, but it will eventually destroy the United States.

Liars and Lies Behind Opium Explosion

One of the most difficult aspects of eradicating opium is to peel off the layers of lies presented as "realities" by the beneficiaries of opium production—and these are not the Taliban militia members. These are corrupt beneficiaries of the bribes to allow opium and heroin production to continue. These beneficiaries also are the offshore and other corrupt bankers who use the drug money, the only cash available in today's Alice-in-Wonderland financial market they have been allowed to create, to meet daily cash requirements. Both these groups obfuscate the drug issue to prevent opium eradication in Afghanistan.

Lie #1: NATO troops in Afghanistan, referred to as the International Security Assistance Force (ISAF), avoid any involvement in eradicating opium, because they claim the destruction of opium would alienate the population.

This lie can be exposed in no time by looking at the reality on the ground. In Afghanistan, 80% of the opium is produced in five southern provinces: Helmand, Nimroz, Farah, Uruzgan, and Kandahar. These are all virtually under the control of the drug lords and their militias (conveniently labeled as Taliban to obfuscate reality). These provinces are manned by more than 8,300 British troops, in collaboration with a few thousand troops from Canada, Australia, and the Netherlands. These troops do not go out and fight the Taliban, and their losses are small. They have little contact with the population, and make sure that the drug lords and their militias remain in control of the opium program.

On March 3, 2008, in Vienna, Hakan Demirbuken, who ran the UNODC opium surveys in Afghanistan for several years, pointed out: "The vast majority of southern Afghanistan is closed to UN operations.... UN people are only in the city centers. They cannot go to the villages. It is very dangerous."

Lie #2: Afghan farmers prefer opium over other crops because it generates more money.

This lie is easy to propagate, since very few Westerners have any possibility of developing contact with Afghan farmers. The truth is, that where the opium production is rampant, the area is under the control of drug lords. The drug lords, with hundreds of militiamen, armed with AK-47s and other assault rifles, make sure that the farmer does not produce anything other than opium in his fields. Opium seed is distributed to the farmer's doorstep, and he is ordered to deliver so many kilograms of opium when it is harvested. The farmer is told how much he will be paid, and that if he does not deliver the said amount, his family will be wiped out. During the opium production, the drug lords place their militiamen armed with AK-47s at the corners of the farmer's field, so that no one can eradicate the poppy crops.

The fact remains, and it is not a difficult fact to assimilate, that farmers have been left at the mercy of the drug lords and their militias. There are numerous photographs showing armed-to-the-teeth NATO troops marching by huge poppy fields in full bloom, guarded by AK-47-carrying militiamen.

In an article for RFE/RL on Oct. 10, "Afghanistan: Poor Helmand Farmers Find Themselves in Eye of Drug Storm," Abubakar Siddique and Salih Muhammad Salih report that Haji Mahuddin Khan, a tribal leader in Helmand, told them that international drug rings are the main benefactors in the province, while poor peasants remain chained to poppy cultivation. "The farmers have never benefited from poppy cultivation," he said. "The profits are taken by those [government officials] who tell farmers to engage in cultivation but then threaten their crops with eradication. The international mafia is the main benefactor, while we are being held responsible for it and portrayed as criminals."while we are being held responsible for it and portrayed as criminals."

How We Treat Our Friends (or Enemies?)

The opium explosion in Afghanistan, which has now been reluctantly acknowledged by the policymakers, has helped the Taliban to regroup, leaving many dead bodies among the foreign troops, far from the much-focussed-on battlefields of

Afghanistan and Pakistan. These dead bodies, and those who have been made dysfunctional because of drug use, are strewn across Pakistan, India, Iran, the nations of Central Asia, Azerbaijan, Georgia, Ukraine, and Russia. Among these nations, are those the U.S. establishment considers to be good friends, some just friends, and Iran, as an exception, is the "enemy."

Now, let us look at what our seven-year "War on Terror" has achieved in the region. To begin with, it is now common knowledge that the entire western part of Pakistan, between the River Indus and the imaginary border known as the Durand Line, which theoretically separates Pakistan from Afghanistan, is in turmoil. The level of turmoil is such, that Pakistani President Asif Ali Zardari had to issue a statement on Feb. 15, that Pakistan is at war with the Taliban. The fact remains that Islamabad's writ does not extend to the Swat Valley, or most of the tribal areas and the North West Frontier Province (NWFP), west of Peshawar city. In other words, if business as usual continues, Pakistan will break apart.

It is to be recognized, even at this late stage, that much of the financing of the terrorists operating to break apart Pakistan (with the exception of the Wahhabis in control of the Swat Valley) comes from Saudi Arabia, drawing money from opium and heroin sales, and taxes imposed on farmers by the drug lords.

The effect on the people of the region has been documented by the UNODC, whose *World Drug Report* includes a section on the annual prevalence of abuse for opiates, cannabis, and other drugs, as a percentage of the population aged 15 to 64, for each country monitored. These rates reflect the percentage of people who used the drug in the 12-month period prior to the survey. Although these statistics undoubtedly understate the extent of drug consumption, they are nonetheless useful to consider.

In 2007, an estimated 434,000 Afghans used hashish; 130,000 used opium; and 41,000 used heroin, according to the UNODC. While the population of Afghanistan is officially listed as 31.8 million, the UNODC figures are based on a figure of 23.8 million.

A flood of Afghan heroin has swept through the Islamic countries of Asia and Central Asia since the late 1990s. Additionally, Afghan opium and hashish is being distributed regionally in Pakistan, Iran, and the Central Asian Republics. Over 10 million Muslims in Asia and the Middle East have used Afghan drugs, leading to the economic and social ruin of millions of families, one report claimed.

Pakistan, a friend of the United States since the 1950s, has been most affected, with a surge in addiction rates during the last 12 years. According to the UNODC, 640,000 Pakistanis used opiates in 2007; of these, 515,000 used heroin and 125,000 used opium. A 2004 survey from Karachi found that 20% of IV-drug users were HIV positive.

The UNODC estimated that in 2007, 371,000 Iranians used heroin, 928,000 used opium, and 1.9 million used hashish. There are over 3 million Iranians who had used drugs during the previous year, but only about 1.3 million of these used opiates, and most of that is opium, not heroin.

Addiction rates have grown by leaps and bounds as the Afghan heroin moved through these areas to the north, reaching Russia and Ukraine. In Kazakstan and

Tajikistan, up to 90% of drug addicts are HIV positive, and 90% of new HIV cases come from drug use.

One report pointed out that, globally, the rate of heroin addiction stands at about 0.3% for people between the ages of 15 to 64, the most commonly used sampling group. It is almost five times that in Afghanistan (1.4%), and more than twice the average in Pakistan (0.7%) and the Central Asian Republics (Turkmenistan, 0.5%; Uzbekistan, 0.8%; Tajikistan, 0.5%; Kyrgyzstan, 0.8%; and Kazakstan, 1.0%).

In addition to Pakistan, Iran, Tajikistan, Uzbekistan, and Kyrgyzstan, the carrier of death and destruction, produced in the five fortified provinces of southern Afghanistan, has made its impact felt in Egypt, Syria, Jordan, Turkey, and Bangladesh.

What To Do Now
The Warriors on Terror have been in Afghanistan for more than seven years. During this time, in addition to aiding the explosion of opium production, the Washington-led policy has also helped the resurgence of the Taliban, and other insurgents funded by drug money. The insurgents, who are battling the U.S. and NATO troops, reportedly tax all aspects of the drug trade, from cultivation to processing and distribution. They also earn money by providing protection for opium fields, heroin labs, drug shipments, and narcotics traffickers.

Despite having all this information, Washington and Brussels continue to flail around, blaming one another for the failure of their poorly defined mission, and for the resurgence of the Taliban. The first to be chastized was Pakistan, for allowing al-Qaeda leaders to move into its territory, and then, failing to annihilate them, and preventing the Pakistani Pushtuns from joining ranks with the Afghan Pushtuns, in the latter's fight against the foreign troops.

The second round of blame was directed against Iran, for allegedly helping al-Qaeda. Although Kabul refused to accept that argument, pointing out that Tehran does not want a Taliban government any more than does Washington, the blame game continues. While it is true that the insurgents coming from Saudi Arabia pass through Iran to Afghanistan and Iraq, Iran is committed to opposing the orthodox Sunnis of the Taliban, who are imbued with anti-Shi'a zealotry propagated by Saudi Arabia.

The third round of the blame game began last year when the failure of the undefined mission was placed squarely on the shoulders of President Hamid Karzai and his government. Mind you, those who are blaming the Karzai government for corruption and inefficiency are also aware that the situation is so dire in southern Afghanistan, that the well-trained, well-armed British/Canadian/Australian/ Dutch troops find it too dangerous to venture out, and thus, leave themselves, de facto, with the task of protecting the drug trade.

In reality, if anyone is to be blamed, it is those troops on whose watch a huge opium/heroin production and trade is conducted; many large heroin labs continue to convert opium into heroin; and acetic anhydride and precursors needed for conversion continue to come in hundreds of tons to these labs.

With a new administration in Washington, the blame game has to stop, and work to shut down the drug production and traffic has to begin. The destruction of the opium empire set up by international cartel with the help of the Afghan drug lords, protected by British troops in five southern Afghan provinces, has to be achieved quickly.

First, all the Afghan drug lords have to be eliminated from the scene physically through capture. If they resist, they should be considered as war combatants.

Once the elimination of the drug lords takes off, the farmers will be "liberated." At this point, a well-organized and well-thought-out plan to eradicate the opium poppy must be implemented. The eradication has to be followed by paying compensation to the farmers that would last them a year at the least.

In a series of article last year, *Middle East Times* writer James Emery pointed out that most of the processing labs are located in southern Afghanistan. These labs are close to opium sources and are jointly protected by the Taliban and the drug lords. Smaller refineries, including mobile labs, are scattered around the country. Taking out heroin-processing labs will help curtail the market for opium.

The UNODC's "Winter Afghan Opium Report" of 2008 noted that a massive quantity of opium is being stockpiled for future sales. The report said that even if the entire 2008 Afghan opium crop were eradicated, heroin labs would remain busy, unless opium warehouses were located and destroyed

Acetic anhydride is the essential precursor used for converting opium into morphine base and heroin. Its sole use in Afghanistan is in drug refineries that have increased their annual demand from about 200 tons to 1,330 tons during the last six years.

None of the precursors are manufactured in Afghanistan. In all, some 11,000 tons of chemicals were required to process opium during 2007. The chemicals are smuggled into Afghanistan from China, India, Pakistan, and the Central Asian Republics, Emery pointed out. The main opium markets in Helmand province are in Musa Qala and Sangin, which were under British control, reportedly for a while, in 2007. Each of the two districts has numerous heroin labs.

It is imperative that Washington engage in serious discussions with the countries from which the precursors come into Afghanistan, and work out a surveillance system at the manufacturing places themselves.

These are the basic requirements to rid Afghanistan of this menace and prevent the region from becoming a safehouse for the terrorists. The only way to defeat the terrorists is to starve them of the opium cash that helps them to proliferate. That would also help the United States earn some respect in the region.

Retired Gen. Barry McCaffrey, former drug czar in the Clinton Administration, wrote an *After Action Report* on an early December 2008 visit to Mexico, in which he described the drug hell into which Mexico is rapidly descending. The southern neighbor of the United States "is on the edge of the abyss," he warned, and "could become a narco-state in the coming decade."

For well over a year, the Mexican and international press have documented that descent on a daily basis, with horrifying accounts of beheadings, random kidnappings, and torture of military and police personnel; shootouts among rival gangs; and psychological terror aimed at the general population.

Mexico's Descent into Hell Can be Stopped

Moreover, Mexico's drug cartels appear to operate with total impunity, and demonstrate the same level of bestiality that Dope, Inc.'s employees like George Soros use to argue for drug legalization. The war on drugs is unwinnable, they insist, so take your pick: Silver or lead?

If you make a deal, as Soros demands, you get silver—you cash in on some drug money. "Tax and regulate" the marijuana crop, and the drug violence will end, the story goes. But if, like current Mexican President Felipe Calderón, you choose to fight, and enlist the Army to do so, you'll get the "lead"—and you will lose, they say.

One example of the lead was delivered on Feb. 1, when cartel hitmen kidnapped Brig. Gen. Mauro Enrique Tello Quiñones (ret.) in downtown Cancún, hideously tortured him, and then killed him. Tello was an experienced veteran of the war on drugs, sent into Cancún in late January by the Office of the Defense Secretary, to clean out a nest of cartel collaborators inside the local police.

On Nov. 5, 2008, a plane crash in Mexico City had killed Calderón's close collaborators in the war on drugs, Interior Minister Juán Carlos Mouriño and the former Deputy Attorney General for the war on drugs, José Luís Santiago Vasconcelos. Although the crash was deemed an accident, there is lingering suspicion that it was caused by the drug cartels as a warning to Calderón to abandon his anti-drug strategy.

U.S.-Mexico Cooperation

Many Mexicans bridled at McCaffrey's talk of a "narco state," viewing the general as the typical arrogant Yankee imperialist, who is looking for any opportunity to attack—or invade—Mexico. They also recall the constant discussion of "failed states" during the Bush years, as a justification for the Bush policy of trying to terminate the institution of the sovereign nation-state altogether.

But McCaffrey has repeatedly stressed that the only way to conduct a successful war on drugs is with U.S.-Mexico cooperation, based on full respect for Mexico's sovereignty. And he placed the full measure of blame on the U.S. government—the Bush Administration, to be precise—for allowing the uninterrupted flow of weapons across the border into Mexico, which keeps the drug mafias armed with weaponry far more sophisticated than anything the underfunded Mexican Army has.

Why is there such "callous disregard" from the U.S. side, McCaffrey asked, "for a national security threat to a neighboring democratic state?" If the situation were reversed, he argued, "we would consider it an act of warfare from a sanctuary state if we were the victim."

The U.S. Department of Justice's National Drug Threat Assessment, published in mid-December 2008, also stressed the logistical and technological sophistication that Dope, Inc. has deployed along the U.S.-Mexico border. "Mexico's DTOs [drug trafficking organizations] maintain cross-border communication centers in Mexico near the U.S.-Mexico border to facilitate coordinated cross-border smuggling operations," they wrote. They use "Voice over Internet Protocol, satellite technology (broadband satellite instant messaging), encrypted messaging, cell phone technology, two-way radios, scanner devices, and text messages to communicate with members. In some cases DTO members use high-frequency radios with encryption and rolling codes to communicate during cross-border operations."

Lyndon LaRouche has called on the Obama Administration to forge an alliance with Mexico, premised on respect for Mexico's sovereignty, to shut down the murderous drug traffic. Shown: Mexican soldiers detain a man following a deadly gun battle in Apatzingan.

The Department of Justice report stated that the DTOs use gang members in U.S. cities, "which insulates DTO cell members from law enforcement detection," noting that the total number of gang members in 2006 was estimated at 785,000, but in 2008 it "may be significantly higher."

But a political commitment on both sides of the border could mobilize even more sophisticated means to be used by the United States and Mexico to defend their citizens from these predators.

Lyndon LaRouche has called on the Obama Administration to forge an alliance with Mexico to fight drugs, premised on respect for Mexico's sovereignty. It's possible to wage war against the cartels using non-lethal means—high-technology, science, and economic development plans, LaRouche said. "Drugs *will* be fought," he emphasized, "but it is preferable to do it largely peacefully, with economic alternatives to what will otherwise be chaos." LaRouche pointed to the proposed Northwest Hydraulic Plan (PLHINO), a huge infrastructure project that would greatly expand land under cultivation in three northern Mexican states, as an example of the kind of projects Mexico needs.

Soros and the British Drug Lords: How the Empire Created 'Decrim'

Feb. 20—British "drug lord" George Soros, banker to the Queen of England, and financier of a worldwide campaign to legalize mind-destroying drugs, received a hammer-blow from the United Nations International Narcotics Control Board today, when the INCB released its 2008 report. Contrary to the legalization campaign into which Soros has poured millions of dollars over the last years, the INCB took its toughest stand against marijuana in years, saying: "The international community may wish to review the issue of cannabis. Over the years, cannabis has become more potent and is associated with an increasing number of emergency room admissions. Cannabis is often the first illicit drug that young people take. It is frequently called a gateway drug. In spite of all these facts, the use of cannabis is often trivialized and, in some countries, controls over the cultivation, possession and use of cannabis are less strict than for other drugs."

In the report's Foreword, INCB President Dr. Hamid Ghodse writes that 2009 is the 100th anniversary of the International Opium Commission in Shanghai, China. "A hundred years ago, substances that are internationally controlled today were unregulated and widely abused," Dr. Ghodse says. "The consumption of opiates in China alone was estimated to be more than 3,000 tons in morphine equivalent, far in excess of global consumption [today]. In the United States, about 90 per cent of narcotic drugs were used for non-medical purposes. *As drug abuse spread, an increasing number of people became familiar with the wretchedness, misery and evil connected with that affliction*" (emphasis added).

Within hours of the report's release, Soros's drug pushers were denouncing the INCB and the United Nations. Soros's Big Dope, Ethan Nadelmann, head of the Drug Policy Alliance, demanded the "abolition of the INCB," because of "its shameful commitment to politics over science ... [and] shocking indifference to the failures and harmful consequences of the global drug prohibition regime." In lockstep, the British-based legalization front-group Transform, complained that "the INCB and the UN Office on Drugs and Crime (UNODC) posed a greater threat to global well-being than drugs themselves." The INCP has turned over narcotics production and distribution to "terror groups, paramilitaries, and organized criminals," Transform wailed.

Soros's drug lobby wants to turn the clock back 100 years, to the era of the slavery under imperial powers!

Ironically, just one day earlier, Nadelmann had been the featured speaker at the fascist economics center, the Cato Institute, where he proclaimed "optimism" that the prohibition forces are losing ground, especially after Soros's three bought Latin American former-Presidents had come out in favor of marijuana decriminalization (see article, this section).

Although the Big Dope got a warm welcome at Cato, especially since Soros paid for the event, the world is moving in a different direction—taking steps to shut down narcoterrorism, and making the long-overdue moves against bank secrecy that could shut down drug money laundering.

The following report on drug pusher Soros, is an update of several comprehensive dossiers by *EIR* on Soros's drug-pushing operations. It is in three parts: how the British oligarchy invented decriminalization; a profile of Soros's legalization operations in the United States: and, the backlash against "Marijuana, Inc."

1. How the Brits Invented Decrim

This section is excerpted from an article in the April 1981 issue of *War on Drugs* magazine, "Why British Aristocrats Invented 'Decrim,'" by Karen Steinherz.

The April 1981 issue of War on Drugs showed how the British invented "decrim," as a foot in the door for the full legalization of all drugs. The U.S. dope lobby, NORML, employed the methods of the British Empire's "India model."

In 1980 the original U.S. "pot lobby," the National Organization for the Reform of Marijuana Laws (NORML), traced its policy to legalize dope directly to the British Empire's "India model," an elaborate tax system which was imposed on the population of India by the British in 1895, at the height of the era when "the Sun never set on the British Empire."

For more than a century, the British have tried to block the prohibition against cannabis and opium. But it is clear historically that the international laws against cannabis came into effect because of the desire of nation-states to make economic and social progress. The countries—like Egypt and China—which fought to outlaw dope, recognized that if there was to be progress in a nation, there could not be rampant drug usage. For the British and Dutch empires in the 19th Century, the reverse was just as true—progress could be blocked if the population in the colonies of the Imperial powers were kept in a stupefied state, and that was precisely their strategy.

In 1893, the British Parliament commissioned what turned into a nine-volume study on "hemp" (marijuana) in India, then a British colony. The India Hemp Commission Report, which took more than two years to compile, was an elaborate justification of an extensive hemp tax system and the continued subjugation of the coolie population by encouraging their use of *ganja*.

In the same way that the British opium trade in China was used to turn China into a drugged nation, incapable of acting in its own interest, the legalization of *ganja* was used to suppress the population of India. The commission report, which was held up by NORML as the model argument for legalization, recommended that cannabis be *legal.*

The testimony of the pro-marijuana witnesses, many of them plantation owners and tax collectors, shows the imperial mindset:

- Mr. Skinner, manager, Gogra Tea company, Tezpur, Darrang, India: "The castes who use it most are Yoosoahe from Gaya ... bricklayers from Calcutta, and of the jungle caste.... I cannot see any harm in the use of the drug. All of those who appear to use it are good, quiet and willing coolies...."
- Mr. Phillips, tea planter: "I advocate no prohibition on *ganja.* ... If prohibited, the health of our coolies would suffer ... and of course, discontent would ensue."
- Deputy Commissioner of the Port Akyar: "It [*ganja*] is now brought in by the crew of the British India Steam Navigation Company."

During the first half of the 20th Century, it was an open secret that United Kingdom officials ran the international marijuana and opium traffic. The resulting problems were so acute that two International Opium Conferences, in 1912 and in 1924-25, were held in The Hague, The Netherlands, to force London to adhere to curbs on drug production. In both cases, the British pronounced themselves in favor of "Free Trade" for opium and cannibis.

At the 1912 conference, which declared a ban on opium production, the assembled nations demanded that a study be done of India's hemp "with the object of regulating its abuses...." But the countries, especially in the Middle East and Africa, whose populations showed the effects of serious abuse of opium and hashish, were blocked by the British Empire.

The Second Opium Conference, in 1925, held under the auspices of the League of Nations, included the countries that had signed the 1912 agreement. This conference focussed primarily on measures to *enforce* the opium ban, and the Egyptian delegation, supported by the Turks, submitted a proposal that prohibition of hashish be included in the list. The British delegation tried to divert the outrage over marijuana and hashish abuse into a proposal for an endless "investigative commission," like the 1895 India Hemp Commission Report. But this time, the British lost.

A committee of doctors, professors, administrators, and ministers from Belgium, Brazil, Canada, the Dominican Republic, Egypt, France, Germany, Great Britain, Greece, Italy, Japan, The Netherlands, Poland, Spain, Switzerland, and the U.S. met to consider complete prohibition of the production and use of cannabis resin. Banning cannabis use was overwhelming voted up—with three absentions: Great Britain, The Netherlands (whose Dutch East India Company ran a Far East dope traffic comparable to the British East India Company), and India, then a British colony.

It was a defeat for the British Empire, and one that they have never accepted. The international law against marijuana, despite frequent challenges by the vestiges of the British ruling circles, has been in effect since the 1925 Convention. In 1961, a Plenipotentiary Conference for the Adoption of a Single Convention on Narcotics Drugs, held under UN auspices, reaffirmed the ban on cannabis, hashish, and other cannabis extracts. In 1968 again, the UN Narcotics Commission supported banning marijuana, and recommended "that all countries concerned increase their efforts to eradicate the abuse and illicit traffic in cannabis...."

Within months, the British counterattacked, and in 1968, the House of Lords created the very first official commission in the world to explicitly recommend the removal of criminal penalties for marijuana possession and use. An official Committee of the British Parliament, it was chaired by the Baroness Barbara Frances Wootton of Abinger, and bears her name. This Wootton Committee report is the founding document for British agent George Soros's dope lobby. Lady Wootton, a Deputy Speaker of the House of Lords, may not be well known, but for over 60 years, beginning in 1922 as a disciple of the evil H.G. Wells, Wootton was a key figure in shaping social policies that would turn modern nation-states—especially the United States—into a version of Aldous Huxley's *Brave New World.*

Wootton joined the board of the Legalize Cannabis Campaign in England, which became the core of an international alliance with the National Organization for the Reform of Marijuana Laws (NORML) in the United States, and a hodge-podge of European groups. Thanks to the Wootton Committee, no longer is the United States known for its "amber waves of grain"; rather, since 1987, marijuana has been the biggest cash crop in America, with an estimated 10,000 metric tons of retail cannabis produced each year as of 2006, according to reports by the United Nations and the U.S. State Department.

2. Soros Model:
Legalization by Deceit

The dope lobby that sprang from the loins of Baroness Wootton today belongs to billionaire Nazi-collaborator Soros, who, since 1994, has poured more than $50 million into elections and resolutions to legalize marijuana in the U.S., along with his co-funders John Sperling of Arizona and Peter Lewis of Ohio. Much more has gone into international efforts.

Soros's dope organizations have morphed several times from the original Lindesmith Center, to the Drug Policy Foundation, and now the Drug Policy Alliance, which also goes by the name of the Drug Policy Alliance Network. There are a multitude of affiliated organizations and websites that get Soros's money for marijuana legalization, including NORML, the Marijuana Policy Project, *High Times* and *Grow* magazines, stopthedrugwar.com, drugsanddemocracy.com, and Americans for Safe Access, to name a few. There is no fight too small for Soros to adopt in the "step-by-step" approach to legalization. In 1998, when Sperling's medical marijuana law was repealed in Arizona, Soros rushed to reinstate it, proclaiming, "I live in one place, but I consider myself a citizen of the world. I have foundations in 30 countries...."

George Soros's step-by-step plan for full legalization of pot now focusses
on promoting the fraud of "medical marijuana." Already, cities like
Mendocino, Calif. have legalized pot for "personal use."

Now Soros's front groups are on a campaign to prevent the Obama Administration from waging an effective drug eradication program using *non-lethal* and *economic development* means, along the lines described by Lyndon LaRouche.

Soros's drug apparatus opposed Obama's appointment of Attorney General Eric Holder, who had led a vigorous, successful campaign in the 1990s to stop "de facto" drug legalization, when he was U.S. Attorney in Washington, D.C.—although they did not dare to say this openly. Instead, the drug apparatus is ramping up for a barrage of resolutions, referenda, and events, to create the myth that there is a mass movement demanding drug legalization. Nothing can be further from the truth. Without Soros's millions, the referenda would fail miserably.

Even Nadelmann has admitted this. In October 1999, Nadelman appeared at the Cato Institute, where one of the main speakers, then New Mexico Gov. Gary Johnson, a "new Republican," came out with guns blazing for legalization: "I am talking about legalization, not decriminalization," boasted Johnson. The drug trade in America is worth about $400 billion—"larger than the car industry."

Nadelmann countered this "legalization" machismo, warning that such open talk had failed over two decades. Instead, the road to legalization is by deceit: New terms were needed, such as "harm reduction" and the "medical benefits" of marijuana. Nadelmann admonished hard-core dopers on the left and the right that although these were just "baby steps," *this* would be the way to success.

Pointing to the 1996 California law, Proposition 215, known as the "Compassionate Use Act of 1996," Nadelmann said this was the *first statewide medical marijuana voter initiative ever adopted in the United States,* and guaranteed that there would be greater achievements to come. Nadelmann was right—until now. From 1999 until Nov. 4, 2008, Soros's dopers won almost all of the medical marijuana initiatives. By 2008, more than 14 states had passed medical decriminalization laws, and about 11 states had some form of decriminalization. The campaign had cost more than $50 million (if not hundreds of millions), mostly from Soros.

Then, in 2008, for the first time in a decade, the dope lobby *lost* in Calfornia. Proposition 5, a plan to replace jail time for drug abusers with rehabilitation program time, got only 40.6% of the vote. Dope pushers had spent close to $10 million on the initiative, including $1.4 from Soros and $400,000 from the Drug Policy Alliance. Making matters worse (for Soros), the Drug Enforcement Administration (DEA) has begun a successful campaign to eradicate marijuana production, and seize the drugs and assets from marijuana "dispensaries" that been set up to sell medical marijuana.

Now the Soros forces are trying to recoup. On Feb. 19, 2009, Nadelmann returned to the Cato Institute to launch a legalization road show that plans to hit 11 U.S. cities in the next month, to try to prevent the Obama Presidency from wiping out drugs. After the California defeat, their strategy will be to bring pro-dope resolutions and laws to city councils and small elected bodies. But already one such effort in El Paso, Texas, was overturned.

3. Welcome to 'Marijuana, Inc.'

In 1999, Gen. Barry McCaffrey, the drug czar under President Bill Clinton, who is hated by the Soros forces, declared that the United States had become a drug producer. Don't blame Peru, Colombia or other foreign countries, said McCaffrey; we have the problem here and the means to solve it. McCaffrey understands the perils of drug legalization, and has again joined the fight against Soros's designs (see *EIR*, Jan. 16, 2009).

Exactly how Soros's step-by-step plan for full legalization of marijuana production, distribution, and use worked, was revealed by CNBC-TV in a documentary, "Marijuana, Inc." which began airing in January 2009. But although the documentary painted a horrific picture of middle school children reeking of pot that is grown and smoked by their parents, and of the rising violence from traffickers in Mendocino County, California, it *never once* mentions Soros or the existence of a dope lobby.

Mendocino County is part of California's "Emerald Triangle," where marijuana growing has been the major industry since about 1998. But, after "medical marijuana," the drug production became bigger—and more insane.

It goes like this: Patients obtain a "medical marijuana" plastic card from a physician for conditions ranging from "anxiety" to terminal cancer; various localities pass ordinances that allow residents to grow marijuana for "personal use," but this turns into a major black market business; "clinics" or "dispensaries" open up, where "patients" buy their marijuana and enjoy their "treatment" on premises.

In economically dead Mendocino County, the marijuana-growing industry brings in about $1.5 billion a year (and this is probably an underestimate), and California supplies about one half of the 10,000 metric tons of marijuana produced in the United States.

The most insane aspect of this is that, under *local laws*, about one third of California's dope production is *legal!* In Mendocino, until recently, a home could have 25 mature marijuana plants on its land. These plants are 8-10 feet tall, and produce about 2 pounds of high-grade marijuana each. With potent marijuana selling for up to $5,000, a "little garden" can gross $200-250,000 in retail sales. These numbers were gleefully explained by Eric Sligh, editor and publisher of *Grow* magazine. But, to the dismay of the legalizers, in the last year, county officials voted to reduce the number of plants to only 6, and added other restrictions. Crime and violence have come to Mendocino, and the community as well as law enforcement, are striking back.

Police have uncovered how multiple houses were bought by major growers/ distributors, who populate them with family members to create virtual "plantations" of legal marijuana. Some houses are nothing but indoor greenhouses filled with sophisticated lighting, fertilizers, and growing solutions.

Another part of the dope empire is the "dispensary," such as the Blue Sky Cafe in Oakland, run by Richard Lee, who spent a lot of time in Amsterdam, where dope cafes are legal. Lee boasted that his cafe has a front section where parents can leave their kids with cafe-provided babysitters, while they shop in the back for up to 20 varieties of high-potency pot. Lee says he pays both state sales tax and Federal income tax. But, he warns, this is all illegal under Federal law, and can be shut down at any time.

Even bigger are the "plantations" hidden deep in the forests and mountains of public lands and national parks, run and populated by the Mexican cartels and their U.S. partners. The cartels bring in Mexican marijuana farmers as virtual slaves, to live in the wilderness, nursing the marijuana farms, setting up long-distance irrigation systems from a water source to a sunny clearing. Many of the Mexicans are under threat that their children or families will be killed if they try to escape.

This is just a snapshot of America's domestic dope business. But as the clear picture of the danger of narcoterrorism now emerges, and as the international community tires of the 100 years of the British Empire's opium war against the rest of the world, time may be running out for George Soros.

LaRouche: 'Medical Marijuana' Is a Fraud

At his Feb. 11 webcast, Lyndon LaRouche was asked a question by a member of Congress, who said, "I'd like to preface my remarks by saying that I am unequivocally opposed to the legalization of drugs in any way, shape, or form. However, the question that I have, regards medicinal marijuana. I am ... deluged with calls about this, mainly from people who are either elderly, or who are stricken with cancer. And they provide me with research, with statistics, and papers and articles, insisting that medical marijuana, prescribed by a physician, does not lead to drug addiction, that it is innocuous, and that it is helpful and merciful to them.

"While I understand the tremendous potential for abuse in legalizing medicinal marijuana—and I think the situation in California speaks to this—it is still something that I think we have to address if for no other reason, than to identify for these people, who really are very much in need, that they may be being manipulated by the drug lobby."

LaRouche replied: "Well, I think we went through this back in the '50s and '60s, and the argument is false. You have people who are desperate, and it is spread also by the 68ers. The 68ers started this thing; and it was started not because marijuana was helpful—people fooled around with this. But the problem was that legitimate medication was not available. And it was a policy of the drug industry not to provide the necessary help.

"The important thing here is, that the promotion of narcotics—and marijuana is a narcotic—the promotion of this in that form, even if you produce medically something very similar to it, if it has clinical value, and producing marijuana, are two different things. So, if you take a drug which has the same effect as is attributed to marijuana, or you take so-called medical marijuana—don't allow the medical marijuana. Get the drug. We should provide, economically, these kinds of things and make them available.

"Now, this is a problem of the drug industry. The drug industry is not necessarily operating in the interests of the people of the United States or Europe. So, therefore, we need a new philosophy on the way medication is generated and provided. The drug industry has become a big financial racket, and its purpose is not medicine; the purpose is money; the purpose is wealth. Physicians need help, not the drug industry.

"But we can provide it, and we should provide it. Even if it's equivalent to marijuana in some symptomatic effect, do it that way; don't do it with marijuana. Why? Because the marijuana is the opening of the control of society by organized crime, international organized crime. And, therefore, if somebody needs something, they get it, but don't give it to them in a way which contributes to organized crime. And what happens is, when you use medical marijuana, it becomes a cover for the use of marijuana in other ways.

"If we're going to have civilization, we have to bring this drug thing under control. It's killing us globally. It's killing us in the United States, and it's a 68er phenomenon. It's a phenomenon which was created by the British, British Intelligence, and we have to defeat that weapon. We have to defeat it entirely; crush it. But we will provide, we have the policy of providing the ill, who need medication, whatever medication they require. But we will do it; we won't have it on the street as medical marijuana."

Soros's Narco-Politicians Demand Drug Legalization

Feb. 19—No one should have been surprised by the Feb. 11 press conference in Rio de Janeiro, in which leaders of the Latin American Commission on Drugs and Democracy (LACDD), an outfit financed and sponsored by Nazi-trained drug-pusher George Soros, issued a statement calling for legalizing marijuana for personal consumption—just for starters—and for ending the "failed" U.S.-backed War on Drugs. These issues must become the subject of a great debate, the LACDD demanded, in which Ibero-American governments would pressure the U.S. into carrying out a "drastic policy shift" toward legalization.

Co-chaired by three former Ibero-American Presidents—Ernesto Zedillo of Mexico, César Gaviria of Colombia, and Fernando Henrique Cardoso of Brazil—the 14-member LACDD has spent the last year spouting off Soros's legalization propaganda at conferences around the Americas. Generously financed by Soros's Open Society Institute and Transnational Institute, the LACDD claimed to be hearing a drumbeat in every country against the "prohibitionist" policies of the U.S. and the Uribe government in Colombia, in favor of a more "humane" approach focussing on "harm reduction" and public-health programs that were more respectful of addicts' "human rights."

Drumbeat? There is none. As the LaRouche movement warned, the LACDD only exists to serve as a fifth column in the British Empire's new Opium War to legalize the global drug trade. The Ibero-American flank in this war is aimed at Mexico in particular, which is fighting for its very survival against the drug cartels, and whose President Felipe Calderón, with aid from the United States, has vowed to follow the Colombia model, and not to cave in to the cartels' terror campaign.

That can't be allowed to happen, the LACDD warns in its statement, "Drugs and Democracy: Toward a Paradigm Shift." The only thing valuable about the Colombian experience, it argues, "is that it is a useful reference for countries not to make the mistake of adopting the U.S. prohibitionist policies."

Colombia's Alvaro Uribe is a problem for the Soros toadies, because he is the only Ibero-American President who has vocally opposed the idea of decriminalizing marijuana for personal use, a policy he charges is a first step toward the full legalization of all drugs.

In a Feb. 12 meeting with Catholic bishops in Bogotá, Uribe repeated that legal consumption stimulates trafficking. "It corrupts children, because it links them with distribution." And, he added, let no one forget that consumption "sustains terrorism."

With few exceptions, most other Presidents are too cowardly to stand up to Soros, stupidly embracing his decrim and "harm reduction" mantra instead. Even Calderón, despite his otherwise tough stance against the cartels, proposed legislation last Fall to decriminalize marijuana. It's not too late for Mexico to fall into line, the LACDD insists. Now that the country has erupted in cartel-linked violence, it is "thus well-positioned" to join *with* the cartels in pressuring the Obama Administration to also legalize.

It's Soros's Drumbeat

The only drumbeat the LACDD's narco-politicians hear comes from their boss Soros, or his various acolytes in the Americas.

Ethan Nadelmann, whose Drug Policy Alliance is spearheading Soros's drug legalization drive internationally, coordinates with the drug kingpin's network of Ibero-American stooges, such as Mexico's former Foreign Minister Jorge Castañeda, who once considered running for President, with Soros's financial backing.

In a Feb. 11 article in the daily *Reforma*, Castañeda admitted that "well-known financier" Soros, and "my friend" Ethan Nadelmann are the "primary sponsors" of the Commission. A mass movement they are not.

This fact notwithstanding, Soros's network is already waging a well-financed public relations campaign whose insidious goal is to make it socially and politically acceptable for governments to debate whether they have the right to defend the minds of their countrymen, and of future generations.

No sooner had the LACDD report been released, than Nadelmann issued a statement describing the report as "a major leap forward in the global drug policy debate," because it breaks the "taboo" of debating legalization of all drugs. He announced that he intends to line up endorsements of the LACDD statement from international political and other leaders, and force through legislative hearings on legalization in national capitals, including Washington, D.C.

Although the LACDD's report is cloaked in sophistry, there is no escaping its central message: that governments must capitulate to the drug cartels and legalize. It complains, for example, that repressive drug policies are so "firmly rooted in prejudices, fears, and ideological visions" such as the "association of drugs with crime," that this "inhibits public debate." For such a debate to occur, it asserts, it will be necessary to break "taboos and acknowledge the failure of current policies."

Brazilian ex-President Fernando Henrique Cardoso spelled it out explicitly in Rio: "The problem is that in the U.S., to date, narco-trafficking is a crime, so any politician is fearful of talking about narco-trafficking or talking about changing policy because they believe that they will be called soft on crime."

The Soros mafia's main objection is that *drug-trafficking* is labelled a crime! What follows from this is the LACDD's insane assertion that "most of the damage associated with cannabis use" doesn't come from the drug itself, but rather, from "the current prohibitionist policies" involving "indiscriminate arrest and incarceration of consumers," and the "violence and corruption that affect all of society."

When a *Wall Street Journal* reporter asked why the Commission hadn't also proposed cocaine legalization, Cardoso was apologetic. Marijuana is about as harmful as alcohol and tobacco, he lied, "so it's possible to consider marijuana to decriminalize … our main idea was to start a debate. So, we are forced to start by saying [let's legalize] marijuana for now, and then let's see what can be done with the rest."

Colombia's Álvaro Uribe Vélez is a problem for the Soros toadies; he is the
only Ibero-American President who has vocally opposed the idea of
decriminalizing marijuana for personal use, a policy he charges is a árst
step toward the full legalization of all drugs.

The Three Stooges

Just how much Soros is paying the three "exes" for their services hasn't been
revealed. But they are all well-qualified for this dirty job. During their respective
terms in office—Cardoso, 1995-2003; Gaviria, 1990-94; and Zedillo, 1994-2000—
each obediently imposed the City of London's free-market and privatization
policies that allowed the drug trade to flourish, and eventually take over entire
economies throughout the region.

At various points over the past year, when Lyndon LaRouche representatives
publicly attacked the LACDD's drug legalization agenda and ties to Soros, the
co-chairmen loudly protested, claiming their position had been misrepresented,
and that they remained "undecided" on the issue. But during a Nov. 26, 2008
conference in Washington, D.C., Zedillo spilled the beans, when confronted by an
EIR correspondent with the sordid details of Soros's collaboration with the Nazis
against his fellow Jews in World War II Hungary. None of that matters, Zedillo
said. "It's completely irrelevant to me" in the current discussion about dealing with
the drug issue.

Gaviria's participation is also telling on two counts. He is infamous in Colombia
for having allowed the drug cartels to infiltrate the 1991 Constituent Assembly
that illegally rewrote Colombia's Constitution, and for also making a deal with the

Medellín Cartel's Pablo Escobar, by which the drug kingpin would only serve a short stint in prison.

Maximiliano Londoño, president of the Lyndon LaRouche Association of Colombia, has recently documented the iron grip which the cartels still hold over that nation's economy and finances, despite the efforts of patriots, at various times, including President Uribe, to drive out the drug trade. Gaviria facilitated the cartel's takeover of the economy.

The former President is also now being mooted as a possible Liberal Party candidate against Uribe in the 2010 elections, should Uribe decide to run for a third term. A Gaviria candidacy should be seen as a virtual death threat against Uribe, Londoño warns. Gaviria could only come close to the Presidency, if Uribe were killed, in the same way he became the Liberal Party's Presidential candidate, after the drug cartels assassinated candidate Luis Carlos Galán in 1990.

How Gaviria would approach the drug issue is revealed in his recent statement that the only problem with the drug trade is that it had been "criminalized" by making it illegal.

Soros/Malloch-Brown Factor in Afghanistan

The Obama Administration must realize that while the Afghan drug lords and their minions, using AK-47s and other weapons, will challenge the opium eradicators on the ground, their battle will be joined at the corporate and diplomatic level by two well-known, and much despised public figures: George Soros and Lord Mark Malloch-Brown. Soros, who has a hook over the world's narcotics cartels, benefits immensely from the explosion of drugs; Malloch-Brown, adequately trained by Her Majesty's Service, serves the interest of the offshore banks and the City of London by helping to procure the much-needed liquidity to keep the imperial wheels greased.

Their common interests have brought the two men close to each other. Malloch-Brown is not merely a collaborator of Soros and his New York house guest, who helped to finance Soros's anti-nation-state war chest with United Nations money; he is a business partner, as well. In April 2007, Malloch-Brown was appointed vice-chairman of Soros's hedge-fund, the Quantum Fund, whence Soros's billions come. The *Financial Times* of London reported that "Sir Mark will also serve as vice-chairman of the billionaire philanthropist's Open Society Institute (OSI), which promotes democracy and human rights, particularly in eastern Europe and the former Soviet Union." The *Financial Times* added in a May 1, 2007 article: "In a letter to shareholders in his Quantum hedge funds, Mr. Soros said Sir Mark would provide advice on a variety of issues to him and his two sons, who now run the company on a day-to-day basis. With his extensive international contacts, Malloch-Brown will help create opportunities for [Soros Fund Management] and the fund around the world."

Now, Lord Malloch-Brown is Minister of State in the Foreign and Commonwealth Office.

In Afghanistan, Soros promotes, while the Afghan drug lords implement—with the help of the militia, illegal cash, and gun power. At the same time, the Soros-funded Senlis Council, having enlisted a number of drug-loving bureaucrats, holds seminars on the "impossibility" of eradication of Afghan opium.

Behind these shenanigans, the prime objective of the Senlis Council, and its benefactor Soros, is to legalize opium production.

In 2005, a visiting scholar of the Carnegie Endowment for Peace, Frederic Grare, in his article, "Anatomy of a Fallacy: Senlis Council and Narcotics in Afghanistan," wrote: "In the present situation, the Senlis proposals would, on the contrary, speed up the transformation of Afghanistan into a narco-economy...."

Soros's pose as a "philanthropist" allows him to use his money to make money through drugs. Soros uses his OSI, Human Rights Watch, and other NGOs to this end.

George Soros (left) and Britain's Lord Mark Malloch-Brown are joined at the
hip, so to speak, in their mutual interest in maintaining the global dope
trade and the billions in cash it produces.

But that is only one side of Soros's face. While promoting needle-exchange
and "harm-reduction" programs, Soros keeps plugging for continuation of drug
production in Central Asia. However, once in a while, somebody sees through his
game plan. For instance, in 2004, Soros's OSI, chanting its "I Love Democracy,"
mantra, moved in to dislodge Uzbek President Islam Karimov. Soros's objective
was to put in place a "democratic liberal government" which would allow, among
other things, huge opium production in the fertile Ferghana Valley to "ease the cash
flow" for both Soros and the country he was planning to control. In 2008, he tried
the same game in Georgia, using his henchman, President Mikheil Saakashvilli.
That effort was thwarted by the angry Russians.

In 2004, Karimov was under security threat from two jihadi groups. One was
the Islamic Movement of Uzbekistan (IMU), funded and armed by the Saudi-
British nexus and protected by the Pakistani ISI in the unchartered tribal areas
of Pakistan. The other group was the Hizb-ut-Tahrir (HT), banned in all Central
Asian Republics and headquartered in South Kensington, England, and which
was extremely active in the Ferghana Valley, calling for unification of Muslims
worldwide under a single caliphate, proclaiming that Western democracy was
unacceptable to Muslims. It is evident that the HT was under British MI5 control.

Karimov, who had taken in a large number of IMU and HT members, soon
discovered the link between the "I Love Democracy" crowd, caliphate-seekers,
and assault rifle-wielding hard-core terrorists.

Karimov shut down the Open Society Foundation.

Drug Money Laundering Keeps the Banks Alive

Feb. 20—Three stunning developments during the past month, focused attention on the world narcotics trade and the laundering of its proceeds, which is virtually the sole source of funds propping up the hopelessly bankrupt Anglo-Dutch world financial system. Were governments to shut down the enormous flow of laundered narco-dollars, which pass primarily through offshore centers such as the Cayman Islands, the Jersey Islands, and the City of London itself, the financial system would seize up, and the world drug trade would come to a dead stop.

- On Jan. 27, in an interview in the Austrian weekly *Profil*, Antonio Maria Costa, director of the UN Office on Drugs and Crime (UNODC), made clear the indispensable role of drugs in holding up the world's banking system. "In many cases," Costa said, "drug money is currently the only liquid investment capital, to buy real estate, for example. In the second half of 2008, liquidity was the biggest problem the banking system had, and therefore, this liquid capital [of drug money flows] became an important factor." On his personal website, the UN's top drug fighter asserted, "with the banking crisis choking lending, these cash-rich criminal groups have emerged as the only sources of credit."

Antonio Maria Costa, head of the UN Office on Drugs and Crime, told an interviewer, "Drug money is currently the only liquid investment capital. . . . In the second half of 2008, liquidity was the biggest problem the banking system had, and therefore, this liquid capital became an important factor."

- On Dec. 11, 2008, FBI agents arrested Bernard Madoff of Madoff Investment Security LLC, on charges of "securities fraud," in connection with a global $50 billion Ponzi scheme. Harry Markopolos, a money manager, testifying Feb. 4, 2009, before a hearing of the House Financial Services Committee's Subcommittee on Capital Markets, isolated the dirty money that was the bedrock of Madoff's operations. Markopolos said:

"Mr. Madoff was running such a large scheme of unimaginable size and complexity, and he had a lot of dirty money. Let me describe dirty money to you. When you're that big and that secretive, you're going to attract a lot of organized crime money, which we now know came from the Russian mob and the Latin American drug cartel. . . .

"The feeder funds that were offshore in tax haven nations attract dirty money. . . . The only reason you go offshore is if it's dirty money. . . . And just given the size, it's statistical. If 5% of the world's currency comes from organized crime, well, Mr. Madoff was going to be at least 5% organized crime for his investors."

TABLE 1: Foreign Positions Held in Offshore Banks, by Country			
	Liabilities June 98 (Billions of $)	Liabilities June 08 (Billions of $)	Population (Thousands)
Offshore			
Bahamas	16	439	306
Bahrain	2	44	586
Cayman Islands	127	1,903	48
Guernsey Islands	N.A.	222	66
Hong Kong	64	627	7,109
Isle of Man	N.A.	97	76
Jersey Islands	N.A.	590	91
Netherland Antilles	43	159	189
Panama	30	106	3,310
Singapore	16	502	4,608
West Indies of the U.K	32	251	3,000
Europe			
Luxembourg	44	1,011	486
Netherlands	127	1,085	16,645
Switzerland	68	1,472	7,582
United Kingdom	134	5,386	60,944

TABLE 1: Foreign Positions Held in Offshore Banks, by Country			
Mideast, Africa			
Israel	17	50	7,184
Kuwait	16	47	3,400
Saudi Arabia	54	161	27,601
United Arab Emirates	47	90	4,621
Total	**851**	**14,347**	**147,919**

Source: Bank for International Settlements.

- On Feb. 17, the U.S. Securities and Exchange Commission charged billionaire and George W. Bush ally Sir Allen Stanford with fraud and multiple violations of U.S. securities laws, for "massive ongoing fraud" involving $8 billion in certificates of deposit, and associated investments. Stanford based his operations on the tiny British-run island enclave of Antigua, in the Caribbean. Functioning through his Stanford International Bank, the Bank of Antigua, and related companies, Stanford's aggregate businesses claimed 30,000 clients, based in 130 countries. The FBI-led multi-agency team raided the Texas-born Stanford's U.S.-based offices in Houston, Miami, Memphis, and Tupelo, Miss.

On Feb. 19, ABC-TV reported, "Federal authorities tell ABC News that the FBI and others have been investigating whether Stanford was involved in laundering drug money for Mexico's notorious Gulf Cartel." Mexican authorities detained one of Stanford's private planes, and, according to officials, checks found on the plane are believed to be connected to the Gulf Cartel.

The Madoff, Stanford, and many other offshore operations now surfacing, are annexes of an international network, under the command of the Anglo-Dutch financial oligarchy, flourishing in scores of offshore centers, that enables the movement of immense volumes of drug money into the world's financial centers. Without the big banks, the drug trade would choke on the physical dollars, and could not get them "out of harm's way" into secured secret locations. The idea that the banks are being taken advantage of by "outside swindlers" should be laughed off the stage—the reality is that drug money laundering is top down, not the other way.

Just how large is the drug money laundering? The accompanying table looks at 20 "offshore" centers, which process the vast majority of the world's dirty money. When money is deposited in a country's banking system by a non-national, it is classified as a "bank's foreign deposit." Deposits are a subset of a bank's liabilities. Therefore, in the table, we report the offshore banks' "foreign liabilities," mostly composed of money that foreigners deposited. Liabilities and assets roughly match, so we could have used either one. Note that between June 1998 and June 2008, the offshore banking centers' foreign liabilities increased from $851 billion to $14.3 *trillion*, an increase of 17 times! This reflects the massive swelling of the monies of the drug trade, and other dirty money, as well as the hedge funds, which operate offshore. The two sources of money are highly intermixed.

Bush family retainer Sir Allen Stanford is under investigation for drug-money laundering for Mexico's notorious Gulf Cartel.

The combined population of the listed countries, most of which are Anglo-Dutch satrapies, is 147.9 million, only 2% of world population, but the banks domiciled here control 44% of the world's foreign liabilities, and a nearly equivalent amount of its assets. *EIR* estimates that the world's drug flow, and associated criminal activity, such as illegal weapons, contraband, etc., amounts to $2 to $3 trillion. The offshore centers are the engines of this operation. Shut them down, and the narcotics trade would go up in smoke.

George Soros Nailed In Dope Banking

George Soros, chief funder and controller of the campaign to legalize narcotics, has been caught in the banking network that launders the criminal proceeds of dope sales.

An *EIR* investigation has uncovered the British-agent billionaire's hand in Colombian and related drug banking, beginning in 1994, when Soros employed his vast offshore funds to shore up the Cali cocaine cartel and its allies against a determined U.S. government effort to shut down the dope.

In January 1994, the Colombian government sold a 75% stake in the Banco de Colombia to Soros's henchmen, the Cali, Colombia-based Gilinski family—Isaac Gilinski and his son Jaime Gilinski, for $432 million. Banco de Colombia had long been identified by the United States Drug Enforcement Administration as under the control of Colombian drug traffickers, for money laundering, in conjunction with the Eagle National Bank of Miami, Florida.

Then in May 1994, the Gilinskis applied to the Colombian government for permission to sell just over 9% of the Banco de Colombia. In August 1994, Soros himself invested an estimated $70 to $80 million to become minority owner with a 9% stake. His man Jaime Gilinski was chairman; Gilinski also acquired the dope cartel's Eagle National Bank in south Florida.

Four years later, Russia's *Argumenty i Fakty*, one of the world's largest-circulation papers, reported (Feb. 18, 1998) on the Gilinskis and the Colombian mafia using billions in cocaine revenue to buy up Russian resort properties, trading cocaine for automatic weapons and surface-to-air missiles that went to narcoterrorists inside Colombia.

Reporter Aleksandr Kondrashov wrote that Russian and Colombian security services were cooperating, and had given out "the valuable information on how the Colombian clan of drug baron Gilinski, is laundering dirty narco-dollars in our country, buying up resorts of Crimea and Russia through figureheads"; and that about $2 billion was estimated to be put into Russia that year, 1998, from cocaine profits.

The report was elaborated on by Dr. Phil Williams of the Strategic Studies Institute at the United States Army War College:

"The Colombian Gilinski family was using drug profits to buy resort property in the Crimea and Russia, and reportedly hired Armenian and Chechen hit men to remove members of Slavic crime groups opposing their activities." (See "Cooperation Among Criminal Organizations," by Dr. Williams, in *Transnational Organized Crime and International Security*, 2002.)

The international banking axis that had been taken over by Soros and his Gilinskis, was bluntly identified in a Public Broadcasting System broadcast Oct. 4, 2000, by Carlos Toro, an informant for the Drug Enforcement Agency who helped put Colombian mafia boss Carlos Lehder and others in jail, and then went into the U.S. Federal Witness Protection Program.

Colombia's Cali cocaine cartel made millions of dollars available to the 1994 Presidential campaign of Ernesto Samper Pizano, as revealed in the famous "narco- cassettes."

"**Mr. Toro**: The Colombian banking industry that ... had subsidiaries in Miami and Panama worked very closely with us [the mafia].... We had Colombian banks, Banco de Colombia, Banco [unintelligible], Banco Cafetero [phonetic], Eagle National Bank of Miami.... In those days ... Eagle National Bank was a powerful aid for us between 1980 and 1984.

"**Interviewer:** But the cartel did not own the bank. It was simply allied with the cartel.

"**Mr. Toro:** The cartel didn't own the bank in front of FDIC, but we own the bank...."

The U.S. Federal Reserve issued a cease and desist order, on March 31, 2005, to Eagle National Holding Co. of Miami, Florida, shutting down suspected money-laundering by the Gilinskis.

The *South Florida Business Journal* reported (Jan. 14, 2005) on Federal actions then in process against Gilinski:

"Eagle National Bank [was] publicly reprimanded by federal banking regulators for violating anti-money-laundering laws.

"The regulators honed in on accounts opened at the bank by foreign political figures and their families, friends and associates that may involve money-laundering, the proceeds of foreign corruption, terrorist financing or other suspicious activity.

"Regulators ... reprimand[ed] Eagle for allowing the bank's largest owner, Colombian businessman Jaime Gilinski and his family, to use the 48-year-old federally chartered bank for personal use with lax oversight.... Gilinski is ... reported to have substantial holdings in Colombia and around the world.... [C] hairman of the Eagle National's holding company, [he] lives in London and could not be reached for comment....

"The bank is prohibited from entering into any new business transactions with Jaime Gilinski, his spouse, children, parents or siblings, [and] any persons who act in Jaime Gilinski's behalf...."

The Soros Group in Colombia
The year that Soros and Gilinski took over Banco de Colombia, 1994, the U.S. government fought to counter the narco takeover of that country. The Clinton Administration, the Justice Department, and Sen. John Kerry (D-Mass.) attacked Gustavo de Greiff, the corrupt chief prosecutor of Colombia from 1992 to 1994, for sabotaging the prosecution of the Cali cocaine cartel, allegedly in exchange for mammoth bribes from the cartel.

Audio tapes were made public (the famous "narco-cassettes" in the "8000 Process" case) showing that the Cali cartel had made millions available to the 1994 Presidential campaign of Ernesto Samper Pizano. De Greiff's daughter, Monica de Greiff, was treasurer of that Samper Presidential campaign. Gustavo de Greiff notoriously dismissed the case, and had to leave his post as chief prosecutor.

In a confidential February 1994 memo, later declassified, U.S. Ambassador Morris Busby had reported on his meeting with Samper Pizano and Monica de Greiff, in which she claimed the Cali cartel would "reduce the amount of cocaine ... on the streets of New York," if the U.S. would strike a deal with them.

In April 1994, Soros's Drug Policy Foundation put Gustavo de Greiff, then still chief proscutor, on a United States tour against drug law enforcement. The Soros group staged a Washington, D.C. press conference for him on April 23, since, "The chief prosecutor has been attacked with increasing vigor by a series of U.S. government officials." At the conference, de Greiff demanded that the U.S. attacks on him stop, and the U.S. War on Drugs be closed down.

The next month, the Gilinskis applied to de Greiff's government for permission to sell part ownership of the Banco de Colombia to George Soros.

Over the succeeding years, Gustavo de Greiff went into exile in Mexico, where he had been Colombian ambassador for a time. He is now the chief spokesman for the Soros-Gilinski partnership, while serving as the spokesman and attorney for the Gilinski family, as they and George Soros have carried out a decade-long legal battle to squeeze more money out of the Banco de Colombia (now called Bancolombia), whose control they have lost.

At the same time, de Greiff is one of the leading hemispheric spokesman for the Soros drug legalization movement, operating for various Soros entities in North and South America (such as the group Law Enforcement Against Prohibition), pulling together the lobbying forces of narcotics producers and their financiers, demanding the surrender of law enforcement.

The Gilinski family continues to operate a string of banks in Colombia and offshore in the Caribbean, including the Colombian bank Sudameris, Banco Tequendama, the cash dispensers and ATM network Servibanca in Colombia, and the Sudameris assets in Panama and in the drug-money-laundering center, the Cayman Islands.

The Opium War
200 Years of British Drug Wars

The British Imperial drug war against civilization got its start with the British East India Company's production of opium in British India, and 29 years of Opium Wars against China, to force the acceptance of free trade in deadly opium upon the 5,000-year-old Chinese culture. The 1840-60 Opium War consisted of two phases of direct British military campaigns against China (usually called the First and the Second Opium Wars), and a British-controlled peasant revolt, known as the Taiping Rebellion, which followed the common Imperial pattern of British-instigated religious fundamentalist movements, aimed at disrupting the national unity of the target population. Altogether, these wars effectively left a broken China under the financial control of the East India Company drug dealers, killing more than *20 million* Chinese along the way.

The British East India Company
In the 17th and 18th centuries, the privately constituted British East India Company established trading houses in Indian cities, and eventually expanded its control over the entire subcontinent, building a 150,000-strong private army in the process, all under the banner of free trade.

The British were less successful in breaking through China's barriers against foreign intervention and trade. The reigning Qing Dynasty strictly forbade foreign presence or trade outside the single trading post in Quangzhou (Canton).

The Chinese banned opium in 1729, a ban that was strengthened in 1799, in the face of British opium smuggling from Bengal. The British ignored the ban, and made lucrative alliances with Chinese merchant families in Guangzhou willing to flout the law, while the Company expanded its smuggling routes to the cities along the southern coast. These criminal activites were led by William Jardine and James Matheson, whose infamous partnership in 1828, Jardine Matheson & Co., became the largest opium business in the world, interlinked with the Hongkong and Shanghai Bank, whose current incarnation, the HSBC, is a bank associated with drug-money laundering throughout its history. By 1836, the East India Company was delivering 30,000 chests of opium to China, enough to supply more than 12 million users. The impact on society was devastating, draining the country of silver, while destroying the minds of millions of Chinese.

In 1839, the Emperor sent leading scholar and statesman Lin Zexu as commissioner to Guangzhou, with orders to crush the opium trade. Lin was already familiar with the moral depravity of the southern merchants who were enriching themselves as compradors for the British poison. They were also the sponsors of a school of thought among scholars, called the Han Learning, which opposed the moral traditions of the national government and educational system, based upon the great Song Renaissance of the 11th and 12th centuries. The Han

Learning school promoted a pragmatic ideology which served the same purpose as today's "Open Society" fanatics, financed by drug promoter George Soros on behalf of his British sponsors: "opening" to drugs and financial thievery at the expense of the sovereign state.

When the scholar Lin Zexu wrote to Queen Victoria, appealing to her to stop the destruction of China with opium, the Empire instead sent its navy to "defend the principle of free trade." Shown, British warships capture Chusan, during a naval battle in 1840.

Lin set up his headquarters at the school run by the leading Confucian scholar in Guangzhou, moving immediately to arrest the Chinese opium merchants, including the local government officials, confiscating every chest of opium from the British. A grand celebration was staged before a gathering of the British drug dealers and much of the population of Guangzhou, where over 20,000 chests of opium were destroyed.

This was the occasion of the famous letter from Lin Zexu to Queen Victoria, appealing to her conscience to prevent her subjects from acting to destroy China with their opium. The Queen refused, choosing instead to follow the instructions of Foreign Secretary Lord Palmerston, to support the East India Company and the British Navy in "defending the principle of free trade" in drugs. A massive British flotilla arrived in 1840, which quickly destroyed the outmoded military defenses of the Chinese, beginning with Guangzhou, bombarding the city until it submitted and paid tribute. The warships then moved up the coast, repeating the process at every city along the way, including Shanghai, before moving up the Yangtze River to Nanjing, the southern capital. At that point, the Emperor sued for peace.

The Treaty of Nanjing, signed on August 29, 1842, ceded the island of Hongkong to Britain in perpetuity as the headquarters for its drug operations, and opened four other ports to British merchants, where British warships were to be allowed entry "when the interests of trade demanded." But the Treaty was a compromise, since the Chinese did not give unlimited access to the opium dealers, although they did grant open access to the merchants' devilish missionaries. This provided the conditions which Lord Palmerston needed to begin making arrangements for phase two—to take over the country in full.

The Taiping Rebellion

The Taiping Tianguo (Heavenly Kingdom of Great Peace) controlled nearly one half of the territory of China at the peak of its peasant revolt, which lasted from 1853 to 1865. It began as a pseudo-religious cult in the countryside near Guangzhou, in the 1840s, in the midst of the spread of opium and demoralization following China's defeat at the hands of the British drug dealers in 1842. Its leader Hong Xiuquan read a Protestant tract from Hongkong, and had a vision that he was the second Son of God, Christ's brother, sent to cleanse China of evil—not the British barbarians, but the Manchurians (who ran the Qing Dynasty)—and Confucianism itself. Their fundamentalist doctrines had Christian wrappings, but had more to do with local Daoist beliefs than anything associated with Christianity. The British quickly took them under their wing.

While the Taiping peasant army rampaged across the countryside, taking over much of the South and seizing Nanjing as their capital, Hong Xiuquan's cousin Rengan was brought to Hongkong, where he receiving intense training from British missionaries, headed by James Legge, the British expert on Chinese religious beliefs. Legge, whose bowdlerized translations of the Confucian, Buddhist, and Daoist Classics are treated as authoritative still today, labored to subvert and destroy the humanist tradition in Chinese Confucianism, while training the leader of a pagan insurgency to impose British colonial rule over China. British intelligence agent Lawrence of Arabia would have been proud.

In a manifesto written by Hong Rengan upon his return to Nanjing: "At present [England] is the mightiest nation of the world, owing to its superior laws. The English are noted for their intellectual power and national strength, are proud by nature, and averse to being subordinate."

W.A.P. Martin, an American Presbyterian missionary, and close friend of Massachusetts politician Caleb Cushing, whose family had become rich in the China opium trade, and who was playing a leading role in instigating the U.S. Civil War on behalf of the British, visited the Taiping in Nanjing regularly. In a series of public letters to Cushing, Martin wrote: "The Tartars [Manchurians] dynasty, too far gone in senility to afford any encouraging prospect of reformation, will now, perhaps, consider the expediency of recognizing its youthful rival [the Taiping] which, catching the spirit of the age, may be prevailed upon to unlock the treasures of the interior and throw open its portals to unrestricted trade.... Divide and conquer is the stratagem to be employed in storming the citadels of oriental exclusiveness."

Although the Western powers were officially neutral in the civil war between the Qing government and the Taiping, British diplomats threatened Beijing that they would grant official recognition to the Taiping, if the government failed to accept all British demands for a new treaty, when the 1842 Nanjing Treaty expired in 1856.

Second Opium War

The British were not interested in negotiations. As soon as the Nanjing Treaty ran out, they immediately launched a full-scale military operation, this time with French support, occupying Guangzhou, then moving up the coast, reaching Beijing in 1860. While the British-sponsored Confederacy was busy trying to split up the United States, British and French forces were burning and looting Beijing.

The Chinese finally capitulated. Opium was legalized and domestic production was introduced, leading to an estimated 30-40 million addicts by the turn of the century (so much for George Soros's argument that legalization will not lead to greater usage). The customs houses were taken over by the British, demonstrating once again the cold advice of Mayer Amschel Rothschild in 1790: "Let me control a nation's money and I care not who writes the laws."

The task remained of cleaning up the mess left by their sponsorship of the Taiping Rebellion, which was no longer needed as leverage against Beijing. The British re-deployed their military forces, led by Charles "Chinese" Gordon, fresh from burning the Summer Palace in Beijing, to join those of the Qing armies, in one of the great slaughters of the century, wiping out nearly every remaining member of the Taiping.

The British were effectively in full financial, military, and political control of the decaying Qing Dynasty. Only when Sun Yat-sen led a Republican Revolution in 1911, based on the principles of the American System of physical economy, inspired by Abraham Lincoln's defeat of the British war to divide the Union, was China able to begin the long, hard struggle to regain its true sovereignty.

Afghanistan Heroin Drives Drug Epidemic in Russia

Feb. 19—In a survey of the world illegal drug trade in 1996, *EIR* identified the newly independent states of the former Soviet Union and the former socialist bloc in Eastern Europe as Dope, Inc's fastest-growing expansion market. The overnight imposition of radical free-market policies in those countries opened them up for a hugely expanded role in drug transshipment from production areas into Europe, as well as for an explosion of addiction among their own abruptly impoverished and displaced populations.

By the middle of this decade, as Afghanistan narcotics production surged after 2001 (see article, this section), international health organizations supporting HIV treatment and control programs inside Russia reported a new pattern within an alarming epidemic: Among the HIV-AIDS hotspots in the country were not only port cities like St. Petersburg, or Moscow, the capital, but also cities deep in the Russian interior. Towns on the lower Volga River such as Samara, Saratov, Volgograd, and the auto industry center of Togliatti began to show HIV prevalence rates in excess of 1% or even 2% of the population. They are on the waterway and road transport routes from Afghanistan. A great majority of the HIV-AIDS victims were young injecting drug users.

A series of reports and proposals made in the past three months by Victor Ivanov, Prime Minister Vladimir Putin's deputy chief of staff at the Kremlin, and now head of the Federal Drug Control Agency, have situated the overwhelmingly Afghanistan-origin drug epidemic as a top public-health and national-security issue for Russia. Bringing the picture up to date at a Feb. 12 press conference, held at the Itar-Tass news agency, Ivanov said: "The increase in the number of drug addicts in Russia is beginning to look like an epidemic. Each day, over 80 people die from drugs and more than 250 become drug addicts."

There are 537,000 officially registered drug users in Russia, but Ivanov cited estimates by international agencies that are five times higher. "Around 90% of the drug addicts in Russia are addicted to Afghan opiates; are hooked on the 'Afghan needle,'" he said.

In a December 2008 interview with the government daily *Rossiyskaya Gazeta*, Ivanov showed starkly how the drug plague which has swept Russia contributes to the country's steep population decline. From a level of nearly 150 million people at the time of the break-up of the Soviet Union in 1991, the population of the Russian Federation has fallen to under 142 million. Most of those 537,000 registered drug addicts, Ivanov noted, are young. Looking back eight years to 2001, the number of registered drug addicts in Russia was 496,000, but the majority of the 2001 group have died. According to Ivanov, 90% of Russian drug addicts have Hepatitis C and 75% have HIV/AIDS. He gives the life expectancy of a newly identified drug addict as five to six years.

But the total numbers are greatly understated; statistics on traffic stops show that as few as 3% of drivers stopped in a state of narcotic intoxication are registered as addicts. At Feb. 18 State Duma hearings on the data from Ivanov's agency, Speaker of the Duma Boris Gryz-lov said, "Since 1990, drug consumption in Russia has grown almost tenfold, and is currently eight times higher than in the European Union."

Quantifying the flood of opium and heroin out of Afghanistan into and through Russia, Ivanov said that 29 tons of narcotics had been seized in Russia as of December, with 10-15 shipments being caught daily. He subsequently gave an updated year-end figure of 38 tons of drugs seized, including 3.5 tons of heroin.

Ivanov told *Rossiyskaya Gazeta* in December that he does not favor increased cooperation with NATO in Afghanistan, which he termed a narco-state, because opium cultivation has boomed in that country, since the beginning of the NATO operation there. For counterterror purposes, Ivanov suggested, what's needed are serious special service operations, not an occupation by 60,000 troops. At that time, he also cited information received on British-linked South Asian narcotics kingpin Dawood Ibrahim's role in the Mumbai, India terror attacks, as a case in point on the need to shut down the Afghanistan opium trade; he also highlighted the role of narcoterrorists in Russia's North Caucasus, a major area of intense activity by London- and Saudi-supported separatist networks. "In Russia, as well, terrorism cannot be overcome without liquidation of the drug shipments out of Afghanistan," said Ivanov.

Ivanov told *Rossiyskaya Gazeta* on Jan. 30 that the Russian government desires to work with the new U.S. Administration in Afghanistan to fight drug trafficking. Noting the spread of drug crops and trafficking from southern Afghanistan to the whole area along the border with the Central Asian countries, Ivanov said, "To reduce this danger, we are vitally interested in working with the new American Administration."

This proposal for U.S.-Russia collaboration, as *EIR* reported Feb. 6, was heartily endorsed by Lyndon LaRouche, who emphasizes that the only way to stabilize the world strategic situation, is for the U.S. to get out of Afghanistan militarily (except for a presence around the capital), and to wage an all-out war on drugs. "Either we stop the drug trafficking, or we lose civilization," LaRouche said.

In the Jan. 30 interview, Ivanov called for con-vening a conference under UN auspices on "Peace and Prosperity in Afghanistan," as a "first step" in such U.S.-Russian collaboration against drugs. "It would be appropriate to hold such a conference in Afghanistan itself, e.g., in Kabul," said Ivanov. All tribes, areas, and political forces "prepared for a constructive dialogue" should be invited, he said, proposing a special role for Russia, as a country "whose forces have not participated in this seven-years-long war." Ivanov said that creation of a "single, independent, and strong nation of Afghanistan" would be the pathway to tackling the explosion of the heroin business.

The language of Ivanov's Peace and Prosperity conference appeal closely echoes a Russian policy discussion paper, published at the end of last year by the Institute for Demography, Migration and Regional Development, under the title, "The Path to Peace and Concord in Afghanistan Will Be Determined by the Position Russia Takes." The just-issued English edition is excerpted in the pages that follow.

Russia's Policy Will Determine The Path to Peace in Afghanistan

The following is excerpted, with permission, from a report by the Institute for Demography, Migration and Regional Development and the Development Movement, Moscow 2008, titled, "The Path to Peace and Concord in Afghanistan Will Be Determined by the Position Russia Takes." It was prepared by researchers Yuri Krupnov (project leader), Ilnur Batyrshin, Andranik Derenikian, Boris Krupnov, and Serafim Melentiev. The full report is available online at http://afghan.idmrr.ru/ afghan.idmrr.ru_eng.pdf.

The main goal of this report is to propose theses for discussion in order to elaborate a new policy on Afghanistan for Russia.

This report incorporates the results of discussions with Russian and Afghan experts, representing different opinions on the situation in Afghanistan. It is also based on data obtained from Afghan, Russian, and foreign experts, the Regional Studies Center of Afghanistan (Kabul), analytical surveys done by the Modern Afghanistan Studies Center (Moscow), as well as the publications of Russian and foreign nongovernmental organizations and mass media.

The Problem of Afghanistan for Russia and the World

The ongoing civil war in Afghanistan, and the essential inability or unwillingness of a number of foreign states and their military contingents to bring peace and concord to the people of Afghanistan are the source of fundamental challenges, threats, and aggression for Russia and other countries, namely:

- the drug threat and drug aggression, as a result of which, the majority of Russian drug addicts are taking Afghan opiates and heroin, while the overall number of people addicted to these most dangerous drugs is steadily increasing; furthermore, over the past five years we have observed a drastic growth in the export of cannabis group drugs from Afghanistan to Russia;
- the threat from transnational criminal groups, closely connected to the drug business and drug trafficking from Afghanistan to Russia via the Middle (Central) Asian republics, gaining strength in Middle Asia;[1]
- the threat from the presence of U.S. and NATO armed forces in Afghanistan and its neighbors in the form of a network of "military super-bases."

In general, due to the ongoing military actions and foreign interference in its affairs, Afghanistan has become a source of growing threats and aggression which affect the Russian Federation directly, as well as through the Middle Asian tes, and increase general instability, undermining Russia's overall capacities and strength.

---

1. The authors have chosen the terms "Middle Asia" and "New Central East" for the English edition of their study, in preference to the traditional imperial "Central Asia."

MAIN ROUTES OF HEROIN TRAFFICKING
FROM AFGHANISTAN TO RUSSIA

At the same time, Russia, at present, does not possess proven methods and technologies to protect the country from the threats and aggression mentioned above. This has to do with the fundamentally new situation existing in Afghanistan, in which routine economic and military approaches and solutions are destined to be ineffective.

Analysis shows that only realistic way of eliminating the above-mentioned threats and aggression is the intensified development of the state in Afghanistan, transforming this country into a strong and self-sufficient nation. This challenge, in turn, requires the elaboration and implementation of totally new approaches, which will be comprehensive and relevant in the -humanitarian, political-anthropological, and socio--economic spheres, contributing to building a strong and prosperous Afghan state.

There need to be new approaches and development methods, which, in their totality, would allow Afghanistan to gain its independence; build up and strengthen its statehood; carry out an intensified transition from a ruined society and economy with an expanding drug business, accounting for over half of the country's GDP, to a prosperous, stable and consolidated society, ensuring a worthy life for every single Afghan citizen and ethnic group.

A Comprehensive Afghanistan Development Plan2

The establishment of a strong, united and independent state in Afghanistan is impossible without reconstruction of the basic conditions for its people's life and activities.

In a situation where real unemployment is close to 80% and more than half of the GDP is formed by cultivation, production and illegal trafficking of drugs, the main task for the Afghan government and the international community is to set up life-support infrastructure, able to provide no less than 1 kWh of electricity, one liter of drinking water and 10 liters of process water per day for each citizen of Afghanistan.

At present, all the proposed so-called "development plans" for Afghanistan have at least one important defect: lack of a strategic horizon. These plans for the most part cover the issues of rendering foreign donor help to Afghanistan, ignoring the issues of promoting the country's economic self-reliance and self-sufficiency. Afghanistan needs a Comprehensive Development Plan built on new principles and approaches.

The method of intense improvement and recovery of the basic conditions for life and human activity requires a combination of elements for accelerated industrialization—advanced development of the means of production and of the real economy, i.e., economic development planning centered on estimated minimum and additional consumption, as well as on practically oriented fundamental science.

A transition from the present state to the one required will be impossible without the creation of strategic life-support infrastructure and full-scale productive forces. The latter should be based on practically oriented fundamental science, with the development of education and innovational advanced industry, which would be set up in Afghanistan through cooperation involving other countries.

Development of the energy sector, especially of the electric power industry, is a high priority for the economic development of Afghanistan. It can give an impetus to the development of the entire productive sector and dramatically raise the level and quality of life for the Afghan people. There is a great need for an Afghanistan State Electrification Plan, similar to the early 20th-Century GOELRO (State Plan for the Electrification of Russia), which provided the impulse for the Russian and Soviet industrialization. In particular, full cascades of power plants must be built on the rivers of Afghanistan, primarily on the Kunduz, Kokcha, Kabul, Helmand, and Hari Rivers. Furthermore, it is necessary to build or modernize the electric power lines from Tajikistan, Turkmenistan, and Uzbekistan to Afghanistan to provide additional electricity for the country's needs.

Efforts must also be focused on solving the problem of providing Afghanistan with adequate drinking and process water. This is a crucial factor in overcoming the imbalance between population growth and the reduction of overall land under cultivation and agricultural output.

---

2. The following excerpts are from Chapters 7-11 of the report.

One of the strategic objectives must be the construction of a railway line on the route Mashhad (Iran)-Herat-Kandahar-Quetta (Pakistan), which would integrate Afghanistan into the global railway network and goods circulation system. This line must become the backbone of the Afghan Development Corridor, which would be a place of concentrated implementation of development projects and would make Afghanistan a strong and economically self-sufficient state, able to take care of its further development and prosperity independently.

It would be appropriate to examine and approve the Comprehensive Afghanistan Development Plan at an International Conference on Peace and Prosperity for Afghanistan, to be held in Kabul.

Exporting Development

In the present circumstances in and around Afghanistan, Russia has a unique opportunity not only to develop a new policy on Afghanistan, but to take that as an opportunity to elaborate new principles for its entire foreign policy.

Russia cannot continue to maintain its own existence as a world power (*mirovaya derzhava*) by further resigning itself to isolationism and provincialism. Russia has always existed and will exist with its full identity only as a world power, i.e., as a state entity which takes responsibility for formulating and working to solve world problems.

Implementation of the *mirovaya derzhava* doctrine requires countering the export of democracy, which currently dominates the world, with the export of development, i.e., the transfer of methods and technologies for the comprehensive development of countries, regions and spheres of activities. Only by exporting development to other countries will Russia be able to deal with civilizational, political, and economic challenges, while simultaneously maintaining its own development.

The export of democracy has revealed not only its forcible and violent nature, but also a plain failure to be effective. Moreover, in practice it has turned out to mean the export of financial and economic crisis and military conflict, i.e., the guaranteed export of instability.

Russia has a unique opportunity to turn its traditional role of helping other countries to develop, into a major principle of its foreign policy. Unfortunately, indiscriminate criticism of the Soviet past and an imaginary intrinsic imperial character of Russia have disavowed and virtually wiped from public memory this central direction of Russian international activity, historically: its fruitful and devoted efforts to train development elites for other countries, providing them with scientific, educational and industrial-technological support.

Today, we must not only set the historical record straight, but also develop this hereditary feature of our nation into a principle of joint development, or co-development, which means the export of development as the targeted transfer of the full-set development capabilities to partner countries, enabling them to make qualitative breakthroughs.

The key idea of exporting development is to create full-fledged productive forces in the country under development, which would comprise three elements: developing education, fundamental practically oriented science, and innovational industry. In this sense, the export of development may be counterposed to the export of democracy, which implies the imposition of alien state organizational and social standards on the country which is a recipient of "democracy." Russia's mission in Afghanistan is to create full-scale production forces, appropriate for the goals which are set.

The necessary preconditions exist for adopting such a doctrine at the government level. *Inter alia*, it is significant that at the meeting of the Council of Heads of Governments of the Shanghai Cooperation Organization on October 30, 2008 in Astana, Prime Minister of the Russian Federation Vladimir Putin said that "values and models of development are becoming the subject of competition. We have to join our efforts to promptly complete the transformation of the global and regional security and development architecture by adjusting it to the new conditions of the 21st Century, when stability and prosperity are becoming inseparable concepts."

Russia needs a strong, safe, and friendly Afghanistan. Therefore, a Russian doctrine of exporting development can become the foundation for solving the current problems of this country. The export of development to Afghanistan would bring peace and prosperity to Central Asia, strengthen economic and political ties between the Middle Asian states and Russia and also would set an example to other great powers.

As a first step, the Russian Federation could propose to Afghanistan and other interested countries the elaboration of a Comprehensive Afghanistan Development Plan, and cover the initial expenses.

Afghanistan Development Projects

One of the main causes of the ongoing war in Afghanistan is that it lacks the economic conditions for its people to lead a decent and comfortable life. Many of those engaged in military actions do so because, in the present socio-economic situation, they are unable to support their families by their own labor.

Therefore, in order to stop the war in Afghanistan and restore peace in the country, a solution to the economic and social problems of the country must be found, above all. The recovery of Afghanistan's ruined economy requires the elaboration of comprehensive development plans and projects, along with a mobilization of the forces and joint labor of all Afghan citizens.

The rural way and pattern of life are traditional for the Afghan people, and the country's development system must preserve and rely on this unique asset. That is why progressive agriculture, organized in an exemplary way, should become the basis of Afghanistan's economy. A farmer confidently looking forward, providing for his family and leading a decent life based on his honest and highly skilled labor could become the symbol of Afghanistan as soon as ten years from now.

On the whole, the development of agriculture must involve not only the cultivation of crops, but also the creation of a processing industry for the types of crops being grown. The southern provinces of Afghanistan are famous for their fruit. Thus, cultivation and processing of fruit would be the most promising area of agriculture industry there.

During 30 years of the civil war, the culture of farming has been almost completely forgotten, such that today many people do not know how to till the soil and cultivate crops. The creation of a nationwide network of agricultural educational institutions, whose graduates will be able to organize highly efficient agriculture, must be one of the major projects. It will become prestigious to study at these universities and colleges, and their graduates will be respected in society as people working for the benefit of the entire Afghan population.

High-quality agricultural machinery is crucial for developing successful agriculture. Therefore, every international conference on Afghanistan's development should focus on issues of arranging deliveries of agricultural machinery to the country, providing maintenance service for the equipment, and sending specialists to the country to teach people how to use the machinery. The international community and donor countries should help, first and foremost, by providing special machinery, equipment, and qualified specialists, as well as by providing a guaranteed market for Afghanistan's agricultural products. This is preferable to monetary grants, most of which do not enrich the Afghan people, but rather line the pockets of intermediary organizations.

It would be reasonable to begin pilot projects in one or two provinces, which would later become models for the organization of development in a specific area. Comprehensive development of these experimental provinces would include agricultural, industrial, infrastructure, and energy projects, as well as road construction, organization of water supplies, etc.

We would propose Nangarhar and Helmand as the model provinces. It would be appropriate to establish special administrative bodies responsible for the suggested projects.

Nangarhar development projects:
1. Reconstruction of the Jalalabad irrigation canal.
2. Reconstruction and construction of a complete cascade of power plants on the Kabul River (Naglu HPP, etc.) and construction of reservoirs along the river.
3. Establishment of sugar-cane plantations and construction of a sugar factory.
4. Revival of olive plantations and construction of an olive oil factory.
5. Setting up rose plantations and a rose essence and perfume production plant.
6. Reconstruction of the vegetable canning factory.
7. Revival of citrus farming for cultivation of lemons, oranges, tangerines, and grapefruits.

Helmand development projects:
1. Setting up pomegranate farms and factories for producing pomegranate juice. Afghan pomegranates are of higher quality than the African ones, making this project very promising for the southern provinces.
2. Establishment of sunflower plantations and factories for producing sunflower oil (this project could also be implemented in Badakhshan).
3. Establishment of saffron plantations. A kilogram of saffron sells for around $2,500 on the world market. There is huge demand for it, making this a very profitable project.
4. Establishment of red pepper plantations.
5. Establishment of production and packaging of dried fruits.
6. Establishment of cotton plantations, as well as launching of clothing and textile production.
7. Establishment of vegetable storage facilities with refrigeration.

The Helmand development projects can also be implemented in other southern provinces, such as Oruzgan and Kandahar. In general, an individual list of development projects should be prepared for each province. The projects must be capable of palpably helping a province and creating jobs for its population. For instance, sugar beet plantations and sugar factories should be established in Baghlan: Afghanistan consumes around 800,000 tons of sugar per year, so there is strong demand for this product.

Such projects would give an impetus to the economic development of the provinces and create jobs for thousands of people.

A national oil and gas company should be established to exploit the Afghan oil and gas fields and organize oil extraction in Lowgar and Paktika, as well as gas extraction in Sar-e Pol and other places. Afghanistan has enough gas for its own needs, but this gas needs to be extracted. Russia's Gazprom could become a partner and supplier of gas transportation and extraction technologies.

Gold mining at the four largest gold deposits of the country, which are now being plundered, should be placed under firm state control.

It is necessary to restore industry rapidly according to a special plan: build a cement plant, a clothing factory, and chemical fertilizer factories in Mazari Sharif and other provinces, reconstruct the Jangalak factory in Kabul, etc. This requires giving up the free-market model in favor of establishing and supporting a class of Afghan industrialists. It is also necessary to restore and organize development of Soviet-built facilities. Afghanistan's development projects must not be limited to economic ones. Socio-cultural projects are also of great importance.

For example, there is a need to solve the problem of providing higher education opportunities for graduates of Afghan schools. There are around 5 million pupils in Afghan schools now, meaning that 300,000-450,000 children graduate each year. At present, the universities can accept only around 15,000 entrants, so there is a great gap between the total number of secondary school graduates and how many are able to receive a higher education. The number of university entrants should be increased up 60,000 people per year in the next ten years, while the overall number of university students should be increased from 45,000 to 250,000. This requires convening an international conference on the development of higher education in Afghanistan.

Cooperation with Neighbors for Development
A lasting peace in Afghanistan depends on two factors.

First, it is unacceptable to regard Afghanistan as an area for testing geopolitical projects. Thus, a timetable for the withdrawal of foreign military forces must be set, and any activity by a global or regional power in its own interests, at the expense of Afghanistan, must be prohibited.

Second, a gigantic resource for the stabilization and development of Afghanistan lies in the implementation by neighboring countries of a unified, coordinated Afghan development policy. Peace in Afghanistan can be achieved much sooner, if its neighbors combine their efforts to ensure security and stability in the country.

That is why Pakistan, Iran, Russia, China, India, Tajikistan, Uzbekistan, Turkmenistan, and Kyrgyzstan must be broadly represented at the International Conference on Peace and Prosperity for Afghanistan, in Kabul, and participate in decision-making on securing peace in the country.

Cooperation with neighboring counties is also necessary for launching the development of Afghanistan. For example, construction of the Afghan Development Corridor Mashhad (Iran)-Herat-Kandahar-Quetta (Pakistan) will be impossible without the involvement of Iran and Pakistan, with the active participation of Russia as coordinator of the international efforts.

Afghanistan needs neighborly cooperation to rebuild itself as a united, sovereign, and economically effective state, which would not only put an end to the export of instability, drugs, and terrorism, but also serve as an example of accelerated industrialization and development.

Afghanistan's neighbors must help it achieve this goal in order to ensure firm cooperative security and stability. This would also help in forming a united, peaceful macro-region, the Novy Sredny Vostok (New Central East). Consequently, Afghanistan's neutral status needs to be guaranteed. This could become one of the key issues on the agenda of the International Conference on Peace and Prosperity for Afghanistan, where all countries of the Novy Sredny Vostok region should be represented.

The SCO Factor

Deepening of strategic partnership between the neighboring countries, aimed at solution of the Afghanistan problem, would be most productive within the framework of the Shanghai Cooperation Organization (SCO). The leading role of this organization in defining and solving key problems of the Eurasian region is widely recognized at the present time. It is also very important that all of Afghanistan's neighbors are either members of the SCO or have observer status, which creates unique conditions for elaborating and mutually agreeing upon a new strategy and plans for supporting the establishment of a strong and independent Afghan state.

3. Dope, Inc. Is $600 Billion And Growing

Dope, Inc. Is $600 Billion And Growing

In the summer of 1996, the editors and staff of *Executive Intelligence Review* conducted the most exhaustive study of the worldwide illegal drug trade to be undertaken in years. The results of that survey were published in the July 26, 1996 issue of *EIR* ("Britain's Dope, Inc. Grows to a $521-Billion Business"). That study was, in part, provoked by an autumn 1995 *EIR* profile of the "new international terrorism," which highlighted the very Afghansi mujahideen and Ibero-American narcoterrorist organizations that have waged war against every nation-state on this planet for the past decade, culminating in the irregular warfare assaults of Sept. 11, 2001.

What linked the two groundbreaking *EIR* reports was the fact that the global $ 1-trillion-per-year underground economy of guns and drugs represented the logistical heart of the new international terrorism. From the opium fields of Afghanistan to the coca plantations of Colombia, the legions of modern irregular warfare combatants, deployed top-down by factions of the Anglo-American oligarchy (with generous assistance from elements within the Israeli military and intelligence structures), survive or fall, on the strength of the "logistics in depth" of the underground economy of illegal weapons and drugs.

To defeat international terrorism today, governments of the world, led by the United States and Russia, must undertake a no-holds-barred assault on the underground economy of illegal drugs and weapons—what the editors of *EIR* first labelled "Dope, Inc." back in 1978. The black market in guns and drugs is the Achilles heel of the modern irregular warfare apparatus. Take out that infrastructure, and the capacity of this network to conduct their warfare is destabilized, decisively.

This means, above all else, that the "Grasso Factor" can no longer be tolerated, if the world is to survive the ongoing drive for a global "Clash of Civilizations" aimed at spreading war and chaos across the entire Eurasian landmass. The "Grasso Factor" refers to the now-infamous visit the chairman of the New York Stock Exchange, Richard Grasso, paid to the Colombian jungles, in June 1999, where he embraced a top leader of the F ARC (Revolutionary Armed Forces of Colombia), Raúl Reyes, and pronounced one of the world's leading narcoterrorists "a man Wall Street can do business with."

Since the Grasso visit, damning new evidence has emerged of the FARC's far-flung drug operations, including evidence of a multibillion-dollar-a-year FARC guns-for-drug alliance with the Mexican Arellano Félix drug cartel, the biggest and most murderous drug gang in that country.

It is now an open secret that the major Wall Street and City of London commercial banks launder hundreds of billions of dollars in illegal drug money every year *as a matter of policy*. U.s. intelligence officials privately acknowledge that all of the major New York commercial banks have emissaries in Colombia,

Peru, Paraguay, and the other capitals of Dope, Inc., soliciting the narcotraffickers' business. There is a fierce competition for narco-dollars—one of the biggest sources of cash flow in the world today, at a moment when the global financial system is on the verge of collapse.

The pace at which the global financial and irregular warfare crises are unfolding, did not permit the *EIR* team to undertake the same painstaking study of the present world illegal drug trade that we were able to conduct in 1996. However, several *EIR* editors have reviewed some of the critical data, and have interviewed senior anti-drug officials from the United States and several Ibero-American nations. The report that follows, while not as comprehensive as the 1996 report, employed the same methodology, and does represent a highly accurate summary profile of the status of Dope, Inc. at the dawn of the new millennium.

A Noteworthy Paradox

The 1996 *EIR* study had concluded that Dope, Inc. had grown to a $521-billion-a-year illegal business—nearly doubling from the $259-billion-a-year revenue of 1985. The recent *EIR* review of U.S. government data, including the "National Drug Threat Assessment 2001" report, produced in October 2000 by the National Drug Intelligence Center, confirms that Dope, Inc. has continued to grow over the past five years, and now certainly represents an annual cash flow of well over $600 billion. This is an extremely conservative estimate. More precise figures, which we are not prepared to state at this time, are likely significantly higher.

EIR's July 26, 1996 cover feature documented a huge jump in dope money volume, which has now increased again

At the same time, it is important to report a significant, seemingly paradoxical phenomenon. According to the March 2000 "International Narcotics Control Strategy Report," the annual State Department study of the world under ground narcotics economy, both opium and coca production, *declined* between 1995 and 1999. The declines were very specific: Bolivia and Peru carried out intensive campaigns to eradicate the coca production there. Over that five-year period, Bolivian coca production fell by a staggering 71 %, and Peru, under the Presidency of Alberto Fujimori, cut coca production by 62%.

During the same time, as the FARC was supplanting both the Medellín and Cali cartels as the country's leading cocaine-trafficking organization, Colombia's coca production shot up by 126%. During the same time frame, Colombia also emerged as an opium-producing and heroin-processing country, which now provides a substantial portion of the highgrade heroin sold on the streets of North America. Colombian anti-narcotics officials who recently visited Washington reported, during a closed-door briefing, that the opium fields and heroin laboratories were established in Colombia, with the assistance of Afghani and Pakistani agricultural specialists and chemists, leading to suspicions about a possible narco-link between the F ARC and Afghan and Pakistani drug lords, who, after 1996, had worked out a drug tax-for-protection arrangement with the Taliban.

Afghan opium production increased 1995 and 1999 by 34%, but at the same time, the government of Burma launched a successful crackdown against opium growers there, reducing the output by 53%.

What is the significance of these countervailing trends over the past half-decade? While overall drug production has been on the rise, countries that showed a determination to crack down on the production of cocaine and opium were not only successful, but their efforts reduced global production figure for cocaine and opium by 18% and 26%, respectively, over the period 1995-1999.

So much for the drug legalizers' arguments that Dope, Inc. is "too big" to defeat. A global, concerted effort, which may now be politically possible, in the wake of the Sept. 11 attacks, *can succeed.* The trillion-dollar question is: Will the Bush Administration, the Putin government in Russia, and allied governments in Europe and other parts of the world, at long last, launch the kind of coordinated effort that aims to win?

Russian President Putin called for precisely such a concerted effort to wipe out the underground narcotics economy, as a means of defeating international terrorism. At the Sept. 28 session of the Russian Security Council, President Putin decribed the "acute" drug abuse crisis in Russia. "This problem is extremely acute today, and not only in and of itself," he told his top security aides. "It is directly connected with the success of the struggle against crime . . . and of course, it is very closely interwoven with topic number one in the world, the struggle against terrorism. The narco-business is one of the main sources of financing for terrorist groups and irregular military units."

He elaborated: "Terrorism and narcotics are absolutely kindred phenomena. They have common roots and a similar destructive force. Terrorism, like the drug trade, has a highly ramified international network, and is transnational. . . . This illegal business produces superprofits, and 'dirty' monies are spent for 'dirty' purposes."

He concluded, "We must put an effective barrier to all forms of penetration of narcotics into illegal circulation, destroy the infrastructure of the narco-networks, and eliminate demand . . . . Therefore our objective is to close off all channels for the proliferation of narcotics, both external and domestic . . . . An important subset of tasks has to do with eliminating the financial channels for the narco-business, which can be done not only by a fight against criminal elements, but also with an entire system of special measures. These include combatting the legalization of criminal incomes."

If the opportunity, posed by the post-Sept. 11 Russian-American cooperation is lost, then the other side of the picture—the continuing overall growth of Dope, Inc.—will dominate and destroy.

Dope, Inc.-$600 Billion and Growing

The local success stories in Bolivia, Peru, and Burma hardly offset the fact that Dope, Inc. continued to grow, albeit at a slower pace, over the 1995-1999 interval. *EIR*'s comparative review of core data—the estimated volumes of production of cocaine, heroin, marijuana, and synthetic drugs; and the changes in retail prices and street-level purity (normally among the most accurate data assembled by national law enforcement agencies)—points to certain conclusions:

First, the dramatic increase in production and use of marijuana and ever-more sophisticated and addictive synthetic drugs, more than offset the decline in raw opium and coca production over the five-year period through 1999. This is confirmed by both statistical data assembled by the NDIC and the State Department, and by anecdotal reports, largely featured in the NDIC's "Threat Assessment 2001." In fact, even in the cases of heroin and cocaine, the NDIC study suggested that pre-existing stockpiles of previous-year production meant that retail use in the United States continued to increase, even as new production declined, as the result of the targeted efforts of Bolivia, Peru, and Burma.

By the year 2000, the proceeds from the illegal drug trade had certainly passed $600 billion per annum, given the continuing growth trends in the United States and mushrooming drug abuse in Central Europe, Russia, and in many of the producer-countries that, in the past, had been immune to large-scale drug abuse, because crops were largely targetted for advanced-sector export markets.

Among the particular findings of the NDIC was that cocaine use continued to grow after 1997, but at a slower rate; and heroin use stabilized after 1997, but after having doubled between 1993 and 1997. Additionally, the continued growth of the "rave" culture has increased adolescent abuse of designer drugs, including combinations of heroin and MDMA. NDIC warned, "The rave culture and the criminal activity that surrounds it pose a major threat to America's youth." In addition to the widespread presence of smokeable and inhalable heroin at rave concerts, the report warned of a big increase in heroin, MDMA, LSD and boutique designer drugs on college campuses "in visually appealing and easy to administer forms."

The reports also noted an explosion in the illegal manufacturing and distribution of methamphetamines. In 1999 alone, more than 7,200 clandestine methamphetamine labs were shut down by police in the United States alone! Canada, in the five-year period since the groundbreaking 1996 *EIR* study, has emerged as a major supply point for precursor chemicals, required for the manufacturing of methamphetamines. Overall, Canada has become a hub of drug abuse and of illegal drug flows into the United States. This may be called "the NAFTA effect."

While methamphetamine and "club drugs" like MDMA (ecstasy, XTC, etc.) were identified by NDIC as the biggest expansion threats, marijuana abuse also continued to increase, with new and far more potent strains of marijuana being produced in sophisticated indoor hydroponic "pot farms." Canada, again, has surfaced as a major production center.

There are no figures available from the U.S. government on domestic marijuana production, which makes any precise estimate of worldwide crop size or cash value impossible. In many U.S. states, marijuana remains the number one cash crop.

The second issue that the recent U.S. government drug surveys highlighted was the links between the illegal drugs and weapons economy and international terrorism have become more and more evident. Whereas, in the past, the argument was often made, in official U.S. government publications, that the narcoterror links were tenuous and opportunistic, the 2001 NDIC study stated, bluntly, that "traffickers used laundered drug proceeds to . . . fund insurgency and terrorist organizations."

Indeed, while the case of the F ARC in Colombia represents perhaps the most clearcut example of the narcoterrorist phenomenon, other cases, with profound implications for Presidents Bush and Putin's "war on terrorism," can be found on every continent. In South Asia, the Taliban case has already been cited.

But in the heart of Europe, the Albanian-minority Kosovo Liberation Army (KLA), with its offshoots operating inside Macedonia, as well, has been exposed as one more narcoterrorist gang. One feature of the links between the KLA and the Egyptian Islamic Jihad (the core component of the so-called Osama bin Laden organization, al Qaeda) is that the KLA serves as the Balkan smugglers of Afghan heroin and hashish, into Russia and Western and Central Europe.

Money-Laundering: Follow the Hedge Funds
Newly elected U.S. Senator Joe Corzine (D-NJ) has recently emphasized that bigtime money-laundering can be carried out far more securely and efficiently through hedge funds, whose activities are subject to virtually no government scrutiny, than through the commercial banks per se. Corzine should know. Until his election to the U.S. Senate, he was chairman of the board of Goldman Sachs, one of the biggest Wall Street brokerage houses.

With combined cash flows surpassing $1 trillion, Dope, Inc. requires enormous access to the global financial system, and its access is from the top-down, as evidenced by the 1999 Grasso visit to the FARC jungle command, on behalf of Wall Street. A recent Senate Permanent Investigations Subcommittee study by the Democratic staffers, commissioned by Sen. Carl Levin (D-Mich), revealed that the private banking units of most of the major New York commercial banks maintained a strict "see no evil" attitude towards their wealthy clientele. And the same banks engaged in the worst kinds of criminal collusion through their corresponding banking relationships with offshore British Commonwealth banks and branches that operate totally outside the law.

4. Britain's 'Dope, Inc.': A $521 – Billion Business

Britain's 'Dope, Inc.' Grows to $521 Billion

Editor's Note: The following section, down through the bibliography to LaRouche's War on Drugs, represents a 1996 update on Dope, Inc. which first appeared in Executive Intelligence Review magazine.

The war on drugs *can* be won. There is no need to raise the white flag of surrender and tolerate legalization. There is no reason to accept yet another generation of American youth being turned into blank-stared, lost souls. We don't have to watch any more Third World nations sink into the slavery of drug-producing dictatorships. And we need not, and must not, allow the world financial system to remain addicted to—and governed by—blood money from the drug trade, just as a heroin addict is hooked on smack.

Shown here is the cover graphic to Dope, Inc.: Britain's Opium War against the United States, the book which exposed the British Crown forces behind the drug trade.

The apparatus which runs the international drug trade—or Dope, Inc., as Lyndon LaRouche and associates have called it for nearly two decades—is an entity which can be known, profiled for weaknesses, publicly identified, and *destroyed* by concerted action carried out by cooperating sovereign nations.

That is the single, most important conclusion to be drawn from the detailed information and analysis presented in the pages that follow.

Does the Queen run drugs?

Who is behind Dope, Inc.? Does the Queen of England really run drugs, as people often ask LaRouche in shocked disbelief? No more than Adolf Hitler killed millions of innocent people. Neither of the two committed the crime personally, with their own hands—at least, not as far as can be proven. But, in both cases, it is their policies, their *intentional* policies, which fit the Nuremberg Tribunal's criteria of "knew or should have known" what the deadly consequences of their actions would be, which are responsible for massive crimes against humanity.

In the case of drugs, it is demonstrably the case that powerful oligarchical financial interests, centered in Great Britain, run the trade today, from the top down, as they have for centuries, almost as if it were a single, multinational firm— thus the sobriquet, "Dope, Inc." As we document below:

- The British Commonwealth and other countries under the British imperial thumb account for 94% of all licit and illicit opium production in the world today, which is the source of deadly heroin. Historically, opium has been *the* British drug par excellence.

- In Colombia, the linchpin country in the world cocaine trade, the narco-dictatorship of Ernesto Samper is being buttressed in power, against the Clinton administration's escalating pressure, by the British House of Lords, whose members describe Sarnper's Colombia as a "model democracy." And British government officials, such as Trade Minister Richard Needham, rub it in by snootily commenting to the media in Colombia on the subject of U.S. concern over drugs: "That is *their* problem."

- Belize, the British Commonwealth nation which borders on Mexico, plays a critical role in the transshipment of Colombian cocaine up through Mexico into the United States. The narco-terrorist Zapatista National Liberation Army in the adjacent Mexican state of Chiapas, was manufactured by British intelligence to aid in this and related projects.

- Most significant of all, the British directly control an estimated 52% of all dirty-money-laundering operations globally—which is the actually the controlling force behind the international drug trade, as we show in the pages that follow.

- Those yearly proceeds from the drug trade, totalling an estimated $521 billion in 1995, are supplemented by some $200 billion from tax evasion, $125 billion from flight capital, $100 billion from illegal gambling and prostitution, $100 billion from contraband commodities, and $70 billion from the illegal weapons trade, to add up to a *trillion-dollar-per-year* flow of dirty money. This is the crucial margin keeping the global speculative bubble afloat—all $75 trillion of it. Cut off that flow of laundered money, and the entire speculative system will implode, more or less overnight

It is this, above all, which is the driving force behind the British sponsorship of drug trafficking, and their use of supranational institutions such as the International Monetary Fund and the United Nations, to impose economic policies which promote the drug trade.

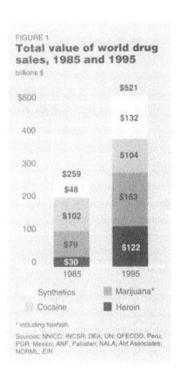

FIGURE 1
Total value of world drug sales, 1985 and 1995
billions $

.

Dope, Inc. doubled in a decade

The yearly "take" from illegal narcotics can be conservatively estimated at $521 billion in 1995, a 101 % increase over the $259 billion of a decade earlier (see **Figure 1**). The sales revenues come from four principal drug categories:

Heroin, which quadrupled from $30 billion in 1985, to $122 billion in 1995, has over 5 million addicts worldwide, most of whom are located, not in the United States or Europe, but in the *producer* nations (for example, Pakistan), where 70% of world heroin consumption occurs.

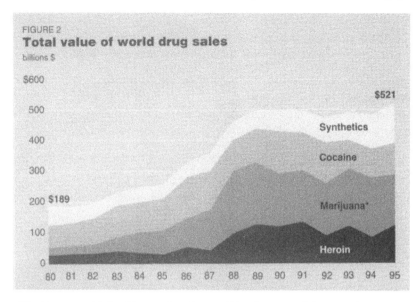

FIGURE 2
Total value of world drug sales
billions $

$600

$521

500

Synthetics

400

Cocaine

300

200 $189

Marijuana*

100

Heroin

0

80 81 82 83 84 85 86 87 88 89 90 91 92 93 94 95

Marijuana, still the "drug of preference" in the United States, where over 10 million people use it yearly, has more than doubled, from $79 billion in 1985, to $163 billion in 1995. Marijuana has been, and remains, the "gateway" drug, which has introduced an estimated 72 million Americans into experimenting with illegal drugs.

Cocaine, whose dollar value was relatively steady over this period, grew from $102 billion in 1985, to $104 billion in 1995. This is because the physical output of the drug grew significantly over the decade (by about 104%), but this was nearly offset by an equivalent drop in the average price per gram of cocaine on the streets of both the United States and Europe.

Synthetic drugs, such as methamphetamines, PCP, and LSD, also grew sharply, from $48 billion in 1985, to $132 billion in 1995, a near tripling in the 10-year interval.

Although the dollar value of the drug trade doubled over the last decade, **Figure 2** indicates that this wasn't an even process: It grew more rapidly in the first half of the decade than it did in the second half. However, it would be a serious mistake to conclude from this that the drug problem is somehow leveling off. Rather, what is going on is a period of relative consolidation, preparatory to a new take-off stage in production, consumption, and the value of total sales—a trend which is already visible in the figures for the last two years. In other words, what we are seeing is a classic "S-shaped" function, whose stage of relatively slower growth has already ended, as the curve accelerates back upwards.

There are two principal reasons for this conclusion.

First, the data used in this study, and reflected in the graphs, do not include information on Russia, or other states of the former Soviet Union or of the East bloc. The reason is that data on this area are simply not available, neither publicly available, nor, according to high-level law-enforcement sources, even privately available to the U.S. government. And yet, it is universally acknowledged that, since 1989-91 especially, there has been an explosion of drug consumption and production in the region, most notably in the former Soviet republics of Central Asia. In fact, this has been Dope, Inc.'s principal "growth market" over the last five years. When data finally do become available as to what has been happening over this period, there is no question but that the totals for 1990-95 will have to be adjusted upwards accordingly. If unchecked, it furthermore portends an ominous, exponential leap over the next few years in all drugrelated parameters in this strategically critical region.

EIR's methodology and assumptions

Over the past two decades, *EIR* has conducted a number of in-depth investigations of the size of the international drug trade. Although the current study is by far. the most detailed and systematic to date, each of these has addressed the matter from the same vantage point: that Dope, Inc. functions like a single, unified, multinational corporation, whose various production, processing, transporta- tion, distribution, sales, consumption, and money-laundering phases are centrally coordinated to a single purpose.

We therefore discard as misleading, and inaccurate, all "demand-" or consumption-based approaches, whose implicit assumption is that the "aggregate demand" for drugs by a collection of autonomous individuals, "causes" drugs to be produced, presumably by a collection of equally autonomous producers who only associate after-the-fact into various criminal cartels. In this view, money laundering is merely an epiphenomenon, and drug bankers are only the occasional bad apples who are corrupted by the producer cartels.

Even the most thorough of such "consumption" -driven approaches inherently underestimate the actual scope of the drug problem, and vastly so, probably by a full order of magnitude. For example, the National Household Survey on Drug Abuse (NHSDA), the most comprehensive survey of drug use in the United States, depends on responses to surveys from purported drug users. But, as the private consultants Abt Associates admit, in their extensive 1995 study prepared for the White House Office of National Drug Control Policy (ONDCP), entitled "What America's Users Spend on Illegal Drugs, 1988-1993," "drug users often misrepresent their drug use when interviewed. . . . Those who are reached probably have an incentive to misrepresent their consumption." No amount of sophisticated mathematics and complex regression analyses can make up for flawed assumptions and methodology: It only makes the problem worse by convincing the gullible layman that it is somehow "scientific."

And what of the rest of the world outside the United States, where even less is known about consumption, and such surveys are non-existent? What of the millions of unsurveyed heroin "consumers" in Pakistan, Afghanistan, or Thailand? How are we to judge Dope, Inc.'s role in such areas of the world?

By its very illegal nature, Dope, Inc.'s size and activities are not directly reported. However, one can obtain a far more accurate—if still not precise— reading, by analyzing the *physical economy* of the drug production process, and estimating what were they fully marketed at retail street prices. In using this approach, *EIR* has made use of official data provided by numerous governments, as verified and corrected by direct *EIR* consultation with knowledgeable sources in various drug-producing countries. We are convinced that our global findings about the dimensions of Dope, Inc. err on the conservative side.

The single most comprehensive, and consistent time series for much of this data is provided by the U.S. government's National Narcotics Intelligence Consumers Committee (NNICC), a multi-agency task force which includes the Drug Enforcement Administration (which chairs the group), the Federal Bureau of Investigation, the Department of the Treasury, the U.S. Customs Service, the U.S. Coast Guard, the Department of State, the Department of Defense, the Internal Revenue Service, the Central Intelligence Agency, the National Institute on Drug Abuse, the Immigration and Naturalization Service, and the Office of National Drug Control Policy.

The NNICC produces an annual report which presents a range of probable hectares under cultivation for each of the major drug crops: coca, marijuana, and opium. These estimates come from aerial surveys, on-site inspections, country reports, and other data. They then multiply their area figures by estimated yields per hectare, which provides an estimated range of output in tonnage. In most cases, *EIR* has used the higher value of the range under consideration, *since* it seems most likely that some of the drug crop escapes detection. In specific cases where other data were available for cross-checking, the higher figures were in fact borne out as the more accurate. Also, where official data were subsequently modified by new estimates for either area cultivated or yields, the modifications almost always increased the earlier estimates.

In some cases, additional physical production data were obtained from the yearly *International Narcotics Control Strategy Report* (INCSR), published by the U.S. State Department, which has more detailed country studies than the NNICC annual report.

If one starts with such figures for total potential crop output, based on the amount sown or cultivated, one must then subtract the amount eradicated before the crop is even harvested. In the case of marijuana, this is quite substantial; with coca and opium, less so. This leaves the total amount harvested, or the total production of the raw material of the drug in question. Then, standard conversion ratios are applied for the respective refining processes, taking into account variations both over time, and from one country to the next For example, 10 kilograms of opium yield 1 kilogram of refined pure heroin—pretty much across the board. In the case of cocaine, back in the mid-1980s, it took about 500 kilograms of coca leaves to produce 1 kilo of pure cocaine HCl; whereas in the 1990s, the productivity improved, and it now requires only 333 kilos of leaves to produce a kilo of cocaine, according to official estimates.

In this way, we generate a time series of the physical amount of output of each of the refined drugs. From that amount, one must subtract the amount lost to seizures worldwide, which leaves a net amount which is potentially available for sale. We say "potentially," because there is no way of determining whether the entirety of this amount is actually sold in a given year, or whether some of it is lost to spoilage, or is stockpiled for use in subsequent years. But as a trend, it is the best available indicator of Dope, Inc. 's marketing process.

EIR then determined, in broad terms, how much of the total net production was consumed locally in the producer countries, and how much was exported, differentiating the share which went to each of the major export markets (the United States and Europe). This breakdown is necessary, because the price of cocaine and heroin, for example, is significantly different in these three markets (local, United States, and Europe).

With this determined, the amount available for sale in each market was multiplied by the respective average retail street sale price for each drug (taking into account variations in purity from year to year). This then yielded the total value of potential sales of that drug per market, which was reaggregated to give world totals.

U.S. retail prices for marijuana, cocaine, and heroin were obtained and cross-checked among various sources, including NNICC (using the median value of the range they report), Abt Associates, and others. It should be noted that price and purity information are the only data generated by the methods of street samples and surveys, which are relatively reliable.

In the case of Europe, no similar time series currently exists for any of these drugs. *EIR* developed the first such published series of which we are aware, based on partial data for a half-dozen European countries, made available in various United Nations study documents. Other empirical studies of purity levels of drugs sold in Europe were then applied, to develop a single series for the estimated price per pure gram of cocaine and heroin. Those findings are presented in the graphics that follow.

More specific assumptions and estimations employed in the calculations are as follows:

Cocaine: quantities of production as per NNICC, and Peru's Executive Office of Drug Control (OFECOD); U.S. sales prices 1977-80 from NNICC, 1981-95 from Abt Associates.

Marijuana: U.S. eradication as per Drug Enforcement Administration (DEA) data, and quantities of production were estimated based on an eradication ratio of 33% in 1985, dropping to 20% in 1995, based on DEA and National Organization for the Reform of Marijuana Laws (NORML) information; U.S. *sinsemilla* equals 25% of the total crop in 1983, rising to 40% in 1995; Mexico production and eradication as per INCSR, NNICC, and the Office of the Attorney General (PGR) of Mexico, with the exception of the period prior to 1989 (see text of article on marijuana for detailed explanation); all other countries' production and eradication as per NNICC and INCSR; on *hashish,* quantities as per NNICC and the National Alliance of Lebanese Americans (NALA) for Lebanon, with retail price assumed equal to that for *sinsemilla* marijuana in the same year.

Heroin: production and eradication data as per NNICC (median value) and INCSR; percentage of total opium that is converted to heroin is based on INCSR and other country sources, including NALA and Pakistan's Anti-Narcotics Force (ANF) (in Burma, 20% in 1980, rising to 70% in 1995; Laos 50% in 1980, rising to 80% in 1995; Thailand 100%; China 50%; Afghanistan and Iran, 50% in 1980, rising to 85% in 1995; Pakistan 70% in 1980, rising to 100% in 1995; Lebanon 100%; India 10% in 1980, rising to 50% in 1995; and Mexico, Colombia, and Guatemala 100%); local or regional consumption of heroin as per INCSR, UN, and country sources; of total Southeast Asia exports, assume 75% shipped to the United States, and 25% shipped to Europe; Southwest Asia exports 25% to the United States, and 75% to Europe; Ibero-America exports 100% to the United States; prices in the United States and Europe as explained above; local price of heroin assumed to be 10% of the current European price.

Synthetic drugs: this is fully explained in the article below on synthetics.

There is a precedent, on a far smaller scale, for this type of phenomenon. In 1989, official marijuana production figures for Mexico were announced that were *twelve times* greater than what was reported for 1988. Actual output didn't grow that much in one year. What happened is that systematic surveillance flights were conducted for the first time during that year, and Mexican and foreign law-enforcement agencies discovered that they had been sitting on a mountain of marijuana, undetected and out of control.

The world will shortly discover something similar regarding Russia and other former Soviet countries: The problem there is *already* probably an order of magnitude greater than anyone has dared to imagine.

The second consideration behind our "S-shaped" curve hypothesis, has to do with Dope, Inc.'s deliberate pricing policies.

If ever there were any doubts about the cartel-like nature of Dope, Inc., the next three figures should put them to rest. When cocaine (and especially crack cocaine) was first introduced into the U.S. market, its price was so high ($640 per pure gram in 1977) that there was not much of a market for the drug. Dope, Inc. then employed a classical marketing technique, taken from a Harvard Business School manual: They deliberately slashed the price of their "product" in order to increase the volume of purchases. It worked for Henry Ford's "Model T," and it worked for Dope, Inc. As the U.S. price was reduced down to $135 per pure gram in 1995, the quantity of cocaine shipped to the United States for sale, shot up from 85 tons in 1977, to 560 tons in 1995 (see **Figure 3**).

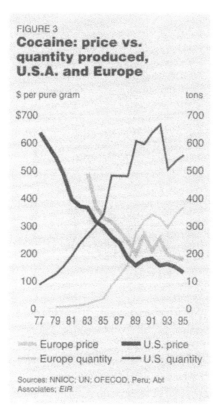

FIGURE 3
Cocaine: price vs. quantity produced, U.S.A. and Europe

$ per pure gram   tons

Europe price   U.S. price
Europe quantity   U.S. quantity

Sources: NNICC; UN; OFECOD, Peru; Abt Associates; *EIR*.

The identical marketing strategy was repeated for Europe a few years later, with equal success. The European street-sale price of cocaine has closely followed the U.S. trajectory down, with a phase difference of a few years: It dropped from $493 per pure gram in 1983, to $180 today. Not surprisingly, the quantity shipped for sale in Europe rose too, from next to nothing in 1979, up to 373 tons in 1995. In fact, as **Figure 4** shows, Europe's estimated share of world cocaine sales has been steadily rising, and today stands at about 40% of the world total. This parameter also does not take into consideration the opening up of the *eastern* European market, which will further shift the proportion in the years immediately ahead.

Back in 1990, *EIR* had already warned of exactly this danger, in a feature story on the drug trade. "Dope, Inc. is now engaged in a vast expansion of its markets in Europe and Japan, which, if not checked, will do to their youth, their cities, and their economies what has already been done to ours in America," we forecast.

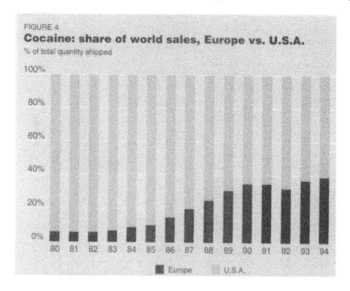

FIGURE 4
Cocaine: share of world sales, Europe vs. U.S.A.
% of total quantity shipped

If one looks at the global pattern, as reflected in **Figure 5,** one sees how success-ful Dope, Inc.'s strategy has been: World cocaine prices dropped from $640 per pure gram to $150 per pure gram between 1977 anti 1995 (a decline by a factor of 4.3), while the quantity produced skyrocketed from 90 tons to 933 tons (a factor of more than 10). Furthermore, world cocaine production is now set for another take-off stage after a few years of relative stagnation, as we document in the section on cocaine below.

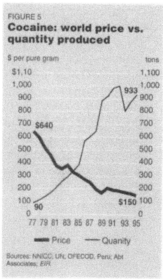

FIGURE 5
Cocaine: world price vs. quantity produced

It should be noted that Dope, Inc. has engaged in similar marketing tactics for heroin: From 1980 to 1995, the U.S. price per pure gram was cut by more than half and the European price by two-thirds, while production rose sixfold.

A war-winning strategy

The LaRouche movement has been at war with Dope, Inc., and its British sponsors, for nearly two decades. The first salvo was our 1978 publication of the best-seller *Dope, Inc.: Britain's Opium War Against the United States.* That was followed by the founding of the National Anti-Drug Coalition and its magazine *War on Drugs;* by numerous exposés and feature stories in *EIR;* by two additional English-language editions of *Dope, Inc.;* and by a Spanish-language edition, called *Narcotráfico, SA,* which was so provocative to the drug bankers that it was banned in Venezuela (and almost banned in Peru).

Cocaine Production Set for A New Takeoff Stage

Nowhere is the foolishness of the standard demand-driven analysis of the drug trade more evident, than in the case of cocaine. The typical official argument goes like this: U.S. "demand" for cocaine has been dropping—for reasons undefined—since about 1989-90, and as a result, hardcore users supposedly fell from 2.6 million to 2.1 million during 1989-93, while occasional users declined from 6.5 million to 4.1 million during the same period. The White House's own showpiece publication, *The National Drug Control Strategy: 1996,* announced hopefully that "cocaine use has fallen 30% in the last three years alone."

The data for these conclusions were drawn principally from surveys of households and of prison populations, where drug "consumers" are questioned about their habits. Reliable information? Hardly.

Not surprisingly, such surveys also produce internally contradictory evidence. For example, the same White House report which talks about an overall 30% *drop* in cocaine consumption, also reports a 1995 increase of cocaine use among high school students. Similarly, the NNICC annual survey for 1994 reports: "Survey results for 8th and 10th graders indicated an increase in all cocaine use categories from 1993 to 1994." So, is cocaine consumption falling or rising? Or, is it falling rapidly among adults, while rising swiftly among adolescents?

The actual picture of the U.S. and the world cocaine market is better approached from the opposite direction: by looking at what Dope, Inc. is physically *producing* for market, in order to generate its gigantic flows of hot money. Consumption levels are a *result* of that orchestrated offensive, not its cause. From that standpoint, it is evident that the supply of cocaine has continued to grow, as has its availability in both the United States and Europe.

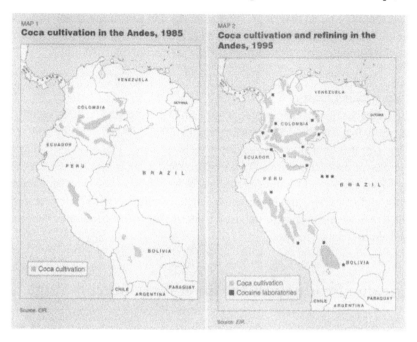

Cocaine production: an 'S-shaped' curve

Cocaine hydrochloride, commonly called cocaine, is produced from coca leaves. Coca plants are grown in significant quantities in only three countries in the world: Colombia, Bolivia, and Peru, all in the Andean region of Ibero-America. The coca leaves are then converted into cocaine paste, and from there into pure cocaine, with the use of a variety of easily acquired chemicals, such as ether and acetone. Although these are legal chemicals that have valid industrial uses, they are obtained illegally by the drug traffickers in large quantities, principally from the United States, western Europe, and also Brazil.

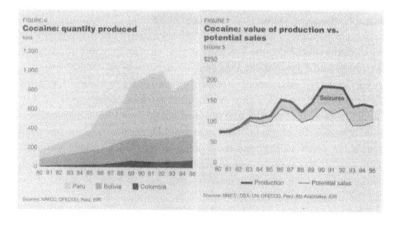

As **Maps 1** and **2** show, there has been a significant increase in the area under coca cultivation in the Andean region, between 1985 and 1995. Most of the coca is grown in Peru, while most of the processing laboratories are located in Colombia. (More recently, laboratories have also been established in the Amazon region of Brazil.) However, Dope, Inc. has woven an elaborate logistical interconnection throughout the region, in which tens, if not hundreds, of illegal cocaine flights occur daily, transporting drugs, chemicals, and dirty money back and forth among the different production and processing sites.

Figure 6 shows total world production of refined cocaine from 1980 to 1995, which rose from 166 metric tons to 933 metric tons over this period—a nearly sixfold increase. On an annualized basis, production has been rising at an average 12.2% per year. Over the last five years, that rate of growth slowed down, largely as a result of the steep drop in production which occurred in 1993.

Over 60% of the total quantity of coca originates in Peru, with smaller shares coming from Bolivia and Colombia. These figures should not be misunderstood to imply a lesser role for Colombia in the overall cocaine trade: They simply indicate that its local production of coca leaves is less than that of Peru and Bolivia, while it plays a larger role in downstream processing.

As is evident from **Figure 6,** the sharp decline in 1993, of almost 20% of total production, can be attributed totally to Peru—in fact, Colombia and Bolivia's output continued to rise throughout the 1990s. What happened in Peru is of the greatest political significance. First, there was an apparently "natural disaster" which struck the coca plantations, especially in the Upper Huallaga Valley, the heart of the producing region. As a result of overcultivation and monoculture growing patterns, soil depletion began to set in around 1991, as did the deadly *fusiarum oxyporum* fungus.

The second factor is referred to euphemistically by the NNICC as "tumultuous" political conditions in the region, and as "the cumulative impact of counternarcotics efforts of all types in the Huallaga Valley," in the words of the U.S. State Department. What actually happened is that, over the course of 1992, the Fujimori government in Peru launched an all-out war against Shining Path and other narco-terrorists in the country. In April of that year, President Alberto Fujimori summarily shut down the country's Congress and Supreme Court, for complicity with the subversives.

And then, in September, his government captured the notorious Abimael Guzmán, the head of Shining Path, and quickly sentenced him to life in prison. From that point on, a series of further devastating blows was delivered to the entire narco-terrorist apparatus across the country.

At no point did the Fujirnori government explicitly target the drug trade. But Shining Path's main rural base of operation is the coca-producing Upper Huallaga Valley, and the terrorists are so thoroughly integrated with the Dope, Inc. apparatus, that their suppression led to a serious disruption of the drug trade.

Dope, Inc., however, reacted swiftly, and moved to shift significant amounts of coca growing to other river valleys in Peru. By 1994, that diversification had led to an additional half-dozen river valleys joining the Upper Huallaga as major coca growing regions. According to informed Peruvian sources consulted by *EIR,*. the 1994 area under cultivation, by valley, was as follows:

Upper Huallaga	28,900 hectares
Aguaytía	21,400 hectares
Apurímac	17,000 hectares
Cuzco	9,900 hectares
Central Huallaga	8,500 hectares
Lower Huallaga	7,500 hectares
Ucayali	2,000 hectares
Others	13,400 hectares

In the Aguaytía and Apruírnac valleys, the area planted to coca grew by 20% in 1994 alone, according to informed Peruvian sources. But it takes a couple of years for a coca plant to mature and produce viable leaves for cocaine production, so the new production sites could not immediately make up for the drop in output caused by the Upper Huallaga problems.

However, as the new areas have come on line, total Peruvian coca production began to rise again in 1994 and 1995, with ominous implications for the future.

In fact, Peruvian experts consulted by *EIR* note that the demonstrated ability to diversify quickly to new areas, means that Peru may well become a super-producer of coca *and poppy.* The same experts also report that, in addition to the 130,000 hectares under active coca cultivation in Peru, there are an estimated additional 100-150,000 hectares that are part of Dope, Inc.'s holdings, but which in any given cycle are either fallow (in-between cropping) or under preparation for future planting.

It is therefore probable that the relative stagnation of total cocaine production of the early 1990s, will not continue as a trend. Rather, it appears to be a momentary leveling off in what will actually turn out to be an "S-shaped curve" which has just begun its second ascent stage. Nor can much be expected in the short term from coca eradication in any of the three producer countries: Only trivial amounts are eradicated in Colombia and Bolivia, and none at all in Peru.

Since the price of cocaine in both major consumer markets, the United States and Europe, has been steadily dropping over the last 15 years (as we noted at the outset of this report), the total dollar value of the output did not rise as rapidly as the physical production. As **Figure 7** shows, the total value of production rose from $76 billion in 1980 to $140 billion in 1995, i.e., it "only" doubled, as compared to the sixfold increase in the volume of cocaine output during that time frame.

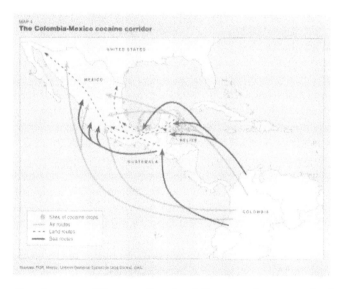

Dope, Inc., however, did not realize that full amount in street sales, because a significant amount of cocaine was seized on its way to market. In 1980, this only amounted to about $3 billion worth, but by 1995, a full 26% of total production was seized, whose sales value would have been an additional $36 billion. So, the value of all potential cocaine sales worldwide—i.e., the total revenue that would accrue to Dope, Inc., if they were to sell their total available cocaine production at street retail prices—came in at $104 billion in 1995. In 1980, the value of all potential sales was $73 billion.

Trafficking routes

Despite the rising share of total cocaine production that is now being shipped to Europe, the United States still consumes about 60% of the world total. Nearly all the refined cocaine entering the United States comes from the Cali Cartel in Colombia, and much of that, perhaps as much as 70%, is transshipped through Mexico (see **Map 3**).

Most of the cocaine crosses into the United States in southern California, Arizona, Texas, and southern Florida, and then proceeds to the four main distribution centers: Los Angeles, Houston, Miami, and New York City. These cities in turn serve as the consolidation centers for the proceeds from the drug sales. Another frequent entry point into the United States is the island of Puerto Rico.

Over the last couple of years, the blows delivered to the Cali Cartel, combined with surveillance and interdiction cooperation between the United States and the Peruvian governments, have disrupted the Peru-Colombia air bridge used by the traffickers to get coca paste to processing laboratories in Colombia, before shipment on to the United States and Europe. The traffickers have increasingly developed alternate routes, including using the Amazon and other rivers to ship into Brazil, and from there, abroad. Similarly, Peruvian and Colombian Pacific Coast ports are being used for maritime shipments to the United States and, to a lesser extent, to Asia. (Cocaine is still not a particularly popular drug in most of Asia, where it is considered too "Western," as compared to the more familiar opium and heroin.)

Most amazingly, there have also been cases of the use of both manned and unmanned *submarines* to ship large quantities of drugs across the Caribbean, to waiting speed boats, known as "go fast boats," just outside U.S. territorial waters.

In both maritime and air shipments directly to the United States, traffickers frequently conceal large quantities of cocaine in legitimate containerized cargo.

Shipments from South America to Europe also go both by air and by sea— although air cargo predominates. Spain, because of its historical and language ties to Ibero-America, continues to be a major staging ground and transshipment center for drugs sent throughout Europe. Another major route goes directly from Surinam, a former Dutch colony in South America, to the old "mother country," the Netherlands, which is an important drug consumption and distribution haven for all of Europe.

Increasingly, cocaine is also being shipped into Russia and the other countries of the former Soviet Union, as Dope, Inc. rapidly develops these new markets

Map 4 presents a "close-up" of the Colombia-Mexico cocaine corridor, through which most of the drug passes on its way to the United States. A tightly knit infrastructure of narcotics trafficking now links the two countries, which is also expressed in the form of close working relations between the Colombian and Mexican drug cartels.

Historically, the Colombian mafia used twin-engine general aviation aircraft to transport cocaine from Colombia, up through Central America (often with a stop in Guatemala), and on into Mexico. In recent years, however, they have increasingly turned to jet cargo, passenger aircraft, and even *full-size commercial jets loaded with cocaine,* which are landed on remote clandestine airfields in Mexico, and then simply discarded.

Another relatively recent innovation of Dope, Inc. is the extensive use of air-drops of large, sealed packages of cocaine into the waters surrounding Mexico. Here again, waiting "go fast boats" pick up the cargo and take it ashore, where it is transported by land up to the border with the United States.

Note the two areas of greatest density of such air drops:

- the Gulf of Mexico coast off the Isthmus of Tehuantepec, where most of Mexico's offshore oil platforms are located, and where there is consequently a significant amount of related onshore ground transportation, construction, and so forth; and
- the Caribbean coast off the Yucatán Peninsula and the nation of Belize, a member of the British Commonwealth which plays a crucial role in coordinating both drugs and terrorism in southern Mexico. This cocaine is then transported overland through southern Mexico, in particular through the state of Chiapas where the British-sponsored Zapatista narco-terrorists are active, and northwards to the United States.

Marijuana: A $150 Billion Chunk Of Dope, Inc. Production

The number-one drug of preference in the United States is still marijuana, and official government surveys indicate that the major decline in consumption over the previous decade and a half has now been reversed, and that consumption is again on the rise, especially among school-age children. Law enforcement officials are par-ticularly concerned over what they call a "gateway effect," by which this age group is introduced to other, still more deadly drugs. That is, by crossing over into illegality through use of a banned substance, these children become increasingly vulnerable to the physical, psychological, *and* financial addiction of the narcotics netherworld.

What is this so-called "recreational drug," which its pushers would have us legalize, putting it in the same category as alcohol and tobacco? Marijuana is the flowering tops and leaves of the *Cannabis sativa L* plant, which are gathered, dried, and smoked in a pipe or cigarette, or in combination with tobacco or other drugs. Both the plant, and the psychoactive chemical delta-9-tetrahydrocannabinol (THC) found most densely in its flowering tops, are considered "controlled substances," that is, their consumption is illegal. Two other substances are derived from the cannabis plant, hashish and hashish oil, which contain a higher THC content than marijuana, but which do not have a significant U.S. market.

World production

Although cannabis is grown around the globe, from South America to Asia, from the Middle East to Africa, the United States has become in the past decade the single largest grower of marijuana in the world, contributing an estimated 34% to total world production in 1995 (see below).

The bulk of marijuana consumed in the United States is also produced domestically. As of 1995, *EIR* estimates that at least 50% of all marijuana consumed in the United States was domestically grown, with the rest coming from Mexico, or through Mexico from points further south, primarily Colombia (see **Map 5**). Because marijuana is a relatively bulky product to ship (unlike cocaine and heroin, for example), it is more cost-effective and less risky to either grow it domestically or to transport the drug to the U.S. market from nearby sources.

After the United States, Colombia and Mexico together account for another 45% of total world production. Colombian cultivation, which, by 1990, had been nearly eliminated altogether through eradication by glysophate, began to climb again in 1991-92, when eradication was abandoned, had a dramatic resurgence in 1993, and has been steadily climbing ever since, surpassing even Mexican production in the last year or two.

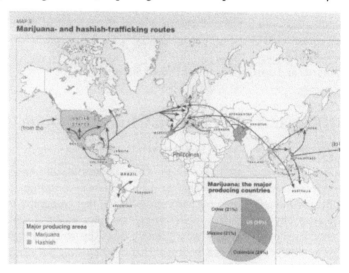

As **Map 6** shows, the bulk of Colombian cultivation is concentrated in the northern Sierra Nevada region, and in the Serranía de Perija in the northeast, a no-man's-land dominated by narco-terrorist bands along the Colombian-Venezuelan border. Current estimates are that at least 5,000 hectares are under marijuana cultivation, with a potential yield of 4,133 metric tons annually.

Because of the consolidation of financial and political power by the cocaine cartels in Colombia during the past decade, marijuana trafficking is no longer an independent affair. Combined shipments of Colombian marijuana and cocaine are now making their way northward to Mexico, by boat and air, through both Pacific and Caribbean routes, and thence across the border into the United States. Although most of Colombia's marijuana heads north to Mexico, the United States, and Canada, multi-ton shipments have also been seized in western Europe in recent years, entering largely through Germany and the Netherlands.

In Mexico, marijuana cultivation is largely concentrated in the western states of Sinaloa, Nayarit, Michoacán, Sonora, Jalisco, Oaxaca, and Durango. Mexico's so-called "golden triangle" of marijuana (and poppy) cultivation extends from Badiraguato in

Sinaloa, to Tomazula in Durango, to Guadalupe y Calvo, in Chihuahua (see map). Although the bulk of Mexican marijuana is of commercial grade, the more potent

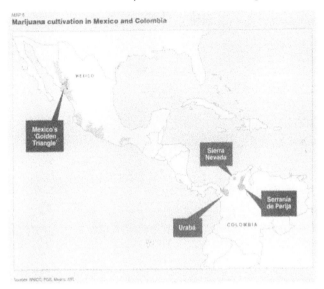

MAP 5
Marijuana cultivation in Mexico and Colombia

sinsemilla has been on the increase here, too, since 1992. It is estimated that Mexico currently has nearly 7,000 hectares under cultivation, with a potential annual yield of 3,650 metric tons. Apart from what is domestically consumed, most of Mexican marijuana is smuggled into the United States, largely via overland routes.

As shown in **Figure 8**, combined Ibero-American production (largely Mexico and Colombia) accounts for an estimated 9,700 metric tons, out of a world total of 17,450. The United States accounts for about 6,000 tons, and Southeast Asia another 1,750 tons.

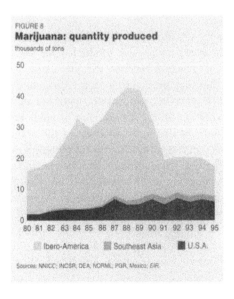

FIGURE 8
Marijuana: quantity produced
thousands of tons

Sources: NNICC; INCSR; DEA; NORML; PGR, Mexico; EIR.

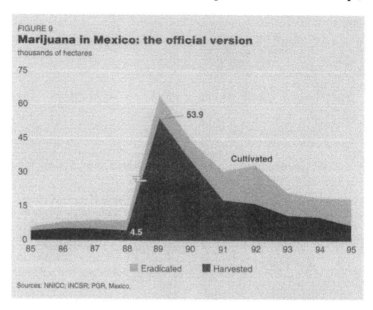

FIGURE 9
Marijuana in Mexico: the official version
thousands of hectares

Sources: NNICC; INCSR; PGR, Mexico.

The informed reader may recognize that the total Ibero-American production during 1980-88 is far higher than the official statistics reported by either the Mexican government or the U.S. Drug Enforcement Administration (DEA), both of which report a dramatic *12-fold* leap in the number of hectares of marijuana harvested in Mexico in 1989, purportedly jumping from 4,500 hectares to 53,900 hectares in that one year (see **Figure 9**). The official sources admit that this does not reflect an actual increase of that magnitude in a single year, but only that new technologies were applied to detection and that new methodologies of calculation were introduced. But they have not altered their own earlier discredited figures to reflect these changes.

EIR has done so, on the following basis. What occurred is that systematic aerial surveillance over Mexico was conducted for the first time in 1989, as a result of agreements reached between the Mexican government and the DEA. They discovered that they were sitting on a virtual mountain of marijuana, and significantly revised Mexican production estimates upward. Those overflights yielded new information on the average size of fields under cultivation, as well as a new method for calculating production. So, the dramatic peak in 1988-89 of quantity produced represents these revised production estimates. But the fact is, that Mexican production throughout the previous period was probably closer, and rising, to that level all along, and had just never been adequately detected.

The precipitous drop in Ibero-American marijuana production after 1989 stems from a combination of adverse climate conditions and aggressive eradication, principally in Mexico, in the aftermath of the new findings.

Other producers in Ibero-America include Jamaica (206 metric tons annually), Paraguay (2-2,500 metric tons annually), and Brazil. Most of Jamaica's production goes to the United States via Florida and the East Coast. Although Brazilian production levels are substantial, no official estimates of hectareage or tonnage currently exist. Brazilian marijuana exports are minimal; the bulk of production is consumed domestically. Paraguayan marijuana is also intended for domestic consumption, or for the market in neighboring Brazil and Argentina.

In Southeast Asia, the major marijuana producers are Thailand and Laos, and Cambodia to a lesser degree. Much of the area's trade appears to be under the control of Thailand-based traffickers, who ship to Europe via Italy, as well as to Australia, Hongkong, Singapore, and the Philippines. The Philippines is also a major producer and exporter of marijuana, as well as transshipment point. It exports mainly to Japan, Taiwan, and Australia. New reports that the Philippines has risen to become the second- or third-largest marijuana producer in the world have not yet been confirmed.

Nigeria is a grower of low-grade cannabis, often smuggling it into Europe via Dutch ports and, increasingly, into eastern Europe. Nigerian smuggling networks have constituted themselves as major traffickers not only of marijuana, but of heroin and cocaine, as well. A recent raid in Bogota, the capital city of Colombia, led to the arrests of more than a score of Nigerians and other West Africans, all part of a Nigerian-run smuggling network which was preparing to transport cocaine out of the country in their stomachs. Substantial amounts of marijuana grown in South Africa are largely consumed domestically, while Kenya is both a marijuana grower and exporter, and a transshipment route for hashish from Pakistan.

Figure 10 shows the reductions from total marijuana cultivated worldwide, due to eradication and seizures, leaving a net available amount for sale of nearly 13,000 tons. This is almost a 50% drop from the 25,800 tons available a decade earlier in 1985. The value of the potential sales, however, did not decline similarly, because of the rising price of the drug. Thus, we see in **Figure 11** that the value of potential sales has zoomed from $21 billion in 1980, to $141 billion in 1995 (even after losing $39 billion to seizures), a seven-fold increase.

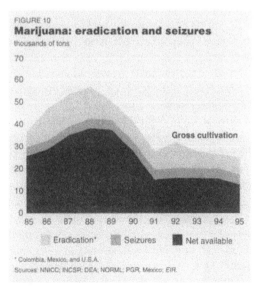

FIGURE 10
Marijuana: eradication and seizures
thousands of tons

Gross cultivation

Eradication*   Seizures   Net available

* Colombia, Mexico, and U.S.A.
Sources: NNICC; INCSR; DEA; NORML; PGR, Mexico; EIR.

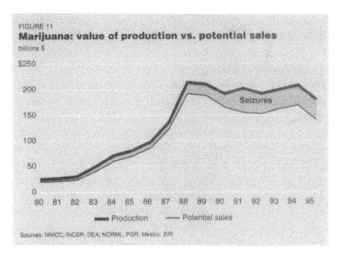

FIGURE 11
Marijuana: value of production vs. potential sales
billions $

Sources: NNICC; INCSR; DEA; NORML; PGR; Mexico; EIR

Hashish

Although the Philippines converts a certain percentage of its cannabis crop to hashish and hashish oil, destined for Australia, Canada, and Europe, the majority of the world's hashish supply comes from North Africa and the Middle East.

According to the National Narcotics Intelligence Consumers Committee (NNICC), world hashish production in 1993 (the last year reported) was 1,150 metric tons, and EIR estimates that the figure for 1995 is equivalent. This amount has a potential sales value of about $22 billion. The main producing countries, in order of importance, are Lebanon, Afghanistan, Pakistan, and Morocco, which service the Mideastern, European, and Canadian markets (hashish has never been popular in the United States). Egypt is one of the countries in the producing regions which is most afflicted with the drug.

Lebanon is the world's primary grower and processor, with cultivation centered in the northern Bekaa Valley, where the Syrian Army has introduced large-scale and sophisticated farming techniques. The area also has been a major producer of opium. Almost all of the cannabis grown in Lebanon is converted to hashish. According to a 1994 report of the NNICC, "Most of the cannabisgrowing region in Lebanon remained under Syrian Army control."

Although Lebanese hashish production is an ancient practice, it underwent massive expansion following Syria's 1977 invasion and occupation of Lebanon, in the midst of the Lebanese civil war. Since that time, Lebanese hashish and heroin proceeds (in part based on refining Central Asian opium) have accounted for a significant amount of Syria's income. Most Lebanese-produced hashish is shipped through Syria, on its way to Europe, Canada, and the Arabian peninsula.

Morocco is another cannabis grower, and while an estimated 15-40% is used domestically, the rest is converted to hashish for export through the Iberian Peninsula to other North African and European countries. Over the last year, Moroccan producing and trafficking organizations have been hit with a series of huge seizures and arrests, indicating that its role as a supplier of Europe may soon decline.

Pakistan and Afghanistan are significant producers of hashish. While a substantial amount of their hashish goes to Canada and western Europe, a growing percentage is making its way into Russia and eastern Europe. Reports of significant marijuana cultivation and export from the states of Turkmenistan, Uzbekistan, Kyrgyzstan, Tajikistan, and Kazakhstan cannot be confirmed, due to a lack of data from or on these areas.

The Dope, Inc. trafficking network used to transport heroin from the Golden Crescent, also is used to traffic in hashish. As with heroin, the land route proceeds through Iran and Turkey, reaching western Europe via the Balkans.

Made in the U.S.A.

The fact that the United States is both the largest consumer and largest producer of a drug that has been proven to be of the utmost danger to its population, is a shocking reality that needs to be understood by the American citizenry. Besides the social and economic consequences, it immediately shatters the myth that all U.S. drugs are imported from drug-producing nations in the Third World, which are "the cause of the whole problem." It shows, instead, that Dope, Inc. is an integrated world cartel which simultaneously controls the production, distribution, consumption, and moneylaundering phases of the total drug cycle.

Marijuana is today the largest cash crop of the United States, whose potential street sale value in 1995 was an estimated $77 billion.

Less than one year ago, the National Household Survey on Drug Abuse released their 1994 results, and announced that drug use has increased markedly among the nation's youth, particularly the consumption of marijuana. For example, according to the report (which probably significantly underestimates consumption), in an average month in 1994, some 13 million Americans used illicit drugs. Of these, 10 million used marijuana, making it by far the most commonly used illicit drug. Even worse, between 1992 and 1994, the reported rate of marijuana use among youths 12-17 years old nearly doubled, from about 14% to 22% of the total age-group population.

Other studies report similar findings. In its most recent annual survey (November 1995), the National Parents' Resource Institute for Drug Education reported significant increases in marijuana use by students in grades 6 through 12, and jumps in cocaine and hallucinogen use by students in grades 9 through 12. "As in recent years, marijuana use increased more dramatically than any drug in the study. One-third of high school seniors (33%) smoked marijuana in the past year, and one-fifth (21 %) smoked monthly. Since the 1990-91 school year, annual reported use of marijuana in junior high school (grades 6 through 8) has risen 111% (from 4.5% to 9.5%) and has risen 67% in high school (16.9% versus 28.2%)."

And the White House's Office of National Drug Control Policy's latest "Marijuana Situation Assessment" study reports "alarming indicators that marijuana is increasing in popularity, particularly among teenagers." Even worse, "the marijuana is at least 10 times more potent than it was 10 years ago."

The potency of marijuana is determined by its percentage content of THC, the main psychoactive chemical it contains. There are two kinds of marijuana grown in the United States, commercial grade and *sinsemilla* (seedless), of which the latter has substantially higher THC content, and today supplies over one-third of the domestic market, up from about 20-25% in the early 1980s.

The THC content of both kinds has been rising significantly over the years, thanks to genetic manipulation. This partially accounts for the significant increase in the street price of marijuana (**Figure 12**). Although commercial grade marijuana prices have been relatively steady since 1991, the cost of *sinsemilla* has continued to rise from 1980 onwards, and is currently selling in the United States for an average of $550 per ounce.

Pot is not only more potent today; average doses are also rising. One study by Monika Guttman pointed out, "Kids today smoke larger amounts than their elders did, thanks to innovations such as 'blunts': short cigars hollowed out and restuffed with pot or a pot and tobacco mix. Marijuana is now often laced with other drugs, as in 'primos' (with cocaine) and 'illies' (with formaldehyde)." The result of such concoctions is that in 1994, some 50% more 12-17-year-olds went to the emergency room for smoking pot than in 1993.

As noted, most of the marijuana consumed in the United States is produced at home. In recent years, U.S. production has undergone a virtual revolution. Although there are no official numbers on production, different estimates can be made based on the figures for marijuana eradication, which are available from the DEA. Not surprisingly, there is a disparity in the approach, depending on the source. The DEA, for example, estimates that what is eradicated accounts for 50% of what is planted. The National Organization for the Reform of Marijuana Laws (NORML) and the Drug Policy Foundation on the other hand, representing the pro-pot lobby, say it is much more likely to be only 15% of the total. *EIR* believes the truth lies somewhere between these two extremes, perhaps at about one-third of the total crop.

Everyone concedes, however, that it is America's number-one cash crop. Even conservative estimates put it undisputedly in first place. For example, take the value of the top six legal crops for 1992, according to the U.S. Department of Agriculture:

Corn	$17.8 billion
Soybeans	$10.8 billion
Hay	$10.5 billion
Wheat	$ 8.1 billion
Cotton	$ 4.0 billion
Tobacco	$ 3.1 billion

Marijuana estimates for the same year, range from $20.9 billion (NORML), to $28 billion (DEA), to $76 billion *(EIR)*.

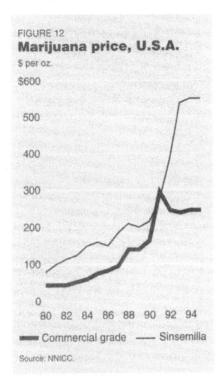

FIGURE 12
Marijuana price, U.S.A.
$ per oz.

Commercial grade — Sinsemilla

Source: NNICC.

MAP 7
The top ten states in U.S. marijuana cultivation

U.S. total, 1995 = 5,950 tons

Sources: DEA, NORML, EIR

Map 7 shows the top ten pot-producing states in the United States, according to NORML. Many of these are states one normally thinks of as agricultural giants. And yet, in Kentucky, in 1992 the marijuana crop was worth about $2.280 billion (NORML), while tobacco brought in only $955 million, hay $375 million, corn $312 million and soybeans $209 million.

When the Cannabis Cup, a convention and festival for marijuana growers sponsored by *High Times* magazine, took place last November in Amsterdam, Michael Pollan, writing for the *New York Times*, noted: "Marijuana growing in America had evolved from a hobby of aging hippies into a burgeoning high-tech industry with earnings that are estimated at $32 billion a year."

How is it possible that a criminal enterprise of this magnitude thrives across the United States today? A cross-gridding of law enforcement reports and sources from pro-drug interests shows the following picture.

The growing business has made a significant shift indoors, not simply to escape detection, but to allow more sophisticated growing techniques. This allows growers to adjust the amount, intensity, and wavelength of the light the plant receives; use computer-controlled irrigation; and adjust the nutrients the roots receive. Ceramic heaters are used to warm the roots, and sodium lamps give them light for extended hours.

Moving indoors has encouraged not only these advanced cultivation strategies, and permitted year-round growing, but has also permitted an overall shift to the cultivation of *sinsemilla* marijuana, the unpollinated female plant. Journalist Pollan explains:

"At the beginning, American growers were familiar with only one kind of marijuana: *Cannabis sativa*, an equatorial strain that can't withstand frost and won't reliably flower north of the 30th parallel. Eager to expand the range of domestic production, growers began searching for a variety that might flourish and flower farther north, and by the second half of the decade, it had been found: *Cannabis indica*, a stout, frost-tolerant species that had been cultivated for centuries in Afghanistan by hashish producers.

"*Cannabis indica* looks quite unlike the familiar marijuana plant: It rarely grows taller than 4 or 5 feet (as compared to 15 feet for some sativas) and its deep bluish-green leaves are rounded, rather than pointed. But the great advantage of *Cannabis indica* was that it allowed growers in all 50 states to cultivate *sinsemilla* for the first time."

Pollan wrote that, at first, the new plants were grown as purebreds. "But enterprising growers soon discovered that by crossing the new variety with *Cannabis sativa*, it waossible to produce hybrids that combined the most desirable traits of both plants while playing down their worst. The smoother taste and what I often heard described as the 'clear, bell-like high' of a *sativa*, for example, could be combined with the hardiness, small stature and higher potency of an *indica*. In a flurry of breeding work performed around 1980, most of it by amateurs working on the West Coast, the modern American marijuana *plant—Cannabis sativa x indica*—was born."

Heroin: Britain's Opium Wars: Two Centuries, and Going Strong

Dope, Inc. came into being as global opium vendor in the nineteenth century. Prior to that time, narcotic use was widespread, but there was no single global organization guiding its distribution internationally. The banking, planning, marketing, and smuggling network that came into being then, in order to destroy China, provided the basis for Dope, Inc.'s expansion in the twentieth century. Because of this global infrastructure, Dope, Inc. not only controls world narcotics trafficking, but weapons trafficking, currency smuggling, money laundering, and related criminal enterprises.

The use of opium to destroy China in the nineteenth century, is the model that Britain is following in its war against the institution of the nation-state today. Dope, Inc. is not merely a commercial enterprise, but comprises the very center of British imperial strategy of re-creating its old empire in a new form. To do that, the British empire must destroy powerful institutions and entire societies throughout the world. Opium and heroin are among the poisons used to that end.

Opium is a narcotic drug prepared from the juice of the unripened seed pod of the opium poppy, a flowering plant indigenous to southern Europe and western Asia, but now cultivated throughout the world. It is usually consumed through smoking or eating. Morphine and heroin are extracted and refined from its juice, and are consumed either by smoking, or through hypodermic injection. The use of opium as a powerful painkiller was known in the ancient world, and is referenced in Greek medical texts as early as the first century B.C. The drug had valid use when other, safer anesthetics were unknown. But its abuse as a narcotic also dates back to that time.

Morphine, the active ingredient in the poppy juice, was first identified in 1805, and the German pharmaceutical house Merck and Company soon began producing it as an anesthetic. In 1874, an Englishman, CR. Wright, first synthesized its more potent form, diacetylmorphine (heroin). The German pharmaceutical house of Bayer and Company began mass production of the drug in 1896, under the patented trade name of "heroin." It said the new wonder drug was a powerful non-addictive cure for various adult and infant ailments. It spread throughout the United States and western Europe as a patent-medicine, and was touted as a general cure-all for the old and young alike, capable of curing everything from the common cold to aging.

Cocaine was also developed and promoted as a wonder drug by the same pharmaceutical houses. But unlike opium and morphine, heroin and cocaine never had any legitimate medical use.

The extraction of morphine from poppy juice is uncomplicated. But the manufacture of heroin requires training and equipment, and a considerable amount of the chemical acetic anhydride—making Southeast Asia the world's largest consumer of an industrial chemical whose only legitimate use is in photography.

The First Opium Wars

The use of opium as a means of social control is as old as its use as a pain killer. In the ancient Near East, pagan cults regularly intoxicated their devotees with opium, hashish, and various powerful psychedelics, to ensure that they remained under total control. Pagan priests also used opium and other drugs to enfeeble, corrupt, and control the ruling aristocratic families.

However, the use of opium to destroy entire societies on a mass scale, was first introduced by the British in the nineteenth century. British use of opium against China then, remains the model for what it is doing with narcotics worldwide, today.

In 1842-44, and then in 1856-60, Britain fought two Opium Wars to force the Chinese government to lift its ban on the sale and use of opium within its territory. The second war was fought because the British were not satisfied by the concessions won by the first. In the interim, Britain organized the Taiping rebellion in southern China to force the government to accept the trade, which killed 20-30 million people directly, and an estimated 70 million indirectly.

As a result of its defeat in these wars, a prostrate China capitulated to British demands, and signed a series of peace treaties which made opium legal, and gave Britain the exclusive monopoly on its sale. Despite continuing efforts by the Chinese government to discourage its use, British traders flooded the country with the poison. By 1850, Britain was exporting 3,210 metric tons of opium to China, then produced in British India, capable of feeding the habit of millions of users. By 1880, this reached 5,880 tons.

Britain also compelled China to open up its interior to opium poppy cultivation. This was not done for commercial reasons, but to further the breakdown of Chinese society. By 1900, opium poppy was cultivated in every Chinese province, in some regions diverting vast peasant populations and lands to its cultivation. Terrible famine was the foreseeable, and desired, result. By 1900, China's addict population had risen to 13.5 million out of a total population of 400 million. Its domestic production for internal use was 22,600 tons. By comparison, opium production in the entire Southeast Asia's Golden Triangle in 1995, was "only" 2,560 tons—about one-tenth of what China was consuming in 1900.

Through this decades-long subversive campaign, China was made a de facto British colony.

Massive opium cultivation in British India to supply the Chinese market, also served British interests there as well. There, too, society was ravaged by famine, and there were related effects of massive poppy cultivation, including local use of the drug. In the 1860s, Britain greatly expanded small-scale opium cultivation in the Iranian and Ottoman Turkish empires, to meet the needs of its Chinese market. This opium was also exported to western Europe, to service Britain's growing market there, as well as feed its own developing addict population.

The explosive growth of opium use in the nineteenth century, led to increasing efforts to ban the drug, particularly as it spread into Europe and the United States. In 1909, the British Empire reluctantly agreed to U.S. pressure to outlaw opium cultivation and sale. Then, as now, narcotics revenues comprised a major part of the profits of its banking system. But despite this legal ban, Britain continued the export of opiates.

As late as 1927, opium was the largest source of official Crown revenue in all of Britain's Asian colonies; it was then primarily sold to her own colonial subjects to keep them subdued. Of the official Straits settlements (Singapore) revenue that year, 37% came from opium trade. At its high point, 60% of Malaya's revenues came from taxes on the opium monopoly.

And under the British claim that morphine is still legitimately needed as a painkiller, opium poppy cultivation still is legal in many British Commonwealth countries, such as Australia and India, and is produced there under government license. Opium is the only important narcotic which remains legal under this guise.

Britain's current opium war

A review of the sites of opium poppy cultivation and heroin manufacture, trafficking routes, and the populations targetted for addiction, corroborates other evidence showing that Britain is currently engaged in another opium war, this time against the entire world.

Map 8 shows the world's three opium poppy production regions, and the main trafficking routes bringing this opium, in the form of heroin, to the external market.

These three producing regions are the Golden Triangle region of Southeast Asia, which produces 57% of total world opium output, and 51 % of its refined heroin; the Golden Crescent region of Southwest Asia, which produces 40% of world opium and 46% of world heroin; and Ibero-America, which produces about 3% of world opium and a like share of world heroin. The Golden Triangle and Golden Crescent are entirely a creation of the British Empire.

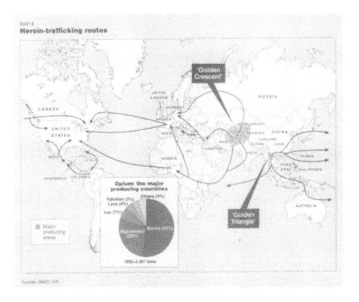

As the map indicates, the broad band stretching from the Balkans in southern Europe, into Central Asia via Turkey and Iran, and on to Southeast Asia via northern India, is the world's primary production and transshipment zone for the drug. There is not one country in that area, which the British sometimes term the "Arc of Crisis," which is not deeply involved in heroin production or trafficking.

This is not an accidental feature that can be explained by either suitable climate conditions, or an ancient tradition of cultivation of the plant, but is a deliberate result of British imperial policy, which systematically introduced opium production throughout the entire area. By placing opium production there, Britain has situated itself to launch broad destabilizations of Asia, and to break up any efforts to develop the interior of the Asian landmass. It is now particularly targetting China and Russia, and opium is one of the means through which it is doing it.

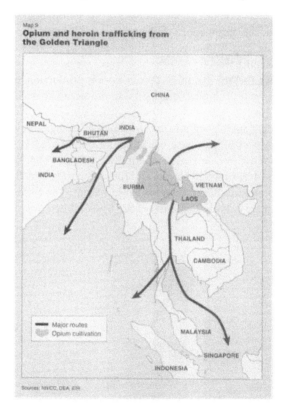

Map 9 shows the Golden Triangle region, the world's largest opium plantation, and the source of about three-quarters of the heroin found on the streets of the United States. The major producing area is Burma, with smaller amounts produced in Laos, and across the border in China and Thailand. Most of this opium is refined into heroin. Thailand is the primary refiner of the drug and the main transshipment point for heroin sent to Europe and the United States. China is another important route to western markets.

This entire production region is in a rugged cross-border area, inhabited by minority backward tribes, which have never been fully controlled by their respective governments. Northern Burma has been in revolt against its central government, since independence. The Shan, Wa, and other minority tribes, which produce almost all of Burma's opium, were patronized by the British during the colonial period, and sustained by them in their revolt since that time. The same minority peoples live on the other side of the porous border, in China. (The area depicted as under cultivation in China is approximate, due to lack of reliable data.)

Contrary to claims one often finds in the western media, opium is not indigenous to the region, but was introduced there at the end of the nineteenth century by the British and French empires, to supply their Chinese market. Both powers continued cultivation there in the twentieth century, in part to fund their intelligence operations, which remain dependent on narco-proceeds, During the Vietnam War, Britain and Maoist China dramatically expanded cultivation in the region, to supply, and demoralize, nearby American troops.

More recently, China itself has become a primary target of the dope trade, as in the nineteenth century. Heroin and opium use there has skyrocketed, particularly along southern transport routes to the Chinese coast.

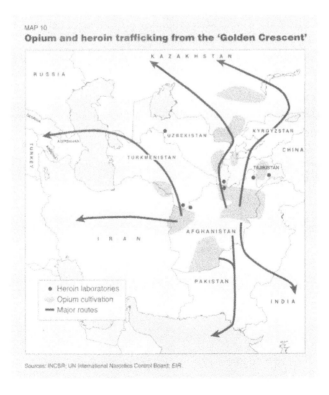

MAP 10
Opium and heroin trafficking from the 'Golden Crescent'

- Heroin laboratories
- Opium cultivation
- Major routes

Sources: INCSR; UN International Narcotics Control Board; EIR.

Map 10 shows the Golden Crescent region, the source of about two-thirds of the heroin found on the streets of western Europe. Most of the poppy is cultivated in Afghanistan, and refined and transported through Pakistan to the coast, for shipment to Europe. As in the case of Southeast Asia, narcotics cultivation is done by minority tribes, in border regions, which largely operate outside the control of any of the governments concerned. An increasing, unknown, but large amount of poppy is also cultivated in former Soviet Central Asia, which is also being used as a route for Afghan opium destined for the West. Iran is also a producer, especially since the rise of the ayatollahs, and is on the main land route to the European market.

Commercial-scale Southwest Asian production began in the nineteenth century, to supply opium for the Chinese market. In the aftermath of World War II, the AngloAmerican-reorganized Italian Mafia used the region to supply opium for the European and U.S. heroin markets.

As recently as 1979, there was almost no heroin refining in the region. Except for Iran, there were *no* heroin addicts anywhere in the area, including nearby India. The opium produced there was almost entirely refined in Turkey and Lebanon, and destined for Western markets.

But the overthrow of the Shah of Iran that year, and the Soviet invasion of Afghanistan, soon transformed the region into the world's major opium plantation and heroin refinery. Afghan mujahideen, trained and equipped by Western secret services to fight a war against Soviet troops, were also instructed to grow opium to finance their needs. Afghanistan produced very little opium before the war. It is now the world's second largest producer.

The collapse of the Soviet Union has drastically worsened this problem. Opium cultivation is now spreading rapidly throughout former Soviet Central Asia, to provide revenue for desperately poor, newly independent states, who are encouraged by international agencies to produce the drug. Clan wars fought over the control of opium production and trade in Central Asia and in the Caucasus, are convulsing the entire region.

Behind these developments stands Dope, Inc., which oversaw the expansion of the Golden Triangle during the Vietnam War, and the creation of the Golden Crescent during the Afghan War. Now, the former Soviet Union is targetted for the same treatment.

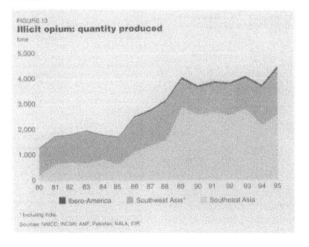

FIGURE 13
Illicit opium: quantity produced
tons

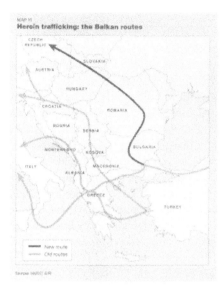

War is not unfavorable to the cultivation, refinement, and trafficking of narcotics, by any means. **Map 11** shows the "Balkan routes," through which most of the heroin destined for western Europe passes. Heroin and hashish trafficking played an important part in the pre-war economy of Yugoslavia, providing an important source of income for the Serbian-dominated military. The trade continues there, in fact aided by the war, providing income for Serbian fascist militias, as well as militias and criminal gangs outside the control of the Croatian and Bosnian governments. And, as in the case of Afghanistan, international agencies have descended on the region, encouraging all sides to cultivate narcotics in order to buy arms. A new route, via Romania and Hungary, supplementing the old Balkan route, has also been added.

Although Ibero-American cultivation of opium is small by comparison with Southwest and Southeast Asia, it takes on relatively greater significance because it is converted, in its entirety, into heroin for export to the United States. Mexico has historically been the principal producer in the region, but Colombia has become a major factor in just the last 3-4 years, and now produces more than Mexico. This is a cause for great concern in law enforcement circles, because the Colombian cocaine cartels are logistically, politically, and militarily well equipped to handle a huge increase of heroin trafficking.

What the numbers show

EIR's review of statistics compiled by several governments and other agencies, show that the British Empire remains the world's major opium and heroin producer, and that it is using the drug to systematically destroy targetted states. **Figure 13** shows that illicit opium production has been steadily rising over recent years, from 1,291 metric tons in 1980, to 4,467 metric tons in 1995. (Poor crop years reported for Burma in the earlier period skew the comparative production of Southwest and Southeast Asia.) That is a growth of 346%, or 8.6% per annum.

Not all of the opium produced in the world is converted into heroin. In 1980, about 40% of the total crop was refined into heroin, but that proportion has been steadily increasing over time, as the far more dangerous heroin has increasingly become the drug of choice of former opium addicts in the producing regions. By 1995, a full 75% of the crop was converted to heroin, both for local consumption and export.

Dope, Inc.'s total revenue from potential sales of heroin increased nearly fivefold in 1980-89, rising from $27.5 billion to $127.4 billion (see **Figure 14**), and has fluctuated around that high-point since. Of this revenue, over 90% comes from the lucrative western European and U.S. markets, despite the fact that the majority of the heroin, by quantity, is consumed in the producing regions themselves, but at far lower prices than in Europe or the United States (see below). Relatively little of world heroin supplies is seized, unlike cocaine and marijuana. The eradication of the poppy plant by government authorities is virtually nonexistent.

Dope, Inc. has the same marketing strategy for heroin that it has for cocaine: slash prices to increase sales, and total profits. Dope, Inc. cut the price of heroin in the U.S. and western European market over 1980-95, by about one-half and two-thirds, respectively (see **Figure 15**). This bargain-basement strategy paid off. The total quantity produced for sale increased almost sevenfold in the same period, from 49 tons in 1980, to 331 tons in 1995.

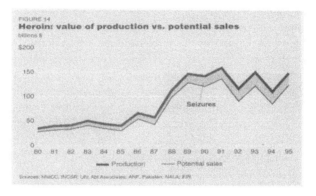

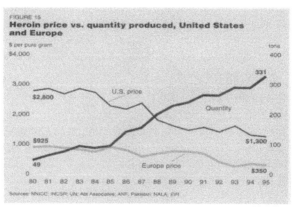

But illicit opium and heroin is only part of the story. There is also *licit* opium production, supervised by pharmaceutical houses, for manufacture of morphine as a prescribed painkiller. As **Figure 16** shows, licit production has remained steady from 1980 to 1995. Although shrinking as a proportion of total opium production, licit output remains vast. Diversion of licit stocks to illegal use is a major problem. According to Indian government estimates, 10-30% of its yearly licit production of 740 tons of opium, is siphoned off for illegal use—equivalent to the entire illegal crop in Laos.

A review of the role of former British colonies, or their satraps, in the production of opium, shows a fact that is never reported in the establishment media, which continues to cover up for the British role in the drug trade.

Figures 17 and **18**, along with the pie chart on Map 8, show that current or former members of the British Empire and Commonwealth, together with countries under its domination, produce virtually all of the world's licit and illicit opium.

Burma and Pakistan, former jewels of the British Raj, produce 55% of the world's illegal opium (with India producing another 3%). Afghanistan and Iran, both former British imperial dependents, produce another 35%. The former French colony of Laos produces 4% of the total. Only 3% of the world's illegal opium production takes place in countries that were not under British rule. And, in all these cases, opium cultivation was introduced by Britain to supply its Chinese market.

With the partial exception of Burma, all these countries remain British dominated to this day.

The case of licit production tells the same story, as Figure 17 indicates. The Crown colony of Australia is the world's largest producer of licit opium. India, the former jewel of the British Empire, ranks second. British-dominated Turkey ranks third.

Non-producing countries involved in trafficking are almost entirely former British, French, and Dutch colonies. For example, Nigeria, now high on the British hit-list, is a major transshipment point. Canada is on the primary route into the United States.

Who is targeted

It may shock the reader to learn that the vast majority of heroin users in the world are in the producer regions themselves, and the numbers (as conservatively estimated by the governments concerned, the UN, and the U.S. government) are staggering.

In 1996, the government of Pakistan, for example, reported that it had 1.5 million heroin addicts and an equal number of opium addicts, constituting over 2% of its 125 million population—the highest addiction rate in the world. Before the Anglo-Americans created the Afghan mujahideen in 1979, there was no heroin addiction in Pakistan at all. By comparison, the United States, with a population of 255 million, has 816,000 heroin users.

Similarly, Thailand, which refines most of the opium produced in Southeast Asia, has 340,000 heroin addicts—largely as a byproduct of the entertainment it provided to U.S. troops during the Vietnam War. India has an estimated 1 million heroin addicts, and another 4.5 million opium addicts. There was also no significant heroin addiction in India before the Afghan War. Thus, out of perhaps 5 million heroin users worldwide, less than a million are in the United States, and perhaps an equivalent number in Europe.

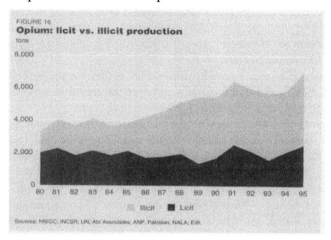

FIGURE 16
Opium: licit vs. illicit production
tons

This is reflected in the consumption figures as such. Out of the 331 metric tons of heroin produced worldwide in 1995, an estimated 83 tons were exported to the United States, 51 tons were exported to western Europe, and 197 tons remained in the producing regions of Southwest and Southeast Asia to feed their own addicts, who usually consume lower grade No.3 heroin, mainly for smoking, as distinct from the No.4 heroin for export, which is usually injected. .

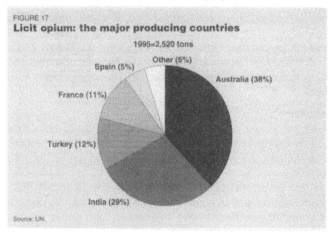

FIGURE 17
Licit opium: the major producing countries
1995=2,520 tons

In other words, 60% of the world's total heroin production in 1995 was consumed in the Southeast and Southwest Asia producing regions themselves. (Relatively little heroin is consumed in Ibero-America.) This was not a one-year anomaly. In fact, over the entire decade from 1985 to 1995, about 70% of all world heroin was consumed in the producing regions. While the revenue Dope, Inc.

earns through this use is comparatively small ($7 billion in 1995) because of the vast difference in price, the devastating effects on the societies concerned are enormous.

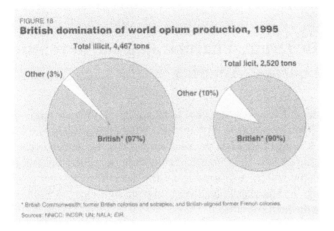

FIGURE 18
British domination of world opium production, 1995

Total illicit, 4,467 tons

Other (3%)

British* (97%)

Total licit, 2,520 tons

Other (10%)

British* (90%)

* British Commonwealth, former British colonies and satrapies, and British-aligned former French colonies.
Sources: NNICC; INCSR; UN; NALA; EIR.

Table 1 shows the disposition of world heroin production in 1995, from its source in Southeast Asia, Southwest Asia, and Ibero-America. Of the 168 tons of heroin produced in Southeast Asia, an estimated 86 tons were consumed regionally, and the rest was exported to the United States and Europe. Of the 151 tons produced in Southwest Asia, about 111 were consumed in the region. In the case of Ibero-America, virtually all the 12 tons produced were exported—to the United States. Of the total 83 tons of heroin exported to the United States from different sources, about 17 tons were seized, leaving 66 tons for sale (most originating in Southeast Asia). Europe, similarly, had 43 tons available for sale after seizures, and most of the supply came from Southwest Asia.

TABLE 1: Disposition of world heroin production, 1995 (tons)				
	Destination			
Source	Local Consumption	Exported to U.S.	Exported to Europe	Total
Southeast Asia	86	61	21	168
Southwest Asia	111	10	30	151
Ibero-America	0	12	0	12
World production	197	83	51	331
Seizures	0	−17	−8	−25
Net consumption	197	66	43	306

Sources: NNICC; INCSR; UN; NALA; EIR.

This table shows that the common media and government distinction between producing and consuming regions is ultimately misleading, in some cases deliberately so. It also leaves no doubt that a new opium war, directed against the same general region as the nineteenth-century Opium War, is now in progress.

Synthetic Drugs: Pharmacological 'Revolution' Sweeps Europe, America

There will be in the next generation or so a pharmacological method of making people love their servitude and producing dictatorship without tears, so to speak. Producing a kind of painless concentration camp for entire societies, so that people will in fact have their liberties taken away from them but will rather enjoy it, because they will be distracted from any desire to rebel—by propaganda, or brainwashing, or brainwashing enhanced by pharmacological methods. And this seems to be the final revolution."

—from a 1961 lecture by Aldous Huxley, at the California School of Medicine in San Francisco, sponsored by the U.S. Information Service's Voice of America

In February 1996, the U.S. Drug Enforcement Administration convened an emergency summit of law enforcement officials from across the country, to chart out a response to an epidemic-proportion jump in illicit methamphetamine ("meth") use in the United States. Two months later, the DEA released a *National Methamphetamine Strategy*, which candidly admitted: "Trafficking of a highly potent form of methamphetamine has been on the rise in the United States over the past few years, and abuse continues to devastate many communities. Although still more common in western areas of the country, methamphetamine trafficking and abuse are no longer confined to anyone region: Methamphetamine is spreading eastward. The production and trafficking structures now in place, if left unchecked, pose the risk that the nation as a whole will experience very serious levels of methamphetamine abuse."

The *Strategy* noted with alarm, that, since 1993, large quantities of meth have been flooding the United States from Mexico. In March 1996, U.S. and Mexican anti-drug authorities captured a large and sophisticated meth lab in the Yucatan Peninsula, and seized one of the largest supplies of the stimulant in history. Multi-drug cartels, in Mexico and Colombia, are now emerging as major suppliers of methamphetamine to the U.S. market (according to the DEA, the Cali and Medellín cartels have, for over a decade, been major suppliers of Quaalaudes, a depressant, to the U.S. black market).

Inside the United States, the growing involvement of the major international drug cartels in the meth trade has meant that methamphetamine distribution is being increasingly dominated by the same apparatus that traffics in cocaine, heroin, and marijuana, and has vast smuggling, distribution, and money-laundering capabilities. DEA sources tell *EIR* that, this year, the California Highway Patrol has made seizures of pure methamphetamine that are larger than any recent cocaine seizures.

Buttressing the evidence of the recent emergence of the Ibero-American multi-drug cartels in the U.S. methamphetamine trade, is the following data, from the *Strategy* document: In 1992, federal agents seized a total of 6.5 kilos of meth at the U.S.-Mexican border. The following year, 306 kilos were seized, and in 1994, 682 kilos were confiscated.

But, the picture presented in the *Strategy*, although alarming, represents just the tip of the iceberg. Meth is but one of a growing number of illegal synthetic drugs flooding the American and world markets. *The National Drug Control Strategy: 1996*, produced by the White House, acknowledges that LSD and stimulant use by 8th, 10th, and 12th graders has increased by 82% and 37%, respectively, in the first half of the 1990s. And, the National Narcotics Intelligence Consumers Committee (NNICC) annual report has, for several years, catalogued growing abuse of PCP (Phencyclidine), a powerful hallucinogen; MDMA (a.k.a. "Ecstasy"), a combination of methamphetamine and MDA (a strong hallucinogen); Methcathinone ("Cat"), a stimulant; and a growing number of "controlled substance analogs," more popularly known as "designer drugs."

The deeper crisis

The tremendous recent increase in Ecstasy abuse in the United States and Europe provides an alarming window into the deeper cultural crisis that the synthetic drug explosion signals.

The May 13, 1996 issue of the *New Federalist* newspaper featured an article by Carol Greene, "Techno-Music Will Destroy Your Brain," exposing computer-generated techno-music as the latest, most mind-deadening, and fastest-growing aberration of the drug-rock counterculture. Greene wrote: "In Germany alone, approximately 2 million sadly bored and under-stimulated members of the middle-class, mostly students, sales personnel, administrative workers, and computer specialists, are members of the 'rave society.' Entertainment specialists in Germany estimate that 56% of the above go to a techno party once a week and some 22% even go more than twice a week." The overwhelming majority of "ravers" use Ecstasy (MDMA) to throw themselves into a trance-like, but energized state, as they spend hours at the techno clubs, dancing in all-night, and sometimes weekend-long, dance marathons, to computer-generated, repetitive noise, playing at 85-120 decibels.

The techno "revolution," like the earlier "Beatle-mania," began in Britain in the early 1980s, and has now spread across Europe and the United States. The Berlin Love Parade in May 1995, a weekend "rave-fest," drew an estimated 350,000 participants, courtesy, in part, of a massive advertising campaign, subsidized by Marlboro and Camel cigarettes, and Adidas sneakers. The Berlin event dwarfed Woodstock, by comparison. German authorities estimate that a half-million German youths participate in rave sessions every weekend.

The rapid expansion of designer drugs, of which Ecstasy is but one currently leading example, offers another crucial look into the future of Dope, Inc. In 1987, Dr. Joseph D. Douglass, Jr. and Neil C. Livingstone coauthored a book called *America the Vulnerable: The Threat of Chemical/Biological Warfare.* They wrote:

"One of the newer complications confronting both civil and military authorities is the spread of 'designer drugs,' high-tech heroin substitutes. These drugs are synthetics designed to mimic heroin—hence the name designer drugs. The drugs are exceedingly potent. The newest ones are up to four thousand times more potent than heroin, and because they are new, they are not illegal. When one drug is identified and declared illegal, less than a month goes by before a new, modified—and legal—variant or analogue surfaces to take its place. And the process continues. The first fentanyl analogue, alpha-methyl-fentanyl, appeared in 1979 in Orange County, California. Since 1981, DEA laboratories have identified seven more fentanyl analogues. Authorities in California now estimate that 20% of heroin addicts are using the fentanyl analogues.

"One of the authorities in the field, Dr. Gary Henderson (a pharmacologist and toxicologist at the University of California, Davis), believes that a world-class medicinal chemist has been responsible for the many analogues of fentanyl that have appeared. . . . The drugs are very pure, and the doses are very uniform. . . . The quality is comparable to what one might expect if the source were a pharmaceutical plant rather than a clandestine basement laboratory."

Douglass and Livingstone then warned: "Because the designer drugs are so potent, tracking the substances down is exceedingly difficult and getting worse. A two-hundred gram batch of fentanyl (less than a half a pound) represents a lifetime supply of two hundred million doses. This potency also greatly magnifies the difficulty of detecting evidence of use in the bloodstream or urine. Extremely sensitive laboratory techniques are required to detect such drugs—techniques capable of detecting concentrations of a few parts per billion. The drugs are astronomically more profitable than heroin. This explains why the supply of these designer drugs can be expected to expand. An investment of $2,000 translates into a street value of over $1 billion."

The DEA does acknowledge that some of the flow of synthetic drugs onto the black market comes directly from large pharmaceutical houses that are wittingly involved in the illegal trade. President Clinton has taken up this problem, in at least one, most egregious case. On Oct. 21, 1995, he signed Executive Order 12978, entitled "Blocking Assets and Prohibiting Transactions With Significant Narcotics Traffickers," which named a dozen Colombian pharmaceutical manufacturers and distributors as fronts for the Cali Cartel, and banned any American companies or citizens from doing business with them.

The DEA acknowledges that large "legitimate" pharmaceutical manufacturers in western Europe, China, and Brazil are now supplying drug cartels with synthetic drugs. in growing volumes. Here, the evidence shows, again, that Dope, Inc. is a top-down structure.

A unique challenge

For years, official U.S. government statistics on the use of illegal synthetic drugs have grossly underestimated the size of the traffic. There are understandable reasons for these errors.

Frenzied youth in Germany, many high on the drug Ecstasy, dance to computer-generated "techno" music

Unlike cocaine, heroin, and marijuana, which are all cultivated drugs, synthetic drugs are far more difficult to track. Through Landsat satellite photo-analysis, low-altitude aerial reconnaissance, and ground surveillance, drug-enforcement agencies can develop reliable estimates of the gross amount of opium poppy, coca plants, and marijuana plants under cultivation at any given time. Synthetic drugs, especially the newer designer drugs, cannot be tracked as easily, because they are manufactured from chemicals that are, for the most part, easily obtainable on the commercial market. This is precisely why many law enforcement specialists agree with Douglass and Livingstone, when they assert that designer drugs are "the wave of the future."

The DEA has developed a number of techniques for measuring the volume of synthetic drug abuse:

- They keep track of the number of underground synthetic drug laboratories, which are busted each year;
- Through the Drug Abuse Warning Network (DAWN) system, they receive data from every hospital emergency room in the United States, indicating the number of patients who come in with traces of synthetic drugs in their bloodstream, and the number of patients who die of synthetic drug overdoses;
- The Justice Department and the FBI try to maintain parallel data on all people who are arrested and tested for drugs;
- The DEA also keeps track of the volume of synthetic drugs seized each year;
- The National Household Survey on Drug Abuse (NHSDA) questions a sample of Americans about their use of illegal drugs;
- And, through undercover operations, the DEA, in conjunction with other law enforcement agencies, maintains generally up-to-date and reliable data

on the wholesale and retail prices of every illegal drug, including all the major synthetics.

In the spring of 1995, the White House Office of National Drug Control Policy published a report, "What America's Users Spend on Illegal Drugs, 1988-1993." The study was prepared by Abt Associates, Inc., a Cambridge, Massachusetts research outfit that has done illicit-drug research for the federal government for years. The Abt study developed data on heroin, cocaine, and marijuana abuse, using two distinctly different methods of analysis. They generated figures based on production data, and figures based on consumption data. The consumption data invariably relied on the highly dubious Household Survey. (Abt, to its credit, admitted this problem in the report: "We do note . . . that the NHSDA undoubtedly misses some users, and those who are reached probably have an incentive to misrepresent their consumption.")

In the case of cocaine, Abt's production-based data were in the same general ballpark as the *EIR* survey. (The consumption-based estimates were significantly lower than *EIR's*, across the board.) But in the case of synthetic drugs, where Abt was unable to obtain any reliable production data, and, therefore, relied exclusively on the NHSDAderived consumption statistics, the figures were grossly underestimated. Thus, for example, in 1993, Abt estimated that the total dollar value of all "Other Drugs" (i.e., not cocaine, heroin, or marijuana) in the United States that year was $1.8 billion. The *EIR* estimate for 1993 was $46 billion!

Even though the National Household Survey is notorious for understating the drug abuse problem, it does present a stark "best case" picture when it comes to the estimates of the number of Americans who are hooked on synthetic drugs. According to NHSDA figures for 1988-93, in each of those years, well over 2 million Americans used inhalants (usually, black market pharmaceuticals), 2.5 million used hallucinogens, and over 3 million used stimulants and tranquilizers.

Our method

EIR researchers reviewed virtually every available DEA and NNICC study from 1977 to 1995, to develop a more reliable approximation of the synthetic drug trade. During 1977-80, the NNICC studies provided precise dollar estimates for domestic synthetics. From 1981-84, the NNICC studies published annual data on the number of doses ("d.u.") of synthetic drugs consumed by Americans. By multiplying the number of d.u.'s by $5 (the average retail cost per dose of synthetic drugs, according to the DEA), *EIR* was able to come up with an estimated dollar value for illegal synthetic drugs, for the 1981-84 period.

The 1987 NNICC study reported that synthetic drug abuse that year was equal to the 1980 figures, and had increased by 30% from 1986. This made it possible to estimate the figures from 1985-87.

From 1987-90, the DEA released figures on the total number of doses of synthetic drugs seized in the United States. By reviewing the percentages of cocaine, marijuana, and heroin seized during the same period, *EIR* was able to estimate that the volume of synthetic drugs seized was approximately 20% of the total illicit trade. Thus, estimates on the size of the synthetic drug trade for the period from 1987-90 were generated.

For many of those years, and for 1990-95, the DEA also published data on the number of kilograms of synthetic drugs seized, the number of laboratories busted, and the number of emergency room cases reported in the DAWN survey. Specific data on the amount of methamphetamine seized along the U.S.-Mexico border during the 1990s were also available, courtesy of the *National Methamphetamine Strategy.*

Based on these statistics, *EIR* developed an index which suggested a pattern of growth in the illegal synthetic drug trade. The figures for 1991-95 were derived, via that indexing method, from the more precise annual figures covering the period from 1977 to 1990. While there is an element of scientific guesswork in the post -1990 data, and, therefore, a possibility of greater margin of error, there is no doubt that the years 1992-95, as described by the DEA and other law enforcement sources, have been a period of geometric expansion of the illegal synthetic drug trade in the United States and in western and eastern Europe. The numbers generated by the *EIR* method are commensurate with the rates of growth described qualitatively in such locations as the DEA's April 1996 *National Methamphetamine Strategy* and the *National Drug Control Strategy:1996.*

The tremendous growth in the synthetic drug market in the United States has, according to DEA and other law enforcement sources, been paralleled in both western and eastern Europe (including Russia). The DEA reports that the distribution of synthetic drugs is usually concentrated in the areas where there are laboratories producing the illegal products. Europe is widely identified as an area where there are concentrations of underground synthetic drug labs, including in such Central European states as the Czech Republic and Poland. The tremendous growth of Ecstasy use all across Europe further bears out this assessment.

For the purposes of this study, given the prevalence of illegal synthetic drugs on the European markets, *EIR* estimates that the U.S. totals represent half the world consumption of illegal synthetic drugs.

The meteoric rise in synthetic drug sales since 1990 (see **Figure 19,** which shows a jump from $70 billion in global sales in 1990, to $132 billion in 1995) correlates with another critical finding of this *EIR* study. In recent years, larger and larger percentages of the total opium crop are being produced for local consumption in the country of production, rather than for the American and European markets. This is greatly expanding the overall addict population worldwide. And, increasingly, synthetic drugs are supplementing, and, in some cases, replacing cocaine, heroin, and marijuana as the "drugs of choice" for so-called advanced sector users.

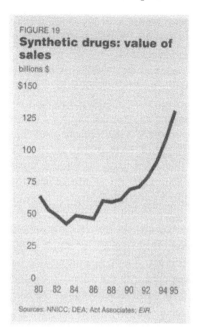

FIGURE 19
Synthetic drugs: value of sales
billions $

The British Oligarchy's Global Drug Money-Laundering Machine

The recent case of the international money-laundering maneuvers of Mexican political figure Raúl Salinas de Gortari, has put a spotlight on the issue of money laundering. Salinas's case involves the laundering of at least $84 million of illicit funds (maybe as high as $600 million), into Swiss and London bank accounts and Cayman Islands shell corporations, through the services of a senior officer of Citibank. The 1989-93 laundering of Salinas's illicit funds, which reportedly included some received from drug-traffickers, such as Mexico's Gulf Cartel drug lord Juan García Abrego, was accomplished with the knowledge and approval of top echelons of Citibank, as well as the U.S. Federal Reserve Board of Governors, potentially including Fed Chairman Alan Greenspan.

This is merely one example out of perhaps 50 that happen every week, but go unreported. It has a long history. During the 1980s and early 1990s, Colombia's Medellín drug cartel overran the world with tens of billions of dollars worth of cocaine per year. The cartel had a desperate need to launder its cash, which itself weighed several tons. According to Rachel Ehrenfeld, in the book *Evil Money*, the U.S. "institutions used by members of the Medellín drug cartel [for laundering] included Chemical Bank, Continental Bank International, Morgan Guaranty Trust, Security Trust International Bank and Republic Bank, New York." Among the international banks identified were Banco de Santander of Madrid, Spain and Miami; Union Bank of Switzerland in New York, Toronto, and California; and Lloyds Bank International of the Bahamas.

How is it possible that over the past quarter-century, since August 1971, the international narcotics and criminal money-laundering trade has survived and prospered? Why do the names of the world's biggest, most powerful, and most prestigious banks, with "impeccable credentials," show up in this trade, year after year? Why are the seemingly best efforts of law enforcement unable to stop them?

The answer is straightforward: No authorities have seriously gone after the real enemy. The people responsible for setting and enforcing anti-money-laundering policy, in particular in the advanced sector, will pursue investigations up to a point, sometimes collaring lower- and middle-level money-launderers. But they pull back at the idea of putting in jail the bankers and political figures "above suspicion." These are the people who run the trade and make it possible.

To be precise, this is the Anglo-Dutch-Swiss financier oligarchy, and the offshore banks based in the "former" British and Dutch colonial empires. The royal Privy Council officially rules in most of the British territories and "former" colonies. If one includes such postage-stamp countries as Liechtenstein and Luxembourg, as well as the British-controlled elements of the American, French, and German banking systems, such as J.P. Morgan and Edmond Safra's Republic National Bank, one has almost the entirety of the world's money-laundering apparatus. This comprises approximately 40 key commercial banks, and 20 investment banks, including English Queen Elizabeth II's personal bank, Coutts, which is an estimable force in the Channel Islands, as well as the Bahamas and Cayman Islands.

The Anglo-Dutch-Swiss financier oligarchy, and their satraps in the British Commonwealth, which total nexus we will call the "extended British Commonwealth empire apparatus," not only runs this criminal money laundering today, but has run it for two centuries, going back to the British Opium Wars against China and before.

Hooked on drugs

The profits and level of cash flow from money laundering are huge: It is the biggest private cash flow in the world. *For this reason, the banks are more addicted to this narco-money stream than* is *the heroin junkie to his* fix. The banks could not give up this money without collapsing. The world banking system is utterly bankrupt, and the only real income stream it earns on its loans and investment is not the electronic entries of derivatives trading, but what it steals from the population. Drug and criminal profits are among the principal sources of these—along with looting of Third World nations and the advanced sector. The British will do everything to protect the narco-money-laundering trade at all costs.

Figure 20 shows the estimated total amount of laundered money for 1995. The drug money component of about $500 billion is computed by methods discussed elsewhere in this study. However, the actual figure may be significantly larger. Author James Adams, an authority on drugs, with sources in British intelligence, stated in the Nov. 15, 1995 London *Times,* "Last year [1994], $400 billion of illegal drug money was laundered in America, of which $320 billion came from the Colombia cartels." If $400 billion is the figure for America alone, then *EIR's* estimate of $500 billion as a world figure is extremely conservative.

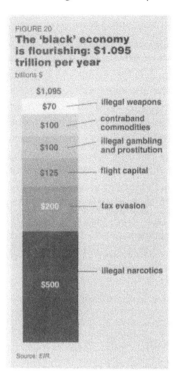

FIGURE 20
The 'black' economy is flourishing: $1.095 trillion per year
billions $

$1,095

$70 ——— illegal weapons

$100 ——— contraband commodities

$100 ——— illegal gambling and prostitution

$125 ——— flight capital

$200 ——— tax evasion

$500 ——— illegal narcotics

Source: EIR.

Our figure of all other criminally laundered money, of $595 billion, is also conservatively estimated. It encompasses such items as contraband of otherwise legal commodities (gold, gems, strategic metals, food, oil); illegal weapons; flight capital; tax evasion; illegal gambling and prostitution. Official figures for these areas do not exist; *EIR* consulted law enforcement officials and experts in each field. For each item, *EIR* chose the smallest reasonable estimate. The total trade of all criminal money is a staggering $1.095 trillion per year. In 1995, world merchandise and commercial services exports were $5.4 trillion. Thus, the criminal money-laundering trade of $1.1 trillion, is equivalent to one-fifth of world exports of all merchandise and services. (The $1.1 trillion may include some double-counting: for example, laundered money from a drug sale may be used to buy illegal weapons for terrorists. But because *EIR* began with very low estimates of the different components of the laundering trade, we believe the $1.1 trillion figure to be in the right ballpark.)

The financier oligarchy's take on the money laundering is immense. When all forms of fees, bribes, money earned by use of the funds, etc. are considered, the profit rate can reach between 10% and 15% of the overall haul. Thus, the rate of financial return alone on this $1.1 trillion can be between $100 and $150 billion a year.

Origins of the problem

The drug trade's dirty money laundering has been around for millennia. By the 1700s, the Middle Eastern portion of the drug trade was centered in Aleppo, Syria, and the Asian portion was run by the Dutch and then the British monarchies, through their East India Companies. During the 1950s and 1960s, organized crime chieftain Meyer Lansky was one of the masterminds of the trade.

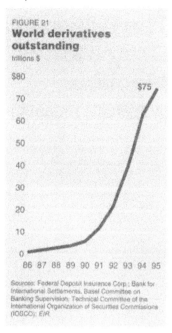

FIGURE 21
World derivatives outstanding
trillions $

In August 1971, a turning point was reached. U.S. President Richard Nixon took the dollar off the gold standard, and the floating exchange-rate system was introduced. The volume of Euro-dollars—hot dollars and other currencies outside their country of origin—exploded, helped by the petro-dollar recycling after 1973-74. From a few billions in the 1960s, the Euro-dollar market zoomed to above $1 trillion by the 1980s.

Once U.S. Federal Reserve Board Chairman Paul Volcker sent interest rates into the stratosphere in October 1979, and the U.S. banking system was deregulated in 1982, two conditions prevailed, both part of Britain's "post-industrial society" policy. First, manufacturing, agriculture, and infrastructure production collapsed. On a per-capita and per-household basis, the market basket of physical goods in the United States has collapsed by 40% since 1967 (see *EIR,* Jan. 1, 1996).

Second, speculative markets, from junk bonds, collateralized mortgage obligations and derivatives, to drugs, increasingly came to determine the geometry of the world economy. The more the physical economy collapsed, the more the speculative flows, which were growing at a hyperbolic rate, dominated. And within this arrangement, drugs and criminal activity, by design, came to rule the speculative markets. It is not an accident, that the leading derivatives-trading centers are also the leading drug-money-laundering centers. There are some legitimate funds in offshore banking centers, representing legitimate business. But this appears to be the minority. The narco and speculative markets are intermingled into one: It is now nearly impossible to separate one from the other.

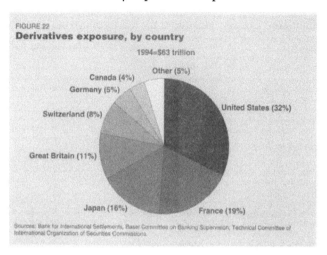

FIGURE 22
Derivatives exposure, by country
1994=$63 trillion

Other (5%)
Canada (4%)
Germany (5%)
Switzerland (8%)
United States (32%)
Great Britain (11%)
Japan (16%)
France (19%)

Sources: Bank for International Settlements, Basel Committee on Banking Supervision; Technical Committee of International Organization of Securities Commissions.

Take the high-flying derivatives markets, the biggest speculative cancer in the world. The derivatives trade has exploded from $1 trillion in derivatives outstanding in 1987, to $75 trillion by 1995 (**Figure 21**). The national banking systems that hold these derivatives are shown in **Figure 22,** although it should be noted, that many of these national banking systems hold these derivatives not simply in their own countries, but in markets such as Hongkong, Singapore, and the Channel Islands. The paper profits on the derivatives are large, but they are only electronic entries in cyberspace. In reality, drug money, sucked from the consumption of the addicted population, is propping them up (**Figure 23**).

The drug trade not only gobbled up the speculative markets, but it started gobbling up the physical economy, turning over trillions of dollars of assets to the British narco-bankers. The corporate takeovers binge of the 1980s and 1990s was financed in significant measure by drug revenues. Further, the drug mob opened gambling casinos (legal gambling revenues in America in 1994 totalled $407 billion, larger than the auto market), houses of prostitution, and more speculative markets. The economy was criminalized and destroyed.

Three steps in money laundering

There are three steps in the process of turning criminal money into "clean" money:

1. The street-level drug dealer must enter the dirty money into the banking system;
2. The money-laundering machine will transport it through several locations, perhaps registering it along the way in a trust, with only a nominee name of a trust officer, perhaps in the Bahamas, indicating who owns the instrument. The trust gives the beneficial owner—the real owner—anonymity. If the

money is then moved through 6-9 jurisdictions, each with bank secrecy, a process called "layering," it could take law enforcement 6-12 months to plow through each jurisdiction—such as going to courts to obtain warrants to search bank accounts—by which time, the statute of limitations on the crime could expire. This presupposes that the law enforcement agency can even trace the money after the second or third level of layering;

3. The money is finally lodged in an investment or a secret, numbered account, with the capability of moving it out at lightning speed, if necessary.

We shall look first at the street level of getting the money into the banking system. Second, we shall examine the ways in which the Anglo-Dutch-Swiss financier oligarchy moves this money many times around the globe, reaping as much as a 10-15% profit on the operation. This will demonstrate the extent of British control. Third, we shall look at how the laundered money is brought back "on shore," and where it is invested. A case study of the Bahamas will be examined.

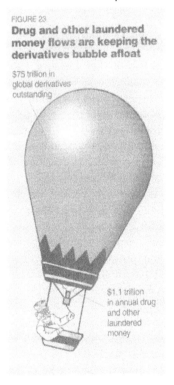

FIGURE 23
Drug and other laundered money flows are keeping the derivatives bubble afloat

$75 trillion in global derivatives outstanding

$1.1 trillion in annual drug and other laundered money

Street-level money laundering
Since 1970, the United States has required all banks to file reports on all cash deposits of $10,000 or more—called cash transaction reports (CTRs)—and in 1986, the passage of the Bank Secrecy Act put a penalty on banks that failed to properly and honestly file CTRs. The CTRs are filed with the Internal Revenue Service, and are made available to law enforcement agencies that demonstrate a need to consult

them. This is to create a barrier to drug money laundering. It is a useful and well-intended step, but even if honestly adhered to (and there are many loopholes), it is simply inadequate as a deterrent against money laundering. However, there are many countries, starting with Great Britain, Canada, Switzerland, the Cayman Islands, and Mexico, that do not even have a CTR reporting requirement or penalty provisions for lack of enforcement.

Entering the street-level drug money into the banking system is a bigger hurdle than it might initially appear. Take a hypothetical drug deal in the United States. Five kilograms of heroin (11 pounds) retails for $6.5 million. But, $6.5 million in $20 bills weighs 370.5 kilograms or 812.5 pounds. The weight of the money is 75 times the weight of the drug smuggled in; $100 billion in laundered drug money, in denominations of $20 bills, weighs 12.5 million pounds. If it was difficult getting the drug smuggled into a country, think of how difficult it will be to smuggle the cash!

The drug dealer has two options. He will either launder the drug money revenues inside the banking system of the country in which the sale was made, or ship a sizable portion of the cash outside the country of sale, using the same smuggling network infrastructure he used to smuggle the drugs in, but in reverse.

Consider some examples of the first instance. Laundering the money in the country where the sale was made, means taking some of the money to the banks; in the United States, that means employing "mules" or "smurfs" to make bank deposits in amounts of, usually, no more than $5,000 to $7,000, so as not to arouse suspicion. To launder $1 million per week that way, would require smurfs to make about 200 deposits per week, within the same area, at multiple banks. This requires a lot of work, and raises the possibility of detection. However, perhaps between $50 and $75 billion annually is laundered this way.

The evidence of this is clear. The Federal Reserve Board of Governors in Washington, D.C. keeps tabs on those Federal Reserve banking regions that turn back to the Fed "excess cash," because it exceeds the cash needs of the region. In 1995, according to Federal Reserve statistics, the regions reporting the largest "physical cash surpluses" and turning these back over to the Fed were: Los Angeles, $13.6 billion; Miami, $7.1 billion; San Antonio, $3.0 billion; Jacksonville, $2.5 billion; and San Francisco, $1.4 billion. These are the cities with the highest street-level drug money laundering.

Gambling casinos are also a vehicle for laundering. The drug money-launderer buys chits with dirty money, waits a suitable period of time, and cashes them in for "clean" money. Since casinos in places like Las Vegas and Atlantic City are often run by Anti-Defamation League-linked organized crime elements, the casinos are compliant, and many take a cut of 1-5% for the service. In January 1996, the General Accounting Office of the U.S. Congress published a study, "Money-Laundering: Rapid Growth of Casinos Makes Them Vulnerable," that shows the danger. It points out that between 1984 and 1994, the dollar amount wagered in gambling casinos in America increased nearly fourfold, from $117 billion to $407 billion. In this time period, nearly 60 riverboat gambling operations were opened. This increased the number of facilities and dollar flows available for the drug money-launderer. While gambling casinos are required to file CTR reports for cash transactions of greater than $10,000, there are ways around that. Moreover, Nevada, the gambling capital of America, does not participate in the federal CTR reporting requirement of the Bank Secrecy Act (although Nevada has its own localized CTR reporting requirement). Prostitution is also legal in Nevada.

A third means of laundering is to use money-wiring services, such as Western Union, and check-cashing parlors, which do have to file CTR reports, but employ 15,000 employees, who are not carefully screened. In both money-wiring and check-cashing services, there have been widespread instances of falsification of records to permit laundering.

In addition, money-launderers use retail businesses with high cash turnover, whose sizable weekly deposit levels are not expected to arouse suspicion at their banks. One example is the La Mina network in California, where gold coin and metal-plating firms in the 30-block Hill Street gold district of Los Angeles, working with the gold district of New York City, laundered $1.3 billion in Cali Cartel drug money between 1987 and 1990. But any and all sorts of stores will be used.

On May 14 of this year, a shocking development occurred on this front. Citing the need to reduce bank paper work, the U.S. Treasury Department lifted the requirement that banks must file CTRs for all business deposits of $10,000 or more. The new ruling, which is for a trial period, but is expected to go into effect permanently in the fall, states that any business whose stock is publicly traded on any American stock exchange is exempt from a CTR filing.

This is remarkable, because to take one example, the stock of Crazy Eddie's, a New York City-based consumer electronics store, was publicly traded on an American stock exchange. However, the store was involved in a number of criminal enterprises, and its principal owner and founder, Eddie Antar, fled to Israel, after siphoning off more than $74 million. He was arrested and is now in jail, though $10 million is unaccounted for.

In the second option, the street-level drug money is physically shipped out of the country where the drugs were sold. The drug-producing network itself will either do this, or hire others to do it for a fee, often at 5-10% of the selling price of the drugs. In the United States, Colombian drug cartels often use Mexican smuggling networks to bring the drugs in and the money out.

Planes, speed boats, and even submarines, which make drug drops to a country, are now employed to ferry the cash supply out.

Smurfs are hired, at $2,000-5,000 a day, to carry the drug money onto airliners, or in the bodies or tires of their cars. Several years ago, federal agents caught Maria Lilia Rojas carrying out of the United States $1.43 million in six "Monopoly" boxes. In February 1986, officials in Texas arrested the pilot and two passengers of a private jet, flying $5.9 million out of the country. Today, that is small potatoes, compared to what some planes carry: $50 million or more.

The 1993 passage of the North American Free Trade Agreement (NAFTA) has facilitated money smuggling across the U.S.-Mexico border, by easing border-crossing restrictions. A Dec. 3, 1995 *Houston Chronicle* article, "Houston Awash in Money Laundering: Authorities Only Dent Export of Drug Profits," reported that "U.S. officials admit that only about one of every 10 vehicles and one of every 30 commercial trucks entering the United States are inspected. *Even fewer vehicles leaving the country are inspected.*" Send 30 trucks across the border to Mexico with cash, and on average, one is stopped. This is 3% of total volume, an acceptable loss to the drug money trafficker.

So-called *giro* houses, which wire money across the border into Mexico, are another option. These are used extensively for legitimate remittances by immigrant laborers in the United States. Naturally, these *giro* houses are located near the border, in states such as Texas. But they are also used to launder dirty money. For example, a launderer enters the *giro* and presents the *giro* operator with dirty cash. The money is wired to a Mexican bank. The launderer, or his associate, picks up clean cash at the *giro's* correspondent bank in Mexico. The *Houston Chronicle* reported, "In all. . . Houston *giro* houses may have laundered up to $250 million, most of it on behalf of the Cali Cartel."

On March 4 of this year, Rayburn Hess, officer of the U.S. State Department's Bureau for International Narcotics and Law Enforcement Affairs, delivered a speech in Panama that presented a "hypothetical" money-laundering example based on real-life composite pieces of the money-laundering operations. We will use Hess's speech for pedagogical purposes. The example is schematically represented in **Map 12.**

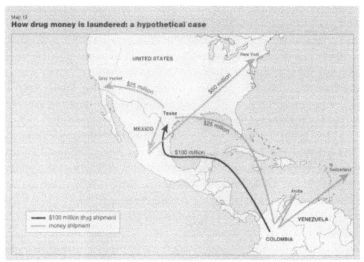

Hess stated, "Assume that the Cali Cartel is moving $100 million over the rather porous border from the United States to Mexico and operating on a 75% profit margin (earnings minus cost) . . . . Cali wants to [receive] $85-90 million in total." It is willing to pay $10-15 million to those who help it move its drug money.

Hess presented the case of laundering the $100 million in three steps, in amounts of $25 million, $25 million, and $50 million:

1. The launderers "will sell $25 million on the gray market." This is an underground foreign exchange market, where Ibero-American businessmen

swap their pesos (or other Ibero-American currencies) for dollars at an exchange rate that avoids the official exchange rate, and avoids taxes. The businessmen take the risk that they are getting dirty dollars. The money-launderer has gotten rid of his dollars and now has pesos. He transports the pesos he has acquired to Colombia, for example, exchanging them there for clean dollars.

2. Next, there is a fake invoicing scheme: "A South American 'clothing manufacturer working with Cali obtains a permit [in his country] to export $25 million worth of suits to New York" (or Miami, as represented in Map 12). The clothing manufacturer exports, however, only $6 million worth of clothing. That clothing is unloaded in the Aruba freetrade zone, and secretly shipped back to Colombia, where it is sold through the underground economy. The crates which held the clothing are then filled with some fake material, and the clothing "manufacturer's agent picks up $20 million in drug proceeds in New York and returns it to Colombia, covered by an export license."

3. The remaining $50 million of drug money is smuggled by various routes described above, across the U.S. border into Mexico. The money is then deposited, by various money-laundering tricks, into one or several Mexican banks, which are more permeable than U.S. banks to laundered funds. The Mexican bank can send the money to New York, either by bank draft or wire transfer. It wires the money to an account at either a Mexican bank or a U.S. bank in New York. Usually, the money is not directly wired, but is settled through interbank accounts. This means that the Mexican bank that is wiring the funds, will have already deposited $50 million, *earned from a legitimate business deal,* at New York Bank A. When the $50 million in laundered money is wired to New York Bank A, it then debits this $50 million from the Mexican bank's account held with it. It gives the money to the money-launderer on whose behalf the $50 million was wire-transferred. The money-launderer now has a clean $50 million sitting in a bank in New York.

The process is aided by the fact that Mexican banks practice banking secrecy, which protects the identity of the person who wired the money.

The above example concerning money-laundering in Mexico, raises a serious question about the Mexican banking system. Under the NAFTA agreement, Section XIII, Financial Accords, the Mexican banking system was further deregulated. Foreign banks, which, with the exception of America's Citibank, had been banned from entering the Mexican domestic banking system, are now allowed in. Since 1995, two Canadian banks have been in the process of acquiring Mexican banks: The Bank of Montreal has bought 16% of Bancorner, Mexico's second largest bank, with an option to increase its share to 55%; and the Bank of Nova Scotia has announced it will purchase 55% of the assets of Banco Inverlat, Mexico's fourth largest. These Canadian banks are experts, on behalf of the British, in money laundering. The Hongkong and Shanghai Banking Corp. is also sniffing around for corporations and banks to buy. This will make the Mexican banking system even more of a laundromat.

Hess's example also reveals a second deadly feature: the ease with which drug money can be laundered. This shows the glaring weakness of an anti-money-laundering approach that simply relies on cash transaction reports, suspicious activity reports (SARs), or the current U.S. anti-money-laundering strictures. So while a U.S. bank has to file a cash transaction report for a deposit of $10,000 or more, it is not required to file a CTR for wire transfers between domestic U.S. banks, or a U.S. bank and a foreign bank, even though wire transfers typically are many times larger than cash deposits.

According to a top Federal Reserve enforcement officer, a U.S. bank receiving a wire transfer is required to keep an internal record, listing only the name and address of the wire-sender and the name of the sending bank. Since Mexico has bank secrecy, the receiving U.S. bank may only receive the name of a dummy corporation, which is registered as a trust, say, in the Bahamas.

We begin to see how easy money laundering is, once the drug money has entered into the system. Wire transfers are a principal means for banks to settle accounts, or for businesses to move funds. The New York City-based Clearing House Interbank Payments System (CHIPS) electronically transfers funds and settles transactions in U.S. dollars for all the major banks that trade through New York City. One hundred and six of the world's biggest banks are members of CHIPS and avail themselves of this facility. In 1980, CHIPS transferred $37 trillion; but by 1995, the per annum level of funds transferred by CHIPS reached a whopping $310 trillion. A few studies have attempted to find out the volume of laundered money that moves through the wire transfer process. The results are inconclusive and even flawed. But were the amount only two-tenths of 1 % of the total—and that could be very possible, meaning that one in every 500 transfers is criminally tainted—that would amount to $620 billion per year.

British control
Once the street-level drug money has entered the banking system, the higher-level laundering takes over. It moves the dirty funds through six to nine jurisdictions, perhaps registering it along the way in a trust, with only a nominee name of a trust officer attached to the instrument, disguising the real owner, making it very difficult for law enforcement authorities to track down the dirty money and the perpetrators.

The British are masters of this, and run the system. The proof is incontrovertible and, for the most part, out in the open for the willing investigator or law-enforcement official to find. Today, the problem is that many law-enforcement figures could uncover the modus operandi of the money-laundering network; but it is run by the British oligarchy, and once the investigators find it is the British, they would have to take them on politically. Most flee in terror and deny what they have seen.

The reader should take a map of the world, and trace out all the key locations where the slave trade was run over 200 years ago. Most of them turn out to be part of the old British and Dutch empires. Now, mark all the places where smuggling and piracy predominated. Next, find the points of production and shipping routes of the 1700s and 1800s drug trade, and the financial centers which serviced them. Now, step back: The map will look strikingly similar to **Map 13,** which shows the key offshore financial centers of the 1990s. **Map 14** shows the Caribbean region, the British-Dutch lake where so many offshore centers and/or tax havens predominate.

This is no coincidence. The British and Dutch simply took these criminal haunts, and the old criminal infrastructure and civil administration, slapped on a fresh coat of paint, and put a sign on the door reading, "Offshore Financial Center." Most investigators take them at their word, as if they knew nothing about history.

The actual command and control over world money laundering today resides in Great Britain (**Figure 24**). A large chunk of today's offshore laundering centers are officially governed by Britain's Queen Elizabeth II as their head of state and sovereign. Officially, the Queen's Privy Council is the ultimate legal authority in a legal system that permits bank secrecy and minimal regulation, and is governed by British law. Or else, these countries are ruled by allied Dutch-Swiss networks. It is not an exaggeration to say that nothing significant occurs in these money-laundering dives without the Privy Council's approval. If the Privy Council wanted to shut down money laundering, it could; it set it up in the first place. The same holds for the Queen herself.

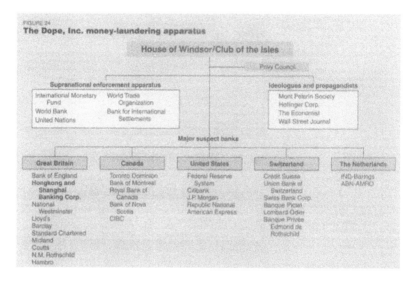

In addition, while sometimes money laundering goes through small, obscure banks, most of it goes through the extended British Commonwealth network of 40 commercial banks and 20 investment banks. The drug-money flow is so large, that no smaller entities could handle it, and consistently hide it. This requires financial sophistication and tremendous political pull.

The list of major banks to be investigated for possible drug- and hot-money laundering, includes: the British clearing banks Standard Chartered, Lloyds, and Barclay; private British banks such as Coutts and Rothschilds; the Canadian clearing banks, led by Scotia Bank (formerly Bank of Nova Scotia), Bank of Montreal, Toronto Dominion, and the Canadian Imperial Bank of Commerce; the big three Swiss banks, Crédit Suisse, Swiss Bank Corp., and Union Bank of Switzerland; some of the exclusive Swiss private banks, such as Banque Pictet and Lombard Odier; the Dutch banks ING-Barings and ABN-Amro; the British-controlled American banks Citibank, Morgan, and the Republic National Bank.

Then, there is a special institution, the linchpin of the drug money laundering, the $350 billion-in-assets Hongkong and Shanghai Banking Corp. The HongShang, as it is called, was formed in the middle of the last century, specifically to finance Britain's opium trade with China. The HongShang is still the primary bank of issue for the British Crown colony and money-laundering center of Hongkong. But the HongShang also spans the globe, owning the powerful Midlands Bank in England; the Bank of the Middle East; Marine Midland bank in the United States; Mocatta Metals (through Midlands bank), one of the five banks that sets the world gold fix. It is active in the Caribbean. With its headquarters moved to London, it still possesses markers of its past: On its board are the Swire, Keswick, and other old-line families, which ran the China opium trade during the last century.

The banks' direct financial profit on laundering $1.1 trillion in drug and criminal proceeds per annum, is up to 10-15% of the volume of money that enters the banking system. (This is aside from any profits made in other phases of the drug trade). To illustrate the point: Suppose that a $100 million deposit is made by a drug lord at one of the hundreds of offshore banks in the Bahamas. The bank, in turn, can charge a standard banking service fee, which can range between 1 % and 3%, depending on what services are billed. Next, the bank has $100 million to lend. According to the June 7, 1996 Financial Times, in the Bahamas, "the spread between typical borrowing and lending rates, currently stand[s] at more than 9%." That is, the bank makes a 9% profit on the money. The bank can lend to anyone, but frequently, it lends back money, aboveboard, to the drug lord who deposited the money in the first place. The loan gets the money "onshore" for the drug lord. As part of the prearranged money-laundering scheme, the drug lord is willing to pay the 9% interest rate spread as compensation to the bank. Finally, the bank can also collect, on top of all this, outright bribes, which can range between 2% and 5% of the proceeds. Total of all fees and charges (assuming that the bank's spread on money is not normally as high as 9%): 10-15%.

In March 1996, the U.S. State Department's Bureau for International Narcotics and Law Enforcement Affairs released its "International Control Strategy Report," which classified 201 nations and territories by the degree of money-laundering in that country. The report listed as either "high" or "medium-high"—the highest two ratings—the following countries and possessions: Aruba, Antigua, Canada, Cayman Islands, Cyprus, Hongkong, Israel, Liechtenstein, Luxembourg, the Netherlands, the Netherlands Antilles, Singapore, Switzerland, the United Arab Emirates, the United Kingdom, and the United States.

Money-laundering havens

There are two ways that the laundered drug money will be held offshore: either as a deposit at a bank, or invested in one of the myriad of offshore investment instruments, such as trusts, mutual funds, and international business corporations.

When money is deposited in a country's banking system by someone who is not a national of that country, that is classified as a "bank's foreign deposit." When a bank lends money—usually the foreign money that was deposited in the bank—to someone abroad, that is classified as a "bank's foreign asset." Since foreign liabilities and foreign assets almost match, for most banking systems, one can talk about one or the other, to indicate the trend of both.

We will look at bank foreign assets, but we caution, this is not all the hot money in the banking system, because if a British money-launderer, for example, deposits money in the British banking system, that is considered a domestic deposit, but it is still laundered drug money. Thus, the volume of the laundered drug and criminal proceeds in the banking system is bigger than that discussed below, although more than half of all drug money is held in banks abroad. On the other hand, not all the money in foreign bank accounts is illegal; these foreign accounts include legitimate business funds deposited and/or lent abroad. But for the countries listed below, the amount of foreign assets is anywhere from 10 to 50 times more than is needed by their domestic economies. What does a postage-stamp economy need with a few hundred billion dollars of funds? Yes, some of these haunts can help one escape taxation. But take away the $1.1 trillion per annum drug and criminal money trade, a portion of which these banking systems capture and accumulate each year, and the category of "bank foreign asset" would fall by more than half, and up to 95% in some places.

EIR chose 14 financial centers to examine (**Table 2**), out of about 62. These 14 have the largest masses of funds, and statistical information is available on them, whereas for several offshore centers, only scanty statistics are available. The table lists the "bank foreign assets" of these 14 money-laundering centers. The British-Dutch-Swiss pedigree is apparent.

The next-to-the-last line in this table ("subtotal") tells quite a story. The level of foreign assets of deposit-taking banks in these 14, predominantly "offshore," centers, rocketed from $263 billion in 1974 to $3.937 trillion in 1994. This is a stunning 1,400% increase in just 20 years. It demonstrates the velocity of the money-laundering network's growth. For 14 economies, only one of which has a population of more than 20 million, to control nearly $4 trillion in bank foreign assets, gives them huge leverage over the world economy. In most of these places, the level of bank domestic assets is virtually nonexistent. Compare the next-to-the-last line to the last line, which shows total world bank foreign assets. In 1995, the 14 financial centers held 52% of the world's total bank foreign assets. These 14 countries represent less than 2% of the world's population.

A country breakdown shows:
- *Cayman Islands—population: 34,000;* bank foreign assets: $410 billion
- *Switzerland—population: 7* million; bank foreign assets: $464 billion
- *Bahamas—-population: 270,000;* bank foreign assets: $170 billion
- *Luxembourg—population: 390,000;* bank foreign assets: $390 billion

Then, there is Britain, the self-avowed speculative capital of the world. With a population of 58 million, Britain holds bank foreign assets of $1.160 trillion, or 15% of the world's total. Britain holds more bank foreign assets than the United States and Germany combined, *despite the fact that their combined economy is seven times bigger than Britain's , and that their combined exports are five times greater than Britain's.*

What does Britain need all that laundered money for? Answer: to maintain its position as the speculative financial capital of the world. The British banking system is bankrupt several times over. But with these laundered funds, it can preserve its share of world financial turnover—and related political muscle. To wit: It underwrites 64% of all trading in equities in markets foreign to those equities' domicile; 45% of all international cross-border mergers and acquisitions; 75% of all debt borrowed in markets foreign to borrowers' domicile; 35% of all currencies swaps; it earns 50% of all shipbrokering commissions, and so forth.

TABLE 2: Foreign assets held In deposit banks, by country (billions of $)				
	1974	1980	1990	1994*
Industrial Nations				
1. United Kingdom	109	356	1069	1160
2. Australia	0	0	11	14
3. Canada	14	35	52	55
4. Luxembourg	15	32	355	390
5. Netherlands	24	105	186	205
6. Switzerland	42	140	444	464
Asia	**20**	**105**	**868**	**1028**
7. Hongkong	7	28	464	582
8. Singapore	9	45	347	363
Middle East	**9**	**77**	**154**	**154**
9. Bahrain	0	31	59	66
10. Israel	2	6	8	11
11. United Arab Emirates	1	6	18	17
Western Hemisphere	**54**	**272**	**619**	**668**
12. Bahamas	25	125	175	170
13. Cayman Islands	15	85	389	410
14. Netherlands Antilles	0	7	16	30
Subtotal 14 offshore centers	**263**	**1001**	**3593**	**3937**
Total of all countries	**466**	**1822**	**6794**	**7565**

Third quarter 1994. Source: IMF

Unlike the American banking system, where the banks are required to file CTRs, the British banking establishment doesn't think that that is a civilized practice. It wouldn't be "cricket" for the money-laundering trade, so such CTR reporting is not required. All the British require is the filing of Suspicious Activity Reports—which the American banking system requires also. In 1994, British banks filed a grand total of 13,000 SARs. In contrast, in 1994, American banks filed 8 million CTRs.

And while the British banking system proper does not formally have bank secrecy (however, just try to penetrate the gnomes of Lombard Street!), if strict bank secrecy is needed, the funds can first pass through any one of 10 British dependencies, ruled by the Queen, which do have bank secrecy, including the

Cayman Islands, the British Virgin Islands, and the Channel Islands, which are off the coast of France, or the Isle of Man, which is off the coast of England.

Meanwhile, for continental money laundering, there is the impregnable Swiss banking system, with $464 billion in bank foreign deposits. Switzerland enacted bank secrecy laws in 1934, largely to help protect money laundered from France. But it was quickly used during World War II to hide Nazi assets and assist the Nazi war machine. During World War II, Swiss banks furnished 90% of Germany's foreign exchange requirements, without which the Nazi regime could not have bought anything abroad. In 1943, Nazi Minister of Economics Walter Funk declared publicly that his government could not afford even a two month break in the Swiss financial connection.

The Swiss bank secrecy code states that bankers, lawyers, and others cannot divulge information about their clients' numbered financial accounts. The penalty for violation is both jail time and a fine. Also, conveniently, tax evasion, and securities and foreign exchange violations are considered fiscal or administrative offenses in Switzerland, not crimes. Therefore, Swiss authorities usually refuse legal assistance to countries trying to prosecute violators of laws in these areas who have parked their money in Switzerland. This paradigm has been emulated by the offshore financial centers.

Nonetheless, the Swiss gnomes have developed a reputation—largely created and promoted by themselves—for financial conservatism and uprightness. This is nonsense: The Swiss are wild speculators; per capita, Switzerland has 10 times the dollar derivatives levels of the United States, making it the highest in the world. The Swiss Banking Commission is not even allowed to regulate Swiss banks, only the auditing firms are, which the Swiss banks hire and pay for.

A second look at **Table 2** reveals something else: the high degree of domination that these 14 financial centers exercise over the bank foreign assets in the regions in which they are located. (This article follows the classification procedure of the International Monetary Fund, from which these statistics are taken, and classified both the United States and Japan as industrial nations, rather than placing them in their respective regions). **Table 2** shows that just two British-run offshore financial centers, Hongkong and Singapore, control 92% of the bank foreign assets of Asia (minus Japan); three British-influenced financial centers, Bahrain, United Arab Emirates, and Israel, control 61 % of the bank foreign assets of the Middle East; and three Anglo-Dutch-owned offshore financial centers, the Bahamas, Cayman Islands, and the Netherlands Antilles, control 91 % of the bank foreign assets of the Western Hemisphere (minus the United States).

These offshore financial centers are strategically located amid the Asian, Middle Eastern, and Ibero-American drug trades and money flows. **Map 14** shows that the offshore centers are midway between the drug-producing region of Colombia, Peru, and Bolivia, and the largest consuming market, the United States.

Table 3 reports the dollar amount of all assets—not just banking assets—of the leading money-laundering centers. This consists of the assets of banks, trusts, mutual funds, captive insurance companies, and offshore shipping. In 1995, the total of all offshore financial center assets stood at $5 trillion, compared to $1.5 trillion at the end of 1989. This is a stupendous growth of $3.5 trillion in six years, or an asset build-up of $550 billion per year.

TABLE 3 British Empire's offshore financial centers	
Total Assets (billions $)	
Cayman Islands	480
Singapore	390
Luxembourg	200
Switzerland	190
Hongkong	130
Lichtenstein	120
Channel Islands	110
Bahamas	100
British Virgin Islands	90
Curaçao	60
Turks and Caicos	30

Sources: ·Comparison of Offshore Domiciles and Asset Protection Planning," by Walter H. Diamond; phone discussion with Mr. Diamond.

The biggest source of tax haven offshore financial assets consists of trusts, which, as of 1995, held approximately $2 trillion in assets. These trusts allow a money-launderer to transfer legal title of possessions to a holding company or some such instrument that provides anonymity, disguising who controls the possession. The areas in which these trusts are incorporated have little or no taxation, and little or no financial or corporate regulation; virtually any criminal, backed by a credit reference provided to him by a banker, can incorporate his dirty holdings into a trust. [1]

The popularity of such trusts is attested to by the fact that the tiny British territory islands of Nevis and St. Kitts, with but 10,000 people, have 60,000 incorporated offshore companies, many of them offshore trusts.

In many cases, these trusts invest in offshore or onshore instruments, bringing a fairly high rate of return, many in the United States, Europe or, Asia. Thus, the money-launderer is able to preserve his illgotten gain and enlarge it.

Bringing the money onshore

A good portion of the money that is deposited offshore, is brought back onshore in the form of a loan, which is what a "bank foreign asset" is. The commercial real estate markets in New York, Hongkong, London, Paris, Frankfurt, and Moscow are perfect vehicles for such loans, since it is widely expected that the purchase of an expensive building will involve borrowed money. Worldwide stratospheric real estate prices, reflect the effect of drug money in these markets.

---

[1] Whereas in Table 2, the level for offshore bank foreign assets is $3.9 trillion, the level used for offshore bank foreign assets in Table 3 is approximately $1 trillion. It appears that the latter only uses net foreign assets, i.e., foreign assets minus foreign liabilities. Were the $3.9 trillion level employed in Table 3, then total foreign assets of all kinds would be closer to $7 trillion.

The point for the drug-money-launderer in buying and selling office buildings, is either to own the property, or to get the money onshore. Let us say that real estate investor A, who is part of the drug cartel, borrows $250 million of laundered money from a Canadian bank, to buy a commercial office building in Manhattan for $250 million. The building may have previously sold for $225 million, so the drug-tainted real estate investor dealer helps bid up the price. The investor holds the building for a certain period of time, and then sells it, perhaps for $260 million. He now has a $10 million profit, but, far more important, he has someone else's $260 million in clean money.

The real estate properties, like hotels on Boardwalk in the "Monopoly" game, are a means to an ulterior end. Purchasing real estate is so popular, that the bidding process, through the use of drug money, has helped to drive real estate prices upward.

A second way of getting the money onshore is to plow the money into the investment market. Many offshore investment trusts are vehicles to purchase stocks, bonds, etc.

This has an established criminal history. During the 1960s, money from the drug- and dirty-money trade was laundered through the Geneva-based, Rothschild-run Investors Overseas Services (IOS) of Bernie Cornfeld and Robert Vesco. Some of this money was the "skim money" from the gambling and drug operations of Meyer Lansky, the financial godfather of organized crime. By the early 1970s, the offshore infrastructure of IOS was brought onshore and folded into the Rothschild-Morgan-run Drexel Burnham Lambert. During the 1970s and 1980s, until its February 1990 bankruptcy, Drexel and its allies laundered hundreds of billions of dollars of drug money and other hot money, using it to take over and asset -strip American industry.

A good portion of corporate takeovers and stock market activity—foreign and domestic—takes place today with drug and criminal money, replicating the vehicle forms and practices of the IOS and Drexel, even though those two particular firms are defunct. Indeed, a survey of the major equity and bond markets of the world, particularly the highly touted "emerging market" stock and bond markets of the former communist bloc and the developing sector, would show a heavy use of drug and dirty money.

This is equally true of the $75 trillion worldwide derivatives market. Brian Bosworth-Davies, a London-based expert on money laundering, who used to investigate derivatives fraud for Britain's Scotland Yard, told *EIR* on March 1 that huge sums of drug money and other illicit funds are laundered through the derivatives market. He described one transaction used to launder money, which, he said, "we encountered so many times, it became monotonous." A money-launderer would set up two companies, one based, say, in the Channel Islands of Jersey and the other in Guernsey. The Jersey company would open a trading account with one commodity broker; the Guernsey company would open a trading account with another commodity broker. "The Jersey company would take a long position [betting the price would rise] in a futures contract, in, say, September soy beans. The Guernsey company would take a short position [betting the price would fall] for the same amount for the same contract."

Whichever company loses, pays for the lose-out of its laundered drug money pool. The winner takes its profits out of the market in clean dollars (the two commodity brokers are not trading with each other, but with the general market). On balance, the transaction is a wash: The money-launderer is not trying to make money on the deal, but to get dirty money into the market, and clean money out.

More dirty money is laundered through the derivatives market than through gambling casinos. This Bosworth-Davies stated, "On the derivatives markets, if you trade a small amount, say $10,000 or something like that, then you might be suspect. But trades of many millions of dollars-that's the norm."

The Salinas-Citibank case

The U.S. Justice Department and at least one grand jury are investigating Raúl Salinas de Gortari's movement of illicit funds through Citibank to hiding places overseas. While the ostensible target of the investigation is Salinas, it appears that Citibank is in the investigative sights as well.

EIR covered the case in depth in our issue of June 7, 1996 ("Money-Laundering Scandal Could Rock Citibank, Fed"). But an illustrative piece of the Citibank story proves conclusively the bankers' witting role in directing money laundering.

According to published reports, between 1989 and 1993, the person who moved at least $100 million of Raúl Salinas's illicit money—and perhaps much more—into bank accounts in Switzerland, London, and the Cayman Islands, using false names, was Amelia Grovas Elliot, the head of the Mexico team of Citibank's Private Bank ($80 billion in assets). Elliot was Salinas's personal banker. She had headed the Mexico team since 1983, and is a 27-year veteran of Citicorp.

At a May 12, 1994 drug trial, Elliot testified as a star prosecution witness, on how a supposedly "clean" bank, Citibank, then America's largest bank, administers banking operations in Mexico. During her testimony, Elliot asserted that she does not act alone at Citibank, and defined a chain of command. She described how Citibank's Private Bank accepts customers who usually have a starting net worth of $5 million, and that the Citibank private banker "knows you [the customer], knows who you are, knows your family . . . recognize[s] your voice." Elliot was then asked to describe the long vetting process, including approval from higher-ups, that Citibank engages in, before it accepts a large deposit from a customer. This is the "know your client" policy. In response to a question about this, Elliot stated:

"The 'know your client,' at least in our bank, is part of the culture. It's part of the way you do things. It's part of the way you conduct yourself. If you come in with a prospect and/or name of a prospect, you will be sure to be asked, 'Who is this person, what do they do, who introduced them to you?' *by at least three or four people higher than you are.* It's just the way it is" (emphasis added).

A Citibank spokesman told *EIR* on May 10 who the "three or four higher people" in Citibank's chain of command would be, who would have to approve Elliot's decision to move Raúl Salinas's tens of millions of dollars around the world. These would include Citibank Chairman John Reed. Further, during part of the time that Citibank was laundering Salinas's money, Citibank, which had blown out in 1991, was under effective Federal Reserve Board receivership, and was being held up by a Fed life support system. Fed supervisors were all over Citibank. Top echelons of the U.S. Federal Reserve Board, including potentially up to Chairman Alan Greenspan, would have seen the paperwork trail of the Salinas money, under whatever name it was being moved.

The Salinas-Citibank-Fed case illustrates the shortcomings in the current fight against money laundering. The basic U.S. anti-money-laundering approach suffers from two glaring flaws:

First, there are numerous loopholes. Just take the CTR reporting requirement. This is waived 1) for all wire transfers; 2) for all cash deposits of $10,000 or more made by businesses whose stock is publicly traded on any American stock exchange; and 3) for Citibank Private Bank customers, with net worths of $5 million or more, such as Raúl Salinas. By simply qualifying to be a preferred client of Citibank's Private Bank (or any other bank's preferred client club), a bank customer can escape such scrutiny, if his banker applies for an exemption because the customer in question is so "valued."

The second flaw is methodological. Money laundering thrives because the entire banking system, under British control, is hooked on $1.1 trillion in annual drug and criminal money flows; it depends on this for its very survival.

To succeed in the fight against money laundering, start at the top. Go after the John Reeds, Alan Greenspans, and the controlling layers of the Anglo-Dutch-Swiss financier oligarchy, and the British Commonwealth political establishment, who run drug- and criminal-money-laundering as a worldwide integrated enterprise and one of the most profitable businesses on earth.

The chairmen and board members of the financial institutions that launder money, have never gone to jail in any major drug-money-laundering case in the last 30 years. They always claim, ingenuously, "I didn't know this was going on at my bank." In most cases, they never even have to set foot in a courtroom.

Put some of these top bankers and the British financier oligarchy in jail for 30 years. Watch the drug-money-laundering trade start to shrivel; watch the drug-trafficking trade collapse.

The Drug-Laundering Haven of the Bahamas

The 300-year criminal history of the Bahamas unites all the different strands of money laundering and the drug trade, revealing how the British orchestrate that trade. Its story could be repeated for each of the other exotic offshore British financial centers.

In 1973, the Bahamas was granted nominal independence. But even though the country elects a prime minister, Queen Elizabeth II is the head of state of the islands, and the Queen's Privy Council's "say so" is final in all legal matters. The population is impoverished, while banking and tourism constitute a huge portion of the Bahamas' fragile economy.

The Bahamas has a dual function: It is both a drop spot and transshipment point for drugs, and a drug-money-laundering center. The Bahamas is an archipelago of 700 islands, of which the closest is 50 miles away from Florida

Since only 40 of the 700 islands are populated, the others make perfect drop points for drugs. During the 1980s, according to U.S. Drug Enforcement Administration reports, up to 75% of the drugs that reached the United States from Ibero-America went through the Bahamas first American authorities, fearful of the drug flow into the United States, forced the Bahamas to take measures to cut back the drug flow. The June 7, 1996 London *Financial Times* reported, "It is guessed that no more than 10-15% of illegal drugs shipments to the U.S. now go through the islands." That may be an underestimation, and the *Financial Times* admits that the drug flow is increasing, now that U.S. radars to monitor drug trafficking were recently taken down in Grand Bahamas, Exuma, and Great Inagua, in a cost-saving measure.

This is part of the Bahamas' historic profile. During the American Revolutionary War (1775-83) and the War of 1812, when Britain invaded America, the British used their colony of the Bahamas as a base for naval assaults on the United States. Because of this, in 1776, the American revolutionaries occupied the Bahamas. After the Revolutionary War, Tory sympathizers fled to the Bahamas, and became part of the establishment. During the British-backed Confederate uprising of the American Civil War, the British used the Bahamas as a base to run ships through the North's shipping blockade against the South. A successful blockade-running voyage could earn $300,000.

During World War II, the pro-Nazi Duke of Windsor was exiled to the Bahamas, but was placed in the very important post of Bahamian governor general. During this time, the duke used Axel Wennergren, the Swedish eugenicist and Nazi agent, to launder money to Mexico. During the 1960s, organized crime godfather Meyer Lansky built the Resorts International casino on Paradise Island in the Bahamas, which served as an international money-laundering center.

The money-laundering Canadian banks dominate the Bahamian banking scene, hiding behind Bahamian bank secrecy and lax Canadian banking laws to shelter drug money. In the Dec. 24, 1985 *Montreal Gazette*, in an article entitled, "How Canadian Banks Are Used to 'Launder' Narcotics Millions," William Marsden wrote that drug money is "hauled to Canadian banks [in Nassau, Bahamas] in huge stacks of small bills—sometimes millions of dollars at once—stuffed into suitcases, duffle bags, paper bags and boxes by narcotics smugglers. . . .

"Trusted drivers and security guards ensure that their cash gets into the banks safely. And once the money is deposited, laws that forbid Bahamian bankers to disclose bank records ensure that it's safe from investigation by foreign narcotics and tax agents . . . .

"Canadian banks, which handle 80% of banking business in the Bahamas, have become key instruments in 'laundering' illicit money—giving it a clean history—for smugglers hiding hundreds of millions of dollars from U.S. and Canadian narcotics agents.

"By taking these huge cash deposits, which is not illegal, the Canadian banks are facilitating criminal activity. . . .

"In the past four years, Bank of Nova Scotia twice stonewalled U.S. investigations by refusing to hand over bank records of drug smugglers to a [U.S.] grand jury. The bank finally yielded after paying nearly $2 million in fines."

Under U.S. pressure, the Bahamian banking system has made changes in its money acceptance practices, but during the past decade, the volume of laundered drug money has gone up.

Russia and Eastern Europe: Dope, Inc.'s Newest 'Growth Market'

There are no official figures showing the extent of narcotics cultivation and production in the countries that formerly composed the Union of Soviet Socialist Republics and its Warsaw Pact allies. However, there is no doubt that since 1989 and the fall of the Berlin Wall, Dope, Inc. has vastly increased its production capacities and consumption market in these countries. The flooding of these countries with easy drugs, the mushrooming of "criminal gangs" and mafias, the jump in drug-related crime, and seizures of tons of narcotics, with a street value in the billions, in a single year, paint the picture.

Dope, Inc. has waged a new opium war against the Newly Independent States (NIS) and Russia, comparable to the first opium wars against China. It would be mistaken, however, to attribute the near takeover of eastern European, Russian, and Central Asian economies by Dope, Inc., and its higher-level controllers, to the fall of communism. The floodgates were opened by British Prime Minister Margaret Thatcher and U.S. President George Bush. The International Monetary Fund supplied the economic "gunboats" that forced open the former Soviet economy to the drug trade. While putting the populations into penury, the International Monetary Fund's (IMF) free-trade regimen, imposed on Russia, gave Dope, Inc. and its local offspring a field-day.

The process is similar to that which has taken place in Nigeria. The emergence of Nigerians in the international drug circuit as couriers, and of Nigeria as a transshipment point for drugs, coincides precisely with the imposition in 1986 on Nigeria of an IMF "structural adjustment program" that reduced Nigerians' per capita living standard by 75% in eight years!

Tons of it

According to the U.S. State Department's *International Narcotics Control Strategy Report* of March 1996, law enforcement authorities in Russia seized more than *90 tons* of illicit drugs in the single year of 1995! As an overpopulation of vermin forces significant of their numbers out into the daylight, so the superabundance of drugs in the Russian economy has netted seizures of huge amounts of drugs. Giving an idea of Dope, Inc.'s expansion, the amount of drugs confiscated has tripled in the last three years. Seizures in other NIS countries point to the same phenomenon:

- In Georgia, 2.5 tons of marijuana were seized in 1995, and 12,000 poppy plants.
- In Kyrgyzstan, 1 ton of opium was seized in 1995.
- In Armenia, 17 tons of cannabis and opium were destroyed in 1995.
- Moldovan authorities say they confiscated 2 tons of illegal narcotics last year.
- In Ukraine, more than 23 tons of illegal narcotics were seized in the first six months of 1995 alone. In 1994, police grabbed one haul of 3.5 tons of narcotics at the Russia-Ukraine border, as Ukraine has not only become a major transshipment point for Golden Crescent drugs into Europe, but also a drug producer itself.
- In Uzbekistan, in 1994, two major shipments of marijuana, each weighing in at 15 tons, were interdicted. The shipments were on their way to Turkey and the Netherlands, from their origin in Afghanistan and Pakistan.
- The seizures are the tip of the iceberg of the actual dope flow through the NIS. This flow includes 1) the domestic distribution of narcotics grown there or synthetic drugs produced there; 2) the flow of domestically grown narcotics out of the NIS states to other points—notably western Europe and

the United States; and 3) the opening up of Russia, Central Asia, and eastern Europe as a major drug transshipment nexus.

Britain's opium war on Russia may ultimately have the same annihilating effect on the population as London's opium war against China in the nineteenth century.

Although, officially, the figure for drug users in Russia is 1-1.5 million, as early as May 1992, the newspaper *Nezavisimaya Gazeta* reported on an explosion of drug addiction: "According to the latest expert estimates, 5.5 to 7.5 million people regularly use narcotics in the territory of the former U.S.S.R. At the beginning of 1991, this figure was only 1.5 million. Specialists believe that the process of headlong narcoticization of the country will continue for the next five to seven years." The International Association for Combatting Drug Addiction and the Narcotics Trade estimates that there are 6 million drug addicts in Russia—4% of the population—and that 20 million have tried drugs at least once. They expect the number to double within the next four years. Official Russian reports state that drug consumption has been increasing at a rate of 50% per year, since 1989.

The streets are virtually flooded with the stuff, in the same way as the inner-city ghetto residents of the United States suddenly found their streets awash with heroin in the late 1950s. *Nezavisimaya Gazeta* further reported that, "while, earlier, a 'new' drug would appear on the Soviet 'market' every five to ten years, in the capital alone," during the first three months of 1992, "three new powerful stimulants had arrived," including cocaine from South America, which has become the drug of "fashion" among Russia's youth elites.

It is noteworthy that the Russian Ministry of Internal Affairs, which had a fig-ure of 1.5 million regular drug users in 1993, estimated that 70% of those users were under 30 years of age, and 8.5% of those users were under-age children. Drug addiction is especially strong in the cities and industrial centers.

The skyrocketing of drug use in Russia is matched by that in other countries, particularly eastern Europe. The Bratislava-West Slovakian region of the Slovak Republic, for instance, reported a more than tenfold increase of heroin addicts referred for treatment from 1992 to 1994, according to the State Department report. Whatever the officially reported figure, it is generally acknowledged that the actual number of regular drug users is ten times the official count, and all sources agree on growth rates of addiction in the range of 33-50% per year.

Drug-related crimes are increasing at even greater rates: According to the wire service Novosti on Nov. 20, 1994, the Russian Internal Affairs Ministry reported that drug-related crime had risen 60% in the first nine months of 1994, over 1993.

In Russia, the newspaper *Vecherny Petersburg* claims for that city the title of the "northern capital of the drug trade," since, as stated in an article on April 1, 1994, "its location is convenient for the transit of drugs from Asia to Scandinavian countries and the Baltic states."

The city's function in Dope, Inc., has taken its toll on the city's populace. The August 1995 *Zakonnost* carried an article by A. Stukanov, head of the Criminal Forensics Directorate, stating that "the total number of enterprises involved in narcotics distribution in St. Petersburg almost doubled in 1994. More than 1,000 criminals were sentenced, 75% of them for illegal manufacture, acquisition, or possession of narcotics with intent to sell. . . . Among the people convicted in 1994 of the production, sale, and theft of drugs, and establishment of drug haunts. . . .84% are criminals under age 30."

The Eastern nexus

Since at least 1992, the criminal gangs in Russia have been operating in cooperation with the international cartel operators, represented, for instance, by the Cali Cartel. In 1992, Cali Cartel mobsters came to Russia to meet with their criminal counterparts. Business started immediately, rising to such levels that in 1993, in St. Petersburg, police seized 1 ton of cocaine originating in Colombia. According to an official of the Russian Ministry of Internal Affairs, the shipment had come from South America to Finland by sea, and then was taken to St. Petersburg by road, where it was seized. The cocaine was hidden in tins labelled as containing meat for Russian consumers. There were 20 tons of cans altogether.

Officials of the Russian Ministry of Internal Affairs and their western counterparts tend to emphasize that the dope trade in Russia, eastern Europe, and Central Asia is run by criminal gangs, most of which are organized along ethnic divides. The widely publicized role of the Chechen criminal clans, and of the Chechen Republic as a processing and transshipment zone in Russia, is a case in point.

But this picture of the dope trade as run by a bunch of individual criminal gangs, is the same as saying that a train is nothing a but a bunch of boxcars. What makes a train a train, are the *linkages between* the boxcars—and the engine. Although each criminal gang may be organized internally along ethnic lines, these gangs are in constant contact with each other, passing and receiving huge shipments of drugs being passed from third parties, often located continents away.

The total picture of the drug-smuggling routes into Russia from Central Asia and the Golden Crescent, back out through Russia into eastern and western Europe, and the flow of drugs from the Western Hemisphere into and then out of Russia and eastern Europe, shows a fully integrated trade, using any criminal gang as the feet on the street. There is one international drug cartel directing the overall flow, market delivery, and price. Its engine is the biggest profiteers of Dope, Inc., the money-launderers and the controlling banks that are raking in the money.

The St. Petersburg bust is but one case exposing the cross-directionality of the drug flows, into eastern Europe and Russia, for transshipment back out to western Europe. The newly independent Baltic states are playing a key role in this routing. One cocaine route travels through Lithuania, according to the State Department report. Cocaine is smuggled from Germany through Lithuania to Russia; the cocaine also flows in the opposite direction. Cocaine is also being smuggled into eastern Europe via airports in Bulgaria, the Bulgarian criminal gangs being more directly allied to the Italian Mafias, which in turn, cooperate fully with the South American cartels. The Czech Republic has also become a depot for transport of cocaine into western Europe.

The Baltic states are also being used for transshipment into western Europe from as far away as the Golden Triangle. Estonian drug couriers have been arrested in Thailand. Opium and hashish cargoes are often transferred to Estonian ships bound for western Europe, especially Scandinavia.

Poland: Dope, Inc. depot

Poland is the "Grand Central Station" for drug flows, reports of the U.S. Drug Enforcement Administration (DEA) show. Marijuana and cocaine come in to Poland from the Baltic Sea from the Western Hemisphere and Africa bound for points east and west. Heroin and marijuana also come into Poland from the eastern border with Ukraine, where it is transported to western Europe. The amount of drugs flowing through the country is so dense that in May 1993, Polish Customs officers seized 4.4 metric tons of hashish. In November 1993, a 2.5 metric-ton shipment of hashish was intercepted; its point of origin was Afghanistan. An additional 2.5 tons of the same shipment had been seized in Belarus. In December 1993, Polish Customs seized half a ton of marijuana that had arrived on a KLM (Dutch airlines) flight from Lagos, Nigeria. On April 18, 1995, 2.1 metric tons of marijuana were seized from a container which had been transported on the Danish ship *Maersk Euroquinto.* Reportedly, the container had been loaded in Rotterdam in a legitimate shipment of ginger. The marijuana shipment was intended for transshipment through Poland to western Europe.

Heroin is also being moved on the roads. Polish police authorities, according to the DEA, say that Nigerians, Turks, Indians, and Pakistanis recruit Polish couriers to transport heroin from the Golden Crescent and Golden Triangle to points west.

Lastly, Poland is itself a major producer of amphetamines for consumption in in western Europe. According to the DEA, Poland ranks second only to the Netherlands in the illicit production of amphetamines for the overall European drug market. But this is not necessarily a rivalry, but cooperation—Swedish authorities have determined that most of the amphetamines consumed in that country are produced in the Netherlands, and smuggled into Sweden through Poland.

Poland assumed its key role as the stationhouse for European drug routes after the launching of the Balkan war. Its services to Dope, Inc. have not left the Polish people unscathed. Officially, there are 40,000 drug addicts in Poland. One-third of its intravenous drug addicts are HIV-positive. But Poles don't consume the high-priced drugs arriving in their ports and airports. Most addicts consume processed poppy seeds with a high opium content, grown in Poland's own illicit poppy fields, but considered of too poor quality for export. In 1993, police located 4,000 illegal poppy fields in Poland. Commensurate with Poland's rise in the drug world, is its crime rate, which has nearly doubled yearly in the 1990s.

Ukraine: the Dope, Inc. Grip

Another country caught in the drug cross fire is Ukraine, once the breadbasket of eastern Europe and the Soviet Union. In only the first six months of 1995, Ukrainian authorities seized 23 tons of illicit drugs, including hashish, opium poppy straw, and amphetamines. Ukraine is also a critical transshipment point for chemicals, such as acetic anhydride, which is produced in large quantities in Russia, for use in opium refining to produce heroin in the Golden Crescent.

As early as 1993, leaders in Ukraine were sounding the alarm on the Dope, Inc. takeover of their country. The New Jersey-based *Ukrainian Weekly* reported in May

1993 that the Ukrainian Security Service had called a special meeting of regional administrators to draw up plans on how to thwart the criminal takeover of the economy.

The *Weekly's* correspondent Dmytro Filipchenko reported: "Profiting from the after-effects of the collapse of the U.S.S.R., various gaps in the existing legislation and enforcement, and a lack of regulation of economic relations between the enterprises and the state, criminal elements have created so-called 'support groups' in the higher echelons of authority in Ukraine. They have also forged strong links with international organized crime groups, and diversified their activities—primarily in banking and trade." On the last point, it was reported by the newspaper *Kiev Pravda* in August 1993, that drug dealers from Russia, the United States, and Ukraine had held a grand council in Zurich, Switzerland, to set goals for drug expansion in eastern Europe.

The *Ukrainian Weekly* article listed the methods to be used: 'The principal goals of the Ukrainian mafia today are perceived to be: to obtain illegal easements in export trade; to illegally obtain raw materials; to use foreign investments to fund criminal activities (such as narcotics, production and traffic, and the sale of nuclear materials); and to embezzle humanitarian aid arriving to Ukraine from abroad.

"As a result, organized crime in Ukraine is struggling *to achieve control over the entire import and export system of the country*" (emphasis added).

As always, Dope, Inc. in Ukraine is feeding on the destruction of young minds. According to the Ministry of Internal Affairs, the spread of drug consumption there has been "alarming." The cause is not only poverty and economic crisis, but, said a ministry official, "superabundance."

"Every year," *Kiev Pravda* reported in July 1993, "more than 6,000 drug addicts are registered in Ukraine, of which more than 40% are minors. More than 90% of all addicts are under 30 years of age. Half of them become addicted as teenagers."

Czech Republic: Shangri-la

To the Czech Republic, Dope, Inc. has given the special role as the "Nepal" of eastern and western Europe—a Dope, Inc. tourist trap. The government signed on, when it passed legislation which permits personal possession of drugs. Simultaneously, drug prices dropped. The combination has made the Czech Republic a drug attraction for tourists from western Europe, especially Austria and Germany, where cocaine and heroin sell for three times their price in the streets of Prague.

The Czech Republic also functions as a launching pad toward the East for the Italian Mafia groups, such as the Neapolitan Camorra and the Sicilian Mafia. Drugs go the other way also: Kosova Albanians, Russians, Turks, and local Czechs move large cargos of heroin from the Golden Crescent to western European markets. South American traffickers are also finding safe passage through the Czech Republic. One ephredine-smuggling route from Mexico has been discovered, and cocaine is now arriving in Czech airports, along with the drug tourists.

The Central Asia bonanza

While the western mafias are walking in the front door opened by the Thatcher-Bush imposition of free-trade globalization on Russia and eastern Europe, by far the biggest flow of drugs coming into and through Russia and eastern Europe, comes in through the back door, from Central Asia and the Golden Crescent of

Afghanistan and Pakistan. As the agency Novosti described it in August 1994: "With the collapse of the U.S.S.R., opium from Afghanistan, Pakistan, and Iran started flooding into the NIS states. And though border guards and customs officers are doing their utmost, the major part of these lethal powders still seeps through the cordons. The new so-called Silk Road is very convenient for smugglers. It has replaced the former mainline into Europe, through Turkey and Bulgaria, which has become far more dangerous because of the political situation in the Balkans."

Hence, even before the opening of Russia and Central Asia to real economic development and trade along rail corridors organized as a new Silk Road spanning from Beijing to Paris, as proposed by American Presidential candidate Lyndon LaRouche, the Thatcher-Bush policies have produced a *drug* Silk Road (**Map 15**).

Evidence suggests, furthermore, that one of the major facilitators of this "Drug Road" is the Russian Army. According to some reports, up to 40% of the Russian and allied soldiers who fought in the Afghanistan War became addicted to drugs. As one official of the Russian Ministry of Internal Affairs admitted in a press conference in 1994, in answer to a question on this point, "Yes, there is some form of cooperation [between servicemen and the drug traffickers]. It's true that the drugs fall into the hands of the servicemen. We carried out a number of operations . . . to check army units deployed in and outside Moscow. A number of cases were revealed in which drugs were trafficked to and fro from the barracks." And in cities such as Dushanbe, Tajikistan, sources report that Russian soldiers frequent the finest restaurants in the city—flush with funds from the drug trade.

The Golden Crescent of Pakistan and Afghanistan was launched with the Afghanistan war. This is the major source of heroin and opium going into the NIS countries.

The price of the heroin goes up every time it changes hands along the route, reported Anatoly Baranov in the Russian daily *Pravda* of Sept. 21, 1994, and has become the most lucrative form of business. "Tajiks have very little money. . . . Even when there is paper money, the Tajiks have nowhere to earn it—all industry is standing idle, agriculture is extremely unprofitable and inadequate, and trade is utterly disorganized." The expanded drug trade, coming in from Afghanistan, says Baranov, is flourishing as a result. In Tajikistan, drugs are called "modeling clay," and a kilogram of it in neighboring Afghanistan costs 80,000 rubles, or about $35-40. "When it crosses the Pyandzh in a smuggler's bag, it increases in price approximately tenfold, and in the border regions of Pamir is valued at 800,000 rubles [$3540,000]." In Dushanbe, it is worth 2.5 million rubles, and in Moscow 10 million rubles.

Baranov reports that Afghanistan accepts anything in payment for the heroin— "hardware, ammunition, flour, military matériel, gasoline, and diesel fuel." He further claims that the Russian Army rear services directorate rides shotgun on food and fuel being sent into Afghanistan, in exchange for the drugs.

In addition to carrying heroin from points southwest, the newly independent countries of Central Asia, which have traditionally grown quantities of opium for local consumption, have now emerged as significant producers in their own right, placing these countries, which were already the poorest sections of the U.S.S.R., under the mercy of Dope, Inc. As Novosti reported in 1995, "Under conditions of war, it is difficult to cultivate agricultural land. Harvests suffer. But the planting of opium, for example, does not require any special conditions, and the profits are incomparably higher than for any of the products of normal agriculture. . . . For example, 1 hectare of a fruit-tree farm yielded in 1991, 15-20,000 rubles, but opium (5 kilos of raw opium) yielded 2.5 million rubles."

- In Tajikistan, drugs are cultivated in the Parnir region in the east of the country, called Badakhshan, whose population are mostly followers of the Ismaili Prince Karim Agha Khan. Sources report to *EIR* that once a traveler steps out of the capital of Dushanbe, he sees poppy fields everywhere in the countryside. Opium grown in Tajikistan is shipped north to Osh, a largely Uzbek city within Kyrgyzstan on the Uzbek border.
- In Uzbekistan, opium poppy and hashish are cultivated in the mountainous regions of Uzbek, particularly in the regions of Samarkand and Syrhandarya, reports the State Department. But Uzbekistan's use to Dope, Inc. is mostly as a brokering center and transshipment point for drug operations.
- In Turkmenistan, opium has traditionally been produced for local consumption. Most opium poppy is grown on the Iranian border in the Akhal Velayat, which contains Ashgabat, and in the eastern regions of Lebap and Mary. As the State Department explains it, "Opium is *bartered by the local producers for scarce commodities like bread and fuel*" (emphasis added).
- Kyrgyzstan is a traditional opium producer, and after the Soviet Union banned its cultivation in 1973, illicit cultivation, mostly in remote mountainous

regions, continued. In 1995, authorities seized 1 ton of indigenous opium. Cannabis is also produced here.

• In Kazakhstan, police seized 6 tons of illegal narcotics in 1995. Marijuana is the most important drug crop, but ephedrine and opium production is on the rise. Most of this production occurs in the vast Chu Valley, which also spans part of the territory of Kyrgyzstan and Uzbekistan. According to some reports, there are some 40,000 hectares of opium fields in the Chu Valley, and 4.5 million hectares of hemp (marijuana). Ephedra plants, from which ephedrine is derived, grow wild in the Taldy-Korgan and Dzhambyule regions, with 2,000 tons harvested in a single summer.

Novosti further reported in 1995 that Russia itself is not immune from the narcotics cash-cropping. "In Russia, 1.5 million hectares of wild-growing hemp are registered. One hectare yields approximately one ton of narcotics material annually. Narcotics plants (hemp, poppy, oil-poppy) flourish in southern Russia, in the non-Black Earth territory, in the Far East, in Tuva, the Caucasus, Buryatia, Siberia, and other regions. *The annual growth of narcotics cultivation is 10-15%"* (emphasis added).

Perhaps nothing better illustrates the Dope, Inc. degradation of the Russian economy, than the way in which Russia, Poland, and other former Soviet satellites have become leading producers of amphetamines. Underground synthetic drug laboratories have become the major employers for thousands of chemists, thrown on the scrapheap by the Thatcher-Bush free-trade regimen, left to try to survive on $20 a month.

The Dope, Inc. Invasion of the Russian Economy

In November 1991, at a conference of the Schiller Institute, only three months after the breakup of the Soviet Union, *EIR* editor Dennis Small presented to an audience of 400 people a documented picture on the disaster that the application of neo-liberal "free trade" dogma, especially its "shock therapy" form, has brought to the countries of Ibero-America. Small warned the audience of representatives of 36 countries, including from eastern Europe and almost all the newly independent states (NIS), that if they accepted the "reform" policy being pushed from the West by such Harvard yuppies as Jeffrey Sachs, "this is what will happen to you." Small cited the case of Bolivia, where Sachs admits that the tin- and oil-sector workers, laid off as a result of his reforms, had gone to work for the coca growers. Now, in early 1996, we read about laid-off fish cannery workers in the Soviet Far East growing marijuana and bartering it for food.

Not only have the populations of Russia and the NIS been reduced to desperate impoverishment, forcing them onto the payrolls of Dope, Inc., as foot soldiers. It is under the financial framework of the shock therapy imposed on Russia and the NIS countries by British Prime Minister Margaret Thatcher and U.S. President George Bush, that the filthy lucre produced by the criminalization of these economies reaches its ultimate destination: the coffers of Dope, Inc., primarily in the West. Thanks to Thatcher and Bush, Russia traded in communism for the British Empire's dope-driven black economy—offshore financial centers, metals speculators, money launderers, crime networks, and drug traffickers.

Meanwhile, in the last six years, Russian industry has been shrunken to 40% of its previous levels. Russian flight capital, on the order of $300 billion, is locked into the global financial system's speculative nooks and crannies, and a vast black economy of smuggling and crime in Russia runs the scale from hard-core criminals to members of the *Nomenklatura* with Swiss bank accounts. But, as much as Russians are accountable for their own country's fate, the logistics for this criminal revolution came from the West, and the Russians who joined whole hog, were often already active in the East- West weapons-for-drugs economy, where the borders between the Warsaw Pact and NATO were faded.

Within Russia, all experts admit that the institutional chaos, associated with the shock therapy reforms, has led to uncontrolled borders, unregulated banking, unbridled smuggling, underpaid police facing mafias flush with dollars, and a collapsing health care system for addicts. How did this Dope, Inc. takeover of the Russian economy happen?

Bust the ruble

A crucial step in the looting of Russia was the destruction of the Russian ruble. This plan went into high gear in January 1992, with the Gaidar reforms. Prices were decontrolled, inflation soared to rates of 2,000% per year, and dollarization of the Russian economy began. By December 1992, the ruble had crashed from 1.81 to the dollar in 1991, to 500 rubles to the dollar. By December 1993, it was 1,250 to the dollar, and by December 1994, it was 3,306 to the dollar. "Doing business" in the ruble became a losing proposition, with the result that transactions generating hard currency became the name of the game. Anything that could get a price in Western markets was bought, stolen, or swindled out of the domestic economy and shipped out.

The street mafias, an outgrowth of black marketeering under the Soviet system, became institutionalized, under International Monetary Fund (IMF) reforms, when Gorbachov privatized much of the retail sales infrastructure in the Soviet Union. These so-called cooperatives were picked up by regional *Nomenklatura* figures and their appended assortment of criminal contacts. According to Yuri Dashko of Moscow's Academy for Economic Security, this was a conscious policy to "integrate the shadow economy into legal areas."

The flood of Western consumer products, increasingly out of the reach of the impoverished average Russian, poured in through the cooperatives, whose clients were the *nouveaux riches*—as the domestic consumer industry shrank. Import-export firms, linked to Western suppliers and staffed by former KGB agents and others, sat on top of the street mafias, and raked in the profits.

Today, estimates of Russian flight capital abroad go up to $300 billion. The October 1995 report of the Swiss Federal police, *Status Report East Money,* estimates that 40-50% of Russia's Gross Domestic Product is in the "shadow economy," and that large sums of Russian criminal money have landed in Swiss banks. In Switzerland, "international trade deals, particularly raw materials, are financially arranged, which never appear in the statistics," it notes.

Simultaneously, Russia was dollarized, reaching such levels that in 1994 and 1995, the New York Federal Reserve sold on a seignorage basis, close to $40 billion newly minted U.S. notes, primarily $100 bills, to the New York-based Republic National Bank of Edmond Safra. Safra had bought them for a select group of Moscow-based banks and their customers, and the dollars were literally flown to Russia.

Enter Marc Rich

Another step in Dope, Inc.'s takeover was to entice members of the Russian and Soviet *Nomenklatura* into get-rich-quick sell-offs of raw material wealth to the "global markets." Russia was sold a poisonous stew of Physiocratic doctrine, the "Bounty of Nature," and Adam Smith free-trade doctrines, that provided the basis for Russian shock therapy czars Yegor Gaidar and Anatoli Chubais, who took office in President Yeltsin's first government in late 1991, and began implementing the reforms in 1992.

After the Fall 1991 breakup of the Soviet Union, and the subsequent chaos in trade and ruble transfer payments among the new republics, Western raw material trading pirates such as Marc Rich, based in Zug, Switzerland, offered their extensive Russian contacts quick access to world market prices for Russian oil, aluminum, gold, and other products normally consumed domestically.

In his heyday, Rich, now a fugitive wanted in the United States, controlled one of the world's biggest commodity trading firms. By the early 1990s, Rich had a large Moscow office, set up by his London partner Felix Posen. From this office was begun the raw materials looting of Russia, which turned into an avalanche of smuggling. The Oct. 24, 1992 issue of the London *Economist* put it bluntly: Russia should shut down its raw-materials-consuming industries and instead ship everything out to Western markets. George Soros, speculator and pro-drug legalizer, boosted this plan.

Prior to his 1984 conviction in a U.S. court on charges of tax fraud, Rich had been a partner with oilman Marvin Davis in Twentieth Century Fox, with Henry Kissinger on the board. Rich was the perfect pied piper, having been the official Western representative for Soviet metals trading in the 1980s, and the architect of the illegal flow of Soviet oil to South Africa, in violation of international sanctions. He was also up to his eyeballs in the 1980s in the triangular trade in weapons, oil, and drugs around the Afghan and Iran-Iraq wars, and George Bush's Iran-Contra drug caper.

Rich was then in a perfect position, in the early 1990s, to set up massive legal and illegal exports of oil and other commodities out of Russia, as well as facilitating the offshore money-laundering channels so that this money stayed abroad.

After the 1991 collapse of trade among the former republics, Rich's contact base was the only network capable of putting together inter-republic trade deals. According to Vsevolod Generalov of the Russian State Committee for Metallurgy, in an April 1, 1996 London *Metals Bulletin* interview, "These companies were only interested in today's profit or 'hit and run' operations. There was a lot of speculation and illegal financial activity."

By 1992, according to the head of Rich's Moscow office, Daniel Posen; Rich and company were doing $2.5 billion in "natural resources" trading with the former Soviet Union. In 1992, Rich's Moscow contact, Russia's "commodities kingpin" Art yom Tarasov, head of the foreign trade ISTOK association, came under pressure and skidaddled off to London with a bundle of money. According to a 1992 *Izvestia* article, in December 1991, Rich was the main beneficiary of a top-down decision assigning substantial hydrocarbon supplies for export. The *Wall Street Journal* in 1993 estimated Rich's trade with the former Soviet Union at $3 billion, "about a tenth of his worldwide business."

Rich has never been shy in bridging the gap between the masters of British geopolitics and the sleazy underworld of the black economy. In Tajikistan, the drug crossroads of Central Asia, Rich's New York agent, Rabbi Ronald Greenwald, has been in charge of putting together aluminum trade convoys, protected by private armies drawn from the area's armed clans, many of which also traffic in heroin.

Since the late 1970s, Greenwald had worked with another Rich-connected operative, Shabtai Kalmanowitch, a KGB agent laundered into the organized-crime faction of Israeli intelligence. Kalmanowitch was adviser to Chief Mangope, head of South Africa's Bophuthatswana Bantustan. "Bop," as the bantustan was dubbed, is known for its casino gambling and for being one of the world's biggest producers of platinum.

Arrested by the Israelis in 1988, Kalmanowitch was freed to return to Russia in 1993, where he took up business with the mafia-connected Duma member Josef Kobzon. Today, the Liat-Natalie firm founded by Kalmanowitch and Kobzon is involved in some of the biggest real estate and construction ventures in Moscow. According to sources, Kobzon hosts Rich whenever the latter visits Moscow. Kobzon and his network had been the focus of 1993 German police intelligence leaks exposing the stay-behind crime networks being built up around the Russian Western Group of Forces still stationed in Germany.

This network encompassed criminal cells, largely operating through import-export companies, that went from Moscow, to Berlin and Antwerp, a center for cutting of Russian diamonds; to Israel and Brighton Beach in Brooklyn, New York, where the Russian emigré mafia had perfected fuel tax frauds running into the billions. Israeli Police intelligence official Leber stated in the Oct. 2, 1995 *Newsweek,* that figures in this network, Boris Nayfield and Rachmiel Brandwain, are handling a heroin and cocaine business stretching from Ibero-America to Europe and Israel. According to a Russian weekly, Kobzon is friends with "thief-in-law" "Yaponchik" Ivankov, who was arrested by the FBI in June 1995 in New York City.

Enter Philip Morris and Transworld Metals

The import flood into Russia is small change, compared to the raw materials out-flow to the West. Here, the volumes of wealth require offshore banking skills, met-als market insiders, secure numbered bank accounts in the West, and protected opportunities for investing the proceeds outside Russia. The unique relationship between a small, London-based metals trading firm, Transworld Metals, the Russian aluminum industry, and Philip Morris, Inc., shows just how close Dope, Inc. has come to succeeding in its conquest of Russia.

The Anglo-Dutch families, grouped into the Club of the Isles, control the bulk of global raw materials production, as a cartel. The only significant area of the world not in their control is the extensive reserves and production capabilities in the former Soviet Union. The London Metals Exchange (LME), with the associated commodities trading houses grouped around it, like Rich and Transworld Metals, is the center for global metals trading. LME-connected metals traders operate like modern-day pirates, descending upon a target, buying, threatening, stealing, much the way the British Admiralty used the Barbary pirates in the 1700s.

According to Russian economics expert Vladimir Panskov, as quoted in the Vienna *Wirtschafts Woche* of Nov. 16, 1995, "20% of oil production, 34% of fertilizers, and 45% of non-ferrous metals are illegally exported out of the country." South American cocaine and Golden Crescent heroin and hashish turn up in the same Baltic ports that handle the metals outflow. The criminal commodities trade provides a means for laundering the proceeds of both raw materials and narcotics smuggling.

According to sources, London's Transworld Metals operates in combination with Rich. It is reportedly the world's third largest aluminum producer. Once owned, and perhaps still, by London interests around Henry Ansbacher Holding, it was assigned to take over the Russian aluminum industry based in Siberia. By 1995, Transworld owned the majority of shares in smelters in Bratsk (50%) and Sayansk (68%), and tried to take over the Krasnoyarsk smelter. These smelters, some of the largest in the world, used to supply the Russian aircraft industry. Within its current borders, Russia has no supplies of the raw materials alumina and bauxite. IMF pressure against Russian state subsidizing of industry made it impossible for these firms to import alumina.

In stepped Transworld, which provided the financing for importing alumina, rented the Russian factories, for about $500 a ton, took possession of "their" aluminum, which was shipped out of a Pacific dock Transworld built in Vanino on the Sea of Japan, and into Rich's market for "Russian" aluminum. Through the rental procedure, called tolling, little money went into urgent maintenance, and nothing was set aside for retooling up to current technological standards. Through corruption and threats, Transworld picked up from within the management, more and more shares of stock.

Most of the deals organized by Rich and others, used the foreign sale of raw materials commodities to launder money out of the country. Zug, Switzerland prosecutors are investigating, for criminal money laundering, the whole gamut of Russian deals by Zug-based commodities firms. The laundry works by falsifying billings, building into the commodity transaction price discrepancies which result in money leaving the country. The LME-connected trade in derivatives permits imaginative variations to the scheme.

With Philip Morris International, Transworld pioneered a variant on this. By September 1990, Philip Morris had made arrangements with Boris Yeltsin, then head of the Russian Federation, for the import of Marlboro cigarettes. Overnight, a black market in Marlboros and other Western brands sprang up in Germany where the Western Group of the Red Army was stationed until 1994. Billions of cigarettes were pumped through the military transportation system, and into the hands of Russian emigré and other mafia black marketeering rings.

Within Russia, Philip Morris was accumulating rubles from their retail and wholesale dealings. Transworld offered a service, used by probably 100 other companies, to unload rubles accumulated within Russia for hard currency abroad. Transworld would use Philip Morris's rubles to pay the tolling fee at the Russian smelters, and simultaneously Transworld transferred to Philip Morris, in a bank account abroad, dollars earned from the marketing of their Russian aluminum.

Transworld ran its alumina supply operation with its Monte Carlo-registered joint venture, Trans-CIS Commodities, a partnership with the Chernoi brothers from Tashkent, Uzbekistan. The Chernois now reside in Israel. Russian investigations into Transworld, Chernoi, and the flight capital scheme have generated press coverage, but no arrests.

But, opposition began to grow inside Russia. In January 1995, the newly appointed head of the State Property Committee, Vladimir Polevanov, who replaced IMF darling Anatoli Chubais, stated that it might be necessary for reasons of national security to renationalize some key industries. He meant the aluminum industry and Transworld, and, was promptly fired as a sacrifice to the IMF.

As 1995 progressed, opponents of Transworld Metals and its partners in Russia began turning up dead. One such opponent was Feliks Lvov. Lvov had been trying to put together with the New York-based AIOC metals firm and some Russian banks a new bauxite-alumina supply operation to break London's stranglehold.

In May 1995, Lvov had testified before a Duma hearing against the looting practices in the aluminum industry, pointing the finger at Transworld's Trans-CIS front, and the Moscow Menatep Bank which had worked with Trans-CIS. Menatep's head is World Bank darling Mikhail Khodorkovsky, who stated in an interview, "I am convinced that there is a chance for Russia to change from an industrial society into a post-industrial one."

In July 1995, two of the bankers working with Lvov were murdered. On Sept. 8, 1995, Lvov himself was gunned down outside Moscow. AIOC was slated for bankruptcy, and Rich began buying up chunks of AIOC's trading divisions.

Cyprus and the Balkan route

Philip Morris also paved the way for the Balkan route that brings drugs into Russia through the back door. From the 1960s on, Philip Morris sold container-loads of Marlboros to wholesale smugglers through Belgrade, Yugoslavia, and Sofia, Bulgaria, who then handled the smuggling to Italy's Camorra and Mafia. Another center for this smuggling was Cyprus, where cargo went by speedboat or ship into Adriatic ports. Beginning in the 1970s, these well-lubricated relations were used to handle a massive heroin pipeline from Southwest Asia's Golden Crescent to western Europe and the United States. With the escalation of the Lebanese civil war, a multibillion-dollar, drugs-for-weapons underground economy emerged, with Cyprus replacing Beirut as the eastern Mediterranean's dirty-money center.

Cyprus, home of two British military bases, is today the main jumping off point for the networks controlling Russia's raw materials trade and flight capital. Over 7,000 Russian offshore companies are registered in Cyprus, and 8 of the 26 foreign banks there are Russian. According to the *Wall Street Journal,* phone traffic between Cyprus and Russia dominates the island's modern telecommunications exchange. Cyprus was used in the 1991 sale of $1 billion in Soviet gold reserves from Tashkent. Cyprus has also conveniently been an outpost of British Empire intelligence operations since the days when the British fleet controlled the Mediterranean. London's Barclays Bank dominates Cyprus, along with France's Banque Nationale de Paris.

Most of Moscow's banks run their currency speculation via accounts in Western banks. Moscow's Stolichny Bank, one of the recipients of large New York Fed dollar sales, has a Vienna company, owned by Stolichny's president, Smolenski, which runs its currency and financial transactions primarily through the Dutch ABN Amro Bank branch in Vienna. Stolichny and its Vienna partners were investigated in 1993 in a $25 million fraud case.

A Winning Strategy: How Drugs Can Be Wiped Out, Totally

Outside of moral indifferentism and the overt promotion of every-man-for-himself hedonism, there are two recurring arguments wielded in defense of the legalization of drugs. The first, is that legalization will cut drug prices drastically, and thereby take the high profitability (and concomitant violence) out of the trade. We addressed that false argument in the opening section of this report, where we proved that Dope, Inc. has itself *deliberately* lowered the prices of cocaine and heroin over the last two decades, as a classic marketing technique designed to increase the market for their "product." Their strategy succeeded. To do more of the same, under the guise of legalization, would only ensure a vast new increase of drug consumption.

The second argument is pure, cultural pessimism: Drugs cannot be stopped, so we may as well learn to live with them. Many then go on to cite the experience of the last decade—but especially of George Bush's phony "War on Drugs"—as "proof" that you just can't win. Even the well-intentioned Clinton administration is promoting the pathetic formulation that "this is not a war" to be won or lost, but rather it is like "fighting cancer"—which presumably means that we are destined to lose the battle.

However, a proper review of the last decade's anti-drug efforts—both the successes and the failures—points to a different set of conclusions:

1. *Crop eradication* is effective. Even with primitive technologies, upwards of 25% of the world's marijuana crop is being eradicated.

2. *Seizures* and drug interdiction can also do serious damage. Again with poor equipment and resources, more than 25% of world cocaine production was seized over the last ten years.

3. *Stopping drug money laundering* will never work . . . if it isn't tried. The story here is that a serious effort has yet to be made, *by any country anywhere in the world*, on this, the most decisive front in the war on drugs.

To effectively dismantle Dope, Inc., it is necessary to act in a coordinated fashion on all three of these fronts. They are the three legs of the stool; without all three, the policy will not stand up.

The final, related consideration, is that the drug trade has to be fought simultaneously, in a coordinated fashion, on a global scale. Since Dope, Inc. is a multinational enterprise with operations in dozens of nations, it does little good to shut it down in one country only: It will simply move its operations to a more favorable environment.

Eradication

Figure 25 shows the disposition of the total quantity of marijuana cultivated worldwide, over the ten-year period 1985-95. Most noteworthy is that a full 26% of what was planted, was eradicated. The United States, the largest producer in the world, eradicates an estimated one-third of its crop (the DEA claims it destroys one-half, but a review of the literature indicates this is overly optimistic).

Mexico, however, is the world leader on the eradication front: In 1995, they eliminated 11,800 hectares of marijuana, out of a total of 18,700 cultivated; that is, about twothirds of the total. How do they do it, with almost no resources, and less in the way of technology? In general, thousands upon thousands of Mexican soldiers are deployed into the drug-producing zones to chop down marijuana plants with machetes and other rudimentary equipment. Aerial surveillance and spraying with defoliants occurs in some cases, but is by no means the rule. As U.S. anti-drug director Gen. Barry McCaffrey reported on April 8, 1996: "The Mexican Army has eradicated more illegal drugs in the last year than any other nation on the face of the Earth. And they did this at the risk of their own lives, and [there was] a lot of hard work and sweat and blood involved in that."

If Mexico is able, with such methods, to knock out two-thirds of its marijuana before it is ever harvested, imagine what could be done with the application of serious resources and technologies. Satellite mapping and sophisticated aerial photography are capable of pinpointing every hectare cultivated, by crop type, on the face of the earth. Such capabilities have existed for almost *two decades*. As *21st Century Science* & *Technology* magazine explained in its January-February 1990 issue, a 1978 joint study by NASA and the Mexican government proved the case:

"The remote sensing techniques developed at NASA's Earth Resources Laboratory to monitor agricultural crops from Landsat satellites [can] be used to detect cannabis. The particular radiation reflectance signature for the marijuana crop was determined to be in the 1.55 to 1.75 micron band, in the infrared part of the electromagnetic spectrum.

"With this knowledge, NASA analysts could find the cannabis fields from the air. A multispectrum scanning instrument (MSS) from NASA, mounted under the wing of a Lear 35 jet, could cover 12,000 square miles of Mexico per day. The entire country could be mapped every 15 days, to allow crops to be targeted for destruction almost as soon as they started growing."

Once the drug crops are detected, highly effective herbicides, such as glysophate, can then be applied massively, using virtual air flotillas protected by the respective national air forces, if necessary. For hard-to-reach mountainous areas and deep valleys, modern, armored helicopters can be equipped for the task.

Environmentalist arguments against such spraying are specious. Herbicides have been designed that are damaging only to the drug crops, and not to other plants. As for the purported harmful effect on the poor, unsuspecting consumers, they should protect themselves by simply not consuming the illegal substances in the first place. In any event, there is some question whether the herbicide does more damage, or the pot or cocaine does.

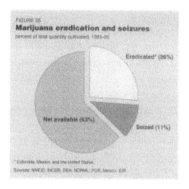

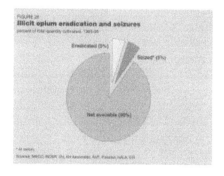

Marijuana cultivation in the United States poses a greater challenge to eradication, but it is far from an impossible task. The first problem is a political one: Much of the marijuana cultivation occurs on national parks land, and the environmentalist lobby is a powerful obstacle to serious eradication. Secondly, over recent years, much of domestic production has been moved indoors or underground, into vast, technologically sophisticated plantations which are not detectable with standard aerial surveillance. Here, however, infrared photography, which is heat sensitive, is very useful. So, too, is the measurement of unusually high rates of water and electricity consumption in areas where they are not warranted. Similarly, the discharge of unauthorized chemical effluents can be readily detected, and point to probable indoor drug facilities. In fact, the Environmental Protection Agency is reportedly already providing the DEA with useful assistance in this regard.

The same basic approach can and must be applied to other drugs, including opium and coca. Today, only 5% of the opium crop is eradicated (see **Figure 26**), while less than 2% of the total coca crop is eradicated.

Eradicating a quarter of a drug crop, as currently occurs with marijuana, is not enough to seriously dent the supply. In fact, it may only serve to maintain market control and weed out the competition. However, what if 90% were to be eradicated? If there is sufficient political will from the national governments in question, and adequate technology and other resources provided by the more affluent nations (the United States in particular), it is not unreasonable to suggest that as much as 90% of all three major illicit drug crops—marijuana, opium, and coca—could be eradicated on the spot.

Seizures

Figure 27 shows what has happened with coca and cocaine over the past decade. Here the level of eradication is pathetically low—2%. There is organized political resistance to such programs in all three producer nations—Peru, Bolivia, and Colombia—by "peasant" associations financed by the drug cartels and their allied UN-based non-governmental organizations (see *EIR,* Nov. 10, 1995, "New Terror International Targets the Americas"). Furthermore, there are major problems at the level of the respective governments: President Samper Pizano of Colombia is owned, lock, stock, and barrel, by the Cali Cartel; President Sánchez de Lozada of Bolivia is a member of the pro-drug Inter-American Dialogue, and has himself openly advocated drug legalization; and President Alberto Fujimori of Peru has staunchly refused to eradicate, for fear of driving millions of Andean peasants into the arms of the Shining Path narco-terrorists, and for fear of losing the hundreds of millions of drug dollars which enter the Peruvian economy every year and without which Peru could not service its foreign debt.

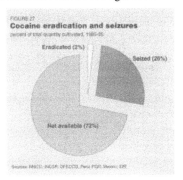

Cocaine seizures, however, are a somewhat brighter picture, with 26% of everything produced between 1985-95 having been intercepted and seized by various national authorities. The United States makes about 40% of the total worldwide seizures, but even here, the resources deployed are woefully inadequate to the task.

First, there is the question of aerial and maritime detection and interception . Cooperation between the United States and various Ibero-American governments has improved somewhat over the recent period, with some U.S. radar equipment and technical support being provided to Peru, Colombia, Mexico, and other countries. But it is far less than what is needed to really dent the trafficking. A full complement of ground radar and linked AWAC capabilities needs to be deployed, which would detect all unregistered flights and immediately transmit the information to national military units each assigned to patrol their own territory and air space. In-depth technical cooperation and intelligence sharing, with strict respect for national sovereignty, is called for in such efforts.

Second, there is the monumental problem of inspecting all of the cargo which *legally* enters the United States. DEA officials estimate that a mere 3% of the 8-9 million containers entering U.S. ports annually are actually inspected today. Similarly, hundreds of millions of passengers cross the borders, as do about 12 million air cargo shipments, and something like 47 million trucks—a mammoth screening challenge. Even in those cases where inspection does occur, the drug traffickers are constantly developing ingenious new ploys to foil existing detection systems: packing cocaine inside concrete posts eludes X-rays; placing packaged cocaine deep inside blocks of frozen shrimp stymies drug-sniffing dogs; hiding cocaine in canned tuna lots, where only one can in a thousand is not legitimate, stands an excellent chance of passing inspection; and so forth.

Only the extensive introduction of new detection technologies will turn the tide. For example, Magnetic Resonance Imaging (MRI) technologies, today applied routinely in the medical field, hold promise for the war on drugs. Here the detection system excites atomic nuclei in the scanned material and, by "reading" the atomic signature of elements, is able to locate the presence of illegal narcotics. Currently, however, only relatively small targets (such as letters or packages) can be effectively scanned this way. Other technologies under development, such as the Explosive/Contraband Detection System (E/CDS) which uses alpha and gamma rays, can handle somewhat larger packages, perhaps 2x2x2 feet—still substantially smaller than standard cargo containers (8x8x40 feet).

Another promising possibility is to use neutron beam technology, developed in the 1980s to verify nuclear and chemical weapons disarmament accords, in the anti-drug war. The technology was designed to put a Soviet nuclear missile through a screening system and count the number of warheads on it, because existing treaties did not allow the physical opening of the missile. The converted version of the technology consists of a kind of gantry through which up to 30 containers per hour can be moved, while a neutron beam scans their contents and tells customs agents what chemical elements they contain.

Although much work is still required, it is evident that such an approach is feasible. Once achieved, all containers entering the United States could be subjected to scanning by such detection systems, and there would be a gigantic jump in the amount of drugs seized. This, combined with the aerial interdiction described above, would be capable

So, if only 10% of the drugs cultivated gets past the eradication stage, and if only 25% of that reduced amount gets past the seizure stage, we are talking about only 2-3% of the total amount initially cultivated actually making it through to the consumer market. That would put a substantial dent in Dope, Inc. But it is still not enough.

Stopping drug-money laundering

The third leg of the stool, and the key to any successful anti-drug strategy, is to aggressively identify and put out of business any and all financial institutions that engage in drug money laundering—which, after all, is the level from which the drug trade is actually controlled. It is at this point in the discussion that people normally start getting very nervous.

The reason, as we have documented elsewhere in this report, is that global money laundering is run from the top by the most powerful financial interests on the face of the Earth: the City of London, the British Commonwealth, and associated forces.

But once the political will is established to carry out the task, here, too, modern technologies are available. Besides introducing anti-money-laundering legislation in countries where it doesn't now exist, and closing all the obvious loopholes in existing reporting regulations in countries like the United States, real-time computer tracking of even the most sophisticated money-laundering schemes is possible. Coupled with banking transparency—the bane of the free marketeers— such computer monitoring and tracking of suspect transactions can identify the vast majority of money laundering globally.

As important as they are, none of the above measures will be effective, however, unless they are carried out on a global scale by a coordinated effort among sovereign nation-states. The following case study shows why.

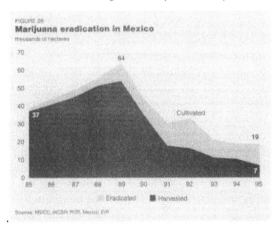

FIGURE 28
Marijuana eradication in Mexico
thousands of hectares

In **Figure 28** we see the growing effectiveness of Mexico's marijuana eradication campaign, beginning in 1989. In 1988, only 4,500 hectares were eradicated; but in 1989, according to official statistics, this more than doubled to 10,200 hectares eradicated. In subsequent years, equivalent amounts, and more, were eradicated, reaching a high of 16,900 hectares eradicated in 1992. As the graph shows, the effect of that campaign was not only to eliminate the specific hectares in question, but it also significantly discouraged cultivation in general, which, as a result, dropped from over 64,000 hectares planted in 1989, to less than 19,000 in 1995—a 70% decline in only six years. The area harvested dropped during that same period by an even greater 87%—from 53,900 hectares in 1989 to 6,900 in 1995. In terms of marijuana output, Mexico went from producing an astonishing 30,200 tons in 1989, to "only" 3,650 tons in 1995.

Was Dope, Inc. concerned? Not particularly.

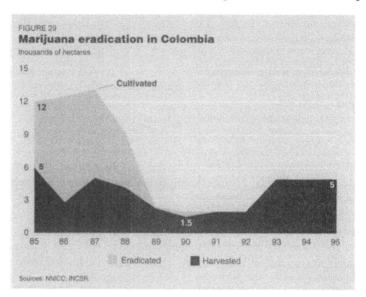

FIGURE 29
Marijuana eradication in Colombia
thousands of hectares

At precisely the point that Mexico began to put a dent in its marijuana output, Dope, Inc. took steps to make sure that another major producer, Colombia—which itself had been successfully eradicating in the mid-1980s—was brought back on line as a major source. As **Figure 29** shows, in 1985, under the government of Virgilio Barco, Colombia was eradicating half of its cultivated marijuana: 6,000 of 12,000 hectares, Over the subsequent four years, the eradication campaign, which made very successful use of glysophate herbicide, in particular, forced the total amount cultivated and harvested to drop drastically, down to a low point of 1,500 hectares harvested in 1990—a 75% drop from five years earlier. But then, under the César Gaviria (1990-94) and current Ernesto Samper governments, *all* marijuana eradication ceased—to the delight of the British-run environmentalists, the British-run legalization lobby, and the British-run drug cartels. Predictably, marijuana production rose back up to nearly the levels it had achieved before the eradication campaign began. Thus, in 1995, Colombia produced 4,133 tons of marijuana, to Mexico's 3,285—beating Mexico out for the dubious distinction of being Ibero-America's biggest pot producer, for the first time since 1982.

The moral of the story is, that Dope, Inc. must be defeated everywhere, if it is to be defeated anywhere. With that in mind, we recall for the reader the prescient remarks by Lyndon LaRouche to an *EIR*-sponsored antidrug conference in Mexico City, held over ten years ago, on March 13, 1985, just as Dope, Inc's "Development Decade" was getting under way:

"It is clear to the governments fighting the international drug-traffickers, that the drug-traffic could never be defeated if each of our nations tried to fight this evil independently of the other nations of this hemisphere. If the drug-traffickers' laboratories are shut down in Colombia, new laboratories open up in Brazil. . . .

"The greatest political threat to democracy in Venezuela, Colombia, Peru, and other countries, is the use of the billions of revenues held by the drug-traffickers to fund terrorist armies. . . . It is impossible to break the ominously increasing political power of the drug-traffickers . . . without capturing the billions of dollars of drug-revenues run through corrupt banking institutions . . .

"Special attention should be concentrated on those banks, insurance enterprises, and other business institutions which are in fact elements of an international financial cartel coordinating the flow of hundreds of billions annually of revenues from the international drug-traffic. Such entities should be classed as outlaws according to the 'crimes against humanity' doctrine elaborated at the postwar Nuremberg Tribunal".

LaRouche's War on Drugs: A Bibliography

Lyndon H. LaRouche, Jr. and his associates have been in the forefront of a campaign for a military war against the global narcotics trade since the 1970s. Below are their principal case-studies and exposes.

Sept. 12-23, 1978: *EIR*, "Why the World Bank Pushes Drugs," details how the international monetary institutions enforce economic policies which have driven Third World nations into producing drugs as cash export crops, in order to pay their foreign debts.

December 1978: *Dope, Inc.: Britain's Opium War against the United States*, commissioned by LaRouche and written by a team of *EIR* researchers. The exposé of the financial and political networks behind the multibillion-dollar international drug trade became an instant best-seller.

June 1980: *War on Drugs*, Vol. I, No.1, is published. The magazine of the LaRouche-founded National Anti-Drug Coalition, it names the names of the "citizens above suspicion" in the drug legalization lobby and behind the dope trade.

July 1980: *The Ugly Truth About Milton Friedman.* Co-authored by Lyndon LaRouche, this book documents the Nobel economist's role in pushing drug legalization as the essence of "free enterprise."

February 1985: *Narcotráfico, SA: La Nueva Guerra del Opio.* The translation of *Dope, Inc.* causes a furor across Ibero-America. Within days, it is banned in Venezuela, on the demand of the powerful Cisneros family. A few months later, Peru's Ulloa family tries, in vain, to do the same.

April 2, 1985: *EIR,* "A Proposed Strategic Operation against the Western Hemisphere's Drug Traffic," a speech by Lyndon LaRouche for a March 13, 1985 *EIR* conference, in Mexico City. The text, along with its 15-point program for a military war on drugs, is published in November 1985, in LaRouche's election platform, *A Program for America,* and in the 1986 edition of *Dope, Inc.*

July 1985: *EIR Special Report,* "Soviet Unconventional Warfare in Ibero-America: The Case of Guatemala," is a case-study of narco-terrorism,

June 1986: *Dope, Inc.: Boston Bankers and Soviet Commissars.* Second edition of *Dope, Inc.,* includes new sections on the dope cartel's command structure, the drug traffic in Ibero-America and Southwest Asia, and the Soviets' role in running the drug trade with the British and their Boston Brahmin retainers.

July 8, 1988: *EIR,* "How the Banks Got Hooked on Ibero-American Drug Money," proves that the international financial institutions encourage Third World drug production to facilitate payment of the foreign debt, and shows how they promote legalization as the next phase to keep their moribund world financial system alive.

June 23, 1989: *EIR,* "Kissinger's China Card: The Drug Connection," is an exposé of the involvement of Henry Kissinger with the major Hongkong dope banks.

January-February 1990: *21st Century Science & Technology,* "Yes, We Can Win the War on Drugs!" describes the technologies—aerial detection, radar, remote sensing scanners—available for a high-tech war on drugs, and counters the naysayers who claim that we must surrender to the cartels.

Nov. 9, 1990: *EIR,* " 'Dope, Inc.' Doubling Every 5 Years; Next Target Europe," debunks the Bush administration's pretense that U.S. drug use is declining; *EIR* warns that the growing narcotics cartel is targeting Europe.

Feb. 8, 1991: *EIR,* "Where Are the Sorties against U.S. Pot Fields, Mr. Bush?" U.S. marijuana production has soared as the economic depression has destroyed American agriculture.

April 1991: *EIR Special Report,* "Bush's Surrender to Dope, Inc.: How U.S. Policy is Destroying Colombia." Official U.S. policy under President Bush fostered Colombia's "truce" with the drug traffickers, turning it into a testing ground for global drug legalization and setting the stage for the current narco-democracy.

Aug. 23,1991: *EIR,* "Dope, Inc. Expands in Asia," The creation of "free trade zones" in Asia's formerly communist regions, became fertile ground for the drug trade.

June 1992: *Dope, Inc.: The Book That Drove Kissinger Crazy.* Third edition of *Dope, Inc.,* adds new material on the phenomenal growth rates of the global drug trade, on China's role in international drug trafficking, and on the Anti-Defamation League of B'nai B'rith.

May 21, 1993: *EIR,* "IMF Free-Traders Turn East Europe into Smugglers' Paradise," under IMF-imposed "free trade" policies; exposé has special focus on Seagram's and Philip Morris.

Nov. 10 and Nov. 17, 1995: *EIR,* "London's Irregular Warfare vs. Nations of the Americas." Eighty pages on the Cuba spawned São Paulo Forum, detail who is behind this "Narco- Terrorist International," created to sow separatism, drugs, and terrorism.

5. Dope, Inc.: The Book That Drove Kissinger Wild

Introduction To Dope Inc., The Third Edition The Book That Drove Kissinger Wild

What follows is the introduction to the third edition of Dope, Inc., *published in 1992.*
Thirteen years after the first edition of this book was released, Lyndon H. LaRouche Jr.—the man who commissioned it, and who has been the world's leading advocate of a genuine War on Drugs—sits in Federal prison in Rochester, Minnesota, the victim of one of the greatest travesties of justice in the history of the United States. The judicial railroad of Lyndon LaRouche and his jailing in January 1989 was the result of a dozen-year effort, spurred by kingpins of the U.S. branch of the international drug cartel we call Dope, Inc.—led by Henry A. Kissinger and the Anti-Defamation League (ADL)—who demanded LaRouche's scalp for his role in exposing their dirty business. The successful frameup of LaRouche is the most telling measure of the political clout of Dope, Inc. inside the United States today.

The book that you have in your hands is one of the crowning achievements of Lyndon LaRouche's campaign to rid the world of the plague of illegal narcotics. In the spring of 1978, LaRouche commissioned the editors and staff of *Executive Intelligence Review (EIR)* magazine to undertake a comprehensive investigation of the international dope trade. LaRouche correctly warned that, unless the United States led an international war to destroy Dope, Inc., the United States itself would be destroyed within a generation. There could be no such thing as "national security" without a serious War on Drugs, LaRouche argued.

LaRouche's words have proven prophetic. The abysmal track record of the Carter, Reagan, and Bush Administrations against the international drug cartel has created a state of affairs in which mind-destroying narcotics are defacto legalized, and where the trillions of dollars in profits from their sale are the dominant force in the international financial system. Even more to the point:

- America's inner cities have been turned into battle grounds where dope trafficking gangs often outnumber and outgun the local police. Ever since the introduction of crack cocaine onto the streets of America's cities during Christmas season 1985, drug addiction and violence have become a fact of life for all urban dwellers, even children under 10 years old;
- America's youth—from the richest communities to the poorest—have been captured by a sub-culture which glorifies drug use and in which the worship of Satan and other pagan gods is posed as a powerful alternative to the Judeo-Christian values that once guided our nation's culture and morality;
- Cocaine is the drug of choice for tens of minions of American addicts, rising from relatively limited use in 1978; and
- Virtually every country in Ibero-America is run by narco-bankers and their armed terrorist gangs, who have seized power over the dead bodies of some of the most patriotic and courageous people in the hemisphere.
- In the first edition of *Dope, Inc.* Lyndon LaRouche declared that the International Monetary Fund and World Bank were committed to

185

systematically imposing narco-economies on many nations of the developing sector as part of a conscious policy of genocide on a scale worse than that of Adolf Hitler. LaRouche identified the IMF-World Bank as being synonymous with Dope, Inc. His words have been borne out with a vengeance.

The ADL and Kissinger React

The first edition of *Dope, Inc.* was subtitled *Britain's Opium War Against the United States.* Even before the first copies rolled off the press in December 1978, leaders of the international narcotics cartel were busy trying to stop LaRouche. Beginning in summer 1978, the Anti-Defamation League of B'nai B'rith (ADL) (which we have nicknamed the "American Dope Lobby" for reasons made clear in our text) launched a multimillion-dollar campaign to smear LaRouche and his political associates as "anti-Semites" for daring to expose the involvement of gangsters like Meyer Lansky and Zionist Lobby leaders like Edgar Bronfman and Max Fisher in the dope business. The fact that LaRouche also identified the powerful British Crown bankers and as partners in the dope trade along with the Jewish crime Syndicate marked him as one of the most dangerous men alive in the eyes of Dope, Inc.

The intensity of the ADL's "anti-Semitic" smear campaign against LaRouche struck us as remarkable, particularly since LaRouche, recognized expert in physical economy, is known internationally through dozens of books and articles, exposing the fascist economic austerity policies at the heart of Nazi genocide. The ADL's insistent slanders prompted *EIR* to dig deeper into the organization's history.

What we found was a 70-year legacy of ADL collusion with Jewish gangsters, from Meyer Lansky and his Our Crowd sponsor Arnold Rothstein, to more contemporary Dope, Inc. figures such as Max Fisher, Edgar Bronfman, Edmond Safra, Meshulem Riklis, and the ADL's own national chairman, Kenneth Bialkin, the lawyer for the Medellin Cocaine Cartel's "American Connection," Robert

Vesco. We also discovered that much of the ADL's financial backing comes from leading families of the Anglo-American Establishment, many of whose fortuness trace back to the British banks and trading companies that ran the opium clipper ships in and out of China in the 19th century.

Given the ADL's vast links to organized crime, it was also no surprise that one of the earliest and nastiest of the ADL-commissioned slanders against LaRouche was published in *High Times* magazine, the unofficial house organ of the dope lobby in America. That article was run under the revealing headline: "This Man Wants To Take Your Drugs Away!"

To this day, the ADL holds the key to the corruption of the American political and judicial system, a corruption that was bought and paid for by the proceeds of the international dope trade. In that sense, the railroading of Lyndon LaRouche was underwritten by drug money, and carried out by government officials and private agencies on the pad of Dope, Inc. . .

By the summer of 1982, the ADL was joined in its Get LaRouche efforts by Henry A. Kissinger, former Secretary of State and recipient of the ADL's Man of the Year Award. Kissinger launched a personal vendetta to get the Federal government to shut down the LaRouche movement.

Although Kissinger has been historically a close ally of the most rabid factions inside Israel and within the Zionist Establishment in the United States, his primary allegiance throughout his political career has been to the British Crown and its intelligence and financial agencies.

This is not a matter of speculation. On May 10, 1982, addressing a celebration at the London Royal Institute for International Affairs (RIIA) at Chatham House in London, Kissinger boasted that throughout his career in the Nixon and Ford Administrations, he had always been closer to the British Foreign Office than to his own American colleagues, and had taken all his major policy leads from London. Kissinger put his money where his mouth is by founding the international "consulting firm," Kissinger Associates, in partnership with Britain's Lord Carrington shortly after he delivered that Chatham House lecture.

Chatham House is a successor to the old British East India Company, and serves as the think tank and foreign intelligence arm of the British Crown. The roots of Chatham House, as we shall see in the chapters that follow, are to be found in Britain's 19th-century Opium War policy.

Kissinger himself is no stranger to the world of international dope trafficking. Kissinger, as first exposed in the original 1978 edition of *Dope, Inc.,* played a pivotal role in covering up the involvement of the Peoples Republic of China in Southeast Asia's Golden Triangle heroin trade back in the early 1970s when he was shuttling between Washington and Beijing playing the so-called "China Card." Tens of thousands of American GIs who became addicted to drugs in Southeast Asia during the Vietnam War can hold Kissinger at least partially responsible for their dope habits. Later, during the 1980s, through Kissinger Associates, Henry became a business partner of some of the very same Chinese opium lords he protected from American drug enforcement for over a decade.

Right after his Chatham House speech, Kissinger threw himself into the effort to railroad Lyndon LaRouche.

Kissinger was furious that LaRouche and his associates widely circulated the official text of his Chatham House speech to document that Kissinger was a loyal asset of the British Crown. He went head-to-head with LaRouche over Reagan Administration policy. A major battle had broken out within the Administration over the emerging Latin American debt crisis, a crisis of which LaRouche had been warning senior White House officials for months. A confrontation evolved between LaRouche and Kissinger over whether Washington would negotiate an equitable solution to the debt crisis, on a government-to-government basis, or back International Monetary Fund policies aimed at further looting our hemispheric neighbors. These events formed the backdrop for Kissinger's personal role in the railroading of LaRouche.

A paper trail of personal letters from Kissinger to then-FBI Director William Webster during the summer and autumn of 1982 documents Kissinger's role.

On Aug. 19, 1982, Henry Kissinger wrote the now-infamous "Dear Bill" letter to Webster, demanding action against the LaRouche movement: "Because these people have been getting increasingly obnoxious, I have taken the liberty of asking my lawyer, Bill Rogers, to get in touch with you and ask your advice, especially with respect to security. It was good seeing you at the Grove[1] . . . warm regards."

Kissinger's own efforts, aided by the ADL's so-called Civil Rights Division, were augmented in January 1983 by a Kissinger-solicited intervention on the part of several members of President Ronald Reagan's Foreign Intelligence Advisory Board (PFIAB), led by Edward Bennett Williams, David Abshire and Leo Cherne. The PFIAB members demanded that the FBI launch an international investigation of Lyndon LaRouche, in effect claiming that LaRouche's expose of Kissinger's record of selling out the United States to British, Soviet and Dope, Inc. interests was somehow "subversive."

Government documents catalogue the role of Kissinger's PFIAB cronies. A memorandum from FBI Director Webster to his chief deputy Oliver Revell dated January 12, 1983 stated in part:

"At the PFIAB meeting today, [name redacted] raised the subject of the activities of the U.S. Labor Party and Lyndon LaRouche. He noted that he and a number of other Americans in public life had been the subject of repeated harassment by LaRouche and wondered whether the FBI had a basis for investigating these activities under the guidelines or otherwise. A number of members present, including the now-deceased Edward Bennett Williams, raised the question of the sources for these U.S. Labor Party activities. In view of the large amounts obviously being expended worldwide, the question was raised whether the U.S. Labor Party might be funded by hostile intelligence agencies."

The PFIAB inquiry led in early 1983 to the opening of a formal FBI investigation into Lyndon LaRouche and his associates. That inquiry provided the legal cover for an all out offensive to drive LaRouche and his associates out of business and into prison. The "guidelines" under which the unconstitutional Get LaRouche campaign was conducted were contained in a little-known White House document,

Executive Order 12333, signed by President Reagan in December 1981. E.O. 12333 gave the FBI and U.S. intelligence agencies a broad mandate to spy on and conduct covert actions against American citizens deemed to be opponents of the incumbent Administration. E.O. 12333 also allowed these agencies to use private citizens as their agents in carrying out these operations. At this point, the ADL became an integral component of the government's Get LaRouche Task Force.

Not surprisingly, the ADL and Kissinger found their most willing collaborators inside the Reagan-Bush Administration among the spooks and White House staffers involved in the illegal secret Iran-Contra program. Once again, the pawprints of Dope, Inc. were everywhere.

In the first years of the Reagan Administration, LaRouche had collaborated with several senior Administration officials in the development of the Strategic Defense Initiative and other national security policies. During the 1982-83 period, LaRouche and his colleagues had been quietly approached and asked to also cooperate with the Administration's effort to support the Contra guerrillas fighting to overthrow the Sandinista regime in Nicaragua. After studying the Central American situation, LaRouche warned the Reagan Administration that the Contra ranks were deeply penetrated by major international drug trafficking organizations and that the entire anti-Sandinista program—and the Reagan Administration's widely publicized anti-drug efforts along with it—were doomed to disastrous failure unless these drug pushers were purged from the ranks of the Contra forces. As an alternative plan of actin, LaRouche proposed the Administration focus its Central American efforts on an all-out War on Drugs which would, among other things, expose Soviet, Cuban, and Sandinista involvement in the dope trade.

By this time, with enormous pressure coming from Wall Street and the Zionist Lobby, Henry Kissinger had been named to head up the Reagan Administration's Blue Ribbon Commission on Central American Policy. Simultaneously, a one-time paid employee of the ADL, Carl Gershman, had been named as the chief of the Administration's National Endowment for Democracy (NED), a covert operations funding agency housed in the State Department's United States Information Agency. The NED was at the center of the secret support for the Contras.

For Kissinger and the ADL-led NED, dealing with cocaine traffickers was no problem. But LaRouche's public expose of leading drug traffickers on the government payroll was a problem that mandated immediate action.

A May 1986 memo from White House Irangate operator General Richard Secord to National Security Council staffer Oliver North confirms that the Contra support apparatus—what Senator David Boren labeled the "secret parallel government"—was gathering "information against LaRouche."

By the time that the Contra effort blew up in the face of the Reagan Administration, as LaRouche had warned it would, the Get LaRouche forces inside the government had built up momentum, especially inside the deeply corrupted Department of Justice and the FBI.

Two of the most zealous of the Justice Department Get LaRouche activists were William Weld and Arnold Bums. Weld was the U.S. Attorney in Boston who led the Federal government's pioneering strike force against LaRouche. He became head of the Justice Department's Criminal Division in September 1986, the number 2 spot at the DoJ. Now the governor of Massachusetts, Weld is the scion of a prominent blue blood family that made its fortune in the China opium trade.

Arnold Burns, the Deputy Attorney General, was a director of the ADL's Sterling National Bank, an outfit founded by mob cronies of Meyer Lansky and implicated in hot money dealings in the United States, Italy, and Israel. Burns himself was nearly indicted in a money-laundering scheme run by Israel's secret service, the Mossad. It would later emerge that Burns's partners in that scheme were part of the Jonathan Jay Pollard Israeli-Soviet espionage ring.

In October 1986, an army of over 400 Federal and state police, accompanied helicopters, fixed-wing planes, and an armed personnel carrier, conducted a raid against the offices of several LaRouche-associated publications in Leesburg, Virginia. This was the largest domestic para-military action by the Federal government since the urban and student riots of the late 1960s and early 1970s. And the purpose was simply to execute two search warrants and make four arrests of people who had no criminal records!

Over the next several years, LaRouche and dozens of associates were arrested and put on trial. A prosecution of LaRouche and a dozen co-defendants in Boston Federal court ended in a mistrial in May 1988. The Boston jury had heard 92 days of testimony from government witnesses. The defense never got to present its case. However, the jurors, according to press accounts, were so angry at the government's behavior that, when polled they polled themselves after they had been dismissed by the judge, they voted LaRouche and the others "not guilty" on all 125 counts. One juror told the Boston Herald on May 5, 1988, that he and his colleague ey were convinced the government had committed crimes against LaRouche. LaRouche told the press that he had been defrauded of a verdict of innocent.

Six months later, the Justice Department re-indicted LaRouche in Alexandria, Virginia Federal district court, on nearly identical charges. The judge and the jury were rigged. The jury foreman, a Department of Agriculture official named Buster Horton, had been a member of a secret government task force that also included Oliver North. The judge, Albert V. Bryan, had been a business partner of the CIA's biggest secret arms dealer, Sam Cummings. In that Federal trial and at subsequent state trials in Virginia, leading officials of the ADL operated as defacto members of the government's prosecution team. In one telling incident, the ADL was caught attempting to bribe a Commonwealth of Virginia trial judge with a promise of a Supreme Court post in return for throwing the book at the LaRouche defendants.

On Jan. 27, 1989, just days after George Bush was inaugurated as President, LaRouche was deprived of bail pending appeal and thrown in Federal prison, along with six colleagues. LaRouche was sentenced to serve 15 years in prison— what amounts to a life sentence for a man already in his mid-60s. George Bush added his personal imprimatur to the jailing, by refusing to release thousands of pages of exculpatory evidence under the control of the White House. Of all of his political adversaries and critics, Lyndon LaRouche was the one man whom George Bush desperately wanted out of the way.

But the carting off of LaRouche and some of his closest colleagues to jail was not enough to satisfy the Dope, Inc. crowd. Two LaRouche-linked publications, including a twice-weekly newspaper, *New Solidarity,* with over 150,000 subscribers, and a science journal, *Fusion* magazine, with over 80,000 subscribers, were seized by the government in April 1987 and shut down in an action that Federal courts after the fact declared to have been illegal.

Patriots Can't Be Pushers Too

When Lyndon LaRouche first warned senior Reagan Administration officials about the drug cartel links of some of the leading Nicaraguan Contras, it was not yet clear just how deep the corruption ran inside the U.S. government and intelligence establishment itself. Just as the Get LaRouche efforts were steamrolling ahead, the Iran-Contra scandal began to unravel, exposing a magnitude of Dope, Inc. contamination of the Reagan-Bush Administration that is even today barely grasped by most Americans. As we shall see, the Dope, Inc. penetration of the Executive Branch was part and parcel of the U.S. government's disastrous "special relationship" with Israel.

The case of Lt. Col. Oliver North is one good example of this corruption, especially because so much media attention has been directed toward building up the image of the Marine-turned- White House super spy as a model of American patriotism.

If Oliver North is a patriot, then Robert Vesco should be hailed as one of the nation's Founding Fathers!

Evidence made public during the congressional Irangate hearings, through Federal and state court cases, and international criminal prosecutions, reveals that Oliver North was in the middle of a major international arms-for-drug trafficking operation which was run out of his National Security Council offices at the Old Executive Office Building next door to the White House.

Colonel North was the day-to-day operations officer for the Contra resupply program. But it was Vice President George Bush, the former CIA Director, who was formally in charge of the entire Reagan Administration Central America covert operations program. Under National Security Decision Directive 3, signed by Ronald Reagan in May 1982, Bush was placed in charge of two little-known White House secret committees: the Special Situation Group (SSG) and the Crisis Pre-Planning Group (CPPG). Oliver North was the secretary of the CPPG, and it was in this capacity that he ran the Central America spooks show—under George Bush.

North's personal notebooks, which catalogued most of his meetings, telephone calls, and personal observations during his White House days, betray the fact that he was well aware that the Contras were being heavily financed by Miami-based cocaine traffickers. For example, a March 26, 1985 handwritten entry in North's notebook read: "Rafael Quintero—Secord's Agent should be on shore when arrivals occur—as liason w/ APLICANO . . . Quintero . . ." Several days later, on April 3, a sequel note read: "0600—RAFAEL QUINTERO-(captured)—known narcotics trafficker—Enrique Cama[rena . . ."

Camarena was a Drug Enforcement Administration (DEA) agent in Guadalajara, Mexico who was kidnapped and tortured to death in February 1985. In 1990, Juan Ramon Mata Ballesteros, a Honduran national who helped set up Colombian cocaine routes through Mexico, was convicted along with several other men in Federal court in Los Angeles of conspiracy to kidnap and murder Camarena. At the time of the Camarena affair, Mata Ballesteros was the owner of a Honduran charter airline, SETCO Air, that was paid over half-a-million dollars by the U.S. State Department to airlift "humanitarian aid" to the Contras in a program run by Ollie North from the White House. Other funds, drawn directly from secret North-Secord bank accounts in Switzerland, were also funneled into SETCO Air.

What's worse, according to a report published in the *Washington Post* on July 5, 1990, a ranch near Vera Cruz, Mexico owned by Rafael Caro Quintero, the mastermind of the Camarena torture-murder and the head of the Mexican drug mafia, was used by the CIA to train Central American guerrillas as yet another feature of the North- White House effort. According to DEA informant Laurence Victor Harrison, the CIA used Mexico's Federal Security Directorate (DFS) "as a cover in the event any questions were raised as to who was running the training operation. Representatives of the DFS which was the front for the training camp, were in fact acting in consort with major drug overlords to ensure a flow of narcotics through Mexico into the United States."

Another North notebook entry, on August 9, 1985, removes any shadow of a doubt that Oliver North was fully aware of the Contra-cocaine connection: "Honduran DC-6 which is being used for runs out of New Orleans is probably being used for drug runs into U.S." The Honduran plane referenced by North was owned by Mata Ballesteros.

North and company were aware of the cocaine connection even earlier, according to other government records. On September 26, 1984, the Miami Police Department provided FBI Special Agent George Kiszynski with an investigative report identifying a network of Miami cocaine traffickers which was pouring money into the Contra's coffers. Within days of the report being turned over to Kiszynski, according to congressional testimony, it had been passed on to Oliver Revell, a key player in the Get LaRouche effort and North's FBI liaison for the White House Central America program.

That Miami Police Department document stated in unambiguous terms: "Frank Castro is a close associate of an individual by the name of Francisco Chanes . . . Chanes is a narcotics trafficker . . . Chanes was giving financial support to anti-Castro groups and the Nicaraguan Contra guerrillas; the monies comes from narcotic transactions . . . Frank Castro contacted Mr. Coutin to give the Legion Cubana financial support to fight the Nicaraguan Sandinista Marxist Government . . . the financial support was from drug monies."

North's indiscreet collusion with dope peddlers was not limited to Central America. In the spring of 1986, according to the congressional Irangate investigation, North, then-National Security Council advisor Robert McFarlane and other Administration officials opened a so-called "second channel" to secretly negotiate the arms-for-hostages swap with the Lebanese-based terrorists holding American hostages. That second channel was a Syrian national named Mansur Al-Kassar. A well-known international heroin, hashish, and cocaine smuggler, Al-Kassar was also implicated in a string of terrorist attacks and kidnappings in the Middle East, including the infamous *Achille Lauro* ship hijacking, in which an American citizen, Leon Klinghoffer, was killed. Al-Kassar provided arms to the Palestine Liberation Front (PLF), the group responsible for the *Achille Lauro* attack, and for years ran a mercenary kidnapping ring inside Lebanon with Abul Abbas, head of PFL. Al-Kassar also sold Soviet-made weapons to the Black September group of Abu Nidal and to the Syrian-sponsored Popular Front for the Liberation of Palestine-General Command (PFLP-GC) of Ahmed Jibril.

Al-Kassar was a black market partner of Syria's Vice President Rifat Assad, the brother of President Hafez Assad. In 1986, Spanish authorities obtained photographs of Al-Kassar and Rifat Assad meeting in the city of Marbella with Medellin Cartel boss Pablo Escobar Gaviria. The purpose of the meeting was to establish expanded cocaine trafficking operations in continental Europe. Al-Kassar, throughout this period, was identified in Central Intelligence Agency files as a Soviet KGB agent who had been a leading smuggler of Soviet bloc arms into the West.

None of this dissuaded North and company from bringing Al-Kassar into the White House "Enterprise." He never succeeded in winning the freedom of any of the hostages, but he did become one of the suppliers of Soviet bloc weapons to the Contras. In 1986, one transaction alone netted Al-Kassar $1.5 million in payments from the North-Secord Lake Resources Swiss bank accounts.

In return for these favors, Al-Kassar's drug-running and terrorist activities were protected by the National Security Council. This protection continued long after the Irangate scandal had blown up in the faces of North, Secord, CIA Director William Casey, et al. And, according to one report. Al-Kassar's cozy ties to the White House may have led to the deaths of 280 people.

On Dec. 21, 1988, just weeks before George Bush's inauguration as President, a bomb exploded aboard Pan American Airlines flight 103 above Lockerbie, Scotland. Everyone aboard the plane, and a number of people on the ground, were killed.

It is still not known exactly how the bomb was placed on board the airplane. The full story may never come out. Attorneys and investigators for the airline, as well as one U.S. Congressman, James Traficant (D-Oh.), have suggested that Mansur Al-Kassar may have been involved. Allegedly, heroin smugglers in his employ at Frankfurt International Airport placed the bomb on board flight 103, and Al-Kassar's men were protected by CIA personnel in Frankfurt as part of the hostage release deal and other features of the new "Syrian-American rapproachmont."

According to syndicated columnist Jack Anderson, in April 1989, President Bush conferred with British Prime Minister Margaret Thatcher and the two ordered British and American intelligence to cover up Al-Kassar's alleged involvement in the Lockerbie bombing. Whether Anderson's charges are true or not, the truth about the Lockerbie massacre has been completely covered up, as has the role of Syria in the flourishing multi-billion dollar Middle East heroin and hashish trade.

One reason for the coverup is that the use of Middle Eastern dope-smuggling networks was as pervasive a feature of the Reagan-Bush era Irangate shenanigans as was the hiring of Colombian cocaine cartel pilots and money washers to supply the Contras. In fact, the Colombian and Middle Eastern dope connections have one recurring common denominator: a very prominent Israeli component.

During the very month—April 1989—that President Bush and Prime Minister Thatcher were allegedly ordering a coverup of the Pan Am 103 bombing, a Drug Enforcement Administration and U.S. Customs Service report was surfaced in the media that New York's Republic National Bank was serving as a money-laundering facility for Middle East and Latin American narcotics-trafficking organizations. Republic National Bank is owned by Edmond Safra, a prominent Jewish banker of Lebanese descent whose worldwide banking operations extend from Aleppo, Syria and to Rio de Janiero, Brazil to midtown Manhattan.

According to a 13-page memo written by DEA agents in Berne, Switzerland and dated January 3, 1989, Safra and Republic National Bank were implicated in a Swiss-centered drug-money-laundering network run out of the Zurich-based Shakarchi Trading Co. U.S. investigators linked Shakarchi to a heroin-smuggling ring that enjoyed the cooperation of the Bulgarian secret police and the state-owned export-import agency, Globus (formerly called Kintex). An earlier DEA report had implicated Kintex's director in the attempted assassination of Pope John Paul II by Ali Mehmet Agca in May 1981. Kintex was identified as the hub of the "Bulgarian Connection" international drug-smuggling network. We provide an inside look at this Soviet-Bulgarian dope ring in a chapter that follows. For now, it is sufficient to note the following:

According to the January 1989 DEA memo, "The Shakarchi Trading Company of Zurich, Switzerland operates as a currency exchange company and is utilized by some of the world's largest drug trafficking organizations to launder the proceeds of their drug trafficking activities . . . Shakarchi Trading Company maintains accounts at the Republic National Bank of New York, a bank which has surfaced in several previous money laundering investigations . . . While he was alive Mahmoud Shakarchi maintained a close relationship with Edmond Safra and the banking institutions in which Safra had an interest, including Republic National Bank. Since the death of Mahmoud Shakarchi, Mohammed Shakarchi doing business as Shakarchi Trading Company has maintained close ties with the Republic National Bank."

"Close ties" is an understatement!

DEA and U.S. Customs investigators tracing the flow of heroin revenues from Lebanon through Turkey and Bulgaria on to the Shakarchi firm in Zurich found that millions of dollars made their way into Account No. 606347712 at the main New York City branch of Republic National Bank. Meanwhile, DEA agents in Colombia and on the West Coast busted up the largest Medellin Cartel cocaine money-laundering scheme ever unearthed as part of the DEA's Operation Polar Cap. Known as La Mina (The Mine), the money-washing circuit involved a string of banks in Colombia and Uruguay and a Los Angeles jewelry wholesale company called Ropex. Millions of dollars in Ropex deposits were traced by the Polar Cap team to Account No. 606347712 at Republic National Bank—the same Shakarchi Trading Co. account!

Not surprisingly, in 1989, as the Shakarchi-Safra story was grabbing headlines in Europe and the United States" banker Safra was donating a reported $1 million to his favorite charity—the Anti-Defamation League!

Banker Safra's ties to the Dope, Inc. money washery go back to at least the mid-1970s, when Republic National Bank sheparded Argentine wheeler-dealer David Gravier into the inner sanctums of Wall Street. Gravier bought up American Bank and Trust in 1975, and in less than a year looted the New York bank of an estimated $40 million. Gravier conveniently "died" in a plane crash in Mexico just as bank regulators discovered that American Bank and Trust's cupboard was bare during an audit of the bank. There was such skepticism over Gravier's disappearance that for years, New York State prosecutors continued to list Gravier as a defendant in the bank fraud case.

Of course, Gravier was simply a front man for a Swiss-based Mossad money-laundering network known as the Cen-trade Group, one of whose leading figures, Tibor Rosenbaum, is profiled at length elsewhere in this book. The point is that for the past 20 years, a large and growing component of Dope, Inc. has been the combined machinery of gangster Meyer Lansky and the Israeli Mossad.

If there were any doubt about the pivotal role played by shady elements within the Israeli intelligence services in the world dope-for-guns bazaar, it was shattered in a hail of bullets in desolate corner of Colombia on Dec. 15, 1989.

On that date, Colombian Army units invaded the compound of Medellin Cartel capo Jose Gonzalo Rodriguez Gacha near the town of Pacho. In the shootout, Gacha and several of his bodyguards were killed. On Jan. 24 and 28, in followup raids on two other ranches owned by Gacha, the army seized large stockpiles of weapons—all of which were made in Israel.

The discovery of the Israeli weapons caches prompted the Colombian government to make a formal inquiry to Tel Aviv: To whom had those particular weapons been sold? The answer came back from the Israeli Defense Ministry: The guns had been sold to the government of the tiny Caribbean island nation of Antigua, in a deal brokered by an Israeli national named Maurice Sarfati. According to the original Israeli version, Sarfati, a resident of Antigua who ostensibly owned a melon farm, had brokered the deal for the Antiguan "national security advisor" —a non-existent post.

Many months and cover stories later, at least a semblance of the truth came out. Israeli intelligence—through a string of front companies—had been providing weapons and terrorist training to the Medellin Cartel's assassination squads. And the entire program had the blessing of senior officials in the Reagan Administration and the CIA.

Among the casualties racked up to the marriage of the cocaine cartel to Israeli intelligence were thousands of innocent Colombian nationals who were victims of cartel gunmen and bombers. During one particular bloody week in June 1990, according to Colombian government reports, over 640 people died violent deaths, the vast majority at the hands of the cartel. In one November 1989 airline bombing that has been linked to Israeli-trained cartel terrorists, 117 people perished. One of the guns provided by the Israeli arms merchants was used in August 1989 to assassinate Colombia's frontrunning presidential candidate, Luis Carlos Galan. Had he survived the armed assault against his campaign rally, Galan would have surely been elected President of Colombia, and he would have pursued an anti-drug policy dramatically in contrast to the total capitulation that has occurred as the result of his murder.

The trainer of Gacha's killer squads was a reserve Israeli Army Colonel named Yair Klein. His company, Spearhead, Ltd. (Hod Hahanit in Hebrew), set up shop in Colombia sometime in the late 1980s. Shortly after the Medellin Cartel assassins school got going, Klein was brought into a sensitive covert action program being run by the Reagan-Bush Administration: the plot to overthrow Panama's General Antonio Manuel Noriega. In 1988, Klein was brought to Miami for a series of secret meetings with Colonel Eduardo Herrera, the recently dumped Panamanian ambassador to Israel. After getting the boot from the Tel Aviv assignment, Colonel Herrera had been relocated to Florida, and put on the CIA's payroll. Colonel Klein was assigned to work with Herrera on a plan to create a Panamanian "Contra" force that would be sponsored by the United States to oust the Panamanian general who had become a thorn in the side of George Bush.

On behalf of this secret project, Klein visited Antigua in early 1989 to solicit permission from the local authorities to establish a "VIP security guard" training academy. Sarfati, a longstanding Mossad operator who had setup so-called melon farms on a string of Caribbean islands as fronts for Israeli shenanigans, made all the right contacts for Klein.

According to Colonel Clyde Walker, who was at the time the chief of Antigua's tiny national defense force, following his meeting with Colonel Klein and Sarfati in January 1989, he made formal inquiries with U.S. CIA officials in charge of the eastern Caribbean. They gave Spearhead and all its personnel a clean bill of health.

In spite of that CIA green light, the powers that be on Antigua decided in March 1989 not to approve Klein's request for the training school.

At that very moment, a shipload of Israeli arms were steaming across the Atlantic on board the Danish- flagged ship *Else TH*. On April 24, 1989, the arms were transferred at the Antigua port onto a Panama registered ship, *Sea Point*, and shuttled off to the waiting Rodriguez Gacha in Colombia. A similar shipment of arms bound for Contra rebels and Peruvian leftist guerrrillas had been seized by General Noriega in 1985 from another Danish-flagged vessel, the *Pia Vesta*—an action that went a long way toward putting the Panamanian Defense Forces chief on the Reagan-Bush team's enemies list.

The money to purchase the 1989 weapons shipment had come from a U.S. State Department-administered account under the control of Elliott Abrams, a major Iran-Contra player who ran the department's Latin American division. The escrow deposit to insure that the hundreds of guns left Israel on time had come through the Miami branch of the Israeli Bank Hapoalim.

If there was any doubt that the arming of the Medellin Cartel hit squads was part and parcel of the same mischief program that also included the December 1989 B.S. invasion of Panama and overthrow of General Noriega, consider the following:

After the smoke cleared in Panama, thousands of dead bodies and billions of dollars in bombed-out property later, the Bush Administration succeeded in installing into the presidency a local Panamanian lawyer, Guillermo "Porky" Endara. A review of court records shows that "President" Endara and several of his law partners were the owners of record of the ship *Sea Point* in April 1989 when the ship had delivered the Israeli weapons to Rodriguez Gacha! They still owned the ship in late 1989, when it was stopped off the coast of Mexico and busted for carrying a masive shipment of cocaine. For good measure, over half of the crew members busted by the Mexican authorities were also on board when the gun delivery was made to the Medellin Cartel. Back on dry land in Panama City, Endara was the co-owner, along with Rodriguez Gacha, of the narco-dollar laundering Banco Interoceanico.

When the lid blew on the Mossad-Medellin connection in early 1990, the Israeli government scrambled to deny that Klein was on "official business" when he trained and armed the narco-terrorists. Unfortunately, Klein had been not only linked to Sarfati in his Caribbean adventures. Back in Miami, Klein's Spearhead, Ltd. had been managed by two rather important Israeli operatives, General Pinchas Sachar and Pesach Ben-Or. Both men were officially designated representatives of the Israeli government's Israeli Military Industry (IMI), and it was Sachar's account at the Bank Hapoalim that had received the funds from Elliott Abrams to purchase the guns routed to Colombia.

Pesach Ben-Or had been installed back during the Carter Administration as the Mossad's principal arms merchant in Guatemala City, a hub of later Contra supply action. According to eyewitness accounts, Carter's National Security advisor Zbigniew Brzezinski quietly informed the Guatemalan junta in 1978—after Carter shut down all American military aid to the country over alleged human rights violations—that Ben-Or would fill all their arms and military training requirements—with the secret blessing of Washington. Ben-Or did just that—at a 600 percent markup. A decade later, Ben-Or was still wheeling and dealing with Guatemala—out of offices he shared in Miami with General Sachar and Colonel Klein.

The CIA-Mossad and Dope, Inc.

The Brzezinski wink-and-nod deal with the Guatemalans backdates U.S.-sanctioned Israeli dirty dealings in Central America to the late 1970s. According to a controversial U.S. Army document, the CIA and the Mossad were carrying out joint cocaine-smuggling ventures even earlier.

A March 1980 affidavit signed by Colonel Edward P. Cutolo, a highly decorated Green Beret commander, suggests that, between December 1975 and March 1976, over 70 undetected cargo flights took place between Colombia and the Albrook Air Station in Panama City. U.S. Special Forces personnel on loan to the CIA were covertly infiltrated into Colombia to man beacon towers that enabled the planes to fly undetected by the Colombian radar.

The project was code-named Operation Watch Tower. The 70 cargo planes, according to the Cutolo affidavit, were loaded with cocaine. Cutolo, who died in a mysterious car crash in England shortly after he signed the affidavit, said that the Colombia-Panama cocaine flights were jointly run by the CIA and the Israeli Mossad. Two CIA men and two Mossad agents were on the ground at Albrook Air Station overseeing the offloading of the cocaine, according to the affidavit.

The U.S. government has denied that Operation Watch Tower ever "officially" took place. They may be right. Some have suggested that the cocaine flights were one of the earliest of the intelligence operations conducted behind the backs of higher-ups. Others have attempted to discredit the Cutolo affidavit altogether, labeling it a forgery.

However, a half-dozen senior Green Beret officers who were close with Cutolo and helped investigate Operation Watch Tower before and after Cutolo's death, also died in a string of mysterious "accidents" and murders over a ten year period. A National Security Agency (NSA) officer who also probed the Cutolo allegations became convinced that the cocaine flights actually occurred. He too died before he could prove the story, although he apparently died of natural causes.

Today, Col. Bo Gritz, one of America's most decorated war heroes, continues to probe the Watch Tower story. In a widely circulating video report, Gritz links the CIA-Mossad Central America cocaine expeditions to some of the same CIA people who jumped on the heroin bandwagon in Southeast Asia during the closing years of the American involvement in Vietnam. Some of the people involved in the CIA's counterinsurgency programs in Southeast Asia and who are named in Operation Watch Tower documents—such as CIA official Thomas Clines and Mossad operator David Kimche—would later emerge during the Reagan-Bush Era as principal players in the Iran-Contra fiasco.

Who was CIA director at the time that the Operation Watch Tower cocaine flights were allegedly taking place? None other than George Bush.

Why a Third Edition of This Book Now

Back in 1978, when the first edition of this book was issued, the United States had not yet been fully captured by Dope, Inc. At the time, we warned you that the United States was the target of a new Opium War, and that you, your children, and your grandchildren would not survive unless this invasion were defeated.

You chose to sit back and allow it to happen. The first chapters of this Third Edition will make clear that the consequences of letting your elected officials sit on their hands as Dope, Inc. ransacked the American economy and took over the streets and schoolyards by force, is that the illegal drug trade is doubling every five years, and marijuana has replaced grain, meat, fruit, vegetables and poultry as the number one cash crop in most states in the United States. The United States is in the throes of a second Great Depression of this century, largely because you chose to abrogate your responsibilities as citizens when Dope, Inc. invaded and seized all the levers of power in Washington and on Wall Street.

This third edition of *Dope, Inc.*—like the previous two editions—is intended to be a military manual, providing you with the ammunition to understand the nature of enemy beast that you must defeat.

Most of the text of the book in your hands is identical to that of the Second Edition. A few details of the command structure of Dope, Inc. have changed over the past six years, and we have reported these changes. Where it seemed especially appropriate, we made some additions and updated some of the information.

Some of the findings that were even considered "extreme" or "exaggerated" in 1986 are by now so universally recognized that they are considered truisms today. Bear that in mind as you read through the text.

And pay special attention to the Fourteen Point War on Drugs platform of Lyndon LaRouche which is included as an appendix to this volume. That war plan was issued in March 1985. It is as valid an approach to fighting and winning the War on Drugs today as it was back then. The only missing ingredient is you—the American citizen who must force the issue onto the policy table in Washington and do whatever else is necessary. There are no alternatives. No one else will do it for you. Are you ready to act?

6. Our Enemies Proved Us Right: Why Dope, Inc. Became Famous

Our Enemies Proved Us Right

1. Why This Book Has Become Famous

When the first edition of *Dope, Inc.* made its appearance in December 1978, it sent shock waves through the international capitals of organized crime—from London to Moscow, from Geneva to Boston and Lower Manhattan, from Tel Aviv to Milan, Sofia, and Montreal. More than seven years later, the multinational narcotics cartel is still desperately scrambling to cover up the truth our book exposed. But fortunately, while several government agencies were confirming the reality of our charges for themselves, the enemy's furious response to the 100,000-copy circulation of the first edition of *Dope, Inc.,* produced much new evidence, implicating a broader net of powerful international figures.

In the spring of 1978, Lyndon LaRouche had commissioned the original investigation which led to publication of *Dope, Inc.,* on the basis of his conviction that unless the U.S. government and the American people moved quickly to crush the international drug mafia, the United States would, within a generation, cease to exist as a nation, and, with its collapse, Western civilization would fall into a new dark age.

The book was conceived as a military intelligence report, a first step toward launching a full-scale war on drugs, employing all of the military, technological, and moral resources which the Allied nations employed in World War II to defeat Nazism. That is still our aim. By the mid-1980s, although the Reagan administration had adopted the phrase "war on drugs" as a slogan, the most energetic battles in the war LaRouche had proposed were being fought in Ibero-America, by such nations as President Alan García's Peru and President Belisario Betancur's Colombia—with scant aid from the U.S.A. On March 9, 1985, LaRouche presented to a Mexico City conference a battle plan for a hemispheric war on drugs that would bring the U.S. armed forces into the fight. The LaRouche plan is published as Appendix A in this book. On March 3, 1986, the President's Commission on Organized Crime recommended to Ronald Reagan: "The Joint Chiefs should be instructed by the highest levels of government . . . that hostile or destructive action from within or without—overt or covert—shall include the . . . invasion of this country by drug smugglers." This conclusion is bitterly opposed by the FBI and the corruption-riddled U.S. Justice Department presided over by Attorney General Edwin Meese, and the go-ahead for the U.S. military's participation in the war on drugs has not been given.

The battle terrain of the drug wars has shifted significantly in the intervening years since the first publication of *Dope, Inc.*

In 1978, the Carter administration was championing the decriminalization and legalization of marijuana and cocaine. "Recreational" drug abuse was being touted as a "victimless crime." Today, with every population group victimized by the dope trade—congressmen, junior high school students, industrial workers, housewives, professional athletes, Wall Street businessmen—such claims of "victimless crime" ring increasingly hollow.

When *Dope, Inc.* was first published, the Latin American "cocaine bonanza" that would open a new, ugly chapter in the annals of organized crime, and boost the annual revenues of Dope, Inc. toward the half-trillion-dollar level, was still a year or two in the future. Indeed, in 1978, Carlos Lehder Rivas, the kingpin of today's Colombian narcoterrorist rebellion and an avowed collaborator of the murderous M-19 terrorist army, was just getting out of jail in Miami on car theft and marijuana charges, and was only first establishing contact with Dope, Inc. financier Robert Vesco.

The concept of narcoterrorism—first elaborated in the first edition of *Dope, Inc.*—was scoffed at in intelligence and law enforcement circles, where images of Sicilian mafia "moustache Petes" and leftist Robin Hoods still blocked officials from discerning a single worldwide underground economy servicing the illegal arms and drug trade. Revelations growing out of the attempted assassination of Pope John Paul II in May 1981 began to open the eyes of a few, particularly with respect to the active role of the Soviet KGB.

With the Soviet invasion of Afghanistan in 1979, the international heroin trade, centered in the Golden Triangle of Southeast Asia where it had operated so successfully during the Vietnam War, began to diversify and expand rapidly in Soviet-occupied Afghanistan and neighboring Pakistan. The coming to power of "Islamic fundamentalism" in Ayatollah Khomeini's Iran, under the auspices of Soviet specialist G. A. Aliyev, together with Soviet-British fostering of separatist insurgencies such as the Sikh "Khalistan," turned southwest Asia into a "Golden Crescent" for Dope, Inc. rivalling the Far East.

In this new edition of *Dope, Inc.*, we have taken account of the changed landscape, by adding new sections on the dope cartel's command structure, the drug traffic in Ibero-America and Southwest Asia, and the major role of the worldwide Soviet Empire.

In one respect, however, the story of *Dope, Inc.* is the same today as it was seven years ago—the unparalleled corruption of so many of the world's "respectable" financial institutions. Since its original publication, this, the central charge leveled in *Dope, Inc.*, has been massively re-documented by official sources—and by the drug bankers of Dope, Inc. themselves, whose uncontrolled and savage attacks on us have demonstrated repeatedly that they regard our efforts as the most serious threat to their continued existence.

'Apocalyptic Vision' or Everyday Reality?

The idea that some of the world's leading private financial institutions were deeply implicated in the witting laundering of hundreds of billions of dollars a year in illegal dope money was seen as the single most shocking fact brought to light with the first release of *Dope, Inc.* We demonstrated that dope was the largest commodity in international trade, with the exception of petroleum, and that the annual revenues of the narcotics traffic exceeded the national product of most of the world's nations, and the revenues of the largest multinational companies.

The American weekly magazine *Saturday Review* described our view as "a truly apocalyptic vision." The intervening years and their unbroken string of revelations have shown that the apocalypse is here. After the November 1984 publication of the report on money laundering of the President's Commission on Organized Crime, the March 1983 report of the Permanent Investigations Subcommittee of the U.S. Senate, and countless congressional hearings on the subject of banks and money-laundering, the core contents of *Dope, Inc.*'s first edition have been restated by official sources.

Among the earliest confirmation for *Dope, Inc.*'s charges came from New York State's banking superintendent: On the basis of evidence presented by its authors, this regulatory body refused to permit the Hongkong and Shanghai Banking Corporation to purchase control of New York's Marine Midland Bank in 1979, delaying what was, until then, the largest foreign takeover plan in American banking history.

The superintendent, Muriel Siebert, demanded detailed accounting of the HongShang's hidden profits, silent subsidiaries, and other paraphernalia of money laundering, and refused its application when the Hong Kong institution predictably refused. HongShang was compelled to employ a subterfuge—ultimately sanctioned by Paul Volcker's Federal Reserve Board—in order to consummate the takeover: it arranged for Marine Midland Bank, one of America's largest, to change its status from a state-chartered to a nationally chartered bank, in order to circumvent the regulatory powers of New York State. The Federal Reserve threw out the rule books and accepted the takeover of Marine Midland in early 1980, preferring to ignore the law and the banking regulator of America's financial center, New York State, rather than jeopardize the plans of Dope, Inc.

In 1978, we asked, "How is it possible that $200 billion and up in dirty money, crisscrossing international borders, can remain outside the control of the law? Again, only one possible answer can be admitted: a huge chunk of international banking and related financial operations have been created solely to manage dirty money. More than that, this chunk of international banking enjoys the sovereign protection of more than a few governments."

Half a decade ago, the charge seemed adventurous to many. Measure it against the conclusions of the study entitled, "Crime and Secrecy: The Use of Offshore

Banks and Companies," issued by the Permanent Investigations Subcommittee of the U.S. Senate in March 1983 after two years of investigations. The investigators estimated the illegal economy of the United States at up to 10% of reported Gross National Product, or over $300 billion. The study reported that London is the leading center worldwide for the concealment of funds, a charge first made in *Dope, Inc.;* that two-fifths of all foreign banking activities conducted out of Switzerland are performed with other offshore centers, Switzerland being the center for the practice of "layering" secret financial accounts so that beneficial ownership is impossible to determine.

We had subtitled the 1978 work, "Britain's Opium War Against the United States." The Senate investigators went to London to ask for British cooperation in dismantling criminal activities in the offshore centers, and complained that British officials rejected the proposal out of hand, asserting for the record that organized crime was an internal American problem and no concern of London's. The British told the Senate investigators:

"As London sees it, the crime problem for the most part rests with the U.S., for whether it is drug money or other fraud it derives primarily from U.S. sources, i.e., criminal transactions in the U.S., and is processed offshore on behalf of American citizens and companies. It is argued by London that control efforts will incur only costs but no benefits. Given these conditions, whatever the U.S. policy, it behooves the U.K. not to involve itself collaboratively."

The SPIS study summarizes the charges of American prosecutors against Swiss, British, and Canadian banks during the preceding several years, with multiple mention of the three big Swiss banks, Britain's largest commercial bank, Barclays, Canada's Bank of Nova Scotia, as well as offshore divisions of American banks. Referring to the Bank of Nova Scotia, nestled into the coziest reaches of the British establishment, the SPIS report complains, "For example, in the Caribbean, one major Canadian international bank has a consistent reputation for encouraging dirty money . . . . Senior bank officials describe instances where headquarters banks have removed competent offshore managers for their failures . . . to optimize profits through corrupt relationships."

Not merely in the specifics, but in the scope of its conclusions, the Senate report corroborated the most controversial judgments we offered in 1978. We had argued that a large part of the world banking structure had come to exist in order to handle dirty offshore-money flows. The SPIS report concluded that illegal financial operations are now so closely meshed with the offshore banking system in general that the movement of illegal funds may constitute a threat to the security of the world banking system as a whole. Citing the case of the 1982 bankruptcy of Banco Ambrosiano, Roberto Calvi's ill-fated vehicle for dirty political and financial operations, SPIS wrote:

"In 1982, Banco Ambrosiano of Milan, Italy, collapsed, crippled by a $1.4 billion exposure in loans to several mysterious Panamanian "shell" companies . . . . The Euromarket is a critically important . . . feature of international commerce. But in the haven countries where money is laundered, it is unregulated. Thus, the same conditions which facilitate international commerce also create criminal opportunites. The criminal use of offshore facilities poses a problem to the stability of entire national banking systems. The fragile condition of the world's banking system today is a result in part of questionable loans, poor controls and the country risk occurring when so many nations cannot pay the interest or principal on their debt. It is not inconceivable that it could be a criminally derived loss, not the failure of repayment of a loan from a sovereign nation, which could be the back-breaking straw to the banking system."

As we will report below, the Senate committee's specific concern in the case of Calvi's Banco Ambrosiano was not merely conjectural. When the financing of the American banking system derives from international flight capital, it is no exaggeration to state that the vagaries of the financial underworld may determine the fate of the entire world banking system.

By October 1984, the role of some of Boston and New York's most prestigious commercial banks and investment houses in washing drug money had become such a public scandal that the Reagan administration drafted model legislation allowing for criminal prosecution of bank corporate executives. And the President's Commission on Organized Crime, a blue ribbon panel established by Ronald Reagan by Executive Order 12435 on July 23, 1983, devoted the entirety of its first published report to "The Cash Connection: Organized Crime, Financial Institutions, and Money Laundering." Among the big league financial houses cited in the commission's report for washing hot money were Chemical Bank, Merrill Lynch, Chase Manhattan Bank, and Deak-Perrera.

When the President's Commission on Organized Crime released its report, the bag of tricks of the narcotics traffic was put on display, at least the best known of them: the use of casinos to launder drug money, the corruption and virtual takeover of banks, the participation of such august firms as E.F. Hutton (which sent security guards to the Waldorf-Astoria Hotel to help a Colombian client bring suitcases full of cash to its offices, and then tipped off its client when informed that he was under investigation as a money-launderer for Colombian cocaine-traffickers).

This corroboration of our original conclusions would be a greater consolation were it not for the continued, massive expansion of narcotics traffic and dirty-money networks. With the consumption of $75 billion per year of cocaine in the United States alone, and the rapid growth of heroin addiction in Western Europe, our original estimate of $100 billion per annum in narcotics sales in the United States and $200 billion worldwide is dwarfed by the present reality. Narcotics traffic grosses a minimum of $200 billion per year in the United States and $500 billion worldwide, and the associated illegal traffic in arms, contraband, and so forth has grown in proportion.

For the first time, the nations of Ibero-America are fighting openly, in their national parliaments and their international gatherings, for their sovereignty, against the professed allies of the narcotics mafias, who dare to openly challenge the power of duly-constituted legal governments. In Colombia, where former president Alfonso López Michelsen has bragged of meeting with the narcotics mafia and advised the government to accept their terms, the narcoterrorist M

-19 has carried out an armed attack on the Justice Ministry, taking hostage and then murdering 11 Supreme Court justices. In Peru, President Alan García has conducted an all-out war on the drug traffickers, but the terrorist guerrillas of Sendero Luminoso have repeatedly crippled the electrical power supplies of major cities, and murdered officials and burned homes in countryside. The Andean Pact countries have been plunged into the same type of inconclusive warfare which has plagued Southeast Asia—the opium region called the "Golden Triangle"—since the middle 1960s, where well-armed and well-organized military bands have exerted control over the territory where the poppy is planted.

Despite President Reagan's promise of a war on drugs, despite the heroic efforts of the Italian police against the Sicilian mafia, despite the destruction of the Calvi gang in Italian freemasonry, despite the mopping-up of money-laundering operations of Florida banks—despite all of this, the international network we called Dope, Incorporated has not merely flourished; it has risen to commanding heights in the world economy. The International Monetary Fund shamelessly does its bidding among the debtor nations of the developing sector.

In June 1983, the International Monetary Fund made its first published comment on the subject, in an appendix buried in its World Economic Outlook report. In its bland, malevolent way, the IMF noted that about $200 billion per year was disappearing from the accounts of national governments who report their balance-of-payments data to the international financial organization. This is referred to in the arcane interchanges of governmental accounts as the "statistical discrepancy in the global current account payments balance." It represents the difference between all countries' surpluses and deficits once they are totaled up. In theory, one country's deficit must be another country's surplus. By 1982, however, the total excess of deficits over surpluses had risen to $89 billion. If all the discrepancies between countries' payments and receipts on current account were totaled up individually, rather than aggregated on a global basis, the total for 1982 would be in the range of $200 billion—representing almost one-fifth of world trade. In other words, the net deficit reported by all countries is $89 billion; the funds not accounted for by all countries is almost $200 billion. Since 1973, the IMF added, the total volume of such discrepancies has accumulated to the fantastic sum of $800 billion.

This is no surprise to the Ibero-American nations hit by waves of flight capital during 1982 and 1983. What the gross numbers state is that the movements of international capital are out of the hands of governments entirely; governments can no longer even identify $200 billion per year in capital flows, much less attempt to influence them!

The IMF report leaves little to the imagination: The origin of the "statistical discrepancy" is international flight capital and related illegal money flows. The 1983 document states:

"The principal factor accounting for the growth of the world payments asymmetry on current account has been the fairly rapid increase in the negative balance on invisibles. After being approximately balanced in 1973, estimated payments and receipts for services and private transfers have diverged progressively more widely in subsequent years, and the excess of recorded payments over receipts in these accounts reached some $800 billion in 1982."

The IMF reports directly that the "invisibles" which account for the "statistical discrepancy," i.e. "shipment," "reinvested earnings," and "other earned income," boil down to flight capital:

"The most readily identifiable part of this large excess of debits over credits is that rooted in the Services provided by fleets flying so-called flags of convenience. The payments for services of these fleets are, for the most part, duly recorded in the balance of payments statistics of the countries using such services. The corresponding credits, on the other hand, are typically not entered in any country's balance of payments," that is, they enter the banking system illegally.

The IMF, the supposed lawgiver of international finance, explains that international finance is now lawless.

The implications of these admissions are breathtaking. After ruining the economies and undermining the political stability of most of Ibero-America, as well as Nigeria, the Philippines, and numerous other nations of the developing sector, the International Monetary Fund admits that the provocation for its actions—the mass exit of capital and associated burgeoning of foreign debt of the victim countries—is out of the victim countries' control. Indeed, according to the IMF, it is out of the control of any national government.

Dope, Inc. Answers the Charges

Long before the law enforcement and intelligence services of the Western nations responded to the challenge posed by the publication of Dope, Inc., the dope cartel itself issued its response. Lyndon LaRouche and his closest associates became the immediate targets of a brutal campaign of libels, attempted murders, kidnappings, and, eventually, an attack by elements of the U.S. Department of Justice, the federal courts, and the Federal Bureau of Investigation, who were themselves under the thumb of the international dope mafia.

Dope, Inc.'s first response came in the form of simultaneous published attacks penned by the Anti-Defamation League of B'nai B'rith and the British import Heritage Foundation, the latter a nominally "conservative" lobbying group that is in fact pushing the British East India Company policies of the opium trade apologist Adam Smith.

While the original edition of *Dope, Inc.* had exposed ADL patrons Edgar Bronfman and Max Fisher among the leading American and Canadian "citizens above suspicion" with deep ties to the international drug trade, it was only as the result of the ADL libel campaign that the full extent of the ADL's role as a public relations front for the dope interests came to the surface.

Current ADL National Chairman Kenneth Bialkin, of the New York law firm of Willkie, Farr & Gallagher, according to U.S. federal court proceedings in the Southern District of New York, was the gray eminence behind dope trafficker Robert Vesco's bilking of Investors Overseas Service (IOS) out of hundreds of millions of dollars, money Vesco then used to build his Caribbean dirty money empire. The Havana-headquartered Vesco, the heir apparent to the U.S. syndicate's original "financial wizard," Meyer Lansky, has most recently fulfilled Lansky's own dream of turning Castro's Cuba into the capital of a hemispheric guns-for-dope and dirty money conglomerate. And, in the course of so doing, ADL Chairman Bialkin's most notorious client became an honorary commissar in Yuri Andropov's army of KGB narco-pushers.

A former ADL chairman, Sterling National Bank President Theodore Silbert, was sued by the Italian government in New York district court in 1983, for alleged criminal conspiracy with mafia financier Michele Sindona. The Italian government's legal brief charges that Silbert knowingly assisted Sindona's looting of the Banca Privata and other companies Sindona controlled, prior to their bankruptcy. Sterling National Bank, which allegedly laundered Sindona's looted funds, manages the ADL's investment and checking accounts.

In February 1985, when *Dope, Inc.* was published in Spanish as *Narcotráfico, SA,* and distributed in countries all over Latin America, the Rockefellers' closest financial allies in Venezuela, the Cisneros family, indulged themselves in a remarkable public tantrum. Pulling wires, the Cisneros clan deployed agents of the Venezuelan political police, the DISIP, to carry out a 2 a.m. raid on *EIR's* offices in Caracas, arrest its correspondents in their homes, subject them to more than 48 hours of illegal jailing, interrogation, threats, and physical abuse, and finally, expel them from the country. Their offense was simply their employment by *EIR,* the authors of *Narcotráfico, SA.* The Cisneros family, an agent of the DISIP announced to *EIR,* "will not permit one single copy of the book to circulate." Shortly thereafter, thanks to a compliant judge, *Narcotráfico, SA* became the first book since the end of the military dictatorship in 1958 to be banned in Venezuela.

You can read what we had to say about the Cisneros family, word for word, later in this book—including the family connection to Castro's Cuba that so embarrassed the Cisneroses.

In August 1985, another Rockefeller ally, the former prime minister of Peru, Manuel Ulloa, brought a slander suit against the Peruvian Anti-Drug Coalition and its head, Luis Vásquez Medina, for repeating the charges against Ulloa made in *Narcotráfico, SA.* With the García government investigating the financial and political interests in the past government which had protected the dope trade, Ulloa hoped to silence his accusers, who had charged his policies had paved the way for the takeover of the Peruvian economy by Dope, Inc. But on October 17, 1985 the court rejected Ulloa's suit, and absolved the ADC and Vasquez of all charges.

On March 22, 1986 a three-judge panel of Peru's Superior Court unanimously upheld the lower-court ruling. The court ruled that the Anti-Drug Coalition's publications, including *Narcotráfico, SA,* were "in the spirit of criticism of the economic policy which the plaintiff executed, . . . which is described as 'superliberal' . . . [and] whose policy permitted the proliferation not only of the drug trade, but also of bingo, finance companies, and real estate which are interconnected and which make up the 'illicit economies.' "

Dope Lobbyists Invade the Halls of Justice

On October 22, 1984, the Boston offices of U.S. Attorney William Weld opened a bogus criminal investigation into the presidential campaign committee of independent Democratic presidential candidate Lyndon LaRouche, on the excuse of several purported cases of credit card irregularities at the campaign's local Boston office.

The Boston "probe" provided the pretext ten days later for First Fidelity Bank of Newark, New Jersey to seize $200,000 on deposit in two LaRouche campaign accounts, thereby blocking a nationwide prime time TV broadcast scheduled for election eve. First Fidelity was the leading institution responsible for bringing Dope, Inc. into Atlantic City under the cover of legalized casino gambling. First Fidelity chairman Robert Ferguson financed the first boardwalk casino construction through an $11 million loan to Resorts International, a notorious front for the old Meyer Lansky syndicate. Ferguson's Newark attorney, Albert Besser, had been the attorney for Robert Vesco in the same series of IOS cases that featured the ADL's Kenneth Bialkin as a virtual unindicted co-conspirator.

Nearly 18 months, and hundreds of thousands of dollars in taxpayers' money later, Weld's "Get LaRouche" witchhunt continues on an expanded scale. The goal? To bankrupt and set up for potential assassination America's leading drug fighter—before the 1986 midterm congressional elections place LaRouche, already a declared and registered candidate for the 1988 Democratic Party presidential nomination, in the political limelight with access to nationwide television advertising. LaRouche's sixteen half-hour nationwide prime time TV broadcasts during the 1984 presidential race prompted Dope, Inc. to loudly declare, "Never again." By the time the reader finishes this book, the reasons for the syndicate's declaration of war will be very clear.

The designation of William Weld as the grand inquisitor was a "family decision" by the Dope, Inc. elite that has ruled New England since the clipper ship days of the opium and slave trade and the traitorous Hartford Convention. Weld's grandfather was the founder of the Lower Manhattan and old Boston investment house of White, Weld and Company. His father, David Weld, was the firm's chief executive officer during a long period in which the company was intermarried with the elite of the Swiss money-laundering institutions, Credit Suisse.

Under its chairman Donald Regan, Wall Street giant Merrill Lynch bought White, Weld in 1978, leaving the White, Weld partners who stayed with Merrill to take over the bigger firm; Merrill's chief administrative officer and next-in-line to the chairmanship is now the former White, Weld legal counsel Stephen Hammerman. But Credit Suisse, which had bought a controlling 31 % share in White Weld from David Weld and his partners, took full control of White, Weld's Geneva and London operations. These operations had provided an estimated two-thirds of White Weld's revenues. Credit Suisse then turned around and bought 38% of the old Rockefeller-Mellon investment bank, First Boston Corporation, bringing White, Weld's foreign operations under a new umbrella, First Boston-Credit Suisse.

The same old White, Weld network now dominates the $150 billion per year "Eurobond" market, the biggest haven for dirty money in the world, and now the most important source of funds for U.S. corporations. Credit Suisse-First Boston is the dominant market maker for "Eurobonds," a form of anonymous international security favored by criminals everywhere. Swiss banker Robert Genillard, the man who set up David Weld's old link to Credit Suisse in the late 1960s, is still chairman of the old White, Weld bank in Geneva, now renamed Clariden Bank under 100% Credit Suisse ownership. Genillard is still a friend and business associate of former White, Weld partner George S. Moore, one of the group that sold White, Weld to Don Regan; Moore is the official advisor to the tainted Cisneros interests of Venezuela.

In fact, on February 7, 1985, Credit Suisse was caught red-handed in a multi-billion dollar money-laundering scheme directed out of the staid offices of the First National Bank of Boston, the flagship institution of the Boston Brahmins' Bank of Boston Corporation. Fortunately for the dope bankers, the case was handled by William Weld, who collapsed 1,163 separate documented cases of criminal felony, involving $1,218,682,281 in hot money, laundered in and out of nine foreign banks, into a one-count indictment—for which Bank of Boston was fined a slap-on-the-wrist $500,000 in a plea bargain! The penalty imposed on the bank amounted to an absurd 1/20 of 1 % of the amount of money laundered in just these documented cases. Bank of Boston chairman and chief executive officer William Brown was forced to admit in testimony before a congressional committee early in 1985 that the bank made enormous profits from the laundering of the dirty money—even after the fine was paid.

The whitewashing of the Bank of Boston was accompanied by no action whatsoever against the nine foreign correspondent banks, led by Weld's own Credit Suisse Bank of Zurich, and including Swiss Bank Corp. of Basel, Union Bank of Switzerland in Zurich, Barclays Bank International of New York, Bank of Boston S.A. of Luxembourg, Bank Leu of Zurich, Die Freie Osterreichische of Vienna, Canadian Imperial Bank of Commerce of Ottawa, and Standard Chartered Bank Ltd. of New York. Meanwhile, a flood of other cases opened up revealing the deeper role of the Bank of Boston in the international narcoterrorist conspiracy.

On February 28, 1985, just weeks after the Bank of Boston case had been swept under the rug by U.S. Attorney Weld, the Venezuelan daily newspaper *El Mundo* published an investigative report by journalist José Cupertino Flores revealing that between October 1983 and February 1984, more than $12 billion in capital had gone from Caracas, Valencia, Barquisimeto and San Cristóbal, Venezuela—all favorite money-laundering holes for Latin America's cocaine and marijuana traffickers—into the coffers of the Bank of Boston. Flores suggested that a study of the "passenger lists of flights between New York and Miami and the Boston airport would find famous names and surnames," although "others come by private jets . . . . After last year's intervention into Continental Illinois, the funds of innumerable personalities of our country were transferred with speed to the vaults of the Bostonian institution."

On February 20, 1985, the Irish High Court in Dublin announced it had seized $1.64 million in cash that belonged to a secret Irish Republican Army fund laundered through Swiss banks, into London, on to the Bank of Boston, before arriving at the secret IRA account at the Bank of Ireland. The laundered money, according to Irish Justice Minister Michael Noonan, represented the revenues of kidnappings, death threat extortions, and robberies.

An earlier investigation by the Senate Permanent Investigations Subcommittee had uncovered another illegal money funnel passing from the Banco Nacional de Panamá through the Federal Reserve Bank of Boston into the Bank of Boston International division during 1982-83. Once again, the hot cash wound up in numbered bank accounts at the Zurich offices of the Weld family-linked Credit Suisse. According to the already-cited report of the President's Commission on Organized Crime, "the cash flow from Panama to the United States is the most significant recorded flow of currency that is likely to be drug money."

If the issue of computer- and electronic mail-generated cash flows between the elite of the offshore international financial community was too pristine a business to warrant the attention of U.S. Attorney Weld, the Boston federal prosecutor had little excuse for blocking the probe into the Bank of Boston's ties to the organized crime Angiulo family, an investigation that Weld apparently had jurisdiction over from no later than 1983. Using an exemption loophole in the federal codes demanding that banks report all cash transactions of $10,000 or more, officials of the Bank of Boston passed tens of millions of dollars in and out of Angiulo family front accounts, taking in cardboard cartons and shopping bags full of ten, twenty, and fifty dollar bills, and issuing cashier's checks. Officials of the U.S. Treasury Department, including the recently departed Assistant Secretary of the Treasury for Enforcement, John Walker, have stated in public forums their belief that the cash laundered by the Bank of Boston, on behalf of the Angiulo family and other shady clients, was dope money.

Testifying before the House subcommittee on financial institutions on March 5, 1985, Walker stated, "There's every indication that the $600 million of small bills that the bank took in was the laundering of drug money. Why else would the money be $20 bills?"

In an earlier public statement, carried by the *Boston Globe* on February 8, 1985, Walker had declared, "The patterns that we saw, which were small bills coming back from Switzerland and large bills going out to Switzerland, are consistent with money laundering going on. There was definitely money laundering in the air."

So confident were the executives of the Bank of Boston in Weld's loyalty to the Dope, Inc. cause that, after the initial flurry of congressional and Treasury Department activity against the bank's laundering adventures, bank officials "discovered" another $73 million in illegally washed funds. The bank executives apologized for the "honest" mistake and Weld took no prosecutorial action.

If there was any doubt that Weld was acting as a defender and advocate of the interests of the Bank of Boston and the Dope, Inc. Brahmins, the U.S. Attorney, who took the federal post only after he was defeated in a statewide election for Commonwealth of Massachusetts Attorney General, received campaign contributions from at least two current officials of the Bank of Boston, honorary director William C. Mercer and Peter M. Whitman—in addition to Canada's Dope, Inc. magnate Edgar Bronfman.

U.S. Attorney Weld's complicity in whitewashing the role of the big Boston banks—including banks associated with his own family business affairs—in the laundering of billions in dope revenues is perhaps only surpassed by the criminal zeal with which he has targeted the enemies of Dope, Inc. for frameup prosecutions.

In addition to the already cited case of Lyndon LaRouche, Weld conducted a brutal five-year-long assault against the Democratic Party political organization of Boston Mayor Kevin White, a campaign that prompted White to retire from the city post when his term expired in 1981, rather than run for a fifth term in a climate defined by Weld's inquisition. Thomas Anzalone, White's leading fundraiser and campaign coordinator, was indicted by Weld's office and convicted before Federal District Court Judge A. David Mazzone, the same judge handling the LaRouche assault. The Weld-Mazzone team committed such a battery of acts treading on criminality that a three-judge panel in the First District Court of Appeals, on July 1, 1985, threw the Anzalone conviction out, characterizing Weld's methods as bordering on the Soviet legal principle of "guilt by analogy." The appellate decision concluded, "We cannot engage in unprincipled interpretation of the law unless we foment lawlessness instead of compliance."

Even as the "Get White" operation was unfolding, the *National Law Journal* published an article on June 13, 1983 describing the Weld action as a "textbook example of a prosecutor misusing his powers to bully witnesses and manipulate the political process." Weld was cited for using improper pressure tactics, unfounded allegations, leaks to the press, and harassment of witnesses, including late-night sweeps by dozens of subpoena-serving FBI agents. These are the identical methods being repeated in the LaRouche case today.

Yet, in early April 1986, according to press reports citing Attorney General Edwin Meese, Weld was about to be promoted to Washington—to head the U.S. Justice Department's Criminal Division!

The role in all this of White House chief of staff Don Regan, the former Merrill Lynch chairman, certainly merits further investigation. According to evidence supplied in the October 1984 report by the President's Commission on Organized Crime, titled "The Cash Connection: Organized Crime, Financial Institutions and Money Laundering," business procedures at Don Regan's Merrill Lynch have been anything but conservative. The report states:

"In 1980 . . . couriers were observed transferring enormous amounts of cash through investment houses and banks in New York City to Italy and Switzerland. Tens of millions of dollars in heroin sales in this country were transferred overseas in this fashion. . . .

One of the couriers for this laundering operation was Franco Della Torre, a Swiss resident. In March 1982, Della Torre deposited slightly more than $1 million in $5, $10, and $20 bills in the "Traex" account at the Manhattan office of the brokerage firm Merrill Lynch Pierce Fenner & Smith. Thereafter, Della Torre made four additional cash deposits totalling $3.9 million in the "Traex" account. . . . "

Merrill Lynch even helped make security arrangements, according to the President's Commission report: "In making large cash deposits at Merrill Lynch, Della Torre's practice was to request that security personnel accompany him from his hotel to Merrill Lynch offices. After several such deposits . . . arrangements were made to escort the money from Della Torre's hotel directly to Bankers Trust, where Merrill Lynch maintained accounts."

According to federal indictments of Della Torre and others in this heroin ring, Merrill Lynch moved the funds directly to Switzerland, where one of the major depositories was—Credit Suisse.

Some direct evidence of Don Regan's attitude toward narcotics trafficking surfaced in March 1984, when he was questioned by Congress on why, as Treasury Secretary, he had dismantled an air interdiction anti-drug program, while shifting $18 million in funds for the program to an administrative fund, to remodel his office.

Marvin Warner Buys a U.S. Attorney

On April 15, 1985, nearly six months into the Weld witchhunt against LaRouche, an associate of the three-time presidential candidate wrote to Attorney General Edwin Meese III demanding an official Justice Department probe into Weld's conflict of interest in the coverup of the Bank of Boston's multi-billion dollar money-laundering schemes. Shortly after the Department of Justice's Office of Public Responsibility opened a brief probe into the Weld-Credit Suisse conflict of interest, a parallel federal grand jury was suddenly opened into the LaRouche campaign in Cincinnati, Ohio, a city where the campaign did not even maintain an office.

What common thread bound the Boston and Cincinnati jurisdictions? Whereas U.S. Attorney Weld hob-nobbed with the elite of the dope bankers in the wood-paneled supper clubs of Harvard Square, the U.S. Attorney's office in Cincinnati was virtually a private fiefdom of Marvin Warner, Jimmy Carter's U.S. ambassador to Switzerland. Warner's dirtyfisted dealings with some of Latin America's biggest cocaine smugglers grabbed coast-to-coast headlines between 1980 and the spring of 1985, when Warner's Ohio banking empire went belly up, triggering a near-collapse of the entire U.S. savings and loan sector.

What the Weld-Warner combination proved, above all else, was the existence of a powerful dope mafia underground pulling the strings from within the U.S. Department of Justice. When push comes to shove, Dope, Inc. occupies the Attorney General's chair.

At the time that the Cincinnati office of the U.S. Attorney obligingly opened a second grand jury against Lyndon LaRouche, the U.S. Attorney was Christopher Barnes, who, at 32 years old, was perhaps the youngest federal prosecutor in the United States. Barnes's father, Earl Barnes, the former chairman of the Ohio Republican Party, handpicked his son for the job—in large measure to protect his financial "godfather" Marvin Warner from federal prosecution for a string of money-fleecing operations generally linked to the Ibero-American drug trade.

According to testimony delivered before an Ohio state legislative committee probing Warner's role in the collapse of his Home State Savings Bank, Earl Barnes was the recipient of a $1 million unsecured loan from Warner, a loan he had never paid a penny on.

While Warner's "contributions" to GOP kingmaker Barnes, and his equally generous treatment of the Democratic Party state machine of Governor Richard Celeste (Warner is widely credited with the multi-million dollar vote fraud operation that stole the Ohio electoral college for Jimmy Carter in 1976) ensured that both the Democratic and GOP-appointed U.S. Attorneys would look the other way when Warner dipped his hands into the Ohio taxpayers' pockets, on December 13,1985, a special state grand jury sitting in Hamilton County, Ohio handed down a 50-count indictment of Warner for willful misapplication of funds, theft of securities, and theft by deception. That indictment was put together without a stitch of cooperation from the U.S. Attorney's office, from the Department of Justice in Washington, or from the FBI.

If the Feds had not covered up for Warner, one of the most protected and hermetically sealed drug-money-laundering operations ever put together in the United States might have been crushed.

It is no coincidence that the Warner money-laundering apparatus can be traced directly back to the Boston Brahmins and White, Weld.

In 1976, a White, Weld securities whiz kid, Allen Nowick, went to Fort Lauderdale, Fla. to help set up ESM Government Securities. The three "out-front" partners of Nowick in ESM were Ronnie R. Ewton, Robert Seneca, and George Mead. In much the same way that White, Weld took control of the vastly larger Merrill Lynch and First Boston Eurobond laundering apparatus, it was White, Weld special operative Nowick who transformed the ESM-Marvin Warner group into a vast hot-money-washing complex over the period from 1976-81, through a string of buyouts and hostile takeovers of banks and other lending institutions stretching from Florida to New Jersey to Ohio.

The merry-go-round got started in 1977, when Warner's Home State Savings Bank, a Cincinnati-based S&L, loaned $17 million to Ewton and Seneca, permitting them to take over the Great American Bank group of Florida. Warner's son-in-law, Steven Arky, a Florida attorney, had put Warner together with Ewton, a close associate of Arky from the National Guard. Warner ignored the fact that Ewton had already been under investigation by the SEC for ESM's unlicensed securities trading.

Warner's cavalier attitude toward his intimate dealings with suspected criminal Ewton was born of two factors. First, by 1978, Warner's Home State already had one federal fraud conviction under its own belt—for issuing phony commercial standby loan commitments (at a lucrative commission) to 47 contractors and developers in 11 states. $800,000 in pay-backs, and a paltry $11,000 in fines were ordered. No bank officials were indicted by name. A spinoff personal tax fraud probe into Warner by the IRS was short circuited by a September 1980 plea bargain arranged by Warner's attorney, Edward Bennett Williams, a prominent Democratic Party fixer, and Justice Department officials John Keeny, head of Carter's Criminal Division, and James Cissell, U.S. Attorney for the Southern District of Ohio.

Second, Warner was richly rewarded for his role in stealing the 1976 presidential elections for Jimmy Carter. In early 1977, he was named U.S. ambassador to Switzerland, a position that never got in the way of Warner's continuing money-laundering activities. It was not merely that Warner enjoyed the political protection and diplomatic immunity of the Carter administration. Warner proved to be a centerpiece of the Florida dirty money machine implicated in the Billy gate affair and the drug empire of fugitive Dope, Inc. financier Robert Vesco.

In 1978, Warner bought back Great American Bank Corp. from Ewton and merged it with ComBank, another Florida banking group he had previously purchased in partnership with Hugh Culverhouse, Sr. In the meantime, Warner issued standing orders to all of his bank officers to conduct their government securities purchases exclusively through ESM. Subsequent investigations by federal and state regulators in the wake of ESM's March 4, 1985, $300 million collapse, revealed that Warner and Arky were the exclusive holders of personal investment accounts with ESM. In effect, ESM was Warner's private little *fondo.*

A review of newspaper accounts and federal court records suggests that Warner used the facilities of his burgeoning empire of Florida banks to draw in the revenues of Ibero-American drug traffickers and wash the funds through ESM and other conduits en route to numbered accounts in Switzerland, Panama, and other offshore havens.

In addition to his own position as ambassador to Switzerland (and lover of Jimmy Carter's personal White House secretary, Susan Clough), Warner enjoyed the protection of the Florida state comptroller, Gerald E. Lewis—his second cousin—and his lifetime friend and business partner, Hugh Culverhouse Sr., whose son, Hugh Jr., up through 1982 directed the division of the U.S. Attorney's office in Florida responsible for prosecuting money-laundering cases.

It was precisely this combination of "guardian angels" who closed ranks to protect Warner when agents of the IRS, DEA, and U.S. Customs Service moved in on the Great American Bank of Dade County on February 27, 1981 as part of Operation Greenback, an early Reagan administration effort to crack down on some of the most egregious instances of drug money-laundering by U.S. banks. In fact, Florida Comptroller Lewis, whom federal officials described as notoriously soft on drug-money-launderers, complained bitterly that the DEA had not informed him in advance of the pending raid.

On December 10, 1982, a federal grand jury in Miami indicted the Great American Bank and three middle level employees—Vice President Lionel Paytuvi, head teller Carlos Nunez, and teller Elaine Kemp—on charges that during the 14-month period leading up to the February 1981 raid, over $94 million had been illegally laundered through the bank on behalf of three Latin American drug-trafficking organizations.

By far the most notorious of the three drug rings was that of Isaac Kattan-Kasin, a Syrian Jew from the smugglers' enclave of Aleppo, who, after spending the early 1960s living in New Jersey as an employee of Robert Vesco, became a Colombian citizen and ran the largest Latin American cocaine smuggling organization of the 1970s. Kattan laundered an estimated $350 million a year into southern Florida, according to Operation Greenback veterans. Those funds were then transferred to numbered accounts at the Swiss Bank Corp. in Zurich, the Banco de Ibero-America in Panama and Banco Internacional, Banco del Crédito and the Bank of Tokyo, all in Lima, Peru.

Although Warner screamed he was only a victim, and managed to sidestep indictment in the Kattan affair, Operation Greenback officials said privately they were convinced that Warner was a mastermind of the laundering scheme. In fact, according to one federal law enforcement source, within days of the arrest of Kattan, Hugh Culverhouse Jr., fresh out of the Miami U.S. Attorney's office, paid a personal visit to the Department of Justice headquarters, lobbying for the International Affairs Section to unfreeze the funds in eight Swiss bank accounts maintained by Kattan.

Once the smoke cleared on the Great American Bank scandal, Warner quietly sold his majority holdings in the bank to Barnett Banks of Florida—at a handsome 325% profit.

Simultaneous to the Great American Bank bust, another one of Warner's flagship institutions, ComBank, surfaced in the middle of yet another DEA investigation, codenamed Operation Groper. On April 13, 1982, a Winter Park, Florida businessman, Robert Govern, and 12 others were indicted for smuggling more than four million pounds of marijuana from Colombia into the United States between 1975-81. Govern laundered the drug proceeds through ComBank into a string of sham corporations in the Grand Caymans and Netherlands Antilles.

According to an investigative report published in the *Cleveland Plain Dealer* on June 18, 1985, one of Warner's prize investors was the Venezuelan Cisneros group that is the subject of another chapter. Suffice it to say here that a Cisneros family retainer, Vincente Pérez Sandoval, was a client of Steven Arky who tried unsuccessfully to take over Freedom Savings and Loan Association of Tampa shortly after Warner, a shareholder in the bank, maneuvered the S&L into buying ComBank at a price estimated to be more than double the book value of the banking group.

Another Florida bank, Metropolitan Bank of Tampa, came under intensive federal investigation on suspicion of laundering drug revenues from the World Finance Corp., a Meyer Lansky-Robert Vesco linked Coral Gables firm also tied to the Cisneros interests in Venezuela through Arky client Pérez Sandoval. Then Warner stepped in through Great American Bank to buy up the Tampa bank. Prior to this "friendly" takeover, overseen by Florida State Comptroller Gerald Lewis, Warner's cousin, Metropolitan had been owned by Edward J. DeBartolo, a Youngstown, Ohio multimillionaire whose name has often been linked to organized crime.

In fact, Warner's association with the very same Ohio-centered criminal circles provoked speculation that the title transfer was a cosmetic change, aimed at clearing the books on Metropolitan's unexplained "loss" of $51 million, drawn from a discount window at the Federal Reserve.

In June of 1985, a Hamilton County judge approved an almost identical "lateral" takeover of Warner's own Home State Savings by Hunter Savings Association, a Cincinnati S&L owned by Carl Lindner. A subsidiary of Lindner's American Financial Corp., Hunter is one of 40 corporations—including the notorious United Brands and Penn Central Railroad—under the control of a holding company board that lists Warner's ComBank partner Hugh Culverhouse, Sr. as one of only three directors drawn from outside Lindner's immediate family.

The taxpayers of Ohio paid for the Hunter takeover of Home State—through a grant of $100 million from the state of Ohio.

This chain of events began on March 4, 1985, when the SEC obtained a federal court order to close down ESM, on the grounds that the Fort Lauderdale hot money laundromat was $300 million short of its current obligations. Within 48 hours, panicked depositors began a three-day run on Home State, which had $570 million admittedly tied up in ESM. By the time Home State Chairman David J. Schiebel announced on March 8 that the Cincinnati thrift was closing its doors, $154 million had been withdrawn.

In early April, a New Jersey government securities firm, Bevill, Bresler, and Schulman folded up in a repeat of the ESM blowout. An even bigger run on the banks seemed possible. Two of the firm's former brokers, Ronnie Ewton and George Mead, had left the firm in 1975 to link up with White, Weld's Nowick in founding ESM. In return, ESM later deployed one of their chief brokers, Andrew Ledbetter, into Bevill, Bresler, and Schulman.

The First Fidelity Case

On November 1, 1984, immediately after U.S. Attorney William Weld announced his investigation of the LaRouche campaign on NBC television, Boston-based FBI special agent Richard Egan contacted the First Fidelity Bank of Newark, New Jersey, then holding deposits for two LaRouche campaign committees. Within hours of the call, First Fidelity had illegally seized $200,000 from the two accounts, thus blocking a scheduled LaRouche election eve half-hour nationwide broadcast on CBS-TV.

At the time of the theft, LaRouche campaign spokesmen charged that top officials of First Fidelity, including bank Chairman Robert Ferguson, were implicated in an organized crime network involving the old Meyer Lansky syndicate and corrupt leading officials of the Democratic Party. The spokesmen documented that the bank's organized crime ties revolved around the Lansky mob's invasion of Atlantic City through the legalization of casino gambling, a project in which bank head Ferguson had played a pivotal role. That Ferguson and First Fidelity shared a lawyer with dope financier Robert Vesco merely added to an already rich mosaic of evidence. The LaRouche campaign committees sued the bank for their money, and the bank countersued for libel.

Fifteen months and thousands of pages of court papers, depositions, affidavits, and motions after the bank's ripoff of LaRouche campaign contributors, the *Wall Street Journal* published a pair of front-page stories putting First Fidelity in the middle of loansharking, bigtime dope-trafficking, a rash of gangland beatings, at least two murders, shakedowns of legitimate—and not-so-legitimate—businesses. First Fidelity bankers had systematically passed $22 million in cash into the mob, and managed, so far, to walk away from the scene scot free.

The January 14 and 15, 1986 *Wall Street Journal* pieces by reporter Jonathan Kwitny exposed First Fidelity's relationship with Richard Mamarella, a professional con man who apparently was picked up by the Gambino organized crime family and assigned to manage a New Jersey loan-sharking and drug-financing operations that made use of the Atlantic City casinos—and the accommodating facilities of a south Jersey branch of First Fidelity. Between early 1982 and September 1983, when he was found guilty of fraud and extortion and sentenced to seven years in federal prison, Mamarella received a total of $22 million in loans from First Fidelity Bank of South Jersey. A total of 139 such loans, all personally approved by the president of the south Jersey branch, John Petrycki, were issued to Mamarella on collateral consisting of non-existent insurance policies, all fraudulently written by shell insurance companies owned by Mamarella himself, on behalf of non-existent corporate clients.

According to court documents and Mamarella's own testimony in a summer 1985 trial of two of his "business associates," the bulk of the $22 million passed into the hands of organized crime to finance loansharking operations from Atlantic City to Chinatown, and to purchase Golden Triangle heroin from mafia refineries in Palermo, Florence, and Milan on behalf of the South Jersey "Pizza Connection."

Was First Fidelity the victim or the perpetrator of the $22-million crime spree? According to *Wall Street Journal* reporter Kwitny, throughout the duration of the theft and fraud, Mamarella's principal front company, IFA Inc., was legally represented by Nathaniel Yohalem of the prominent Newark, New Jersey firm of Greenbaum, Greenbaum, Rowe & Smith—a firm that had represented First Fidelity Bancorp. for the past 20 years. It was Yohalem who submitted the original letters to First Fidelity assuring the bank that Mamarella and IFA were worthy of millions of dollars in credits—no questions asked.

The Mamarella fraud and organized crime ties came out publicly, following his April 29, 1983 Chinatown arrest on extortion charges. Mamarella and four associates were grabbed by the FBI while in the process of beating up a recalcitrant borrower who had fallen behind on his payments to Chinatown dope financier and loan shark Louis Chung. First Fidelity responded to the "news" that it had handed $22 million to a mafia hoodlum—by hiring Mamarella and his mob "toughs" to get the money back! At a time when Mamarella was under Federal indictment for extortion, he and his gang were put on the payroll as "consultants" to aid in the collection of an estimated $14.5 million in outstanding loans from the bank to Mamarella.

The "special arrangement" with Mamarella was sanctioned by no less an official of the bank than First Fidelity's chairman Robert Ferguson, according to the July 19, 1983 issue of *American Banker*.

In a statement issued to the shareholders of the bank, Ferguson stated:

"In February of 1982, one of our banks began purchasing a third party paper from a corporation licensed by the Department of Banking of the State of New Jersey, engaged in the business of insurance premium financing . . . . In early June of this year [over a month after Mamarella's extortion arrest in Chinatown—ed.], we began to question and investigate the authenticity of that paper. . . . At the present time, outstanding obligations total approximately- $15.5 million. . . . We are continuing to receive payments and, in the opinion of our counsel, unpaid balances, if any, after comprehensive collection efforts, will be covered by our blanket and fidelity bonds."

And what were those "comprehensive collection efforts" referred to by Ferguson?

According to Kwitny and other sources, from the very outset of the scam, Mamarella regularly reached out to his mob sponsor Joseph Paterno, a New Jersey syndicate captain who had fled to Fort Lauderdale, Florida to avoid state court subpoena, and to other criminal elements, to help with "collections" on funds lent by First Fidelity.

For Mario Stacchini, a New Jersey restauranteur, and Anthony Turano, a New York shoe manufacturer who used his business as a distribution point for Sicilian-refined heroin, these "comprehensive efforts" cost them their lives. Both Stacchini and Turano were forced by Mamarella's mob higher-ups to take out personal life insurance policies as "collateral" on their First Fidelity loans, once they had fallen behind on their payments.

Anthony Turano was arrested by U.S. Drug Enforcement Administration agents in late 1982 in New York City, as he was about to take possession of 15 kilos of Golden Triangle heroin, purchased with $290,000 provided by Mamarella. Clearly Turano was in no position to keep up his payments. However, when his bullet-riddled body was found wrapped in a deserted lot in Queens, New York, the mob, Mamarella, and First Fidelity all collected on his $1 million life insurance policy.

Such are the characteristic methods of *Dope, Inc.* In our next chapter, we travel up the ladder from casino bankers and mafia hoodlums to the top command of Dope, Inc., where the moral atmosphere is somewhat worse.

2: The Dope, Inc. Command Structure

The international drug traffic works like a single multinational firm, not unlike the Swiss-based pharmaceuticals cartels—controlling production, supply, distribution, stockpiling, and financing through a single, integrated management. Its objective, at least at the highest level of its command structure, is not profit. What we call Dope, Incorporated constitutes a strategic capability in the service of a deal between the Western European financial oligarchy and the masters of the new Russian Empire known as the U.S.S.R. The deal is the same one concluded between Bertrand Russell and representatives of the Soviet Union through the so-called back-channel discussions initiated through the Pugwash Conferences of the late 1950s, among other locations. The world shall be re-divided, according to this deal, which the late Soviet President Yuri Andropov characterized as a "New Yalta" in early 1983: The Western European nations shall become a satrapy of the Soviet Empire, and the United States shall be reduced to 25% of its former post-World War II influence, and relegated to the Western Hemisphere, the brutal debt-collector for Anglo-American and Swiss banking interests which hold Ibero-America's debt.

Through global control of the means of exchanging dirty money for clean money, through control over the supply of narcotics, through a dominant position in the international markets for precious metals and gemstones, and, above all, through its ability to bring a multi-hundred billion dollar annual cash flow to bear upon the corruption of the legal organs of sovereign national states, Dope, Inc. exercises a unique sort of political control. What American intelligence in the 1920s called the "Nazi-Communist synarchist international," works alongside the Italian, Jewish, Chinese and other branches of organized crime in the United States, the criminal wing of Italian masonry, the narcoterrorists of Ibero-America, the Sikh separatists of Southwest Asia, and separatist movements throughout Europe and the developing sector.

Beyond the specifics of this or that business deal or political arrangement, is a shared world outlook of a sort that has been around since at least the days of the Chaldean-Babylonian empire. It is an *oligarchical* outlook that views man as essentially a "talking beast," a creature of appetites to be governed through the manipulation of a priesthood whose business it is to apply pleasure and pain to achieve desired results. Narcotics have always played a central role for oligarchs.

It is therefore hardly surprising that the same oligarchy that controls the filthiest elements of the financial underworld today, dominates, and bends to the same purposes, the leading institutions of international finance: the International Monetary Fund and the Basel-based Bank for International Settlements. The same international political figures who, conceding world supremacy to the oligarchs of the new Soviet Empire, advance the policies of "New Yalta"—policies of depopulation, destruction of national sovereignty, debt collection, decoupling of the Western alliance—are enmeshed, in their private business affairs, with the dirtiest elements of the financial underworld. Henry Kissinger, together with his international political directorate known as Kissinger Associates, is the individual who stands at the intersection point of everyone of these networks: the back-channel with the Soviet Union, the drug and terror networks from Italy to Ibero-America, and the highest levels of finance—including his directorship in American Express, the entity into which has merged a major portion of Dope, Inc.'s command structure.

This command structure contains the following main groups:

The British combination that controls offshore banking and precious metals trading, i.e., the Hongkong and Shanghai Bank, the Oppenheimer gold interests, top British financial institutions such as Eagle Star Insurance and Barclay's Bank, and their Canadian cousins such as Bank of Montreal and Bank of Nova Scotia;

The major Swiss banks;

The continuity of Venetian-Genoese financial manipulations in the personage of the late Roberto Calvi of Banco Ambrosiano, and the shadowy Edmund Safra of American Express;

The combined offspring of the Swiss bankers and the old European *fondi*, the international grain cartel of Cargill, Continental (Fribourg family), Bunge, and Louis Dreyfus; The Boston Brahmin families and the big American financial institutions associated with Henry Kissinger, including Citibank, Chase Manhattan Bank, and American Express.

This monster has devoured North American finance. The United States is now financially dependent upon capital inflows exceeding $120 billion per year (as of the third quarter of 1984). It is also a matter of the International Monetary Fund's official admission that the major source of such capital flows is the so-called "flight capital," i.e., funds moved across borders despite tax or foreign-exchange laws of national governments.

The London Network

In the following chapters taken from the 1978 edition, we identify a tightly closed financial network whose origins lie in the Dutch and British East India Companies and the modern origins of the narcotics traffic in the British Opium Wars of the 1840s. The paradigm for this network is the London Committee, or British-based directors, of the Hongkong and Shanghai Bank, the central bank for Dope, Incorporated. It ties in directly and immediately to the five big London clearing banks, the five London "gold pool" dealers, and the big Canadian international banks.

This network, we demonstrated, provides the offshore banking, precious metals, and related capabilities to cause several hundred billion dollars per year to disappear from the streets of New York, Amsterdam, Frankfurt, and Hong Kong, and reappear as apparently legitimate assets wherever convenient. We showed further that Anglo-Chinese collaboration in the Asian opiates traffic was a matter of official policy on the part of the People's Republic of China, and "business arrangements" of the British elite dating back to the first corruption of the Imperial Chinese bureaucracy by the British East India Company.

As noted, the core of this evidence has been confirmed multiply by the official U.S. reports cited above, among others. Six years of additional research by the hundreds of researchers and correspondents of the *Executive Intelligence Review* has reconstructed the three-dimensional character of Dope, Inc., whose most obvious, outward facade is British. Its other dimensions, equally integrated into the single world command structure, are Swiss-centered continental European, and Soviet.

The Hongkong and Shanghai Bank, as reported, now controls the twelfth-largest American bank, and its close collaborators among the British clearing banks have moved massively into American banking, through the Midland Bank takeover of Crocker National Bank in California, the Rothschild takeover of California's BanCal- TriState, and similar expansion into the American market.

The Oppenheimer mining group, heirs to the empire of Cecil Rhodes, is the dominant force—in collaboration with HongShang and its Mideast subsidiaries—in the illegal traffic in gold and diamonds through which so much dirty money is turned into untraceable, portable assets. Through its diamond monopoly, De Beers, its mining corporations, Anglo-American Mining and Consolidated Gold Fields of South Africa, through its commodity trading organization, Phibro, the Oppenheimer group has expanded its tentacles across the world and, most of all, in the United States.

Eagle Star Insurance, the mediating link between the British oligarchy and the Canadian banks, has extended its branches to the continental insurance companies, and sunk deep roots into the United States at the same time. In the chapters taken from the 1978 edition, the reader will find that Eagle Star controls the family trusts of those barely rehabilitated Prohibition-era mobsters, the Bronfman family. The Bronfmans, in turn, control a variety of lower species of criminal life in Canada and the United States. The Canadian real estate firms which operate under the umbrella of Eagle Star control have come to dominate the major urban real estate markets in the United States, from New York to Texas.

But even more important is the role that Eagle Star assumed as of November 1983, when it became the principal overt link between the British high command of the narcotics traffic, and the Swiss-German financial interests centered around the great South German family fortunes. Allianz Versicherung of Munich, continental Europe's largest insurance company, bought 30% of Eagle Star in a well-publicized takeover battle whose sound and fury disguised the underlying cooperation and identity of interests between the British and German sides. Close financial relationships had existed for some time between the HongShang in the Far East and the nastier elements of German finance.

Allianz represents a coalition of the oldest and nastiest German family *fondi,* or trust funds, including those of the old Bavarian Wittelsbach dynasty, and the most evil family in German-speaking Europe, Thurn und Taxis. It is the Thurn und Taxis family and their in-laws, the defunct Portuguese royal family of Braganza, who created and funded the terrorist organization Tradition, Family, and Property, implicated in plans to assassinate Pope John Paul II. TFP's Venezuelan chapter was banned by the Venezuelan government.

The old United Fruit Company, renamed United Brands in the 1960s, has been the center of American organized crime since the turn of this century, we showed in 1978, through a merger between the Sicilian mafia of New Orleans and the shipping interests of the Boston Brahmins; since the beginning of the Ibero-American narcotics traffic, United Fruit's banana boats coming into Baltimore harbor have been the freest vehicle for the physical passage of contraband into the United States. In its successive corporate reorganizations, United Brands has since wound up in the hands of Cincinnati, Ohio insurance financier Carl Lindner, the principal business partner through the last three decades of Michigan organized crime heir Max Fisher. And through an entanglement of financial interests that might have been invented by a gaudy but unimaginative mystery novelist, the fate of United Brands has been intertwined with that of American Express, the world's most efficient silent money-mover, and the prince of Levantine money-laundering, Syrian-Swiss financier Edmund Safra. American Express, the monster that devoured half the old great houses of Wall Street, ties together the United Brands crime and smuggling capability, the financial networks who created and funded the Argentine Monteneros and other terrorist organizations, as well as the Swiss-based interests who have acted, for a generation, as the private couriers of the Soviet Union in the international gold markets.

But more ominous than the spectacular rise of the tainted financial institutions of the West is the role of the Soviet Union, the subject of a chapter newly written for this edition. There was a pattern to the failure of narcotics-related financial enterprises during the years 1973-1975, when the great shakeout occurred. At the same time that Watergate disposed of Richard Nixon's administration, and the American intelligence services were abandoned to the claws of the U.S. Senate's Church Committee, a grand reorganization came about in the affairs of the financial underworld.

The rotund Bernie Cornfeld was unceremoniously expelled from the money-laundering organization par excellence of the 1960s, Investors Overseas Services, with the connivance of Baron Edmond de Rothschild and the Swiss authorities, to be replaced by Rothschild "discovery" Robert Vesco. Fugitive from justice Vesco is now the guest of Fidel Castro's Cuba, vigorously and personally defended by Castro, and documented to be a key ally of Cuban efforts to milk the narcotics traffic as a slush-fund for dirty political operations in the Caribbean, as we show in a later chapter.

Romanian banker Tibor Rosenbaum, reportedly a senior official of the Israeli Mossad and a principal crony of former Israeli Finance Minister Pinhas Sapir, died in disgrace after the failure of his Swiss-based BCI. His role in the Israeli covert weapons traffic fell to such men as Ariel Sharon and his unpleasant runabout, Meshulem Riklis of Rapid-American Corporation. It is not merely that Riklis and his company have been a top-priority target of U.S. Customs narcotics investigators since the mid-1970s; his patron in Israeli politics, the bloodthirsty Ariel Sharon, belongs to an evil faction which believes that Israel, in order to maintain itself, must cut a deal with the Soviet Union to betray the United States.

Michele Sindona's fall in 1974 was no loss to humanity. But the man who stepped into his role as the Vatican's private banker was the doubly unfortunate Roberto Calvi of Banco Ambrosiano, and his allies in Italian Masonry, Licio Gelli and Umberto Ortolani. We will document in later chapters that Gelli, the ex-fascist enforcer, was the Italian leg of the now-infamous "Bulgarian connection," the heroin-for-armaments network uncovered by Italian police in 1982, and the source of the protection for the would-be assassin of Pope John Paul II.

The great shakeout of the mid-1970s was the point at which the Soviet Union muscled its way into a critical partnership position in the underground of world finance. Through the expansion of its own imperial banking apparatus, through the emplacement of organized crime elements under Soviet influence, and, most of all, through deals with such Western interests as the Oppenheimer group, the Soviet Union took over dirty-money networks. It did this in the service of its global strategic aim: the imposition of Soviet hegemony over the Eurasian landmass, and the relegation of the United States to a hemispheric power presiding over the social collapse of the entire Ibero-American world.

How Dope, Inc. Bought Up American Finance

Parallel to the shakeout of the financial underworld during the mid-1970s was a much more publicized shakeout—the weeding out of the big Wall Street brokerage firms, a process which has continued through to the present. It is no less relevant to the transformation of the world financial system into the instrument of the allied European and Soviet oligarchy. It is no longer possible to tell how much American equity is, in fact, American; it can only be stated as a matter of public record that investment banking in the United States is now almost wholly controlled by the ancient European *fondi,* that is, family trust funds whose pedigree goes back to the financing of the Crusades by Genoa and Venice.

From 1971 to 1981, in the decade after then-Treasury Undersecretary Paul Volcker removed its gold backing, the U.S. dollar fell to a mere 60% of its predevaluation level, while the combined effects of inflation and lower stock prices devalued American equity to about 30% of its 1971 level in terms of gold. From the standpoint of the old oligarchical *fondi,* secured through gold, American equity could be had for a fifth of its pre-1971 price during the late 1970s. This is the period of the grand reflow of capital to the United States, measured by the International Monetary Fund as the "statistical discrepancy in the world current account balance."

A similar collapse of the dollar and equity values occurred during the years 1929-1933. With stock prices at a fraction of their previous values, and the economy in ruins, President Franklin Roosevelt was persuaded by the American friends of John Maynard Keynes to force a devaluation of the dollar in 1932, giving the old *fondi*—particularly the fortunes of the Franco-Swiss- Italian "gold bloc" —the chance to buy into American equity at distress prices comparable to those available during the late 1970s.

Among modern financial institutions, the *Assicurazioni Generali* of Venice, the heir to the old Venetian fortunes, provides the most clues to the operations of the *fondi.* The "Generali," as an insurance organization, is a clearing house for the operations of numerous *fondi,* each one represented by its frontman, one of the principal European investment banks. Its board of directors consists of the principal banking fortunes of Western Europe, each of whom is to be found in the succeeding chapters drawn from the 1978 edition of *Dope, Inc.* These directors included:

Baron August von Finck, reputedly the richest man in Germany until his recent death (with the possible exception of Johannes von Thurn und Taxis), owner of the Merck und Finck investment bank. However large Finck's personal fortune might be, the bank's importance is a function of the *fondo* of the old Bavarian royal family of Wittelsbach.

Elie de Rothschild, of the French Rothschild family; Baron Pierre Lambert, the Belgian cousin of the Rothschild family and proprietor of the Banque Bruxelles-Lambert (and a force on Wall Street through Drexel Burnham Lambert);

Jocelyn Hambro of Hambro's Bank, which owned a quarter of Michele Sindona's Banca Privata when it went under in 1974;

Pierpaolo Luzzatto Fequiz, of the ancient Venetian Luzzatto family, whom we shall encounter later in this chapter in the company of the notorious Banco Ambrosiano;

Franco Orsini Bonacossi of the ancient Orsini family, whose origin includes members of the ancient Roman Senate.

Europe's two most powerful investment banks, Lazard Frères (of the 1,000-year-old David-Weill family) and the Banque Paribas (founded by Venetian Jews based in the Ottoman Empire trade) are the largest stockholders in the Assicurazioni through a variety of shells. The sister Venetian insurance company of the "Generali," the Riunione Adriatica di Sicurtà, includes among its directors members of the Giustiniani family of Genoa and Venice, descendants of the vile Roman Emperor Justinian; the Doria family, the chief Genoese financiers of the Spanish Hapsburgs; as well as the current Duke of Alba, descendant of the brutal

Spanish marcher-lord whom the Genoese bankers sent to the Netherlands four centuries ago to crush their independence.

Assicurazioni Generali and the Bank for International Settlements of Basel (the "central bank for central banks"), are the world's only financial institutions to keep their books in the old pre-war Swiss gold franc, the "hard currency" which the *fondi* employed to buy American equities at a dime on the dollar during the first fumbling years of the Roosevelt administration.

They waited long to avenge themselves against the upstart United States. Their chance came with the break of the dollar from its gold backing in 1971.

Given the collapse of Wall Street stock prices during the long agony of the dollar between the 1967 collapse of the pound sterling and the aftermath of the 1971 debacle, it is not surprising that every major brokerage firm ran into trouble no later than the mid-1970s. Lehman Brothers, once the most powerful firm on the Street, was the first to raise the white flag. It secured, through offices of George Ball, a 7% investment from Banca de la Svizzera Italiana, a Swiss bank which functioned as a virtual Swiss subsidiary of the Banca Commerciale d'Italia— the bank at whose headquarters the infamous Propaganda-2 lodge of Italian freemasonry had been founded years earlier.

The Banca de la Svizzera Italiana (BSI), based in Lugano, Switzerland, specialized in covert movement of Italian flight capital into the United States.

One by one, the other major Wall Street houses fell under the control of the old European *fondi*. The dominant mergers and acquisitions operation on Wall Street, Lazard Frères, had never been an American house in any event; it was always dominated by the French-Jewish David-Weill family, and only managed for the interim by its then chairman, Andre Meyer, when no suitable family member was available.

Drexel Burnham Lambert, the sixth-largest house, sold out its entire capital to the Lambert family of Brussels, the Belgian cousins of the Rothschild family.

A.G. Becker, an old-line Chicago brokerage firm, merged into a *ménage à trois* with S.G. Warburg, the supposedly independent branch of the Warburg banking family, and the ancient French-Ottoman Empire firm, the Banque de Paris et des Pays-Bas (Paribas), to create Warburg-Becker-Paribas (subsequently merged into Merrill Lynch during 1984).

With virtually no exceptions, Wall Street's major houses sold out to the *fondi*. Finally, in 1981, Wall Street's most powerful investment bank (with the possible exception of Henry Kissinger's employer Goldman Sachs), Salomon Brothers, merged with Phibro, the trading arm of the Oppenheimer interests. As we shall see below, the absorption of Salomon Brothers, investment bankers to New York's Citibank, had the most devastating implications of all.

In a July 1981 study, *Executive Intelligence Review* applied the results of an ingenious measure of foreign investment designed by the Securities Industry Association to available data for foreign control of U.S. equities. The Securities Industry Association showed the absurdity of Treasury data: Under the law, brokerage houses must report the nationality of securities transactions of foreign origin. The results of this survey proved enlightening; the Treasury data showed that foreign investors turned over their stock portfolios several times as fast as American investors. This was unlikely, the association argued; it was more likely that the Treasury had badly misestimated the total of foreign investment. If foreign investors behaved the same way as American investors, then the total foreign equity investment in U.S. stocks as of 1980 was $225 billion, three times the $75 billion figure estimated by the Treasury! That rough figure represents 20% of the value of all U.S. stocks. However, 20% of the total appeared to represent a much greater concentration of effective control.

We know that the European *fondi* and their investment banking frontmen launder funds from deficit countries, and turn these into anonymous investments in surplus countries, creating the supposed "statistical discrepancy." Once the nature of the swindle is known, the discrepancy disappears. Armed with a rough and ready estimate of the extent of Dope, Inc. infiltration of the American financial system and control over American corporate equity, we may complete the sordid tale of the dope traffickers' intimate relations with the most prestigious American financial institutions.

Hong Kong, Oppenheimer and Banco Ambrosiano: Flight Capital Is King

Salomon Brothers was the last of the big Wall Street firms, and most important, to go, merging in 1981 with the trading arm of the Oppenheimer empire, Phibro. In the process, the Oppenheimers acquired effective policy control of the largest American commercial bank, Citibank. A month after the Phibro-Salomon merger, Costanzo's deputy George Vojta quietly left for Phibro, to cement a transatlantic relationship between the biggest American bank and the biggest Anglo-South African raw materials empire. Harry Oppenheimer had stated earlier that year, "We mean to expand into North America," and proceeded to create a $3-billion vehicle with which to do so: the Bermuda-based investment firm Minorco, which Oppenheimer created the same year. Both Citibank Chairman Walter Wriston and Citibank's chief lawyer, Shearman and Sterling managing partner Robert Clare, joined the board of Minorco. A year earlier, Oppenheimer had taken control of 28% of the only South African gold firm to rival his Anglo-American, Consolidated Gold Fields of South Africa, the country's second-largest gold producer. With 28% control also of Engelhard Minerals, the largest American precious metals refiner and the parent organization of Phibro, Oppenheimer came to dominate world precious metals and related markets in a way that Anglo-American's nineteenth-century founder, Cecil Rhodes, could only have dreamed of.

Even more obscure than the ultra-secret operations of Phibro is Anglo-American's role in the Caribbean offshore market, the main dumping ground for international flight capital in transit to a more permanent home. About $100 billion in banking assets in the Bahamas alone, as well as substantial operations in the British Virgin Islands, Netherlands Antilles, Cayman Islands, and other Caribbean banking centers, move the money that disappears from the world's balance sheet in the form of the $200 billion "statistical discrepancy" described earlier. Chief investment banker to the region is the International Trust Corporation, or Itco, created by Anglo-American in consortium with Barclays Bank of the U.K., the

Royal Bank of Canada, and N.M. Rothschild of London—whom we will meet again and again in the pages that follow. Itco creates banks, investment companies, commodities firms, tax shelters, trust funds, and insurance and reinsurance outlets throughout the Caribbean, smoothing contacts with local bank regulators and backstopping the legal position of the offshore market operators with which it deals. Itco is, in effect, the offshore-banking sister subsidiary of Phibro.

Citibank, Oppenheimer's direct partner in the Caribbean funny-money business and indirect partner in the Phibro-Salomon combination, was not new to the flight capital game. In the early 1960s, Robert Meyjes of First National City Bank suggested to Chairman Walter Wriston that the bank establish a division for "private international banking" to conduit funds from wealthy individuals abroad into U.S. investment markets. Wriston backed the plan.

When the new division for international private banking opened, it had a staff of six, and managed $250 million. Twelve years later, the "private banking" division of the renamed Citibank was responsible for a $12.5 billion investment pool, and contributed 10% of the bank's annual profits.

The individual who had first proposed the new department was a Dutchman named Robert Christopher Portomas Meyjes. In a 10-year period, Meyjes rotated 600 bank trainees through his division. Today, his protégés manage the private banking divisions of most of the big American banks from Boston to San Francisco. Meyjes is now based at Citibank's Paris office.

The former bank trainees to whom Meyjes played Fagin during the 1960s maintain an active "old boys' " network, according to participants. Many have gone into business for themselves, handling private investments for clients referred to them by associates at the big commercial banks. Each "private international banker" keeps a black book of former colleagues who now operate on their own as "investment advisers." When a client abroad requests services that are too sensitive for the bank to handle—e.g., the creation of dummy subsidiaries or the chartering of non-existent aircraft—the banker will refer the client to one of the "advisers." The adviser will accomplish the required skullduggery, and the funds extracted by the client from his business or investment portfolio in his home country are then invested through the "private banking division" of the commercial bank which made the referral.

David Rockefeller's Chase Manhattan Bank did not take long to imitate Citibank's imaginative program for obtaining new deposits. In 1966, a memo circulated in Chase's international division arguing explicitly that the bank should seek illicit international funds as new sources of deposits. In Chase's international department, this became referred to as "looking for mafia money." Chase found that this was more easily proposed than accomplished. It had made the Asian market a priority, but found that Hong Kong, the central, Asian offshore market, was too closed a club to afford easy access to an American bank. Until Chase brought the billionaire shipowner Y.K. Pao onto its own board of directors, establishing a link to the Hongkong and Shanghai Bank (where Y.K. Pao is vice chairman), Chase could not begin its subsequ ent expansion into the Hong Kong market.

Bank of America, looking westward from its headquarters in San Francisco, also made Hong Kong its top priority. Rudolph Peterson, its former international chief, once told a reporter, "The Hongkong and Shanghai Bank is the dominant institution there, but we found a way to work with them so that they wouldn't see us as a threat."

When the now-infamous Banco Ambrosiano went down in the financial scandal of the 1980s, the chairmen of the major American commercial banks could not have been more embarrassed had they been forced to tell their wives that they had contracted a social disease. Ambrosiano was a financial brothel; by itself it is of no interest past the police blotter, but for the fact that its ownership, and clientele included the financial elite of Europe and the United States. Not merely the major Italian banks, including the Banca Commerciale Italiana and its Swiss offshoot Banca de la Svizzera Italiana, but Bank of America and Chase Manhattan Bank were up to their ears in the scandal.

The most prominent financier of the Italian Socialist Party and the treasurer of the Propaganda-2 lodge of Italian freemasonry, Calvi built the $6-billion Banco Ambrosiano into the core of a $20-billion international empire of merged and associate companies. But Ambrosiano itself fit tightly into a larger series of Chinese boxes, a publicity-shy but powerful international syndicate called "Inter-Alpha," i.e., "among the first." Inter-Alpha was founded as the bridge between the Levantine money-wash of Roberto Calvi and the Far Eastern operations of the Hong Kong dope financiers: its British members are the Royal Bank of Scotland and its English counterpart, the Williams and Glyns clearing bank. At the time of the Ambrosiano bankruptcy in 1982, the Royal Bank of Scotland was negotiating for a merger with none other than the Hongkong and Shanghai Bank.

Remarkable are the intimate ties between Calvi and the major American banks. The Inter-Alpha group capitalized a small securities firm in New York under the name "Ultrafin," leaving the management to Roberto Calvi and his close friend, the late Club of Rome founder Aurelio Peccei, the former chief of Fiat's Argentina operations. At Peccei's suggestion, Calvi brought in the chief economist of David Rockefeller's Trilateral Commission, Professor Richard Gardner, to act as intelligence chief for Inter-Alpha in New York. Gardner became a board member of Ultrafin in New York with this special assignment.

Richard Gardner, personally close to Chase Manhattan chief Rockefeller, drafted all the major financial documents of the Trilateral Commission, including the 1976 plan to replace national governments' control of economic policy with a truly global central bank. His wife, Daniele Luzzatto, is the daughter of Bruno Luzzatto, the aristocratic Venetian who controlled the Paris office of the Marshall Plan after World War II.

Bank of America, meanwhile, together with the Banca Nazionale della Agricoltura, the Banca d' America e d'Italia had capitalized a joint venture with Banco Ambrosiano, the $3-billion-in-assets Interbanca Spa.

Almost to the end, Bank of America defended its connection to Calvi. As reported in EIR July 7, 1981, the chief of the San Francisco bank's international department, Rudolph Peterson, said, "Banco Ambrosiano is a fine upstanding bank of good reputation." Peterson, whose close ties to Italy earned him the country's Grand Order of Merit, added, "I'm sure this scandal concerning them will wash away. Even when there is chaos all around them, the bankers and especially the central bankers know how to get through. The banks and central bank will continue with their direction, while they pull through and the scandal washes away."

Kissinger and the New Directorate of Dope, Inc.

The Bank of America's Peterson was wrong. Calvi ended up hanging beneath Blackfriars Bridge in London, and Dope Inc. was reorganized again—this time from the top.

These capabilities, as we reported them six years ago, were impressive in their day. But they are no longer needed. The grand redeployment of the oligarchical *fondi* onshore to the United States made them superfluous.

When Henry Kissinger was elected to the board of directors of American Express in March 1984, a circle was completed which had begun with the wave of foreign takeovers of American securities houses during the 1960s and 1970s. George Ball's old firm, Lehman Brothers, had long since been absorbed by its great rival among the old-line German-Jewish Wall Street houses, Kuhn Loeb, to form Lehman Brothers-Kuhn Loeb. Shearson Hayden Stone, the second retail broker after Merrill Lynch, had repeated Merrill Lynch's march into investment banking by absorbing the third of the old-line German-Jewish firms, Loeb Rhoades. Now American Express, in turn, swallowed up Shearson-Loeb Rhoades and Lehman-Kuhn Loeb, bringing under a single umbrella a large part of what we identified in 1978 as the supposedly respectable interests behind organized crime and the drug traffic. The American Express board member and chief attorney responsible for handling the serious of mergers is Kenneth Bialkin, the current chairman of the Anti-Defamation League of B'nai B'rith; his predecessor, Theodore Silbert of the Recanati family's Sterling National Bank, currently faces a civil suit initiated by the Italian government, charging that Silbert helped Michele Sindona to launder money for the bankrupt Banca Privata.

Shearson Lehman American Express, as the ultimate Wall Street merger calls itself, is the phoenix which has arisen from the ashes of the offshore money markets. The new entity is effectively controlled, in turn, by two of the world's shadiest financiers, Edmund Safra and Carl Lindner, each of whom owns about 4% of the stock. Lindner, as noted earlier, owns the old United Fruit dope-pushing apparatus. Safra's case is more interesting.

Safra's controlling share of American Express derives from the January 1983 merger of his Trade Development Bank of Geneva with American Express International Bank where Safra briefly served as chairman. Amex took control of the Swiss institution and its global network, in return for 4% of its outstanding shares. Safra is the reported frontman for the Syrian-Jewish banking families who served the Venetian Genoese *fondi* from Aleppo through the long history of Levantine finance.

Safra's Republic National Bank of New York, in the person of its chairman, Theodore Kheel, made the introductions that permitted shady Argentine banker

David Graiver to buy up the American Bank and Trust. Graiver subsequently looted $45 million from the American Bank and Trust, in cooperation with John Samuels, a New York frontman for Safra's original backers, the Recanati family of Israel Discount Bank. The Argentine swindler subsequently disappeared after his plane crashed over Mexico. Graiver had been the principal financier for the Argentine terrorist organization, the Monteneros, and functioned as the Argentine connection for the old Tibor Rosenbaum-Meyer Lansky money wash, before his short-lived fling in New York.

These are current employers of Henry Kissinger, who also serves as vice chairman of the International Advisory Board of Chase Manhattan Bank (he was chairman until David Rockefeller retired from the bank and moved to its International Advisory Board); adviser to Goldman Sachs; and a consultant to dozens of leading corporations and financial institutions through Kissinger Associates.

The members of Kissinger Associates represent a de facto board of directors for the entity we call Dope, Incorporated. Just as Kissinger is represented on the board of American Express, it is represented on Kissinger's, in the person of Mario d'Urso. D'Urso came to Shearson Lehman American Express through the old Kuhn Loeb firm, whose international department he directed before it merged into Lehman. He is also the New York chief for the Jefferson Insurance Company, the joint arm of the Venetian insurance giants Assicurazioni Generali and Riunione Adriatica di Sicurtà; as we saw earlier, these are the central clearing-houses for the ancient Venetian *fondi*. The New York chairman of Jefferson Insurance is an old State Department crony of Kissinger, Nathaniel Samuels, also of the old Kuhn Loeb firm; Nathaniel Samuels is also the New York chairman of the Banque Louis-Dreyfus Holding Company in the United States and director of the Banque Louis-Dreyfus of Paris. This bank owns the grain company of the same name, one of the grain-cartel firms which hook into the Venetian insurance companies. Another board member of Jefferson Insurance for many years was the former British Intelligence station chief in New York City, financier Arthur Ross, an intimate of Lazard Frères' late chairman, André Meyer.

Britain's Lord Carrington, the cofounder of Kissinger Associates until his move to NATO headquarters in Brussels, is a former director of both Hambro's Bank (one of the constituent *fondi* of the Assicurazioni Generali) at the time that Hambro's bought 25% of Michele Sindona's Banca Privata, and also former director of Barclays Bank, the principal financier and partner in Caribbean skullduggery of the Oppenheimer interests.

Lord Carrington was replaced on the Kissinger Associates board in mid-1984 by the chairman of the London merchant bank S.G. Warburg, Lord Eric Roll of Ipsden. Lord Roll had just completed a reorganization of London Warburg interests under the umbrella of the Warburg holding company Mercury Securities.

The Oppenheimer family's London vehicle (which we shall encounter later when we examine the offshore finances of the Soviet Union), Charter Consolidated, meanwhile bought a 9% stake in the new Warburg consortium. Warburg has a mutual ownership with the Paris Banque de Paris et des Pays-Bas, the major stockholder of the Assicurazioni Generali of Venice.

In Asia, Kissinger Associates is represented by Sir Y.K. Kan of Hong Kong, who represents the four overseas Chinese families which control the Hong Kong-based Bank of East Asia.

The staff of Kissinger Associates is headed by Lawrence Eagleburger, the former highest-ranking member of U.S. foreign service, and a Kissinger protégé since the Nixon days. In a 1984 series on Jamaica's marijuana economy, the *New York Times* ridiculed Eagleburger's claims that, in supporting the Edward Seaga regime in Jamaica, he had no idea that Seaga had intentionally made marijuana the country's principal cash crop. Seaga had announced his intention to the *Washington Post* and on the U.S. network television program "Face the Nation."

The intertwining of interests represented in Kissinger Associates is not new. On the contrary, these are representatives of the ancient *fondi* who have collaborated for centuries. What is new and ominous is that the men who perform the dirty work of the *fondi* have moved out of shadows of Caribbean offshore banking and Hong Kong smuggling, and into the board rooms of the most powerful American financial institutions, and close to the councils of the United States government itself. It is even more ominous that the major conduit for the political influence of the Soviet Empire in American politics has now become the point of interchange of the constituent parts of Dope, Inc., doubly so in the context of the Soviet move into the financial underworld which we shall document in a later chapter.

As the International Monetary Fund attempts to destroy, one by one, the friends of the United States in the developing world, creating the conditions in which Soviet influence may extend itself to nations inherently hostile to Soviet designs, so the dope-peddling policies of the IMF finance the Soviet Empire's covert operations. The monster we identified in 1978 has moulted, shedding such skin as the Banco Ambrosiano and Investors Overseas Services, only to multiply in extent and influence. Six years ago, the narcotics traffic menaced all future generations of youth. Now it is the center of the gravest threat to Western civilization since the fourteenth century. Slowly, belatedly, the governments of the West have acknowledged the extent of the problem, and, in their lumbering fashion, accepted parts of the analysis we offered six years ago. But effective, ruthless, action has yet to be taken, against the citizens and institutions who have brought the dregs of the financial underworld to the apex of power in political life.

7. From Dope, Inc.:
Britain's First Opium War

Britain's First Opium War

Introduction: To Sap the Vitality of a Nation

This is the setting for what follows below: Narcotics are pouring in from abroad through a well-organized, efficient group of smugglers. One-fifth of the population abuses drugs, an epidemic surpassing any known since the Great Plagues. Not only the poor, but the wealthy and the children of the wealthy have succumbed. Within the nation, organized crime displays its drug pr ofits without shame, ruling local governments, and threatening the integrity even of national government. None of their opponents is safe from assassins, not even the chief of state. Law enforcement is in shambles. The moral fiber of the nation has deteriorated past the danger point.

And one of the leading dope-traffickers writes to his superiors abroad, that as along as drug use continues to dominate the country, "there is not the least reason to fear that she will become a military power of any importance, as the habit saps the energies and vitality of the nation."[1]

The familiar description is not of America in 1986, but China in 1838, on the eve of the First Opium War, when Great Britain landed troops to compel China to ingest the poison distributed by British merchants.

During the last century, British finance protected by British guns controlled the world narcotics traffic. The names of the families and institutions are known to the history student: Matheson, Keswick, Swire, Dent, Baring, and Rothschild; Jardine Matheson, the Hongkong[1] and Shanghai Bank, the Chartered Bank, the Peninsular and Orient Steam Navigation Company. Britain's array of intelligence fronts ran a worldwide assassination bureau, operating through occult secret societies: the Order of St. John of Jerusalem, its Zionist branch centered in the Jerusalem Foundation, Mazzini's Mafia, the Triads, or Societies of Heaven in China.

Paging back over the records of the narcotics traffic and its wake of corruption and murder, the most uncanny feature of the opium-based Pax Britannica is how shamelessly, how publicly the dope-runners operated. Opium trading, for the British, was not a sordid backstreet business, but an honored instrument of state policy, the mainstay of the Exchequer, the subject of encomia from Britain's leading apostles of free trade—Adam Smith, David Ricardo, Thomas Malthus, James Mill, and John Stuart Mill. The poisoning of China, and, later, the post-Civil War United States, did not lead to prison but to peerages. Great sectors of the Far East became devoted to the growing of the opium poppy, to the exclusion of

---

1. As quoted in Jack Beeching, *The Chinese Opium Wars* (New York: Harvest Books, 1975), p. 258.

food crops, to the extent that scores of millions of people depended utterly on the growing, distribution, and consumption of drugs.

The Keswicks, Dents, Swires, and Barings *still* control the world flow of opiates from their stronghold in the British Crown Colony of Hong Kong. Jardine Matheson, the Hongkong and Shanghai Banking Corporation, and the Peninsular and Orient Steam Navigation Company *still* control the channels of production and distribution of the drugs from the Far East, through the British Dominion of Canada, into the United States. By an uninterrupted chain of succession, the descendants of the Triads, the Mafia, and the *Hofjuden* of the British Chamber of Jewish Deputies *still* promote drug traffic, dirty money transfers, political corruption, and an assassination bureau that has claimed the life of an American President. Of course, the drug revenues of this machine are no longer tallied in the published accounts of the British Exchequer. But the leading installations of the drug traffic are no more hidden than they were a hundred years ago. From the Crown Colony of Hong Kong, the HongShang bank does what the Keswicks set it up to do: provide centralized rediscounting facilities for the financing of the drug trade. The surnames of senior management are still the same.

Even today, the grand old names of Prohibition liquor and dope-running rouse the deep awareness of Americans: e.g., Bronfman and Lansky. Are the denizens of the India opium trade, of the Prohibition mob, imprisoned in the history books and behind the movie screen? Not infrequently, the observer feels a momentary lapse in time, and sees not a history book, but the morning newspaper, not the late-night movie, but the evening television newscast.

The story we have to tell happened twice. It first happened to China, and now it is happening to the United States. Emphasizing that neither the names nor the hangouts of the criminals have changed, we begin by telling how it happened the first time.

Banks were the key to organizing the drug trade, La Rouche argued. Shown here: the Hongkong and Shanghai Bank, an original British Drug bank, plus Chase Manhattan Bank, and a non-banking drug-money-laundering front, Resorts International.

1. The East India Company's War Against China

In 1715, the British East India Company opened up its first Far East office in the Chinese port city of Canton and began trading in opium. Between that time and the First Opium War against China in 1840, Great Britain did not take over the dope trade. The dope trade took over Britain. The vehicle was the 1783 near coup d'état by Lord Shelburne (the British prime minister who concluded peace negotiations with the American colonies after Yorktown), which brought to power in London the financial and political faction that had conducted the Asian opium trade.

Shelburne's ruling combination centered on the East India Company, a group of Scottish merchants, and an alliance on the continent with the chivalric order of the Knights of St. John of Jerusalem and the Society of Jesus. Unable to rule in his own name—he was known as the "Jesuit of Berkeley Square" —Shelburne wielded the power that kept William Pitt the Younger in the prime ministership for twenty years.

The East India Company had begun its business in dope in 1715, but they were not the first. The Portuguese and later the Dutch took over the centuries-old dope-trading routes paved by Arab and Indian traders, including opium trade between Canton, and Portuguese-controlled Macao. The Dutch later negotiated an opium monopoly for the entire northern part of the Indian subcontinent that included Bengal, Bihar, Orissa, and Benares. The Dutch traders were permitted to force-draft Indian peasants to produce opium in exchange for taxes paid to the Mogul court. By 1659, the opium trade had become second only to the trade in spices, for which opium was a medium of exchange. By 1750, the Dutch were shipping more than 100 tons of opium a year to Indonesia.

Opium has always been an extraordinarily lucrative commodity, but the Dutch did not fail to notice its side benefits. According to one historian, the Dutch found "opium a useful means for breaking the moral resistance of Indonesians who opposed the introduction of their semi-servile but increasingly profitable plantation system. They deliberately spread the drug habits from the ports, where Arab traders used opium, to the countryside."[2]

The East India Company remained on the sidelines of this trade until the 1757 military victories that made Bengal a crown colony. But the beneficiary of the new move into the opium trade was not Britain, nor even the company itself. The company had paid the costs of the 1757 military expeditions, but saw none of the profit, as the lucre from the opium trade went to line the pockets of the company's officials in India. Repeatedly, the East India Company had to apply for a parliamentary bailout, until Shelburne moved in, reorganized the company, and made it the central instrument of loot for the maintenance of the British Empire.

Shelburne took two bankrupt entities, the East India Company and the British Empire, and combined them to make a going concern. By the end of the Revolutionary War with the American colonies, Britain's national debt had swollen to the then-stupendous figure of £240 million. Like today's under-

---

2 Philip Woodruff, The Men Who Ruled India (London: J. Cape, 1953)

developed countries, Britain's yearly debt service consumed more than half of all government tax revenues. More serious, through the League of Armed Neutrality, the European alliance that had formed against Britain during the war, England had lost to France most of the European market in staple items such as linens, textiles, and ironware.

To alleviate the crisis, Shelburne proposed a two-pronged strategy: expand the opium traffic and subvert the United States—both under the banner of free trade. The first achieved crowning success with the Chinese Opium War; the second not until the twentieth century.

First, Shelburne struck an alliance with the East India Company faction around Laurence Sullivan, whose son had subcontracted for the private opium monopoly in Bengal, and Francis Baring, the Anglo-Dutch banker prominent in the Atlantic trade. With the money from the opium trade and the monarchy's patronage machine, Shelburne bought the Parliament in 1783 lock, stock, and barrel, and consolidated a financial power that far outweighed the landed families of the 1688 Glorious Revolution that had so bungled British policy toward the American colonies.

Shelburne's chief propagandist was Adam Smith, the paid official of the East India Company, whose 1776 tome *The Wealth of Nations* set forth British policy to maintain the American colonies as backward raw materials producers and the mandate to expand the opium trade. Smith blasted the East India Company's practice of "ordering a peasant to plough up a rich field of poppies and sow it with rice or some other grain," in order to maintain high opium prices in the existing restricted markets. Opium was to be transformed from the source of fortunes for a few East India Company officials into the lifeblood of the Empire. Wrote Smith in *The Wealth of Nations:*

"The servants of the company have upon several occasions attempted to establish in their own favour the monopoly of some of the most important branches, not only of the foreign, but of the inland trade of the country . . . . In the course of a century or two, the policy of the English company would in this manner have probably proved as destructive as that of the Dutch . . . Nothing, however, can be more directly contrary to the real interest of those companies considered as the sovereigns of the countries which they have conquered. . . . . It is in [the sovereign's] interest, therefore, to increase as much as possible that annual produce. But if this is the interest of every sovereign, it is peculiarly so of one whose revenue, like that of the sovereign of Bengal, arises chiefly from a land rent. That rent must necessarily be in proportion to the quantity and value of the produce, and both one and the other must depend upon the extent of the market."[3]

The "produce" was opium.

In 1787, British Secretary of State Dundas had proposed that Britain storm China for the creation of the opium market. The East India Company meanwhile established a set of cutouts, or intermediaries, to conduct the exports of opium from India to China on the Company's covert behalf. Among the first of these was Jardine Matheson, which maintains an active hand in Far East heroin-trafficking to this day.[4]

---

3. Adam Smith, Wealth of Nations, Representative Selections (New York: Bobbs-Merrill, 1961).
4. *Beeching, Chinese Opium Wars*

Under the direct sponsorship now of the Crown, Jardine Matheson and others fostered an epidemic of opium-trafficking into China. By the year 1830, the number of chests of opium brought into China increased fourfold, to 18,956 chests. In 1836, the figure exceeded 30,000 chests. In financial terms, trade figures made available by both the British and Chinese governments showed that between 1829 and 1840, a total of 7 million silver dollars entered China, while 56 million silver dollars were sucked out by the soaring rise in opium trade.[5] In fact, by 1830; opium was the largest commodity in world trade.[6]

'The Chinese Have Fallen Into the Snare'

In 1840, the Chinese Emperor, confronted with a drug addiction crisis that was destroying the Mandarin class and the nation, tried to restrict the British trading companies. Britain's answer was war.

The year before, the Emperor had appointed Lin Tse-hsu commissioner of Canton to lead a war against opium. Lin launched a serious crackdown against the Triad gangs, who were sponsored by the British trading companies to smuggle the drugs out of the "Factory" area into the pores of the communities. The Triad Society, also known as the "Society of Heaven and Earth," was a century-old feudalist religious cult that had been suppressed by the Manchu Dynasty for its often violent opposition to the government's reform programs. The Triad group in Canton had been profiled and cultivated by missionaries and recruited into the East India Company's opium trade by the early nineteenth century.

When Lin moved to arrest one of the British nationals employed through the opium merchant houses, Crown Commissioner Capt. Charles Elliot intervened to protect the drug smuggler with Her Majesty's fleet. And when Lin responded by laying siege to the factory warehouses holding the tea shipments about to sail for Britain until the merchants turned over their opium stockpiles, Elliot assured the British drug-pushers that the Crown would take full responsibility for covering their losses.

The British Crown had its *casus belli*. Matheson of the opium house Jardine Matheson joyously wrote his partner Jardine—then in London conferring with Prime Minister Palmerston—on how to pursue the pending war with China:

"The Chinese have fallen into the snare of rendering themselves directly liable to the Crown. To a close observer, it would seem as if the whole of Elliot's career was expressly designed to lead on the Chinese to commit themselves, and produce a collision."

Matheson concluded the correspondence: "I suppose war with China will be the next step."[7]

Indeed, on October 12, 1839, Palmerston sent a secret dispatch to Elliot in Canton informing him that an expeditionary force proceeding from India could be expected to reach Canton by March 1840. In a followup secret dispatch dated November 23, Palmerston provided detailed instructions on how Elliot was to

---

5. Ibid., p. 43.
6. Ibid.
7. Beeching, *Chinese Opium Wars,* p. 80.

proceed with negotiations with the Chinese—once they had been defeated by the British fleet.

Palmerston's second dispatch was, in fact, modeled on a memorandum authored by Jardine dated October 26, 1839, in which the opium pusher demanded: (1) full legalization of opium trade into China; (2) compensation for the opium stockpiles confiscated by Lin to the tune of £2 million; and (3) territorial sovereignty for the British Crown over several designated offshore islands. In a simultaneous memorandum to the prime minister, Jardine placed J&M's entire opium fleet at the disposal of the Crown to pursue war against China.'[8]

The Chinese forces, decimated by ten years of rampant opium addiction within the Imperial Army, proved no match for the British.

The British fleet arrived in force and laid siege in June of 1840. While it encountered difficulties in Canton, its threat to the northern cities, particularly Nanking, forced the Emperor to terms. Painfully aware that any prolonged conflict would merely strengthen Britain's bargaining position, he petitioned for a treaty ending the war.

When Elliot forwarded to Palmerston in 1841 a draft Treaty of Chuenpi, the prime minister rejected it out of hand, replying, "After all, our naval power is so strong that we can tell the Emperor what *we* mean to hold, rather than what *he* should say he would cede." Palmerston ordered Elliot to demand "admission of opium into China as an article of lawful commerce," increased indemnity payment, and British access to several additional Chinese ports.[9]

The Treaty of Nanking, signed in 1842, brought the British Crown an incredible sum of $21 million in silver—as well as extraterritorial control over the "free port" of Hong Kong—to this day the capital of Britain's global drug-running.

The First Opium War defined the proliferation of and profiteering from mind-destroying drugs as a cornerstone of British imperial policy. Doubters need only consider this policy statement issued by Lord Palmerston in a January 1841 communiqué to Lord Auckland, then governor general of India:

"The rivalship of European manufactures is fast excluding our productions from the markets of Europe, and we must unremittingly endeavor to find in other parts of the world new vents for our industry [opium] . . . . If we succeed in our China expedition, Abyssinia, Arabia, the countries of the Indus and the new markets of China will at no distant period give us a most important extension to the range of our foreign commerce. . . ."[10]

It is appropriate to conclude this summary profile of Britain's First Opium War by quoting from the fifteenth edition of the *Encyclopaedia Britannica,* published in 1977. This brief biographical sketch of Lin Tse-hsu—the leader of the Chinese Emperor's fight to defeat British drugging of the Chinese-makes clear to the intelligent reader that British policy to this day has not changed one degree:

"He [Lin] did not comprehend the significance of the British demands for free trade and international equality, which were based on their concept of a

---

8. Ibid., p. 98.
9. Ibid., p. 127.
10. Ibid., p. 95.

commercial empire. This concept was a radical challenge to the Chinese world order, which knew only an empire and subject peoples. . . . In a famous letter to Queen Victoria, written when he arrived in Canton, Lin asked if she would allow the importation of such a poisonous substance into her own country, and requested her to forbid her subjects to bring it into his. Lin relied on aggressive moral tone; meanwhile proceeding relentlessly against British merchants, in a manner that could only insult their government."

Britain's Opium Diplomacy

Not a dozen years would pass from the signing of the Treaty of Nanking before the British Crown would precipitate its Second Opium War against China, with similar disastrous consequences for the Chinese and with similar monumental profits for London's drug-pushers. Out of the Second Opium War (1858-1860), the British merchant banks and trading companies established the Hongkong and Shanghai Corporation, which to this day serves as the central clearinghouse for all Far Eastern financial transactions relating to the black market in opium and its heroin derivative.

Furthermore, with the joint British-French siege of Beijing during October 1860, the British completed the process of opening up all of China. Lord Palmerston, the High Priest of the Scottish Rites of Freemasonry, had returned to the prime ministership in June 1859 to launch the second war and fulfill the "open China" policy he had outlined twenty years earlier.

Like the 1840 invasion of Canton, the Second Opium War was an act of British imperial aggression—launched on the basis of the first flimsy pretext that occurred. Just prior to his ordering of a northern campaign against Beijing (which permitted the British to maintain uninterrupted opium-trafficking even while a state of war was under way), Lord Palmerston wrote to his close collaborator Foreign Secretary Lord John Russell (grandfather and guardian of the evil Lord Bertrand Russell). "We must in some way or other make the Chinese repent of the outrage," wrote Palmerston, referring to the defeat suffered by a joint British-French expeditionary force at Taka Forts in June 1859. The expeditionary fleet, acting on orders to seize the forts, had run aground in the mud-bogged harbor, and several hundred sailors attempting to wade to shore through the mud had been either killed or captured. "We might send a military-naval force to attack and occupy Beijing," Palmerston continued. Following Palmerston's lead, *The Times* of London let loose a bloodcurdling propaganda campaign:

"England, with France, or England without France if necessary . . . shall teach a lesson to these perfidious hordes that the name of Europe will hereafter be a passport of fear, if it cannot be of love throughout their land."[11]

In October 1860 the British-French expeditionary force laid siege to Beijing. The city fell within a day with almost no resistance. Despite French protests, British commander Lord Elgin ordered the temples and other sacred shrines in the city sacked and burned to the ground—as a show of Britain's contempt for the Chinese.

---

11. Ibid., p. 272.

Within four years of the signing of the Treaty of Tientsin (October 25, 1860), Britain was in control of seven-eighths of the vastly expanded trade into China. This trade amounted to over £20 million in 1864 alone. Over the next twenty years, the total opium export from India—the overwhelming majority of which was still funneled into China—skyrocketed from 58,681 chests in 1860 to 105,508 chests in 1880.[12]

With its war against China, Britain established its method of control over the international opium trade:

1. Sponsorship of mass-scale opium addiction of targeted colonial and neocolonial populations as the way "to sap the vitality of the nation";
2. Willingness of Her Majesty's government to deploy Britain's national military forces to protect the opium trade; and
3. Use of the gigantic profits reaped from the trade to fund allied terrorist and organized criminal infrastructure within the targeted nation to carry out the trade and to act as a fifth column of British interests.

Beachhead in the United States

Plantation cotton, of the Southern states of the United States, was not merely a facet of the same trading operation that produced the dope trade; for all purposes, it was the dope trade.

Opium was the final stage in the demand cycle for British-financed and slave-produced cotton. British firms brought cotton to Liverpool. From there, it was spun and worked up in cloth in the mills in the north of England, employing unskilled child and female labor at extremely low wages. The finished cotton goods were then exported to India, in a process that destroyed the existing cloth industry, causing widespread privation. India paid for its imported cloth (and railway cars to carry the cloth, and other British goods) with the proceeds of Bengali opium exports to China.

Without the "final demand" of Chinese opium sales, the entire world structure of British trade would have collapsed.

It is around the slave production and transport of cotton that Britain gathered allies in the United States into the orbit of the East India Company's opium trade cycle. The southern cotton and slave trade were run to a significant degree by the same Scottish-based families that also ran the opium trade in the Orient. The Sutherland family, which was one of the largest cotton and opium traders in the South, was first cousin to the Matheson family of Jardine Matheson. The Barings, who founded the Peninsular and Orient Steam Navigation Company that carried the dope, had been the largest investors in U.S. clipper shipping from the time of the American Revolution. The Rothschild family, as well as their later "Our Crowd" New York banking cousins, the Lehmans of Lehman Brothers, all made their initial entry into the United States through the pre-Civil War cotton and slave trade.

In the North, John Jacob Astor became the first "American" to make his fortune in Chinese opium sales. "We see that quicksilver and lead from Gibraltar and opium from Smyrna, as well as some iron and steel from the North of Europe, began in

---

12. Ibid., p. 264.

1816 to take a conspicuous place in the list of Astor's imports into China," reported one of Astor's biographers. "Since according to Dr. Kenneth Latourette, quicksilver and opium did not become regular articles of import into China by Americans until 1816, Astor must have been one of the pioneers in their introduction."[13]

Astor poured his opium profits into Manhattan real estate—an arrangement between the two fields of enterprise that still remains intact.

Participation in the China opium trade, a de facto monopoly of the East India Company at the time Astor took part in the traffic, was a privilege extended only to Americans the East India Company thought deserving. Other American firms active in the Canton trade did not touch opium. Possibly, Astor's trading privileges were a British pecuniary reward for services as a British intelligence operative in the United States. Astor provided funds for the escape of his attorney Aaron Burr after Burr murdered Alexander Hamilton: At the time, Burr was a British intelligence agent. Burr's controller and the man to whom he fled after the murder of Hamilton, was East India Company employee Jeremy Bentham.[14]

Apart from the Astor group in New York City, the East India Company developed similar networks in Philadelphia and Boston, among other American cities. The leading British merchant bank, Baring Brothers, acquired a group of business partners (and brothers-in-law) in Quaker Philadelphia. The family the Barings married into was William Bingham's, reportedly the richest in the United States at the turn of the nineteenth century. One historian describes how closely the Bingham group aped the British oligarchy:

"Bingham was a most enthusiastic admirer of the British financial system which he desired to see copied in America. . . . Immense wealth enabled the Binghams to import fashions, and copy the Duke of Manchester's residence in Philadelphia . . . they gave the first masquerade ball in the city, encouraging what soon became a mania among the American rich—a passion for dressing up as aristocrats.

"The Binghams finally achieved their ambitions by uniting two daughters to foreign aristocrats: one to Count de Tilly, and the other to a member of the London banking house of the Barings, who later became Lord Ashburton."[15]

Another Philadelphia family that united itself with Baring Brothers was that of millionaire Stephen Girard,[16] whose interests survived under the family name, in Philadelphia's multibillion-dollar Girard Bank and Trust.

Several of the old "Boston Brahmin" families, however, made it into the mainstream of the nineteenth-century opium traffic, alongside the well-remembered British names of Jardine, Matheson, Sassoon, Japhet, and Dent. The Perkins and Forbes families achieved notoriety in the traffic after the East India Company's monopoly expired in 1832, and after the Astors had ceased to be an important factor. William Hathaway Forbes became so prominent an associate

13. Kenneth Wiggins Porter, *John Jacob Astor, Business Man*, (New York: Russell and Russell, 1966).
14. Ibid., p. 604.
15. Miriam Beard, *History of Business, Vol. II* (Ann Arbor, Mich.: University of Michigan Press, 1963), p. 162*ff*; see also Joseph Wechsberg, *The Merchant Bankers* (Boston: Little, Brown and Company, 1966), 104*ff*.
16. Wechsberg, *Merchant Bankers*, p. 123.

of the British trading companies that he joined the board of directors of the Hongkong and Shanghai Bank in 1866, two years after its founding.

Hathaway, Perkins, and Forbes operated through a joint outlet, Russell and Company, formed around the Perkins family shipping empire, a "business reaching from Rio to Canton." The fortunes of these families, as with the Philadelphia group, began with the slave trade—handed to them when the British dropped it as unprofitable in 1833. The China clippers of Russell and Company made not only Perkins's fortune, but most of the city of Boston's. A biographer reports, "By merging and creating Russell and Company, he was responsible to a large degree in the establishing of all of Boston's merchant families—Cabots, Lodges, Forbes, Cunninghams, Appletons, Bacons, Russells, Coolidges, Parkmans, Shaws, Codmans, Boylstons and Runnewells."[17]

Baring Brothers, the premier merchant bank of the opium traffic from 1783 to the present day, also maintained close contact with the Boston families. John Murray Forbes (1813-1898) was U.S. agent for Barings, a post occupied earlier by Philadelphia's Stephen Girard: He was the father of the first American on the HongShang board.

The group's leading banker became, at the close of the nineteenth century, the House of Morgan—which also took its cut in the Eastern opium traffic. Thomas Nelson Perkins, a descendant of the opium-and-slaves shipping magnate who founded Russell and Company, became the Morgan Bank's chief Boston agent, through Perkins's First National Bank of Boston. Morgan and Perkins, among other things, provided the major endowments for Harvard University.[18] Morgan's Far Eastern operations were the officially conducted British opium traffic. Exemplary is the case of Morgan partner Willard Straight, who spent the years 1901-12 in China as assistant to the notorious Sir Robert Hart, chief of the Imperial Chinese Customs Service, and hence the leading British official in charge of conducting opium traffic. Afterwards he became head of Morgan Bank's Far Eastern operations.[19]

Morgan's case deserves special scrutiny from American police and regulatory agencies, for the intimate associations of Morgan Guaranty Trust with the identified leadership of the British dope banks. Jardine Matheson's current chairman David Newbigging, the most powerful man today in Hong Kong, is a member of Morgan's international advisory board. The chairman of Morgan et Cie., the bank's international division, sits on the Council of the Royal Institute of International Affairs. The chairman of Morgan Grenfell, in which Morgan Guaranty Trust has a 40% stake, Lord Catto of Cairncatto, sits on the "London Committee" of the Hongkong and Shanghai Bank.

But perhaps the most devastating example of continuity among the corrupted American families involves the descendants of old John Jacob Astor. American citizen Waldorf Astor, his direct descendant, was chairman of the Council of the

---

17. Brett Howard, *Boston: A Social History* (New York: Hawthorn Books, 1976).
18. Ibid.
19. Brian Ingles, *The Forbidden Game: A Social History of Drugs* (New York: Charles Scribner, 1975), chapter 11.

Royal Institute of International Affairs during World War II, while Harvard-trained American citizens of its branch, the Institute for Pacific Relations, smoothed the transition to People's Republic of China opium production.

The Chinese Entry

The first shipments of opium into the United States for consumption were not brought in Astor's clipper ships, but via the "coolie trade," referred to by its British Hong Kong and Shanghai sponsors as the "pig trade."

Even before the Civil War, the same British trading companies behind the slave trade into the South were running a fantastic market in Chinese indentured servants into the West Coast. In 1846 alone, 117,000 coolies were brought into the country, feeding an opium trade estimated at nearly 230,000 pounds of gum opium and over 53,000 pounds of prepared (smoking) opium.[20] Although Lincoln outlawed the coolie trade in 1862, the black marketeering in Chinese (the term "Shanghaied" referred to the merchant company kidnapping—through the Triad Society—of impoverished and often opium-addicted Chinese) continued at an escalating rate through to the end of the century. Often these Chinese "indentureds" would put their entire earnings toward bringing their families over to the United States. This traffic in Chinese immigrants represented one of the earliest channels of opium into the country, and laid the foundations for the later drug trade out of the Chinatowns developed in San Francisco, Vancouver, and other West Coast cities during this period. The amount of opium coming into the United States during the last quarter of the nineteenth century is measured by the fact that in 1875, official government statistics estimated that 120,000 Americans— over and above the Chinese immigrant population—were addicted to opium![21]

Adding to the opium addiction, British pharmaceutical houses had begun commercial production of morphine in the years leading up to the Civil War and made large quantities available to both armies. The British firms misrepresented the morphine as a "nonaddictive" painkiller and even had the audacity to push it as a cure for opium addiction.

Protecting the Opium Market

In 1911, an international conference on the narcotics problem was held at The Hague. The conference participants agreed to regulate the narcotics trade, with the goal in mind of eventual total suppression. The conference was a major step forward; in the early days of the dope trade, neither opium nor morphine were considered illegal drugs, and heroin would not be outlawed as a prescription drug until 1924. But this conference and subsequent efforts to stem the opium plague ran up against Britain's open diplomatic posture on behalf of its unrestricted profiteering from a commodity known to destroy its consumers.

The success of the Hague Convention, as it was called, depended on strict enforcement of the earlier Anglo-Chinese agreement of 1905. Under that agreement, the Chinese were to reduce domestic opium production, while the British were to reduce their exports to China from British India correspondingly.

---

20. Beeching, *Chinese Opium Wars*, p. 178.
21. Ibid.

The Chinese, who had subscribed enthusiastically to both the 1905 and 1911 protocols, soon discovered that the British were completely evading both by sending their opium to their extra-territorial bases, Hong Kong and Shanghai. Opium dens in the Shanghai International Settlement jumped from 87 licensed dens in 1911 at the time of the Hague Convention to 663 dens in 1914![22] In addition to the trafficking internal to Shanghai, the Triads and related British-sponsored organized crime networks within China redoubled smuggling operations—conveniently based out of the warehouses of Shanghai.

In yet another act of contempt for the Hague Convention, Britain issued a large new loan to Persia in 1911. The collateral on that loan was Persia's opium revenues.[23]

Even with the post-Versailles creation of the League of Nations, Britain flaunted its drug-trafficking before the world. During this period, His Majesty's opium trade was so widely known that even the Anglophile U.S. newsweekly *The Nation* ran a series of documentary reports highly critical of the British role.[24]

At the Fifth Session of the League of Nations Opium Committee, one delegate demanded that the British government account for the fact that there were vast discrepancies between the official figures on opium shipments into Japan released by the Japanese and British governments. The British claimed only negligible shipments, all earmarked for medical use, during the period from 1916 to 1920; while the Japanese figures showed a thriving British traffic. When confronted with this discrepancy as prima facie evidence of British black market smuggling of opium into Japan, the British delegate argued that such black marketeering merely proved the case for creating a government-owned opium monopoly.

As late as 1927, official British statistics showed that *government opium revenues*—excluding the far more expansive black market figures—accounted for significant percentages of total revenue in all of the major Far East Crown colonies.[25]

British North Borneo	23%
Federated Malay States	14%
Sarawak	28%
Straits Settlements	37%
Confederated Malay	28%

In India as well, official Crown policy centered on protection for the opium market. According to one recently published account, when Gandhi began agitating against opium in 1921

"his followers were arrested on charges of 'undermining the revenue.' So little concerned were the British about the views of the League of Nations that after a commission under Lord Inchcape had investigated India's finances in 1923, its report, while recognizing that it might be necessary to reduce opium production

22. *Ingles, Forbidden Game. chapter 11.*
23. Ibid.
24. Ibid.
25. Ibid.

again if prices fell, went on to warn against diminishing the cultivated area, because of the need to safeguard 'this most important source of revenue . . . .

While the British government was professing to be taking measures to reduce consumption of opium and hemp drugs, its agents in India were in fact busy pushing sales in order to increase the colony's revenues."[26]

Lord Inchcape—who chaired the India Commission which endorsed continued opium production in British India—was a direct descendant of the Lord Inchcape who during the previous century had founded Peninsular and Orient Steam Navigational Company and subsequently helped establish HongShang as the clearinghouse bank for opium trade. Through to the present, a Lord Inchcape sits on the boards of P&O and the HongShang.

In 1923, the British-run opium black market was perceived as such a serious international problem that Congressman Stephen Porter, chairman of the U.S. House of Representatives Foreign Affairs Committee, introduced and passed a bill through Congress calling for country-by-country production and import quotas to be set on opium that would reduce consumption to approximately 10% of then-current levels. The 10% figure represented generally accepted levels of necessary medical consumption.

Porter's proposal was brought before the League of Nations Opium Committee—where it was publicly fought by the British representative. The British delegate drafted an amendment to Porter's plan, which called for increased quotas to account for "legitimate opium consumption" beyond the medical usage. This referred to the huge addicted population in British colonies and spheres of influence (predominantly in Asia) where no regulations restricted opium use. The enraged U.S. and Chinese delegations led a walkout of the plenipotentiary session; the British rubbers tamped the creation of a Central Narcotics Board designated with authority to gather information and nothing more; and the journalists stationed in Geneva henceforth referred to what remained of the committee as the "Smugglers Reunion."[27]

Nothing had been accomplished; the U.S. and Chinese governments were powerless in face of the fact that the deal between organized crime in the United States and the operatives of Hongkong and Shanghai Bank for a dope pipeline into the East Coast of the United States had already been set.

---

26. Ibid.
27. Ibid.

2. Britain's 'Noble Experiment'

In the years 1919 and 1920, two events of critical strategic importance for Britain's opium war against the United States occurred.

First, the Royal Institute of International Affairs was founded.

The purpose of this institution had been set forth over forty years before in the last will and testament of empire-builder Cecil Rhodes. Rhodes had called for the formation of a "secret society" that would oversee the reestablishment of a British empire that would incorporate most of the developing world and recapture the United States. Toward this objective, Rhodes's circle, including Rudyard Kipling, Lord Milner, and a group of Oxford University graduates known as "Milner's Kindergarten," constituted the Roundtable at the turn of the twentieth century. In 1919, the same grouping founded the Royal Institute of International Affairs as the central planning and recruitment agency for Britain's "one-world empire."

The second event occurred on January 6 of the next year. Britain declared its opium war against the United States. Americans knew it as Prohibition.

Prohibition brought the narcotics traffic, the narcotics traffickers, and large-scale organized crime into the United States. Illegal alcohol and illegal narcotics made up two different product lines of the same multinational firm. The British "Company" networks, through their distilleries in Scotland and Canada, and the British, from their opium refineries in Shanghai and Hong Kong, were the suppliers. The British, through their banks in Canada and the Caribbean, were the financiers. Through their political conduits in the United States, the British created the set of political conditions under which the United States might finally be won back.

Two tracks led to the drug epidemic in the United States, one in the Far East, and the other in the United States and Canada. Against the outcry of the League of Nations and nearly the entire civilized world, the British stubbornly fought to maintain opium production in the Far East, expanding the illegal supply of heroin, just as the drug went out of legal circulation in America in 1924. In North America, Canada—which had had its own period of Prohibition—went "wet" one month before the United States went dry.

In interviews with the authors, Drug Enforcement Administration officials have emphasized the similarity of the alcohol and narcotics modus operandi. When the agents of Arnold Rothstein and Meyer Lansky made their first trips to the Far East in the 1920s, they purchased heroin from the British with full legality. What the American gangsters did with the drug was their own business; the British opium merchants were merely engaging in "free enterprise." When Britain's leading distilling companies sold bulk quantities of liquor to Arnold Rothstein and Joseph Kennedy—for delivery either to the Bahamas or to the three-mile territorial limit of the United States coastal waters—they had no responsibility for what happened to the liquor once it reached American shores. (The identical explanation was offered by an official of the British Bank of the Middle East, which now services the Far East drug traffic through a smugglers' market in gold bullion in Dubai, on the Persian Gulf. "We only sell the gold, old boy," the banker said. "What those fellows do with it once they get it is up to them.")

Which of the American syndicates obtained this month's franchise for drug or liquor distribution was immaterial to the British traffickers. The greater the extent of intergang bloodshed, the less obvious their role would be. In fact, the British distillers could provoke such events at will by withholding needed inventory of bootleg alcohol.

The "Noble Experiment" was aimed at degrading the American people through popular "violation of the law" and association with the crime syndicate controlled by the Our Crowd banks of Wall Street. New York's Our Crowd is an extension of the London Rothschild banking network and British Secret Intelligence into the United States. For example, Sir William Wiseman was the official head of British Secret Intelligence in the United States throughout the World War I period. He became a senior partner in the investment house of Kuhn Loeb immediately on demobilization. Wiseman was a personal protégé of Canadian Roundtable founder Lord Beaverbrook and one of the most prominent public figures in the Zionist movement.[28]

With this lower Manhattan-Canada centered grouping acting as the political control, the Prohibition project was launched during the early 1910s under the shadow of the United States' entry into World War I.

It is a fraud of the highest order that Prohibition represented only a mass social protest against the "evils" of alcohol. The Women's Christian Temperance Union (WCTU) and its Anti-Saloon League offshoots enjoyed the financial backing of the Astors, the Vanderbilts, the Warburgs, and the Rockefellers.[29] Then as now, the funding conduits were principally the tax-exempt foundations—especially the Russell Sage Foundation and the Rockefeller Foundation. John D. Rockefeller I was hoodwinked by Lord Beaverbrook colleague and former Canadian Prime Minister Mackenzie King into not only bankrolling the WCTU, but providing it with the services of the foundation's entire staff of private investigators.[30]

One strand of the Temperance Movement was run by Jane Addams, who studied the Fabian Society's London settlement house Toynbee Hall experiment, and came to the United States to launch a parallel project which later produced the University of Chicago.[31]

These three British-spawned cults agitated nationally for Prohibition. While the WCTU and Anti-Saloon League staged well-publicized raids against saloons, the more sophisticated Fabian settlement house social workers of Jane Addams used the unique conjuncture of the recently passed Seventeenth Amendment certifying women's voting rights in national elections and the concentration of much of the adult male population on the war effort to vote up the Eighteenth Amendment making Prohibition the law of the land. The amendment was fully ratified by 1917; however, the Volstead Act that defined the federal enforcement procedures was not scheduled for implementation until January 6, 1920.

28. Who's Who in *America and Who's Who in World Jewry.*
29. John Kobler, *Ardent Spirits* (New York: G.P. Putnam's Sons, 1973).
30. Ibid.
31. Jeffrey Steinberg, *"Robert Hutchins: Creator of an American Oligarchy," The Campaigner* (May-June 1978) 10:73-77.

In Canada, a brief Prohibition period (1915-1919) was enacted by order of His Majesty's Privy Council principally to create the financial reserves and bootlegging circuit for the U.S. Prohibition. In this period, Canada's Bronfman family established the local mob contacts in the United States and consolidated contractual agreements with the Royal Liquor Commission in London.

In New York, primarily out of Brooklyn, teams of field agents of the Russell Sage Foundation conducted a reorganization and recruitment drive among local hoodlum networks—already loosely organized through Tammany Hall's New York City Democratic Party machine. "Legitimate" business fronts were established, replacing neighborhood nickel-and-dime loan-sharking operations, and specially selected individuals—largely drawn from the Mazzini "Mafia" transplanted to the United States during the late 1800s Italian migrations—were sent out of Brooklyn into such major Midwest cities as Chicago, Detroit, and St. Louis in the twelve months leading up to the Volstead enforcement. One such Brooklyn recruit was Al Capone.

The British oligarchy did much more than supply the gutter elements of the crime syndicates with their stock in trade. To a surprising extent, the Anglophile portion of America's upper crust joined the fun. The case of Joseph Kennedy, who owed his British contracts for liquor wholesaling to the Duke of Devonshire, and later married his daughter into the family, is notorious. In some respects more revealing is the strange case of Robert Maynard Hutchins, the president of the University of Chicago from 1929 to 1950. Hutchins had American citizenship, but was so close to the British aristocracy that he became a Knight Commander of Her Majesty's Venerable Order of St. John of Jerusalem, swearing an oath of chivalric fealty to the head of the order, the British monarch.

Under the guise of "social studies research," several well-known University of Chicago postgraduate students received their apprenticeships in the service of the Capone gang.

In 1930, University of Chicago graduate student Saul Alinsky, the godfather of the "New Left," entered the Capone mob in Chicago. Alinsky for several years was the accountant for the gang—at the height of the Prohibition profiteering.[32] Alinsky went on to be one of the most important British Fabian-modeled social engineers in the United States for the next thirty years, specializing in the creation of dionysian cults among the nation's youth and ghetto victims.

Alinsky, in fast, used the organizational model of the Capone mob to build up a criminal youth gang infrastructure in Chicago during the early 1960s that assumed street-level control over drug-trafficking and related criminal operations run thirty years earlier through the Capone gang. When the Our Crowd sponsors of Capone's initial deployment to Chicago determined at the close of Prohibition that a more "civilized" cutout was desired, Alinsky was the channel for bringing Frank Nitti into the mob.

As late as the 1960s, retired University of Chicago President Hutchins himself was under investigation for his involvement with drug-trafficking and other black market enterprises. Through the late 1960s his Center for the Study of Democratic

---

32. Saul Alinsky, *Reveille for Radicals* (New York: Random House, 1969).

Institutions was financed principally through Bernie Cornfeld's Investments Overseas Service (IOS)—an international pyramid swindle and drug money-laundering enterprise. Furthermore, Hutchins was simultaneously the president of a little-known Nevada foundation called the Albert Parvin Foundation, which -several congressional committees investigating organized crime cited as a front for Las Vegas gambling receipts.[33]

Mounting the Drug Invasion

The United States' fourteen-year experiment in Prohibition accomplished precisely what its British framers had intended. Ralph Salerno, an internationally recognized authority and historian on organized crime, a law enforcement consultant and former member of the New York City Police Department's intelligence division, succinctly summarized the effect of Britain's Prohibition gameplan in his book, *The Crime Confederation:*

"The most crucial event in the history of the confederation 'organized crime' was a legal assist called Prohibition . . . .

Prohibition helped foster organized crime in several ways. It was the first source of real big money. Until that time, prostitution, gambling, extortion and other activities had not generated much capital even on their largest scale. But illegal liquor was a multibillion dollar industry. It furnished the money that the organization later used to expand into other illegal activities and to penetrate legitimate business. Prohibition also opened the way to corruption of politicians and policemen on a large scale. It began the syndicate connection with politics and it demoralized some law enforcement groups to the point where they have never really recovered. . . .

"The manufacture and distribution of illegal liquor here and the importation of foreign-made liquor gave the men who were organizing crime experience in the administration and control of multi-billion dollar world businesses with thousands of employees and long payrolls. Men who had never before managed anything bigger than a family farm or a local gang got on-the-job training that turned them into leaders developing executive qualities.

"Mass evasion of the Volstead Act also put the average citizen in touch with criminals, resulting in tolerance and eventually even romantic approval of them. It permanently undermined respect for the law and for the people enforcing it. Ever since Prohibition the man in the street has accepted the idea that cops can be bought."[34]

The combined revenues of the illicit whiskey and drug trade during Prohibition had constituted a multibillion dollar black market booty. While families like the Kennedys and Bronfmans "made out like bandits" in the early 1930s transition to "legitimate" liquor trade, the overall financial structure for maintaining an organized crime infrastructure demanded diversification into other areas of black market activity only marginally developed previously. The market for illicit

---

33. Hank Messick, *Lansky* (New York: Berkley Medallion Books, 1971), p.172.
34. Ralph Salerno and John S. Tompkins, *The Crime Confederation* (New York: Doubleday and Company, 1969), pp. 275; 278-279.

drugs in the United States—though significantly expanded as the result of the Prohibition experience—was not to become the foundation of multi-billion dollar traffic for several decades.

In the interim, the Our Crowd-British crime syndicate turned to casino gambling and associated enterprises as the immediate area for expansion. The Lansky syndicate took the opportunity of Nevada's 1933 passage of specific regulations legalizing casino operations to turn that no-man's-land into a desert resort to house all the West Coast criminal operations that had previously been run on pleasure boats twelve miles off the coast of Hollywood. Lansky also moved into the Caribbean, preparing the way for the British offshore complex of unregulated banking.

Through the investment of the phenomenal profits derived from Prohibition into gambling casinos, professional sports stadiums, and racetracks, organized crime established the support structure during the 1930s and 1940s for the drug-trafficking that would begin in the mid-1950s—once a cultural climate had been created that was conducive to fostering drug addiction.

8. From Dope Inc.: Organized Crime

Organized Crime

1. The Bronfman Gang

The Bronfman family is best known to Americans through its ownership of Seagrams, the biggest liquor company in North America. The family's holdings stretch from whiskey, banking, mining, to real estate, and—although somewhat less publicized—narcotics. Today they are regarded as respectable and outstanding "philanthropists" whose name is attached to everything important in Canada—and Israel—be it government, business, or cultural affairs.

This was not always the public profile of the Bronfman family. Less than fifty years ago, they were known to be the biggest bootleggers in North America and were referred to by the less prestigious title "the Bronfman gang."

The Bronfmans have always been beholden to the Hofjuden elite. The first member of the family to come to North America was Yechiel Bronfman, a grist mill owner from Bessarabia, Romania, who later anglicized his name to Ekiel. Yechiel emigrated to Canada in 1889 under the sponsorship of the Moses Montefiore Jewish Colonization Committee.[35]

This enterprise had been initiated at an 1872 meeting between Baron Maurice de Hirsch, Baron Alfred de Rothschild, and other Zionists who established a Jewish Colonization Association to bring selected Russian and Eastern European Jews to agricultural settlements (kibbutzim) in the Canadian provinces of Manitoba and Saskatchewan.[36] The same period marked the transfer of the Warburg, Kuhn, Loeb, and related Our Crowd migration from Germany and Britain into lower Manhattan. In 1912, William Sebag Montefiore arrived in Montreal where he lived until his death in 1950. Lord Harold Sebag Montefiore, current head of the Jerusalem Foundation (the Zionist wing of the Most Venerable Order of St. John of Jerusalem) was sent to Canada for his early education. In the same period, Baron de Hirsch established the De Hirsch Foundation in Canada as the umbrella for all Canadian Jewish "philanthropic" activities, and the Montefiores created a club (named after the family) to service the resident elites. The Rothschilds, too, planted a branch of their family on Canadian soil.

Meanwhile, in Saskatchewan, the Bronfman family found little interest in eking a living out of the plains of midwestern Canada. The family first turned to selling wood, then to horse trading, and then most successfully to the hotel business (and prostitution).[37]

In Yiddish Bronfman means "liquorman," and the hotel business put the Bronfmans in a good position to take advantage of the 1915 advent of Canadian prohibition. Bronfman hotels became "boozeriums." Prohibition—enacted on orders from the Privy Council as the prelude to the 1920s Prohibition in the

---

35. Canadian Jewish Congress Report, 1967-68, in commemoration of Samuel Bronfman.
36. Ibid.
37. Peter C. Newman, *Bronfman Dynasty, The Rothschilds of the New World* (Toronto: McClelland and Stewart Ltd., 1978), pp. 66-73.

United States and the birth of organized crime—catapulted the Bronfmans into the multi-millionaire bracket and a status as the untouchable kingpins of crime in North America.

During Canada's four dry years from 1915 to 1919, the Bronfmans established their contacts with U.S. criminal figures for illegally importing liquor into Canada. In 1916, the Bronfmans established their first link with the opium trade proper. Samuel and Abe Bronfman, two of Ekiel's four sons, collaborated with the Hudson's Bay Company—in which the Keswick family of Jardine Matheson had controlling interest—to buy the Canadian Pure Drug Company. In this way the Bronfmans rushed into the loophole in the War Measures Act that permitted the distribution by pharmacists of alcohol for "medicinal" purposes.

When Prohibition in Canada ended in 1919 and Prohibition in the United States began, the Bronfmans simply turned from whiskey importing to whiskey exporting. After it was all over in May 1936, the Bronfmans agreed to pay $1.5 million to settle their account with the U.S. Treasury; the sum amounted to an admission that half the liquor that came into the United States during Prohibition was from the "liquormans."[38]

The "Seagram's Chickencock" the family poured across the border was a mixture of pure alcohol, sulfuric acid, caramel, water, and aged rye whisky. Between 1920 and 1930, some 34,000 Americans died from alcohol poisoning.

The strong links between Dope, Inc. and organized crime, including assassinations, are personified in Edgar Bronfman (lower right), whose family fortune came from the Seagram's Company, and William Weld (left above), of the White Weld banking family (and formerly Governor of Massachusetts). Also shown in the 1958 founding meeting in Paris of the Permanent International Exposition, Permindex, which was key to the Kennedy assassination.

Their control of the liquor flow during Prohibition U.S.A. gave the Bronfmans life-and-death control over American crime. Refusing to play ball with the Bronfman gang usually spelled death, and independent-minded gang bosses were often known to be executed by their lieutenants on the Bronfmans' behalf. One of the buyers best liked by the gang was New York City beer baron Arthur Flegenheimer, a.k.a. Dutch Schultz, who succeeded in wiping out his competition, including the notorious killer Legs Diamond. Schultz himself was later rubbed out when he took it into his head to murder crusading New York District Attorney

---

38. Newman, *Bronfman Dynasty*, p. 64.

Thomas Dewey. (There is some question about what Dewey was crusading for, as we shall see in the story of the Mary Carter Paint Company.)[39]

In the first years of Prohibition, Ekiel Bronfman's four boys ran all bootlegging from the prairie states of Canada to major distribution sites south like Chicago. To secure the shipment lines, Harry set up a dummy firm, Transcanada Transport Company. Transcanada was a protective cover for the Canadian Pacific Railway owned by respectable gentlemen back in London, which ran the whiskey across the border.[40] The Bronfmans also bought up stretches of barren farmland along the border and even built an underground pipeline to pump their "chickencock" into the United States.

In 1922, Bronfman brother-in-law Paul Matoff was executed gangland-style by the Chicago mob in a dispute over profit-splitting. A scandal ensued, public hearings were convened, and the Bronfman crimes came spilling out into the light of day. The Bronfmans received a mild reprimand from the Canadian government and relocated their operations to Montreal.

The year 1922 also marks the point when the Bronfmans procured their own distillery, hauled, with workmen included, from Kentucky to Montreal.

Since 1920 the Bronfmans had been importing British whiskey from the Distillery Company of London (DCL), which controlled more than half the world market in Scotch whiskey. DCL was owned by the higher echelons of the British nobility, including Field Marshal Haig, Lord Dewar, Lord Worlavington, and others. The dispensation of distribution rights was a decision made by His Majesty the King. In 1926, upon the request of Samuel Bronfman, the DCL agreed to go 50-50 in the Bronfmans' distillery, and the Distillery Corporation Limited was formed as a holding company with Bronfman and Seagram's distilleries. Headquarters were established at the Bronfmans' corporate castle in Montreal, but it was the Distillery Company of London's William Ross who was installed as president with Sam Bronfman as vice president. The British elite had given the green light to the Bronfmans.

Despite the big infusion of capital and the newly gained legitimacy the link-up with DCL afforded them, the smell of Bronfman smuggling and bribery grew too strong. In 1928, the Royal Commission on Customs recommended the immediate prosecution of Harry Bronfman on charges of attempted bribery. Shortly thereafter, the Bronfmans created the Atlas Shipping Company and moved their smuggling operations to the French islands of St. Pierre and Miquelon, fifteen miles off the Newfoundland coast. With licenses in Bermuda, Saint John, New Brunswick, Belize, and British Honduras, the Atlas Shipping Company was one of the first ties nailed down in the dirty money-drug underground railway between Canada and the Caribbean.[41]

A little ditty popular during the time indicates the amusement with which the British viewed the entire operation:

39. Hank Messick, *Lansky* (New York: Berkley Medallion Books, 1971), pp. 230-31.
40. James H. Gray, *Booze* (Toronto: Macmillan Co. of Canada, Alger Press, 1972).
41. Newman, Bronfman Dynasty, p. 127.

Four and twenty Yanks
Feeling very dry,
Went across the border
To get a drink of rye.
When the rye was opened,
The Yanks began to sing:
"God bless America,
But God save the King."

Organized Crime Comes of Age

With Prohibition, crime became a bigtime business. It was no longer based on small-scale prostitution, loan-sharking, or petty protection rackets. Now it was centralized around the marketing of one precious and outlawed commodity whose supply was controlled from London and from the British colony of Canada. Crime was reorganized from top to bottom into an integrated wholesale and retail distribution chain with well-defined marketing districts, quotas, and uniform pricing. Crime became syndicated.

Hundreds of movies spewed out of Hollywood about the "Roaring Twenties" have glamorized the truth: With Prohibition, Britain—through its Bronfman gang cutout—had created a nationally syndicated crime cancer. Within a decade of the Roaring Twenties, the Bronfman syndicate would be peddling heroin, cocaine, and every other available poisonous drug through the same wholesaling, transporting, and retailing system that bootlegged booze.

Bronfman's counterpart in the United States was one Arnold Rothstein. Just as Bronfman made it into the bigtime under the auspices of the Hofjuden elite, so Arnie Rothstein was sponsored by Our Crowd Zionist investment bankers who arrived in New York as the Montefiores were setting up business in Canada. Arnold Rothstein—the godfather of organized crime—was the son of a wealthy Our Crowd dry goods merchant.

At the turn of the century, the Russell Sage Foundation had issued a well-publicized field study of loan-sharking in New York City.[42] The report's wide publicity resulted in the bankrupting, jailing, or takeover of the petty gangsters by Rothstein, who emerged as a powerful Tammany Hall figure with a fabled loan-sharking business estimated at several million dollars.

Regionwide combines were formed up and down the East Coast for smooth distribution. The Reinfeld Syndicate—named after the Newark, New Jersey bootlegger and accused murderer Joseph Reinfeld—functioned as the middleman between the British liquor distilleries and the "rum rows" of Boston and New York. Its controlling shareholders were the four Bronfman brothers, Allan, Sam, Abe, and Harry. The U.S. leg was handled by Reinfeld and Abner "Longie" Zwillman, later the boss of Atlantic City, and Rothstein's gangs in New York.[43]

---

42. *Russell Sage Foundation, 1870-1946* (New York: Russell Sage Foundation, 1947), Volume 1. Loan-shark operation surveys were also conducted in Illinois and Kentucky.
43. Hank Messick, *Secret File* (New York: G.P. Putnam's Sons, 1969), pp. 277-78

In 1927, the Big Seven combine consolidated the entire East Coast distribution system. Its organizer was John Torrio—a dapper little gentleman who, without benefit of family, racket, or turf had gained notoriety for eliminating any local crime bosses who stood in the way of national syndication. Torrio was a Bronfman man who had murdered his own uncle to prove it. Brought into Chicago in 1910 by his uncle, racketeer "Big Jim" Colosimo, Torrio sniffed the wind on the eve of Prohibition and demanded that his uncle start making the right contacts to get into the lucrative business of bootlegging. When "Big Jim" refused, Torrio had him murdered and took over the Chicago mob as the distribution point for the Bronfman liquor.[44]

In 1925, Torrio suddenly left Chicago, heading for Havana and then landing in Italy. Returning to the United States in 1927 after he miraculously escaped Mussolini's purges of the Mafia, Torrio came back with one goal: to build a nationally organized crime syndicate.

While the mad killers and punks like Dutch Schultz, Legs Diamond, and Al Capone made the headlines every day and provided good material for gangster movies, John Torrio quietly continued the work that Arnold Rothstein (assassinated in 1928) had begun, now with the aid of Rothstein's successors Meyer Lansky and Lucky Luciano. Torrio could do what Lansky and the Bronfmans were prohibited from doing for reasons of ethnicity: Discipline the scores of family local crime chieftains and "moustache Petes" into one centralized business that could penetrate every sector of the economy. Known as the "assassin who never carries a gun," Torrio presented himself as the elder statesman of organized crime and commanded respect from the Mafia locals. "Cooperation is good for business" was his slogan.

The Big Seven had been Torrio's first step. The cooperative of East Coast bootleggers controlled from the top down to the local levels all prices, membership, centralized distribution points, corruption, and protection.

By 1928 Torrio was able to call a Cleveland meeting to establish a nationwide crime syndicate.[45] The gathering was unique in that it had succeeded in bringing together into one room all the crime bosses of every major organized city. There were three items on the agenda. First, how to use the huge profits of Prohibition and invest them in legitimate businesses that would permit a steadily increasing take for the syndicate. Second, how to deal with the Italian question. The ritual vendetta murders of the mafioso families were good for the newspapers, said Torrio, but bad for business. Immediately after the meeting the Castellammarese gang

44. Torrio's rise to power has been chronicled in hundreds of books and press accounts dealing with the history of organized crime and with the "Capone" Chicago organization in particular. See Don Maclean, *Pictorial History of the Mafia* (New York: Pyramid Books, 1974); Ralph Salerno and John S. Tompkins, *The Crime Confederation* (New York: Doubleday & Company, Inc., 1969); Martin A. Gosch and Richard Hammer, *The Last Testament of Lucky Luciano* (New York: Dell Publishing Co., Inc., 1974). Additional insight was provided through numerous interviews with law enforcement officials at the U.S. Customs Bureau and Drug Enforcement Administration.
45. Maclean, *Pictorial History of the Mafia*, p. 150; see also Donald R. Cressey, *Theft of the Nation: The Structure and Operations of Organized Crime in America* (New York: Harper and Row, 1969), pp. 29-53.

wars broke out in New York as the test case for Torrio's syndicate. Under the auspices of Lansky and Torrio, Lucky Luciano succeeded in wiping out all recalcitrant
godfathers. During the last night of the war—the infamous "Night of the Sicilian
Vespers" —over forty people were gunned down.[46]

With cartelization came the need for more long-lasting regulation—gangland
style. In the early 1930,s Murder, Inc. was formed as a regulatory commission of
sorts to police any overzealous "free enterprise" advocates who might try to buck
the syndicate. A special assassination bureau was set up by Meyer Lansky and
Benjamin "Bugs" Siegel. The "Bugs and Meyer Gang" had been distinguished by
the fact that it owed allegiance to no one (except maybe Arnold Rothstein); it
had originally been used to protect Bronfman liquor shipments across the border
against "freelance" hijackers.[47]

By 1932, Torrio was strong enough to pull together another meeting of the
syndicate, this time in Atlantic City, where a National Commission—the board of
directors of organized crime—was officially formed. Aside from the leading Italian
mafiosi who had survived the transition, Meyer Lansky, now regarded as the
financial and enforcement wizard of the syndicate, and Atlantic City's Zwillman
were in attendance as honored guests.

For the British, Prohibition was a roaring success. What had begun as a three-
way contract between Britain (the supplier), Bronfman (the cutout), and Rothstein
(the distributor) had become within the space of a decade a nationally organized
crime syndicate, a private, secret army under British banking and political control.

The Rothstein-Hong Kong Connection

To pick up the story of the modern-day Dope, Inc., let us return to Cleveland and
John Torrio's first 1928 meeting of the syndicate. The third item on the agenda was
what to do after Prohibition. The commodity, Torrio proposed, that would replace
liquor as the black-market, big-profit taker was narcotics.

When Prohibition began in 1920 Arnold Rothstein had personally gone to
Great Britain to establish the liquor pipeline with the British distilleries. At the
same time he had dispatched his underling Jacob "Yasha" Katzenberg to Shanghai
to begin negotiations for a dope pipeline from the Far East into the East Coast of
the United States.[48] (The West Coast had been sewn up in the 19th century with
a pipeline from Shanghai straight into the Pacific Chinese coolie communities.)

It was projected that the same networks established to bootleg liquor could
just as easily smuggle and retail narcotics. By 1926, U.S. narcotics agent-on-the-
scene in the Far East, Ralph Oyler, wrote back to his boss Levi Nutt, chief of the

---

46. Maclean, *Pictorial History of the Mafia*, p. 461. Figures vary for the death toll reached during the
    war period; however, on the night that New York boss Salvatore Maranzano was assassinated—
    September 11, 1931—and the immediate 48-hour period following, it is estimated that 40 gang
    leaders were killed in the overall purge. *See also:* Donald R. Cressey, *Theft of the Nation*, pp. 29-
    53, and Peter Maas, *The Valachi Papers* (New York: Bantam Books, 1968).
47. Messick, *Secret File*, pp. 96-97. Corroboration of the analysis presented here was provided
    through numerous and exhaustive interviews with law enforcement officials at the DEA and
    U.S. Customs Bureau.
48. Messick, *Lansky*, pp. 90, 97-98. Additional corroboration was provided by DEA officials in in-
    terviews in December 1977.

U.S. Narcotics Division, that the opium market had expanded so much that to meet market demand, Britain was "even taking shipments of crude opium from the Near East to add to her gigantic supply of Asian opium." The traditional opium families of Keswick, Sassoon, and Inch cape were preparing for the future.[49]

Let us now stand back and review—in light of this history—the jigsaw puzzle pieces that fall into place with Yasha Katzenberg's trip to Shanghai and the sealing of an opium pact.

First, Arnold Rothstein, Yasha Katzenberg's employer, was a product of the Rothschild dry goods empire that included the Seligman, Wanamaker, and Gimbel families. During Prohibition, according to the Bronfmans' own testimony, Rothstein, Meyer Lansky, and Lucky Luciano were the Bronfmans' main distributors. As Prohibition came to a close, Bronfman associates traveled to Shanghai and Hong Kong to streamline and expand the drug trade into the United States, negotiating with the foremost Chinese drug runners who were not only encouraged but pressured by the British business community to pull together an opium cartel.

The man dictating the opium policy to China in this period was Sir William Johnston Keswick of Jardine Matheson and the Hongkong and Shanghai Bank. From the period of the Shanghai Massacre to 1942 when he was interned by the Japanese, Keswick directed the International Settlements of Shanghai—the period of gross expansion of Shanghai heroin into the United States. The same Sir William Keswick was until very recently the director of the Hudson's Bay Company of Canada, the same company, it will be recalled, that collaborated with Sam and Abe Bronfman in 1916 to found the Pure Drug Company for illegal distribution of whiskey into Canada.

Working for Hudson's Bay along with Keswick is Sir Eric Drake, who not only sits on the board of several Bronfman-run banks and companies, but is also an employee of the Inchcape family and presently the deputy chairman of the Inchcapes' Peninsular and Orient Navigation Company. The current chairman of the board is the son of the Lord Inchcape who in 1923 called for the expansion of "that most valuable source of revenue" —the opium trade.

Sir Eric Drake is also a member of the board of Canadian Pacific, which plays a most vital role in the transshipment of drugs through Canada into the United States, just as it did with alcohol during Prohibition. Along with Lord Trevelyan, who heads up the HongShang's "gold for dope" exchange from his position at the British Bank of the Middle East, and Lord Inchcape, Sir Eric Drake sits on the board of British Petroleum, as does Sir William Johnston Keswick.

Sitting on the board of the Bank of Montreal along with Charles Bronfman and two Seagram's directors are J. Bartlett Morgan, William Arbuckle, and F.S. Burbridge, who in turn sit on the boards of Hudson's Bay, Canadian Pacific, and a host of other banks and corporations in which the drug families of the HongShang nexus play a policy-making role.

---

49. Report from Narcotics Division Agent Ralph Oyler to Narcotics Division Chief Levi Nutt, March 30, 1926 (DEA Library, Washington, D.C.).

We are not charging guilt by association, but rather making note of the fact that the series of legitimate enterprises the Bronfmans moved into toward the close of Prohibition are indistinguishable from and intermeshed with companies controlled by Keswick, Inchcape, and other leading opium traders. During the same period, these gentlemen openly supervised the drug trade into the United States. This association not only continues to this day, but it remains the mainstay of the Bronfman empire.

Going Legit

With the repeal of Prohibition, the Bronfmans, like so many of their partners across the border, "went legit." Organized crime sunk its millions in legitimate businesses that both acted as cover for illegal activities and set up the laundry networks for dirty money. The new phase of respectability signaled that the most successful bigtime whiskey bootleggers were switching to bigtime narcotics.

In the early days, the Bronfmans had to run all the risks of the smuggler's profession. They had to dodge the law, stay one step ahead of the desperados on the other side of the border, and whenever things went wrong, face the humiliation of public exposure and scandal. As a result, the family acquired a considerable reputation.

Looking expectantly toward the fast increase in drug trade in America, the British could not afford to leave their leading cutout in such an exposed and precarious position. Nor could they simply dispose of the Bronfmans after Prohibition. The family had become irreplaceable due to its in-depth control over the syndicate. Yet, the Bronfmans would be a liability if they continued to work as openly with their distributors in narcotics-trafficking as they did running Prohibition.

The problem was resolved by bringing the Bronfmans into the lower rungs of the Hofjuden caste. Almost overnight, the Rothschilds, Montefiores, de Hirsches, et al. took Mr. Sam, the crime czar of North America, and transformed him into a rising star of the Canadian Zionist movement.

- In 1934, Mr. Sam was given his first respectable post as chairman of the National Jewish People's Relief Committee (Canada).
- By 1939 he had been appointed head of Baron de Hirsch's Jewish Colonization Association, the same association that had brought Yechiel to Canada.
- In the same year, the Canadian Pacific Corporation invited Mr. Sam to establish a new refugee organization for Eastern European Jews.
- Within five years, the prince of crime was transformed by the good grace of His Majesty's oligarchists into a Zionist philanthropist. One post followed after another. He became head of the Canadian Jewish Committee, replacing Lyon Cohen, the son of Lazarus Cohen, the founder of the Jewish Colonization Association and the official agent of the de Hirsch family interest.

After World War II, Mr. Sam established the National Conference of Israeli and Jewish Rehabilitation, using his considerable smuggling skills to run guns to the Haganah.

Similar posts were awarded to the other Bronfmans. Allan Bronfman was named president of the Zionist Organization of Canada, a member of the board of trustees of the Federation of Jewish Philanthropists and of the national council of the Canadian Jewish Congress. Abe Bronfman was posted to the Joint Distribution Committee and also to the national council of the Canadian Jewish Congress.

Finally, in 1969 the Bronfmans were given the highest reward issued by Her Majesty. Sam was made a Knight of Grace of the Most Venerable Order of St. John of Jerusalem. His brother Allan and his son Charles were appointed to the highest rank, Knight of Justice of the order. These appointments are emphatically not ceremonial, but are only bestowed on those who have carried out the most dangerous and fruitful missions for the British Crown.

The Bronfmans' time had truly come. Sam's children were welcomed into the Hofjuden elite by intermarriage. Minda married Baron Alain de Gunzberg, himself an extension of the Rothschild family tree. De Gunzberg sits on the board of Seagram's, is managing director of the Banque Louis Dreyfus, and controls the Seligman-Louis Hirsch investment house that has close Rothschild ties. Edgar Bronfman's first marriage, to Ann Loeb, brought him instantly into a command position within the Wall Street house of Loeb, Rhoades, and Co. While taking over the Seagram's main branch in New York, Edgar's marriage clinched the tie to Our Crowd that had begun during Prohibition. His second marriage, to Lady Caroline Townshend, was unsuccessful. Phyllis Bronfman married Jean Lambert of the Belgian banking and mining interests.

Yet, despite their mountains of wealth, despite their hard-won entry into the realms of good breeding, it would be a mistake to think the Bronfmans were a power in their own right. When it comes to the question of control, they are treated as if the money were not their own.

Take, for example, the case of Trizec, the holding company through which the Bronfman brothers ostensibly run their various corporations, including Seagram's. Since it was formed in 1960, the Bronfmans have never held a majority position within Trizec! Trizec is run by Eagle Star Ltd. of London, a holding company whose directors have been described by one author as "the most notable of the British aristocrats."[50] Evelyn de Rothschild, the earls and dukes who control Lloyds of London and other banking and insurance firms, and leading lights of British intelligence such as Sir Kenneth Strong and Sir Kenneth Keith, all converge on the board of Eagle Star. This extraordinary company owns English Property Corp. Ltd.—whose principal individual shareholder, Laurie Marsh, has gained notoriety in Britain as the Prince of Pornography, for his ownership of the majority of pornographic movie theaters, massage parlors, and red light district real estate in London.[51] English Property Corp. Ltd. owns majority holdings in Trizec.

Neither are the brains behind the Bronfman empire situated between the ears of the members of the Bronfman family. The source lies elsewhere—in the family's law firm of Phillips, Bloomfield, Vineberg and Goodman (now called Phillips and Vineberg).

---

50. Henry Aubin, *Who Owns Montreal*.
51. Ibid.

The personage of family arbiter and attorney Lazarus Phillips, in particular, was a constant sore to Mr. Sam. Born into the upper crust of the Zionist elite, Lazarus Phillips succeeded in gaining all the recognition and respect that Mr. Sam could never seem to win. Phillips was a holder of the Order of the British Empire, a senator in the Canadian Parliament, a member of the board of directors of the Royal Bank of Canada, invited into the exclusive Mount Royal Club as a member, and was a powerbroker for the Liberal Party.

But without Phillips, the Bronfman family empire could not survive. It is likely that through him the Bronfmans received the input of cash that allowed them to proceed steadily from bootlegging to a "legitimate" corporate empire. Certainly it was Phillips who unfroze enough funds under export control from the grip of the Bank of Canada to finance Seagram's wartime expansion into the United States. As the final judge in all family matters—legal and otherwise—Phillips has sat on the board of Seagram's since 1940 and on every other company and philanthropic front nominally run by Mr. Sam. He is still the codirector of Trizec and the other major Bronfman holding company, Edper (named after Edgar and Peter Bronfman). Phillips is also the expert who managed to get the Bronfmans off every legal hook on which they ever got caught.[52]

Phillip F. Vineberg is part of the Vineberg family of Abraham Moses Vineberg, chairman of the Moses Vineberg Investments firm and the De Hirsch Institute. Cochairman of all the Bronfman holding companies, Vineberg runs the Canadian Israeli Bond Drives and the Canadian Council of Christians and Jews. He is also a member of the Hofjuden elite's Montefiore Club.

Major Louis Mortimer Bloomfield, also of the firm Phillips, Vineberg, and Bloomfield is the most colorful of the Bronfman brains behind the scenes, and this may explain why his name was left out of Peter Newman's 1978 book *The Bronfman Dynasty* (rumored to have been commissioned by the Bronfmans themselves). In addition to his position as a Bronfman family lawyer up to the late 1960s, Bloomfield remained a close banking associate until his death in the mid-1980s. The major was involved in a nest of corporations including the Israeli Continental Company. He was chairman of the Canadian Histadrut Campaign, and a president of the Israeli Maritime League. He also held the post of consul -general in Liberia, under whose flag vast quantities of opium and narcotics are shipped. He was a high-ranking member of the Most Venerable Order of St. John of Jerusalem and ran its subsidiary Canadian Red Cross Ambulance Corporation.

Major Bloomfield also ran Britain's International Assassination Bureau, an entity we will soon examine in detail.

Are They Really Clean?

The answer, of course, is no. Since the days they sent their chickencock across the border to their claim as the world's finest whiskey blenders, the Bronfmans' ties to North America's crime syndicate have never been broken, but merely undergone corporate reorganization. Later, we will analyze their criminal activities at length. At this point, a few examples will suffice.

---

52. Newman, *Bronfman Dynasty,* pp. 55-61.

Take the case of Bronfman family intimate Murray Koffler. A leader of the Jerusalem Foundation in Canada, Koffler was the subject of a major scandal in 1976 when his business associates, Starkman stores, were busted by Canadian police after their pharmacists were caught manufacturing illegal amphetamines and funneling them into the black market.[53]

Charles Bronfman's sister Phyllis Lambert was the subject of a simultaneous scandal over her involvement in Heritage Canada, a government-funded social service program that got caught conduiting drugs onto Canadian college campuses.[54]

In 1975, the Bronfmans again made the front pages when Edgar Bronfman's eldest son Samuel II was reported kidnapped. The case revealed the chief kidnapper to be Sam II's homosexual lover. When the police found them, Sam's kidnappers pleaded that the Bronfman youth had blackmailed them into the hoax as a way of extorting money from his father. The jury agreed; the two abductors were declared innocent of kidnapping, but found guilty of the lesser charge of extortion. The press also aired the kidnappers' pleas that their lives were now in danger for having sung about Sam II.

Since he took over the reins of Seagram's New York branch in the 1950s, Sam II's father, Edgar, has built the Seagram's distilleries network into a multinational global empire. The Bronfmans, for example, have entered into a most profitable business partnership with the Cuban rum Bacardi family. After Fidel Castro took over the island in 1959, the Bacardis switched their base of operations to Puerto Rico and Miami, taking along with them a small army of anti-Castro Cuban exiles. The Bacardis, headed by Manuel Cutilla Bacardi, have been pinpointed by law enforcement agencies as the funders and political controllers of entire networks of Cuban exiles, including terrorist networks. Drug runners in the Bacardi-Cuban exile networks, José Medardo Alvero-Cruz and Antonio Cruz Vásquez, were arrested in 1978 for drug-trafficking in the Caribbean and Mexico.[55]

Seagram's has also staked a conglomerate empire in Mexico. Bronfman's contact is former Mexican President Miguel Alemán, who demanded the revival of casino gambling in Mexico, and who owned and operated Acapulco, until his death in the mid-1980s. In the 1930s, nationalist President Lázaro Cárdenas threw the casinos, and with them Meyer Lansky, out of the country.

In short, wherever Seagram's branches appear on the map, they are thoroughly intermeshed with narcotics runners, gambling, and crime.

Starkman stores' connections to Koffler were widely publicized at the time in the Toronto *Globe and Mail*.

The Bronfmans' gutter connections are most visible in the case of Mitchell Bronfman. The son of Knight of Justice Allan Bronfman, Mitchell is reportedly never without his automatic strapped to his shoulder and his stiletto strapped to his left calf. He is on record with the Montreal Police, the Quebec Provincial Justice

---

53. Starkman stores' connections to Koffler were widely publicized at the time in the Toronto *Globe and Mail*.

54. *See also* Newman, *Bronfman Dynasty*, pp. 167-169.

55. The *Washington Post*, November 6, 1978, p. 2.

Ministry, and the Royal Canadian Mounted Police as a kingpin of organized crime in Montreal.[56]

A 1972 report by the Montreal Crime Commission names one Willie Obront as the head of the syndicate in the area and describes the relationship between Obront and Mitchell Bronfman as "almost a brotherly relationship."[57]

"This relationship extends into illegal activities in which they have mutually or jointly indulged . . . the special kinds of favors they did for each other and the resulting advantages of each in the fields of loan-sharking, gambling, illegal betting, securities, tax evasion and corruption."[58]

"Everything was on a strictly friendly basis," says Mitchell.

Obront first came to the attention of the authorities after two of his Quebec nightclubs used as hangouts for Montreal's underworld were raided. It was revealed that Mitchell's friend was one of Montreal's top movers of dirty money from narcotics, prostitution, and loan-sharking.

Together with Obront, Mitchell Bronfman is a minority partner in the Pagoda North, a Miami restaurant that has been identified by U.S. and Canadian law enforcement agencies as the headquarters for a continent-wide illegal bookmaking syndicate run by Vito Genovese.

Willie Obront was convicted in 1976 of tax evasion and put behind bars. Mitchell Bronfman narrowly averted the same fate.

Another one of Mitchell Bronfman's business partners is Sidney Rosen, who was also arrested and convicted in 1975 for looting thirty-five Canadian and American companies of $7 million through an asset-stripping clearinghouse called Value Trend Holding Company. Value Trend in turn laundered these stolen assets, along with other dirty revenues from illegal gambling, extortion, and narcotics, through Corporate Bank and Trust Company of Freeport, Grand Bahamas and Flendon Ltd., of the same address. Both companies are jointly owned by Rosen and Mitchell Bronfman through another holding company called the Milton Group. When Rosen went off to jail (again leaving Mitchell Bronfman scot free), the $7 million passed unscathed into offshore accounts in Barclays Bank in Freeport.[59]

But the two major corporations out of which Mitchell has operated are the mysterious Securex and Execaire Aviation.

Securex was disbanded in 1977 by Quebec Provincial Justice Minister Bedard. Although the Official Secrets Act has kept the reasons behind this hidden, it can be stated with reasonable certainty that Mitchell Bronfman and the company were discovered to be up to their necks in the wave of FLQ (Front pour la Libération du Québec) terrorism that had plagued the province since 1970—not to mention the narcotics trade.

The two directors of Securex at the time of its banning were Donald McCleary and Gilles Brunet, formerly sergeants in the Royal Canadian Mounted Police in charge of the G-4 (Secret Service Division) of the Mounties. Both were fired

56. Newman, *Bronfman Dynasty*, pp. 233.
57. Ibid., p. 231.
58. Ibid., p. 225.
59. Ibid., p. 232.

from the Service in 1972 when it was discovered that they were close associates of Mitchell BronfMan.[60] McCleary and Brunet were in charge of counterterror efforts in 1970 when the FLQ kidnapped a provincial official and a British government officer, an affair that led to the declaration of a state of emergency. The emergency period was used as a pretext to go after the French Canadian networks that had been built up by Charles de Gaulle in conjunction with the Vatican to liberate Quebec from British colonial status.

In point of fact, the FLQ was itself funded by Bronfman family networks as an extension of earlier efforts to assassinate French President de Gaulle. The Bronfmans' FLQ option was the North American version of the British Special Air Service's control over both the Provisional Wing of the Irish Republican Army and the British Army's counterterror efforts.

Securex advertises itself as a consulting firm specializing in "anti-terrorism, anti-kidnapping, and guerrilla warfare training."[27] All things considered, it would have to be regarded as both a semi-official covert branch of British intelligence in Canada and as a bridge to the criminal underworld.

Its affiliated Execaire Aviation emerges as yet another scarcely concealed front for crime. Execaire is the largest private charter airline service in Canada, specializing in jet service for business executives . . . and narcotics.

Is Mitchell Bronfman just the black sheep in the Bronfman family? It is unlikely. Cemp, the Bronfman family trust, signed a guarantee for part of Execaire's line of credit at the Bank of Montreal.

Nevertheless, the publicity the Bronfmans have received over the years for such exploits as Mitchell's have prevented the family from receiving that degree of respectability they have always coveted. In the 1950s, Mr. Sam looked across the fence at the status of his friend then U.S.-Senator Jacob Javits and decided that he would buy the ultimate title to confer respectability to his name: He sought to become a senator of the Canadian Parliament. All told, he spent $1.2 million in bribes. The Liberals took his money but wouldn't give him a seat. The Bronfman name was still too dirty to be permitted in the ranks of Canadian politics.

2. Britain's International Assassination Bureau: Permindex

According to an unpublished manuscript on the assassination of John F. Kennedy authored by "William Torbitt" (an apparent pseudonym), during the spring, summer, and autumn months of 1963, a series of top-secret conspiratorial meetings took place behind well-guarded closed doors at an exclusive resort spot at Montego Bay on the Caribbean island of Jamaica. The location for those meetings was the Tryall Compound, built at the close of World War II by Britain's highest-ranking secret espionage agent, Sir William Stephenson. Reportedly present at various times for the planning sessions were: Major Louis Mortimer Bloomfield,

---

60. Ibid., p. 227.

in 1963 still a top officer in Sir William Stephenson's British Special Operations Executive (SOE); Ferenc Nagy, a wartime cabinet minister in the pro-Hitler Horthy government of Hungary and later its Prime Minister; Georgio Mantello, a Rumanian-born Jew who had served as a trade minister under Mussolini; Colonel Clay Shaw, a former officer in the U.S. Office of Strategic Services (OSS) who in 1963 was the director of the New Orleans International Trade Mart; Jean de Menil, a White Russian emigré who at that moment was the president of the Houston-based Schlumberger Company, a heavy equipment manufacturer frequently used as a covert conduit for weapons; Paul Raigorodsky, another White Russian active in the right-wing Solidarist movement. The purpose of the meetings, the manuscript alleged, was to plot the assassination of President John F. Kennedy.

Left: McGeorge Bundy, Special Assistant to President John F. Kennedy for National Security Affairs, and a player in helping steer the investigation of Kennedy's assassination away from the actual culprits and toward 'patsy' Lee Harvey Oswald (right).

Whether or not the meetings took place as described in the manuscript, the authors of Dope, Inc. have been unable to confirm. But through interviews in the United States and Western Europe and through reviews of the evidence presented before the Warren Commission and before the grand jury proceedings and trial of Clay Shaw in New Orleans, the authors have established links between the named individuals and the Permindex trading company at the center of the Kennedy assassination plot.

Permindex was an obscure international trading exposition company, incorporated in Switzerland and housed in Montreal; Permindex is a contraction of "Permanent Industrial Expositions." Its president and chairman of the board from its inception in 1958 was Major Louis Mortimer Bloomfield. The individuals named as plotting at the Tryall Compound were, at the time, board members, officers, and investors in Permindex.

Each of these individuals was also a longstanding trusted asset of the British SOE. Unlike any other trade expositions company in the world, the employees and investors in Permindex had all been selected for specific operational capabilities that they represented; capabilities that would be indispensable to the conducting of high-level political assassinations.

As we delve into the Permindex international assassination bureau and discover the suppressed facts behind the assassination of President John F. Kennedy, we shall encounter three capabilities in particular already familiar to us as Dope, Inc.

First we shall encounter an international web of dirty money outfits, responsible for channeling millions of dollars in black market revenues into the hands of the professional killers deployed on behalf of Permindex and its SOE control. Not surprisingly, we shall discover that these dirty money channels are hard-wired into the Hongkong and Shanghai Bank-centered apparatus that launders the $400 billion in annual revenues from illegal drug sales.

Second, we shall discover an international band of protected killers, drawn from the ranks of the Nazi and Fascist gestapos of World War II—many now in the employ of the Soviet KGB—from the street-level crime syndicate responsible for the retail distribution of narcotics; and from a secret capability established by the Stephenson organization at the outset of World War II, operating under the cover of missionary activity in Latin America and the East bloc. Their missions? Political assassinations employing high-powered rifles at a distance of 1,000 yards.

Third, we shall encounter a British SOE fifth column embedded deeply into the American official intelligence community. This fifth column, linked directly to Permindex and its chairman Major Bloomfield, represents perhaps the single most crucial component of the international assassination bureau: its cover-up capability. Seventeen years after the assassination of John F. Kennedy, Permindex remains one of the best kept secrets in the world—despite the fact that it has been exposed on more than one occasion as the agency behind high-level political exterminations touching on top political officials of no fewer than three sovereign nations.

Louis Mortimer Bloomfield

At the time of the Kennedy assassination, Major Louis Mortimer Bloomfield was acting on behalf of his superiors in the British Special Operations Executive, including "retired" chief Sir William Stephenson, at that time a permanent resident of the Tryall Compound on Montego Bay, Jamaica.

As president and chairman of the board of Permindex, Bloomfield was the designated chief operations officer for the Kennedy hit.

Who is Louis Mortimer Bloomfield and what had brought him to the point of becoming, by 1963, the unofficial successor to Stephenson as Her Majesty's top secret agent in North America; the man entrusted to carry out the execution of John F. Kennedy, an American President who dared to violate the "special relationship" with the British Crown?

Louis Mortimer Bloomfield was recruited into the SOE in 1938,[61] the year that Stephenson, acting as personal emissary of Winston Churchill, negotiated an agreement with U.S. President Franklin Delano Roosevelt allowing British intelligence to set up shop in the United States and to effectively merge its operations

61. "The Nomenclature of An Assassination Cabal," unpublished manuscript by William Torbitt, 1970, p. 21.

with those of the FBI and military intelligence.[62] Under SOE commission, Bloomfield was given an officer's rank in the U.S. Army and assigned to the newly created Office of Strategic Services (OSS), the wartime predecessor to the Central Intelligence Agency.

As a major in the OSS, Bloomfield was detailed into the Federal Bureau of Investigation as the contracting (recruitment) agent for its counterespionage Division Five.[63] Bloomfield, described by numerous authors and associates as a practicing homosexual, developed a deeply personal friendship with FBI Director J. Edgar Hoover. Through that relationship, Bloomfield was able to retain his powerful position in Division Five long after the end of the war. As late as 1963, when Bloomfield was case officering the assassination plot against John F. Kennedy, he was still a top official in Division Five.

When the SOE "formally" dissolved its U.S. operations at the close of World War II, Bloomfield returned to Montreal, Canada to resume his career as a prominent attorney. He had been a founding partner in the prestigious law firm of Phillips, Vineberg, Bloomfield and Goodman, the firm that represents and controls the Bronfman family's holdings. Bloomfield's name was only removed from the firm's letterhead in 1968, after French President Charles de Gaulle publicly exposed the role of Bloomfield's Permindex company in acting as a conduit for funds into the Secret Army Organization (OAS) to finance the 1962 assassination attempt against him.[64]

From the outset, the British SOE had made a point of operating though commercial fronts. For example, Stephenson set up the SOE command center in the United States in the Radio Corporation of America building in New York City's Rockefeller Center under the sign of an import-export firm.[65]

Montreal attorney and SOE operative Bloomfield created a nest of corporate entities following his return to Canada, all of which served as vehicles for ongoing SOE activity. Among Bloomfield's corporate holdings were the Israeli Continental Corporation; the Canadian subsidiary of the Heineken Breweries of Holland; and Crédit Suisse of Canada, a correspondent bank to the Crédit Suisse of Geneva that

---

62. This pre-war controlling beach-head of British intelligence within the U.S. intelligence services was arranged through the services, in particular, of John J. McCloy on the American side. Mc-Cloy, then a partner of Cravath, Swaine, and Moore law firm in New York, became the post-war U.S. high commissioner for Germany. This arrangement almost immediately brought into a controlling position over U.S. wartime intelligence capabilities, the notorious British "triple agent" Kim Philby, who is now a KGB general in Moscow.

63. Torbitt, *op. cit.,* pp. 231-232.

64. A series of articles appearing in *Paese Sera* on March 4, 12, 14, 1967; see also *Les Echos* during spring 1962 for numerous news and editorial references to Permindex' s role in the assassination attempts against President de Gaulle.

65. Virtually all the book-length material on Sir William Stephenson and the British Security Co-ordination—Special Operations Executive is "official cover story" commissioned by the SOE to provide limited exposure to aspects of its operations while withholding the most illegal and anti-American activities. Two books that fit this "official cover story" description, but which provide numerous references to Stephenson's methods of operation, including his penetration into every level of the U.S. military command with his SOE agents, are: H. Montgomery Hyde, *Room 3603* (New York: Ballantine Books, 1962); and *William Stephenson, A Man Called Intrepid,* (New York: Ballantine Books, 1976.)

was among the holding companies exposed by President de Gaulle's intelligence bureau SDECE as a laundering point for hit money into the OAS.[66] As the Bank of Boston case covered up by U.S. Attorney William Weld demonstrates, today Crédit Suisse is at the center of drug-money laundering.

All of these companies would later be documented as investors in Permindex.

Like his law partner Lazarus Phillips and his former "clients" the Bronfmans, Bloomfield also established himself at the top of the Zionist movement in Canada. Among his numerous honorary positions, Bloomfield is the annual chairman of the Histadrut campaign of Canada. No ordinary charity, the Histadrut owns over one-third of the gross national product of Israel; controls the second-largest bank in Israel, the Bank Hapoalim; and has been caught on more than one occasion laundering money into overseas operations of the Israeli secret service, the Mossad. Some of those funds, passed directly back into Major Bloomfield's Permindex, were also used to bankroll unsuccessful hit attempts against de Gaulle.

Among Bloomfield's other "charitable" activities was his chairmanship of the Canadian Red Cross Ambulance Service, a position traditionally held by a top-ranking knight in the Queen's official chivalric order, the Most Venerable Military and Hospitaller Order of St. John of Jerusalem. As an operating arm of the Sovereign Order, the Red Cross Ambulance Service is an official intelligence arm of the British Monarchy, frequently called upon to carry out espionage and terrorist activities.[67]

In addition to his corporate and "charitable" activities in his native Canada and his continuing post in Hoover's FBI Division Five, Major Bloomfield was given special responsibility following the war to develop the international network of clandestine shipping routes that would be essential to the planned skyrocketing of narcotics traffic, dirty money, and related black-marketeering.

First, Bloomfield assumed the directorship of the Israeli-Canadian Maritime League, a trade association whose significance will become clear shortly. Simultaneously, he became the consul-general in charge of the Western Hemisphere of the African state of Liberia. Liberia was a notorious tax shelter and smugglers' port of call. With no shipping regulations, Liberia—under Bloomfield's consularship—became the flag of convenience under which a sizeable portion of the ships bearing bulk cargos of Far East narcotics are registered. Liberia is also one of the secondary offshore banking centers employed by the directorate of Dope, Inc. The unregulated "banks" of Liberia account for $7 billion in average daily transfers—the vast majority of which are related to black market transfers.

The only other foreign-stationed consul-general for Liberia, as of 1978, was Bloomfield-Permindex associate and former Israeli Mossad official Dr. Tibor Rosenbaum.

One final deployment in the immediate postwar period by the SOE's Major Bloomfield would set the stage for the future emergence of the assassination bureau, Permindex. In 1952, Bloomfield became a ranking official of the United

66. Louis Wiznitzer, "Will Garrison's Inquiry into Kennedy Assassination Lead to Montreal?" *Le Devoir,* March 16, 1967, Montreal; also *Canadian Dimension,* Sept.-Oct., 1967 (reprint).
67. Ibid.

Nations Organization, one of its leading advisers on international law. Bloomfield accomplished this by assuming a position as overseas representative of the International Executive Board of the International Law Association. Established in 1873, the International Law Association was from the beginning an arm of Lord Milner's Roundtable group responsible for developing a code of law compatible with the "one world" designs of Britain's leading oligarchical families. After World War II, the ILA became an officially recognized Non-Governmental Organization of the UNO and its principal advisory body on all matters of international law.

Major Bloomfield's particular area of "expertise" on behalf of the UNO: international terrorism, piracy, and civil aviation. To this day, the United Nations' International Civil Aviation Commission is housed in Montreal, under one of Major Bloomfield's closest collaborators, Gerald Fitzgerald. Fitzgerald, on advisement from Bloomfield, has drafted every United Nations convention on hijacking, piracy, and terrorism. In 1962, the year before the Kennedy assassination, Fitzgerald and Major Bloomfield coauthored a history of political assassinations in the twentieth century, focusing particularly on the activities of the Zionist clandestine army, the Irgun, and its 1940s murder plots against Sweden's Count Bernadotte and Britain's Lord Moyne.[68]

1958: Better than ten years have passed since Major Bloomfield's "official" retirement from the SOE-OSS and his return to his native Canada. Sufficient distance has been created from his past activities as a master spy within Her Majesty's most secret spy army to warrant Major Bloomfield a place on the list of "citizens above suspicion." And so, in 1958, on orders from his superiors at Montego Bay, Bloomfield created Permindex and its international subsidiaries Centro Mondiale and the Italo-American Hotel Corporation to house an international assassination bureau.

The Permindex Board of Directors

At the outset of this chapter on Dope, Inc's international assassination bureau, we looked in on the behind-closed-doors sessions at Tryall in which the Kennedy assassination was planned out. At that time, we were introduced to several members of the board of Permindex. It is worth briefly returning to that board of directors roster to get a closer glimpse of the sorts of individuals recruited by chief of operations Major Bloomfield to carry out the most hideous crimes of the century.

According to corporate records on file in Berne, Switzerland, the following individuals were officially listed as officers and board members of Permindex at the time of its incorporation by Major Bloomfield.

- Louis Mortimer Bloomfield, president and chairman of the board of Permindex;
- Ferenc Nagy;

---

68. Bloomfield, Louis M. and Fitzgerald, Gerald, *Crimes Against Protected Persons: Prevention & Punishment* (New York: Praeger, 1975).

- Roy Marcus Cohn, attorney, New York City, former general counsel to Senator Joseph McCarthy, chairman, American Jewish League Against Communism, president, Lionel Corporation;
- Joseph Bonanno, syndicate boss of Montreal and Phoenix; chairman of the board, Lionel Corporation;
- Jean de Menil, millionaire owner of the Schlumberger company of Houston; married into one of the oldest European banking families deployed to reverse the American Revolution;
- Paul Raigorodsky;
- Count Guitierez di Spadafora, former undersecretary of agriculture to Mussolini; sponsor of the Sicilian Separatist Movement;
- Hans Seligman, banker, Basel, Switzerland;
- Carlo d' Amelio, attorney, Rome, representing the financial holdings of the House of Savoy and the House of Pallavicini; attorney for "circolo Rex"; general counsel Centro Mondiale Commerciale;
- Max Hageman, editor, Munich *National Zeitung;*
- Munir Chourbagi, uncle of King Farouk of Egypt;
- Giuseppe Zigiotti, head of the Italian political party Fascist National Association for Militia Arms;
- Ferenc H. Simonfay, former Nazi collaborator in Hungary; leader of the Solidarist movement;
- Colonel Clay Shaw.

Several of these individuals represented a decade-long asset of the British SOE, called into active service for a very specific role in a very specific series of operations.

Bankrolling an Assassination

In 1967, the French Intelligence Bureau SDECE released the results of a five-year investigation into the 1962 aborted assassination attempt against General de Gaulle, carried out by the rabidly right-wing Secret Army Organization (OAS). While the SDECE report traced the origins of the assassination plot to the Brussels headquarters of NATO and to a specific group of disgruntled French and British generals, as well as the remnant of the old Nazi intelligence apparatus, it also singled out Major Bloomfield's Permindex trading company as the agency responsible for conduiting $200,000 into the OAS to bankroll the attempt. The source of the funds was FBI Division Five, the secret counterespionage branch of Hoover's agency that was run out of the Montreal law offices of Major Bloomfield.

As the result of the de Gaulle exposé of Permindex's role in the OAS hit squads, Permindex was forced to shut down its public operations in Western Europe and relocate its headquarters to Johannesburg, South Africa.

As a related feature of the de Gaulle crackdown, Israel's overseas intelligence branch, the Mossad, was temporarily kicked out of France. We have already noted that Permindex's Major Bloomfield established himself as one of the leading Zionists in Canada and had extended that "charitable" activity to a prosperous business relationship extending into international shipping and banking. We shall now see that Bloomfield's efforts "on behalf of Israel" represented an extension of British SOE penetration and control over sections of the important capabilities that were consolidated with the 1958 creation of Permindex. In the course of unraveling this piece of the Permindex web, we shall encounter those operatives within the international assassination bureau designated with the responsibility of providing the laundered millions of dollars for the financing of political violence.

We begin with Basel banker Hans Seligman. According to a suppressed manuscript on the Permindex assassination cabal, the Seligman Bank of Basel, Switzerland was a subsidiary of Permindex responsible for laundering funds into Major Bloomfield's various operations, one of a dozen such subsidiaries of the Montreal trade expositions company.

Hans Seligman is the last remaining European-based member of the Seligman family that made its vast fortune in the United States during the nineteenth century, first in dry goods and later in banking. The Seligman family of New York was one of the "Our Crowd" group that turned its experience in retailing dry goods into a lucrative black market in booze following the passage of the Eighteenth Amendment.

Like the De Hirsh family, the Seligmans originated in Bavaria as part of the entourage built up around the Wittelsbach and Hapsburg courts. It was the joint efforts of the de Hirsh and Seligman families that led to the founding of the De Hirsh Foundation and the Jewish Colonization Association, the agencies responsible for transplanting the likes of Yechiel Bronfman to Canada as an indentured servant. At the time of the Bronfman migration, the de Hirsh Foundation was being run out of New York City by Jesse Seligman.

By the 1890s, the Seligman, de Hirsh and Gunzberg interests merged with the Louis-Dreyfus family interests. Today all four families share control over the Bank Louis-Dreyfus, As we have seen in earlier chapters, Bank Louis-Dreyfus maintains financial control over the Bronfman family holdings, one of the important fronts for the channeling of the revenues of Dope, Inc. Hans Seligman's placement on the board of Permindex, headed by "former" Bronfman family attorney and financial adviser Bloomfield, constitutes one closed circle through which drug revenues can be passed to finance the activities of Permindex.

In addition to the Seligman Bank of Basel, the unpublished Permindex manuscript lists a number of additional banking entities wholly owned by Permindex. These include: Astaldo Vaduz of Miami, De Famaco Vaduz of Liechtenstein, and De Famaco Astaldo Vaduz of Geneva.

These entities appear to have amounted to little more than post office boxes serving as money drops in locations where virtually nonexistent banking laws facilitated such blind passes.

Bloomfield ran the Canadian subsidiary of Crédit Suisse, a far more formidable banking institution with deep ties into the financial circuitry behind Dope, Inc.[69]

---

69. Canadian *Who's Who* (Toronto: TransCanada Press) Vols. 7, 8, 9, 10; and (Toronto: Who's Who Canada Publishers) Vols. 11, 12, 13.

But the most formidable banking entity in the Permindex family was the Banque du Crédit Internationale (BCI) of Basel, Switzerland, which remained in business until 1974.

Dr. Tibor Rosenbaum, BCI, and Permindex

BCI was the creation of Dr. Tibor Rosenbaum, a Jewish Hungarian who migrated to Palestine under the sponsorship of the Jewish Agency. Back in Hungary, Rosenbaum had been associated with Dr. Rudolph Kastner, whose activities as a personal collaborator of Adolf Eichmann in sending an estimated 800,000 Jews of Eastern Europe to the gas chambers at Auschwitz created a major scandal in Israel in the early 1950s, and served as the basis for Ben Hecht's famous suppressed book *Perfidy*.

Following Israel's statehood, Tibor Rosenbaum was appointed the first minister of supply and finance for the foreign intelligence branch, the Mossad. In 1951, Rosenbaum was deployed to Geneva, ostensibly as the director of Israeli migration, holding full diplomatic papers. As there was no migration from Switzerland to Israel during this period, speculation that Rosenbaum was already involved in setting up funds-laundering operations on behalf of the Mossad is well-founded. According to a recently published book-length expose of the Israeli mafia, by *L'Express* journalist Jacques Derogy,[70] Rosenbaum traded his Israeli diplomatic papers for Liberian documents in the mid-1950s on the eve of his launching the Banque du Credit Internationale. Rosenbaum incorporated the BCI in 1958, the same year that his fellow "Liberian diplomat" Major Louis Mortimer Bloomfield established Permindex.

According to Derogy, Dr. Rosenbaum was designated as the "Swiss connection" in an international money-laundering apparatus created to facilitate the diamonds-for-dope trade that was to make up an increasingly large share of the foreign trade of Israel. Despite the cosmetic cover provided to Rosenbaum's operations by his Liberian papers, his Banque du Crédit Internationale was so deeply meshed with Israeli high finance and big time politics that when the scandal of Rosenbaum's dirty-money operations broke in Israel in the early 1970s, Israeli Finance Minister Pinchas Sapir immediately resigned, creating a government crisis.

What can be said about Rosenbaum's Swiss laundering operations and how did his BCI intersect the operations of Major Bloomfield's Permindex?

According to a 1967 *Life* magazine exposé, Rosenbaum's Banque du Crédit International was on the receiving end of $10 million in illegal funds, laundered through the World Commerce Bank of Nassau, Grand Bahamas. The Nassau bank was a joint venture of North American syndicate kingpin Meyer Lansky and several of his closest associates in the gambling, smuggling, extortion and dirty money rackets. The World Commerce Bank was managed by Lansky accountant Alvin Malnick. Another official of the Nassau laundering-hole was a Swiss national and well-known Lansky bagman, Sylvain Ferdmann. According to the Life magazine investigators, Ferdmann was simultaneously listed as the chief operations officer of Rosenbaum's BCI.[71]

---

70. Jacques Derogy, *The Israeli Connection: The Mafia in Israel* (Paris: Librarie Plon, 1980).
71. Torbitt, "Assassination Cabal," p. 105; Messick, *Lansky.* p. 248; *Life.* October 8, 1967.

The picture of BCI, however, remains incomplete without the inclusion of yet another board member of Dr. Rosenbaum's Swiss establishment: Ernest Israel Japhet.

Japhet's presence on the board of directors of the Banque du Crédit International brings us full circle back to the London boardrooms of the Big Five commercial banks that command the international narcotics cartel top down.

Who is Ernest Israel Japhet, in addition to being a board member of the BCI, an entity servicing the black-market money needs of the Mossad, the Israeli mafia and the "wizard" of North American syndicate financing, Meyer Lansky? Japhet was, at the time, the chairman and president of the Bank Leumi, the largest bank in Israel—a bank that we have already identified as a critical component of the diamonds-for-dope traffic into Hong Kong. The current heir of a German banking family that traces its roots back centuries, Japhet sold the family's trading company to the Quaker Barclays Bank of London, which in turn placed him on the board of directors of its thus-created subsidiary Charterhouse-Japhet. Charterhouse-Japhet, like the Japhet Company before it, deals exclusively in the diamond trade between Israel and Hong Kong—trading those precious stones for the same Golden Triangle opium that launched the Japhet family's career in international finance 150 years ago.

Joining Japhet as a trustee of Bank Leumi is Baron Stormont Bancroft, a member of the Samuel family, a former lord-in-waiting to the Queen of England and the deputy chairman of Cunard Lines, a shipping company strongly suspected of shipping large volumes of Far East heroin over its Asian and Mediterranean routes.[72]

Bank Leumi keeps its hands in the drug trade through its 100 percent-owned subsidiary Union Bank. Ernest Israel Japhet is the chairman of Union Bank, which handles over one-third of the world's financing in diamonds.

Bank Leumi was not the only Israeli bank to interface its operations with the Geneva laundering-hole of Dr. Rosenbaum, Even more heavily involved in the BCI is the Bank Hapoalim.[73] The second largest bank in Israel, Bank Hapoalim was founded as an offshoot of the Jewish Agency. Its founder and present board director, British High Commissioner Viscount Erwin Herbert Samuel, belongs to the same Samuel family behind Bank Leumi and the Cunard Lines. Viscount Samuel presides as head of the Israel Red Cross, an official branch of the Most Venerable Military and Hospitaller Order of St. John of Jerusalem—the same order held by Major Louis Mortimer Bloomfield of Permindex.[74]

According to the already cited Derogy exposé of the Israeli mafia, Bank Hapoalim figured prominently in the same diamonds-for-dope apparatus. Illegal

72. *Who's Who in Great Britain; see also, 1977 Annual Report of the Bank Leumi.*
73. *See also New York Times* index citation on "Banque de Credit Internationale" and "Tibor Rosenbaum," particularly covering the period of exposure of Bank Hapoalim and related institutions' involvement in money-laundering; see also Katherine Burdman, "The British Crown's Secret Financial Capability: Israeli Banking," *Executive intelligence Review* 44 (1978).
74. Col. Sir Edwin King and Sir Harry Luke, *The Knights of St. John in the British Realm—Being the Official History of the Most Venerable Order of the Hospital of St. John of Jerusalem* (London: Hills and Lacy, 1924).

revenues from the diamonds-for-dope exchange run between Israel and the Golden Triangle banks of Thailand, would be initially deposited in an escrow account in London, for transfer to protected accounts in Johannesburg, South Africa. From South Africa, the same funds would be laundered through the Bank Hapoalim into Dr. Rosenbaum's BCI.

The "South African connection" for this diamonds-for-dope operation, according to author Derogy, was Zwy Peer, the Israeli director of the Investors Overseas Service (IOS).

IOS, until its demise in 1975, was indistinguishable from the Banque du Crédit Internationale. Nominally an international mutual fund founded by Bernie Cornfeld, and eventually taken over by Robert Vesco, IOS in reality was a laundering service deploying an army of "salesmen" in every comer of the globe, often carrying phenomenal volumes of cash which the IOS directors claimed were the investment deposits of thousands of small investors. These investors for the most part remained anonymous. According to author Hank Messick, a significant number of the so-called small investors were local operatives of the Meyer Lansky-Israeli mafia apparatus.[75]

The convergence of the drug syndicate and the intelligence services of Great Britain and Israel in the person of Dr. Tibor Rosenbaum is further amplified by a brief look at the Swiss-based banker's other major financial holding, the Swiss-Israel Trade Bank of Geneva.

Among its principal holdings, the Swiss-Israel Trade Bank owns one-third interest in the Paz conglomerate. Owned until the early 1950s by the Rothschild family, the Paz group of corporations maintains a virtual monopoly over the Israeli oil and petrochemical industry, including the vital shipping lines transporting oil and petrochemicals in and out of the Middle East. In 1978, police authorities in New York City seized a Paz ship as it attempted entry into New York Harbor. Police found its hold loaded with liquid hashish.

Sharing the Paz ownership with Dr. Rosenbaum's Swiss-Israel entity are Max Fisher, a Detroit, Michigan-based "businessman-philanthropist" about whom we shall learn a great deal more in a later chapter; and Sir Isaac Wolfson, a London department store magnate whose family traces its lineage back to the thirteenth century. It was Wolfson whose family mantle provided prestige for the Paz group following its sale by the Rothschild interests. Sir Isaac was the chairman of the British Board of Jewish Deputies, the most prestigious and powerful Zionist organization in the British Empire. More recently, his son has been a principal policy adviser to British Prime Minister Margaret Thatcher.

The Swiss-Israel Trade Bank, the third owner of Paz, is a who's who of the combined British-Israeli Mossad apparatus, beginning with Dr. Tibor Rosenbaum. The manager of the Swiss-Israel Trade Bank until his recent semi-retirement was General Julius Klein. We shall encounter General Klein on several occasions as we unravel the complex web of front companies, offshore banks, and official government services that together comprised the Permindex international assassination bureau.

---

75. Hank Messick, *Lansky*, p. 248.

As early as 1922, following his service as a U.S. Army counterintelligence officer during World War I, Klein was picked up by Sir William Wiseman, then head of all British intelligence operations in the United States and later a neighbor of Sir William Stephenson at the Tryall Compound on Montego Bay, Jamaica. Under Wiseman's instructions, Klein was brought onto the staff of Colonel House, the special adviser to President Woodrow Wilson who led the U.S. negotiating team at the Versailles Treaty negotiations. The presidential adviser was a neighbor of the British spook, and House rarely made a serious political decision without first consulting Wiseman.

By 1932, the young Klein was on the inside track of the Anglo-American intelligence establishment. In that year, he was appointed director of the first anti-subversive section established in the U.S. Department of Justice. This appointment brought Klein into close working relationship with FBI Director J. Edgar Hoover, and particularly with the FBI's Division Five. In 1938, Klein's operations, for all intents and purposes, became a subordinate feature of the British Special Operations Executive. In addition to his Justice Department anti-subversive role, Klein that year founded a dirty tricks unit of the Jewish War Veterans, the first of several private organizations that he would create as recruiting grounds and intelligence fronts for Stephenson's SOE.

Sir William Stephenson's access to the intelligence facilities of the Zionist movement in the United States and Canada was greatly facilitated by the fact that from 1922, he had employed Chaim Weizmann as his principal adviser on scientific and technical espionage activities. The fact that Stephenson's own mentor, Sir William Wiseman, was a leading figure in the Anglo-Zionist movement also provided the future SOE head with an inside track to the resources and talents of the Zionist networks. According to Richard Deacon, a semi-official historian of British and Israeli intelligence, Stephenson was the single most important figure in establishing the Israeli intelligence services following independence.[76] As we have already seen in the case of Perm index chief Major Louis Mortimer Bloomfield, many of the postwar commercial fronts through which the SOE operated were joint ventures with the Mossad.

In the effort to create an Israeli intelligence apparatus married to the British SOE, Julius Klein would play a major role on behalf of Sir William Stephenson. From his position at the close of World War II as head of the U.S. Army Counterintelligence Corps responsible for Western Europe, Klein—by his own admission—illegally rerouted whole shiploads of medical supplies, trucks, construction equipment, etc. from earmarked destinations in Germany and Austria to the Haganah in Palestine. Throughout the early 1950s, Klein made frequent trips to Israel to aid in the training and structuring of the Mossad. We shall turn our attention once again to General Klein at a later point in our inquiry when he emerges as a principal, background figure in recruiting of the board of directors for Permindex.

Another Rosenbaum associate in the Swiss-Israel operation was Shaul Eisenberg, the top weapons procurer and scientific spy for Israeli intelligence during the 1950s and 1960s. According to the *Washington Post*, Eisenberg was

---

76. Richard Deacon, A *History of the British Secret Service* (New York: Taplinger Publishing Company, 1970).

officially the Mossad station chief in Vienna during much of this period. Born in Shanghai, Eisenberg was the unofficial trade representative for the Israelis in the Far East. Official statistics show that 90 percent of the Israeli business in that region involved sales of diamonds.

Shaul Eisenberg also ran a string of scientific consulting firms in New York City that maintained contracts with the major Canadian firms engaged in the exporting of nuclear technology. These companies have been publicly identified as part of the nest of high technology firms created by the Stephenson SOE following the war.

Completing the board of directors of Dr. Tibor Rosenbaum's Swiss-Israel Trade Bank were:

- Abe Feinberg, the head of the Americans for Haganah, a thinly veiled front for SOE-Zionist espionage and laundering operations during the pre-independence period;
- Phillip Klutznick, self-described protégé of Julius Klein and secretary of commerce in the Carter administration;
- David Graiver, the enigmatic Argentinian banker who was indicted in the early 1970s in New York on charges of bribery and extortion and subsequently disappeared in a mysterious plane crash over Mexico that had Federal court officials and investigators debating for years whether or not he was still alive.[77] Indictments were handed down against Graiver after considerable evidence surfaced that he was serving as a "financial consultant" to a number of Latin American terrorist organizations kidnapping American executives and government officials for fantastic ransoms.

How did this enormous international network of black market banking ventures service the operations of Major Bloomfield's "trading company"?

According to the findings of the SDECE, $200,000 in black market revenues were channeled into the Banque du Crédit Internationale accounts maintained by Permindex. Among the sources of those funds was the Bank Hapoalim, the Israeli banking institution owned by the Histadrut, for which Major Bloomfield was the chief Canadian fundraiser.

Those funds were passed onto the New Orleans station chief of the FBI's Division Five, Guy Bannister. From New Orleans, Bannister deployed one of his agents, Jerry Brooks Gatlin, directly to Paris with a suitcase full of cash for hand delivery to the OAS generals.[78] In 1966, at the very outset of the Garrison investigation into the assassination of President Kennedy, Gatlin—who operated a Permindex-Division Five front called the Anti-Communist League of the

---

77. The U.S. government later went on record as believing that David Graiver was indeed still alive. Graiver gained notoriety when his American Bank and Trust Company in New York City went bankrupt in 1976, amid charges that Graiver had siphoned off some $50 million from the bank and then disappeared. A Federal indictment was sought and those charges were dropped. In June 1978, the U.S. Attorney for the Southern District of New York petitioned for the charges to be reinstated. The petition was granted the same month. See *The New York Times* and the *Wall Street Journal* of June 3-30, 1978.
78. Torbitt, "Assassination Cabal," p. 73.

Caribbean—died when he was thrown out of a sixth-floor window in a San Juan, Puerto Rico hotel. By this time, FBI Division Five spook Bannister had already died under equally mysterious circumstances.[79] Sources in New Orleans reported at the time of Bannister's death that within hours of his demise, agents of Division Five had invaded his office and his home and carted off all of his files. Those documents never materialized again.

Colonel Clay Shaw

There was no coincidence to the fact that the Permindex funds for the 1962 aborted assassination attempt against Charles de Gaulle were laundered through a New Orleans-stationed agent of Division Five. By 1962, New Orleans had already assumed the role of field operations center for the assassination cabal headquartered offshore on the island retreat at Tryall.

The reason that New Orleans assumed a special role in the cabal is that it headquartered the major U.S. subsidiary of Permindex, the International Trade Mart, directed by Colonel Clay Shaw.

Within the overall organizational chart of Permindex, Colonel Shaw maintained two principal roles. Through his International Trade Mart, Shaw retained a secondary capability for washing large volumes of money on an international scale. But first and foremost, Shaw was responsible for "handling" the nest of agents deployed through Permindex's various fronts to carry out the assassination of John F. Kennedy.

By the time that the Kennedy conspiracy was placed on a fully operational footing in the spring of 1963, Colonel Clay Shaw had already put in over twenty years of duty under the direction of Stephenson's SOE.

In order to situate the special role of the New Orleans colonel and the International Trade Mart that he presided over in the Permindex assassination cabal, it is first necessary to return briefly to the Montego Bay outpost of SOE chief Sir William Stephenson and to retrace the process through which the Special Operations Executive turned its wartime capabilities into a postwar fifth column devoted to destroying and capturing the American republic.

As we have already noted, both during and after World War II, it was the modus operandi of the SOE to operate principally through commercial fronts. In 1945, immediately following the "official" curtailment of SOE operations within the territorial United States, Sir William Stephenson founded the Newfoundland Development Corporation in partnership with Newfoundland's top colonial official Jerry Smallwood. (It was not until 1948 that Newfoundland was admitted as a province to Canada). The following year, Stephenson set up BRINCO, an energy exploration company also located on Newfoundland, with financing from Rio Tinto Zinc, an already familiar component of Britain's Dope, Inc. apparatus, and staffing by leading figures from wartime British intelligence. These Newfoundland ventures were the prototypes for the vast string of "offshore" ventures that the Stephenson apparatus would create over the next decades.

---

79. Ibid., p. 161.

In 1949, the same year that BRINCO was launched, Stephenson relocated to Jamaica, where he founded the "retirement colony" at Montego Bay. At the same time, the Stephenson-centered group created the British-American-Canadian Corporation. According to David Ogilvy, another SOE executive who drafted the corporate prospectus, BAC was to be "a profitable company of merchant adventurers." Ogilvy himself became the vice president of the company, with John Pepper, the chief of Stephenson's wartime Washington, D.C. bureau becoming president. Ogilvy subsequently founded the New York City blue ribbon advertising agency Ogilvy & Mather, drawing upon his wartime black propaganda experience as well as his pre-war stint with the Gallup Polls organization.

BAC was financed through the Hambro's financial group in London.

British-American-Canadian Corporation was soon renamed the World Commerce Corporation. By the late 1940s, WCC was doing such a large share of the U.S. and British trade activity into Latin America that one contemporary source commented that if there were "several World Commerce Corporations, there would be no need for the Marshall Plan." Stephenson and company were quietly and systematically building up the infrastructure of trading companies, banks, and shipping lines, etc. through which to conduct their multi-billion dollar opium war against the United States.

By 1946, Colonel Clay Shaw was already a part of that covert command structure. Shaw's association with the Stephenson circle dates back to at least the outset of World War II. At that time, Shaw served as an OSS officer stationed in London. According to Shaw's own testimony, published in *The Kennedy Conspiracy* by New Orleans District Attorney Garrison's investigator Paris Flammonde, he served as an OSS liaison officer to the headquarters of British Prime Minister Winston Churchill. Through that experience, Shaw developed such a feeling of attachment to the British Empire that he seriously considered emigrating to England at the close of the war. It is not difficult to imagine the raving anglophile Shaw (another practicing homosexual in the mold of his Permindex superior Major Bloomfield) choosing instead to assume the role of agent of Her Majesty's government "behind enemy lines" in the United States.

Shaw did return to the United States, to his birthplace New Orleans to assume the directorship in 1945 of the International House/World Trade Center, a "nonprofit association fostering the development of international trade, tourism, and cultural exchange."

Almost immediately, Shaw left the World Trade Center to found the International Trade Mart, also in New Orleans. Very much a profit-making venture, the International Trade Mart sponsored permanent industrial expositions, focused particularly on the Caribbean region then being "colonized" by the Stephenson World Commerce Corporation.

Was Shaw's New Orleans International Trade Mart a front for SOE activities from the beginning in 1946? It is a fact that in 1958, as soon as Major Bloomfield established his own "permanent industrial expositions" firm, Clay Shaw became a board member and with that, his New Orleans Mart became a subsidiary of Permindex's international arm, Centro Mondiale Commerciale.

What sort of evil design did Shaw and Stephenson share back in 1946 when they launched their International Commerce ventures?

Today, there are over fifty "world trade marts" located in thirty countries around the world. Each of these world trade marts is made up of over 1,000 corporate subscribers.

Since 1968, all of the world trade marts have been hooked together through a massive computerized data bank. That data bank now functions through an intelligence-transmitting satellite system, one of the largest privately owned satellite systems in existence. The satellite-computer control point is maintained by the World Trade Center Association—the offspring of the very New Orleans World Trade Center that Clay Shaw assumed the directorship of at the close of World War II on behalf of the Stephenson SOE apparatus.

The computer-satellite system maintains a tracking of all international trade routes, carriers and rate scales; a virtual inventory and tracking map of every air-land-sea shipping medium and bulk cargo in the world.

Among the fifty-plus world trade marts hooked into the WTCA satellite-computer complex is the Hong Kong World Trade Center—a joint venture of the Hongkong and Shanghai Bank and Jardine Matheson. HKWTC is the single largest and highest-priced chunk of real estate in Hong Kong. Dope, Inc., through this Hong Kong center, thus maintains a transnational tracking system that is more sophisticated and technologically advanced than the capabilities at the disposal of any government attempting to combat its deadly traffic.

History of an Assassination

In 1958, however, Permindex had not yet emerged as an international octopus of trading fronts hooked up through satellite-based computers, possessing the resources for global money-laundering at the push of a button on a computer console. Yet, as court records in New Orleans, Montreal, and Paris document, millions of dollars in "hit money" passed through the Permindex organization to bankroll the most deadly assassination plots of the century.

We have already met the black market bankers, many of them linked to the financial, political, and intelligence establishment of the state of Israel, whose special role in the Permindex cabal involved the laundering of the "hit money" into the hands of FBI Division Five couriers for delivery to the designated assassin teams.

We shall now investigate the second major component of the Permindex assassination bureau, the network of protected killers whose actions have irreversibly shaped the course of history for the last two decades.

Garrison Hands Down an Indictment

In February of 1969 proceedings began in the New Orleans Parish Court in the case of *The State of Louisiana v. Clay M. Shaw*. New Orleans District Attorney Jim Garrison, flouting the findings of the Warren Commission, had gone before a grand jury and successfully petitioned for a murder conspiracy indictment against Permindex board member Clay Shaw.

It would take the mysterious deaths of seventeen key prosecution witnesses and the launching of a nationwide media witch-hunt against the New Orleans DA to defeat Garrison's effort to get to the bottom of the assassination of President John F. Kennedy in Dallas on November 22, 1963.

What evidence had Garrison compiled against the New Orleans colonel and his co-conspirators on the board of directors of Permindex?

At minimum, Garrison had "cracked" the Kennedy assassination plot at the operational level; at the level directed by New Orleans case officer Shaw. On March 14, 1967, Garrison brought Perry Raymond Russo, an insurance salesman from Baton Rouge, Louisiana, before a three-judge criminal district court panel. Russo testified that during the middle of September 1963, he had been witness to a conversation between Clay Shaw, David Ferrie and an individual he identified as "Leon Oswald." The topic of the conversation was the assassination of President John Kennedy. In that conversation, Ferrie, an agent of Division Five about whom we shall learn more later, emphasized the importance of using at least three marksmen in order to create a "triangulation of fire." He added, according to witness Russo, that a scapegoat would be required to secure the escape of the actual assassins.

According to the Garrison investigation, the individual introduced to Russo as "Leon Oswald" at the September 1963 meeting, was in all likelihood not the Lee Harvey Oswald charged by the Warren Commission with having conducted the "lone assassination" of President Kennedy. According to the unpublished manuscript by "William Torbitt," the individual (bearing a striking resemblance to the actual Lee Harvey Oswald) was William Seymour, an agent for a Miami-based private detective agency called Double-Chek. Double-Chek, according to "Torbitt," was a U.S. subsidiary of the Rome Centro Mondiale Commerciale, and functioned as a frequently used front for Division Five and CIA activities. Double-Chek was reported to be the CIA channel for weapons into the Bay of Pigs invasion force. Those weapons were provided through the Schlumberger Company of Houston, Texas; the Schlumberger Company whose president Jean de Menil was reported by "Torbitt" to have been present at the Tryall Compound on Montego Bay for the meetings at which the Kennedy "hit" was planned.

Seymour, according to the "Torbitt" manuscript, was one of several individuals responsible for impersonating Lee Harvey Oswald in the several months leading up to November 22, 1963. Seymour traveled throughout Texas, into Mexico under the name "Lee Oswald." He left a trail of witnesses who would testify that they had spoken with "Oswald," that "Oswald" was an avowed Cuban Communist sympathizer, and that "Oswald" had made statements that in retrospect pointed strongly toward his intention to kill the President of the United States.

Seymour and the other "Lee Oswalds" were deployed under the direction of FBI Division Five southern chief Guy Bannister, the same Bannister who oversaw the laundering of $200,000 in Permindex money into the hands of the OAS generals in France.

According to evidence presented in the course of the Garrison inquiry into the Kennedy assassination, Clay Shaw, Georgio Mantello, and Ferenc Nagy, all of the board of directors of Permindex and its subsidiary Centro Mondiale Commerciale, were in place in New Orleans, Dallas, and Los Angeles on November 22, 1963, handling aspects of the assassination and coverup. That deployment had been set by Major Bloomfield several months earlier. Evidence gathered during the Garrison grand jury and published by Garrison investigator Paris Flammonde, established that several members of the Permindex cabal were present at the airport restaurant in Winnipeg weeks before the assassination in Dallas to review the final details of the plan. Witnesses identified one of the individuals at the Winnipeg airport as Major Louis M. Bloomfield.

Who were the assassins deployed to carry out the "triangulated firing" on President Kennedy in Dallas on November 22? According to the "Torbitt" papers, the assassins—seven expert riflemen in all—were part of a special team of the most expert killers in the world that had been put together in 1943 at the combined initiative of FBI Director J. Edgar Hoover and SOE Commander Sir William Stephenson. Members of that team would be implicated in the assassinations of Reverend Martin Luther King, Jr. and Senator Robert F. Kennedy.

We have identified a number of the specific individuals implicated in the actual execution of John Kennedy. We have traced their personal chain of command into the FBI's Division Five and into the board of directors of Perm index. To fill out the picture, however, it is now necessary to delve further into what particular operational capabilities these individuals represented. As we probe these protected assassins, we shall return over and over again to the unavoidable fact that Dope, Inc. killed Kennedy.

The Solidarists

Three of the principals in the Permindex assassination of John F. Kennedy were Eastern European and White Russian emigrés. Each of these individuals, Jean DeMenil, Ferenc Nagy, and Paul Raigorodsky, was a leading figure in the Solidarist movement of fascists.

As we have already noted, Ferenc Nagy was a minister in the wartime Horthy government that ruled Hungary on behalf of Adolf Hitler. After the war, Nagy was himself briefly installed as prime minister during 1946-47. Nagy resigned from that post with a telephone call placed from the lobby of a Swiss bank where he had just opened up a sealed account with the government funds he had looted on his way out of Hungary.

On his departure from Hungary, Nagy immediately became involved in the Solidarist movement.

What are the Solidarists?

The Solidarists were Eastern European and White Russian feudalists and fascists, predominantly former officials of the wartime "Quisling" governments of Eastern Europe and veterans of the Nazi eastern front intelligence apparatus.

By no later than 1943, as a part of the Yalta process accepted by FDR, both the Soviet and Anglo-American intelligence services had begun recruiting from the ranks of the most rabid Nazis for postwar intelligence work. (Anglo-Soviet cooperation in such projects actually reflected a longstanding deal struck between Churchill and members of the Soviet Cheka of Felix Dzherzhinsky during Lenin's lifetime.) Among those recruited were the Eastern European Solidarists who became an all-purpose asset of combined British and Soviet networks in the postwar period. Among the services rendered by these Eastern Nazis was the penetration of rightwing circles in the West.

This infiltration based on the early Bolshevik Trust operation, was facilitated by the severe shortcoming of U.S. intelligence agencies in particular, in understanding the Russian Orthodox Church. The ROC is an integral part of the Soviet state apparat, integrated into the overseas operation of the KGB. Many Russian and Eastern European exiles picked up by British Intelligence "on loan," function as shared assets of Moscow and London. It would be through this channel that Moscow, too, would add its endorsement to the plot to kill JFK. Agencies such as Permindex function as derivative agencies integrating shared objectives of multiple states—with one state, in this case Britain, directing the on the ground operation and the cover-up. Were such an operation as the JFK hit to be carried out in Eastern Europe or the Soviet Union, it would be the KGB rather than the SOE directing the derivative agency.

Among the leading components of the Solidarist movement was a highly professional espionage, sabotage and assassination network called Narodnyi Trudovoy Soyuz ("National Alliance of Solidarists"), Founded in the late 1920s out of the old Menshevik circles in Russia, NTS functioned as one of British secret intelligence's premier spy rings inside the Soviet Union. NTS was bankrolled by Royal Dutch Shell chairman Sir Henry Deterding and by Vickers Arms president Sir Basil Zaharoff.

At the close of World War II, NTS established offices in Munich and New York City. From 1939, the principal Western financial backing to the NTS and all of the other "Solidarist" groupings was provided through the Tolstoy Foundation, a self-described refugee relief and cultural fund. The current office of the Tolstoy Foundation in New York City is located in a West 57th Street building that has been the property of the British SOE since the middle of World War II, when it housed the offices of a dozen front companies all involved in smuggling arms and other military equipment to the Haganah in Palestine. In 1978, one of the Tolstoy Foundation's neighbors in the West 57th Street office building was Julius Klein Associates, the public relations company owned by the same General Julius Klein we have already encountered in our investigation into the dirty-money branch of the Permindex organization.

Among the officially listed board members of the Tolstoy Foundation since the early 1960s height of Permindex activity were Paul Raigorodsky and Jean DeMenil.

Raigorodsky was the owner of Claiborne Oil Company of Baton Rouge, Louisiana. He later became an official United States government liaison officer to NATO.

Jean DeMenil, the millionaire owner of the Schlumberger Company of Houston, was one of the principal financial "angels" behind the cultural activities of the Tolstoy Foundation and its allied Solidarist movement. Following the Russian Revolution, DeMenil's family fled their native country, winding up in France.

There, Jean DeMenil married into the powerful Schlumberger family of the de Neuflize, Schlumberger, Mallet banking empire.

As Anton Chaitkin has documented in *Treason in America,* the Mallet-de Neuflize Swiss financial networks have been at the center of evil operations against the republican institutions of the United States since the time of the French Revolution. In November 1981, Mme. Dominique Schlumberger, the wife of Jean DeMenil, hosted a gathering of the fanatical Muslim Brotherhood in Houston, Texas—to celebrate the Brotherhood's assassination of Egyptian President Anwar Sadat. It is no exaggeration to say that the Schlumbergers have been involved in every derivative assassination of political significance for the past 200 years.

In the 1950s, Schlumberger diversified into the oil diagnostic equipment industry. The company created for that purpose is now the largest company in the field worldwide, accounting for the production and sale of 50% of all of the equipment in existence. In 1958, son-in-law Jean DeMenil became president of the company, headquartered in Houston. That company, as we noted earlier, served as a weapons conduit for the CIA and FBI Division Five. Those smuggling operations were conducted in conjunction with the Double-Chek Company of Miami, Florida.[80]

During the mid-1960s, de Gaulle's intelligence services established that the de Neuflize, Schlumberger, Mallet Bank was channeling funds to Jacques Soustelle to bankroll OAS terrorist activities.

The American Council of Christian Churches

One of the principal agencies through which the Solidarist movement maintained contact with its operatives worldwide was the Old Orthodox Catholic Church of North America and its affiliated Synod of Bishops of the Russian Orthodox Church Outside Russia. This splinter church out of the Russian Orthodox Church had been established originally as a front for British intelligence espionage activities inside Russia following the Bolshevik Revolution and retained that function in North America after many of its operatives had relocated to the West following World War II. Throughout this period a section of Soviet intelligence maintained equal control over the network. This Anglo-Soviet deal came to be known as the Trust.

The Old Orthodox Catholic Church of North America was an affiliated Church of the American Council of Christian Churches (ACCC), an umbrella organization nominally representing those traditionalist churches of all denominations that opposed the ultra-liberal outlook of the World Council of Churches and its U.S. subsidiary National Council of Churches.

Many "conservative" churches are to this day affiliated with the ACCC for precisely this reason stated above. However, there is another side to the ACCC that prompted District Attorney James Garrison to identify it as one of the agencies deeply involved in the Kennedy assassination conspiracy; and to issue an indictment against the ACCC's West Coast Director E.E. Bradley, on charges that he aided Colonel Clay Shaw in assassinating the President.

---

80. Ibid., p. 213.

In 1941, J. Edgar Hoover, in consultation with British SOE head Sir William Stephenson and Division Five recruiter Louis M. Bloomfield, arranged for his close friend Reverend Carl McIntyre to found the American Council of Christian Churches. McIntyre was already a contract agent of Hoover's FBI Division Five. The ACCC was to conceal an extensive espionage and intelligence unit to be deployed throughout the United States, Canada, Mexico and Latin America. The spies and saboteurs were to operate under the cover of Christian missionaries.

As part of the ACCC espionage net, Hoover, Stephenson, and Bloomfield created a secret assassination unit in 1943 under the direction of ACCC Minister Albert Osborne. It is not clear that McIntyre was ever let in on this sinister aspect of the ACCC by his "friend" Hoover. The unit consisted of twenty-five to thirty of the world's most skilled riflemen. It was housed in a missionary school for orphans in Puebla, Mexico. Up through at least 1969, the special "kill unit" remained intact under the personal supervision of J. Edgar Hoover, operating through his trusted agent of thirty years, Albert Osborne.

According to author "Torbitt," it was Osborne and a team of seven expert riflemen from the Puebla "kill unit" who carried out the assassination of John F. Kennedy in Dallas on November 22, 1963.

The records of the Warren Commission establish that Albert Osborne had been a charter member of the ACCC. In 1942, while working for the Hoover-Bloomfield Division Five, Osborne had directed a Nazi blackshirt group called the Campfire Council in the rural area around Knoxville, Tennessee. At that time he had nearly been arrested following an incident in which he burned an American flag in protest against the U.S. entry into the war against Nazi Germany. He shortly thereafter left Tennessee to relocate to Puebla, Mexico.

Garrison documented that on October 10, 1963, Osborne had visited New Orleans, making three stops in town. First he visited the offices of Clay Shaw at the International Trade Mart building. Later the same day he visited the offices of FBI Division Five courier Jerry Brooks Gatlin, whom we encountered earlier in probing the 1962 assassination attempt against French President Charles de Gaulle. Osborne's final stop in New Orleans was at the office of FBI Division Five southern chief Guy Bannister, at 544 Camp Street.

From New Orleans, Osborne traveled directly to Mexico City where, according to the records of both the Garrison investigation and the Warren Commission, he was seen repeatedly in the company of the "Leon Oswald" whom we met earlier in New Orleans with Clay Shaw and David Ferrie.

This circle of assassins closes a bit further as we return to the case of yet another Division Five operative who maintained a cover as a priest in the employ of the American Council of Christian Churches: David Ferrie.

In 1946, Ferrie dropped out of a Roman Catholic seminary in Ohio and joined the Byelorussian Liberation Front, simultaneously being ordained as a priest in the Old Orthodox Catholic Church of North America, an agency we have already identified as a front for the Solidarist movement, the KGB, and FBI Division Five. Ferrie was subsequently redeployed to the southern region of the FBI, where he operated as a Division Five recruitment officer (placing him under the direct jurisdiction of Major Bloomfield).

According to testimony before both the Warren Commission and the Garrison grand jury, given by FBI operative Jack Martin, Lee Harvey Oswald was recruited into the FBI Division Five in 1956 by none other than David Ferrie. While nominally in the Marine Corps, Oswald received special training in covert espionage activities at the Naval Intelligence School on the Memphis Naval Base. One aspect of this training included special instruction in the Russian language, provided by an agent of the Solidarist movement operating in San Francisco under the cover of the Federation of Russian Charitable Organizations, a West Coast branch of the Tolstoy Foundation.

From 1956 until his untimely death in the basement of the Dallas Police headquarters in November 1963, Lee Harvey Oswald had been on a secret Division Five payroll, maintained through a secret account concealed in the budget of the Immigration and Naturalization Service, a unit within the Department of Justice.

During the six-month period leading up to his murder in Dallas, the real Lee Harvey Oswald had been operating out of New Orleans and Dallas under the immediate supervision of Division Five regional director Guy Bannister. In fact, the New Orleans headquarters of the pro-Castro Fair Play for Cuba Committee, a group that Oswald actively participated in during 1963, was located in the same Camp Street office building that housed Bannister. Unknown to Oswald, his "infiltration" into the pro-Castro grouping on behalf of Division Five had a far different purpose than he imagined; a purpose that would become clear only after he assumed the role of the "patsy" that David Ferrie had discussed with Clay Shaw and William Seymour.[81]

The Lionel Corporation Connection

We have now seen two components of the network of protected killers who carried out the assassination of John Kennedy on behalf of Permindex. In the case of both the Solidarists and the American Council of Christian Churches, we have seen the fruit of Sir William Stephenson's wartime penetration of the national security apparatus of the United States.

One further note must be made here concerning Stephenson's wartime activities as they would later surface in the Permindex assassination plot against Kennedy. Stephenson oversaw the recruitment of U.S. organized crime figures into the SOE-OSS during World War II. The best-known case in point was the "rehabilitation" of convicted drug runner, pimp and suspected murderer Charles "Lucky" Luciano. Luciano was dispatched to Sicily under joint SOE-OSS direction to reconstitute old networks that had been dispersed or expatriated during the Mussolini period.[82] In this effort, Luciano would actively collaborate with Count Guitierez di Spadafora, a board member of Permindex.

---

81. Ferrie was found murdered days after he was subpoenaed to testify before Garrison's grand jury on the Kennedy killing. See Torbitt, "Assassination Cabal," p. 164.

82. Rodney Campbell, *The Luciano Project* (New York: McGraw-Hill Book Company, 1977); see also Julian Semyonov, "Capriccio Siciliano," *Ogonyok* (Moscow), October-November, 1978.

Luciano has been widely identified as the case officer on the scene in Sicily for the 1962, assassination of Italian oil minister and close de Gaulle collaborator Enrico Mattei.[83]

Mattei died when his plane went down over the Mediterranean after having been tampered with during a brief, unscheduled stopover at an obscure airport in Sicily.[84] According to sources, the decision to go with the plane sabotage was made by Luciano only after the options of hiring an OAS hit team or an American "leftist" controlled by a Texas oil company had been rejected as too politically explosive. The Texas oil company in question was an investor in Major Bloomfield's international trade expositions firm.

Luciano was by no means the only syndicate figure co-opted into the employ of Permindex.

According to official incorporation papers on file in New York City and Berne, Switzerland, mob attorney Roy Marcus Cohn and Montreal crime boss Joseph Bonanno were both personal stockholders in Permindex through their ownership of the Lionel Corporation of Hillside, New Jersey.

At the time of Permindex's initial incorporation, 50% of the corporate stock was purchased by Major Bloomfield. A significant minority position was purchased by Lionel Corporation. Several years before the Permindex investment, Lionel had been bought up by Cohn and Bonanno. Sources indicate that the Lionel buy into Permindex was financed through a $600,000 "loan" that Cohn arranged through contacts in Hong Kong. New York City corporate records show that as of 1958, Joseph Bonanno was the chairman of the board of Lionel and attorney Roy Cohn was the president.

Lionel was principally involved in defense contract work. At the same time the nest of corporate fronts was used to carry out other "business" on behalf of Major Bloomfield's trade expositions company in which, as we noted, Lionel had been an enthusiastic investor.

At the end of 1963, Cohn, et al. sold off Lionel and all of its subsidiaries. One of the most lucrative pieces of the Lionel "empire," the Intercontinental Corporation of Garland, Texas, was sold to Robert Vesco. It became one of Vesco's earliest financial scores.

It was the same Intercontinental Corporation that author "Torbitt" identified as the front through which a group of Cuban exiles, all veterans of the Caribbean gambling and narcotics syndicate and the Bay of Pigs paramilitary operation, were assigned to Permindex board member Ferenc Nagy to play supporting roles in the assassination of John Kennedy.

We have already seen how Sir William Stephenson and a coterie of SOE spooks moved in on Montego Bay at the very close of World War II and built that spot up into a cross between paradise and Fort Knox. In the case of Acapulco, the guiding figure behind its postwar emergence as a watering hole for the super-rich and the

---

83. Semyonov, "Capriccio Siciliano," reprinted English translation from *Ogonyok* in *Executive Intelligence Review* 43 (1978), p. 38.
84. Giuseppe Pantaleone, "An Interview," *Panorama,* April 1970.

super-secretive was former Mexican President Miguel Alemán, himself a central figure in the international narcotics and assassination cartel.

It was during Alemán's tenure as interior minister (1940-46) and President of Mexico (1946-52) that J. Edgar Hoover's Division Five was given carte blanche to set up shop in that country. Combined SOE-Division Five operations were set up all over Mexico and very few were shut down at the end of the war. Reverend Osborne's Christian boys school has already been identified as one such case in which a "hundred-year lease" was signed between Alemán and SOE-Division Five.

When President Alemán formally retired from politics in the 1950s, he built up a vast real estate empire in Mexico that today includes a string of resort hotels, among them one of the largest resort spots in Acapulco.

Not coincidentally, all of Alemán's hotel acquisitions are managed by the Canadian Pacific Corporation—the biggest covert importer of Golden Triangle narcotics into North America and a heavy investor in the Caribbean islands that house some of the most important black market money houses in the Dope, Inc. international portfolio.

Among Alemán's other major holdings is a lion's share of the stock in the fifth largest company in Mexico, Tavos de Acero de Méjico (TAMSA). The director of TAMSA, Bruno Pagliai, is the cousin of Princess Beatrice of Savoy, herself a resident of Mexico and a frequent guest at Alemán's own Acapulco jet set parties.

It is through two Alemán confidants that the Mexican end of Dope, Inc. begins to emerge more clearly. Alemán's personal banker and one of his most intimate friends is Max Schein, president of the Banco Mercantil de México. Schein's bank is the correspondent bank to Bank Leumi, the Israeli banking giant that we have already encountered as a major laundering vehicle for the revenues of international dope traffic. Schein is the chairman of the Sociedad Technión de Mexico, the local branch of the Israel Technion Society—the Mossad's overseas scientific espionage front. Among the board members of the Technion International is Major Louis Mortimer Bloomfield of Permindex.

Alemán's other, far more exposed flank into Dope, Inc., is Gonzalo N. Santos, a former aide and well-publicized personal friend of the ex-President. Santos was a business partner of a Guadalajara-based Cuban exile named Alberto Sicilia Falcón. Falcón, once an asset of the Division Five apparatus in Miami and later Mexico City (and also widely believed to be on the payroll of Cuban intelligence, DGI), was arrested in 1975 as the head of a major heroin-importing ring that stretched from Thailand to Turkey to Marseilles. The Falcón ring had an entire fleet of private planes that ran drug pickup and dropoff routes throughout Latin America into the United States. That ring also ran a string of heroin laboratories.

While Falcón's associate and Alemán staff officer Santos survived the 1975 bust unscathed, he was the subject of a 1977 Mexican Senate inquiry into the guns-for-dope traffic across the United States-Mexican border. Santos was labeled as the major conduit of illegal weapons acquired in the United States and smuggled into the hands of some of the leading oligarchical families in Mexico. Many of these weapons were believed to have been subsequently passed into the hands of the Liga 23 de Septiembre, Mexico's equivalent to the terrorist Italian Red Brigades.

The Coverup

As we unravel the web of government agencies, media channels, and private spook armies that were set loose both immediately after the Kennedy assassination, and once again when New Orleans DA Garrison launched his own independent probe into the Clay Shaw cabal, we shall discover that the cover-up of the Kennedy plot is perhaps the single most damning piece of evidence pointing to a high-level conspiracy behind the death of the President. Once again, we shall discover the guiding hand behind the operation to be that of Dope, Inc.

Immediately after the assassination, there were more than six months' active disruption efforts against the investigation on the part of a very special secret agent of the national security establishment. The agent was Walter Sheridan, the man that Attorney General Robert F. Kennedy had earlier entrusted to head up the highly irregular "Get Hoffa" unit of the Department of Justice. Despite such appearances of closeness to the Kennedy family machine, strong evidence suggests that Walter Sheridan had already been a longtime asset of the' British SOE circuitry inside the U.S. intelligence establishment at the time of his "recruitment" into the Kennedy camp in the late 1950s.

Walter Sheridan, after graduating from the Jesuit-run Fordham University and briefly attending Albany Law School, was recruited into the Federal Bureau of Investigation, where he worked for four years. From the FBI, Sheridan moved over to the newly established National Security Agency. The NSA was established in the early 1950s as the most secretive, high technology-oriented snooping agency in the U.S. government. To this day, for example, the NSA is the one intelligence service that operates under a total Official Secrets Act screen. Neither the Congress nor any other Federal agency has oversight or even access to information concerning the NSA.

Walter Sheridan evidently already had heavy backing. He was appointed chief of the Counterintelligence Section, Special Operations Division, Office of Security of the NSA. He was subsequently appointed assistant chief of the NSA Clearance Division.

The NSA had been an outgrowth of the sophisticated telecommunications and coding operations developed by the Allies during World War II. In this effort the United States had been thoroughly trained by the British Special Operations Executive. Early in the war, Sir William Stephenson had established a special "code breaking" unit at Bletchley Park, England, which served as a training center as well as an encoding unit employing a select group of Americans and Englishmen. Among the Americans trained at the Bletchley Park center were Robert Sarnoff and William Bundy. Sarnoff was the son of General David Sarnoff, the founder and president of the Radio Corporation of America (Robert Sarnoff would replace his father as president on the latter's retirement during the early 1950s) and a wartime member of the SOE elite in the United States. Bundy would later become the editor of the Council on Foreign Relations' quarterly journal *Foreign Affairs* while his brother assumed the National Security directorship under John F. Kennedy.

After the War, Sarnoff's RCA became the technological core of the capability that later was brought under top secret government control as the NSA. In that sense, the NSA is perhaps the branch of the U.S. intelligence establishment most directly run by the Stephenson SOE apparatus.

Sheridan's high-level placement in the NSA Counterintelligence Division—the unit most closely interfaced with the FBI Division Five-belies the popular idea that Sheridan was first and foremost a Kennedy family loyalist.

In 1958, a "church friend" introduced Sheridan to Robert Kennedy, who immediately hired the NSA veteran as the special investigator for the Senate Rackets Committee, the "McClellan committee" that RFK was then serving as general counsel. When John Kennedy was elected President, Sheridan was appointed "confidential assistant" to Attorney General Robert Kennedy—a position that placed him in the inner circle of both the Justice Department and the White House (where he maintained a secret office adjacent to the Oval Office).

As "confidential assistant" to RFK, Sheridan created the "Get Hoffa" unit of the Justice Department. According to sources who served close to Robert Kennedy at that time, the "Get Hoffa" unit rapidly became a private fiefdom of Sheridan that even the Attorney General could not penetrate.

Kennedy Justice Department historian Victor Navasky described the Sheridan unit in the following way: "Its modus operandi was pure cloak and dagger. . . . Sheridan's relations with the FBI were highly irregular, in that it received little or no cooperation from the top, yet Sheridan, an ex-FBI man, had a degree of line cooperation in the field that was, in some respects, unparalleled. He actually coordinated FBI agents with his own men—told them where to go and when, and they went."[85] Sheridan had similar access to the resources of the Internal Revenue Service, the Secret Service, the U.S. Marshals, and the Alcohol, Tobacco and Firearms Division of Treasury. In effect, Sheridan replicated the operational capabilities and the targeting methods of the wartime SOE. Sheridan's private army replicated the methods of the SOE in another significant area. In addition to the "official" channels that Sheridan was able to navigate through every Federal agency even remotely involved in intelligence and enforcement, he apparently created a nest of clandestine agencies—under corporate cover—that were deployed to carry out those special operations that were so flagrantly illegal that they could not even be remotely associated with the government.

According to author Jim Hougan, Sheridan created a private investigative agency known as "Five Eyes": International Investigators Incorporated of Indianapolis, Indiana. Although the firm was officially incorporated on October 3, 1966 (two years after Sheridan left the Justice Department), Five Eyes maintained offices in Indianapolis, Chicago, Detroit, Louisville, Nashville, Memphis, and Minneapolis by no later than fall 1961. For its first five years of existence, no corporate records existed anywhere in the United States even suggesting its existence.[86]

Sheridan's Five Eyes (also frequently referred to as Three Eyes, for International Investigators, Inc.) went out of business in the late 1960s at the same time that another Three Eyes was being founded by some of Sheridan's top operatives in the

85. Victor Navasky, *Kennedy Justice*.
86. Jim Hougan, *Spooks* (New York: Bantam Books, 1978).

"Get Hoffa" unit. This Three Eyes, International Intelligence, Incorporated, is more commonly known as Intertel, the private security arm of the Caribbean gambling and dope center known as Resorts International. We shall return to this offshore paradise in our next chapter.

In February 1967, Walter Sheridan was hired by the National Broadcasting Company (NBC) as an "investigative journalist" attached to the NBC White Paper television documentary series. Sheridan's assignment for NBC? To do a special television report on the investigation into the assassination of President John F. Kennedy that had just been launched by New Orleans District Attorney Jim Garrison. By July of that year, Sheridan would be indicted by Garrison on four separate charges of public bribery—all revolving around Sheridan's efforts to wreck the Garrison probe.

According to evidence submitted by Garrison, Sheridan had engaged in flagrant witness-tampering aimed at both publicly discrediting the Garrison probe and preventing key witnesses from appearing before the New Orleans grand jury.

One of the witnesses targeted by Sheridan was the Baton Rouge insurance salesman Perry Raymond Russo, whom we met earlier as the "fourth man" in the assassination planning session convened by Clay Shaw.

On June 19, 1967, Assistant New Orleans District Attorney Andrew J. Sciambra delivered a memo to Garrison proving that Sheridan had used his NBC team to harass Russo on a round-the-clock basis, had gotten to Russo's employers at Equitable Life Insurance to pressure them to relocate Russo outside of the Louisiana jurisdiction of Garrison, and had succeeded in smuggling Russo out of the state for a "vacation" in California. Once out of Garrison's hands, Russo was to be put on nationwide television to denounce Garrison for having "doctored" his testimony to create a phony conspiracy case against Clay Shaw.

The Sciambra memo further reported that the NBC White Paper crew was working closely with a research team from the *Saturday Evening Post* on the "Get Garrison" operation. The *Saturday Evening Post* had just been purchased by Bert SerVaas of Indianapolis. SerVaas's name appeared in October 1966 on the incorporation papers of International Investigators, Incorporated as its president.

A second bombshell exploded in the face of the Sheridan operation on August 19, 1967 in a Chicago courtroom. There, an official of the International Brotherhood of Teamsters, Zachary Strate, testified that he had been offered a deal by Sheridan. In return for his joining Sheridan in the propaganda blitz against Garrison, Strate would be provided with classified government documents proving that his conviction on extortion in a case involving Teamster president and Sheridan target Jimmy Hoffa, had been obtained through the use of illegal wiretaps.

Extortion, blackmail, kidnapping, bribery; these were not the only weapons unleashed in the war against Garrison. By the time of the 1967 Garrison probe, over a dozen key witnesses had died under mysterious circumstances. Guy Bannister, the FBI Division Five chief in New Orleans, was dead.

Lee Harvey Oswald was dead, shot at point-blank range before a nationwide television audience in the basement of the Dallas Police headquarters. His assassin, Jack Ruby, far from being the "distraught good samaritan," had been a business, partner of Guy Bannister and David Ferrie in a series of Cub an casino ventures before the fall of Batista; and had been involved in the Schlumberger-Double-Chek gun-running adventures, first into Fidel Castro's forces and later into the anti-Castro army put together by the CIA after the Cuban President's turn to the Soviet Union.

David Ferrie was also dead, the victim of a "suicide" overdose of narcotics on the very eve of his appearance before District Attorney Garrison's probe. According to Jules Rocco Kimble, a witness before the Garrison probe, he and Jack Helms had entered the Ferrie apartment just hours after the former Division Five contract employee had died and removed a file cabinet full of documents. Kimble and Helms, both admitted members of the Ku Klux Klan, then fled to Canada. Their flight, and their future lodgings and safety, had been guaranteed by Walter Sheridan of NBC. Kimble "coincidentally" showed up in the files of the House Select Committee on Assassinations as a neighbor of James Earl Ray, when the assassin of Martin Luther King fled New Orleans for Montreal after his jailbreak.

Sheridan's blast at Garrison did eventually air on NBC national television and did serve as the trigger mechanism for a barrage of attacks on the New Orleans DA from the national media.

NBC was from its founding a wholly owned subsidiary of the Radio Corporation of America. At the time of the airing of the NBC White Paper on Garrison, the president of NBC was Robert Sarnoff, the wartime veteran of Sir William Stephenson's SOE retreat at Blechley Park, England. In retrospect, President Dwight Eisenhower's efforts to break up the RCA monopoly were among the clearest, most important—and unheeded—legacies of his presidency.

What apparatus within the government stood behind Walter Sheridan and his "Get Garrison" apparatus? We have already identified the NSA and FBI Division Five pedigree of this Jesuit-trained spook. Evidence further exists that another secret police agency—one that we have already encountered in our probe of Permindex—was instrumental in the effort to cover up the cabal behind the Kennedy assassination.

According to author "Torbitt," a New Orleans employee of the Double-Chek agency named Gordon Novel had infiltrated the Garrison investigation staff in spring 1967, and determined that Double-Chek and the FBI's Division Five were being actively investigated for their parts in the Kennedy assassination. Novel was put in contact with Walter Sheridan. When Garrison discovered the double-agent role being played by Novel, he subpoenaed the former "staff investigator" to appear before his grand jury probe. Novel left Louisiana under the protection of Sheridan and was delivered to a Virginia safehouse where the results of a doctored lie detector test were released to the press by Sheridan, claiming that Novel had provided conclusive proof that the Garrison probe was a pure publicity stunt with no substantive evidence.

More than two decades have passed since the assassination of John Kennedy in Dallas; and at this very moment, Permindex and the British command that ordered the cold coup by assassination remains one of the best-kept secrets in the world.

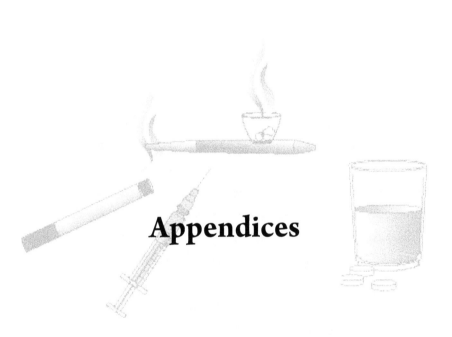

Appendices

Appendix I
Wall Street and the IMF Love Drug Money: The case of Colombia's FARC

The following was adapted from a package which appeared in the July 16, 1999 issue of EIR.

There is no question that the biggest and most murderous narcoterrorist organization in the Americas is Colombia's FARC, the self-proclaimed Revolutionary Armed Forces of Colombia. This army of at least 20,000 soldiers, has a deserved reputation for the utmost brutality, controls approximately half the territory of Colombia, and functions as the largest drug cartel in the nation which is the number one producer of coca and its deadly derivatives, cocaine and crack cocaine.

Yet, in June of 1999, no less a major U.S. political and financial figure than Richard Grasso, president of the New York Stock Exchange, purportedly answered the invitation of the Colombian government, and made a highly publicized visit to the jungles of Colombia, to meet with the "treasurer" of the F ARC, Raúl Reyes. The embrace which they shared—which we at *EIR* have dubbed the Grasso Abrazo, and is featured on the cover of this Special Report—has since been sent around the world, on the official web page of the Colombian government. The picture reflects the ugly reality: Wall Street and the biggest drug cartel of the Americas are loving partners in the business of drugs, terrorism, and drug-money -laundering.

This evidence of a close collaborative relationship was shocking in its public nature, but it was hardly a surprise to *EIR*. This news service had been following the process of incremental drug legalization for more than 20 years, including the easing of financial regulations for drug money. But on June 9, 1999, the process of de facto legalization had taken a new step, when the Colombian government's National Administrative Department of Statistics (DANE) released a report on new procedures for calculating Gross National Product. Included were new methods for measuring a different product—*illicit crops*. That meant illegal drugs.

In investigating the basis for this change in "accounting" procedures, *EIR* discovered that the mandate for including illegal drugs in the National Product was none other than the world's most powerful financial authority, the International Monetary Fund itself. Such an action makes a total mockery out of "official" attempts to fight the drug trade—as now Colombia's "wealth" depends upon it.

In fact, what these two events show is that, while the narcoterrorist FARC may be a scourge of Colombians, and supply the wherewithal for illegal drugs and weapons all over the world (including, recent reports have indicated, the Afghani drug-runners), the world's leading financial institutions consider it a friend and necessary partner in the business of making money, no matter what the cost.

Wall Street's Affair with the FARC

It was June 26, 1999 that Richard Grasso returned from the southern jungles of Colombia, to announce that he had just struck a pact with the FARC. Grasso hailed the FARC leadership as "extraordinary," said they had discussed a "mutual exchange of capitals," and announced that he had invited the FARC's "Supreme

Commander," with other leaders, to "walk the trading floor with me" at the New York Stock Exchange.

Grasso hailed his FARC pact as part of the Stock Exchange's strategy of being "very aggressive in trying to pursue international markets and opportunities," and he declared that he hoped his visit "will mark the beginning of a new relationship between the FARC and the United States."

Does this mean that the FARC—which is on the U.S. State Department's list of international terrorist organizations, and is feared and despised throughout Colombia for its wanton murders, kidnappings, and extortion rackets—has changed? Not in the least. Does it mean that Grasso, and the officials of the NYSE who went with him—vice president of international relations Alan Yves Morvan, and head of security and protection James Esposito—don't know with whom they are meeting? Not unless they are mentally retarded.

The New York Stock Exchange delegation met with Raúl Reyes, the member of the FARC's secretariat who heads the group's finances, and received the translation services of none other than Colombian Finance Minister Juan Camilo Restrepo. At the June 29 press conference which Grasso gave in New York City to report back on his meeting, he could hardly keep from gushing about his experience.

Grasso said that Colombian President Pastrana (a former kidnap victim of another Colombian narcoterrorist group, years earlier), who has been kowtowing to the terrorists from the moment he came into office, had urged him to visit right before the scheduled opening of "peace" talks on July 7.

Those talks, of course, have never resulted in "peace" at all; the more concessions the government has made, 'the more demands the FARC has put forward, Just a few more concessions, the FARC says, and we will stop the violence. Grasso's statements also imply that the FARC is looking forward to days when Colombia is not "viewed solely as a narcotraffic economy," and that the days of that being the principal industry are over. He is *very* well-attuned to the subject of "alternative investment, what will happen when a peace is arrived at in Colombia, and is very open to the dialogue we had on the whole process of democratization of capital."

Why should Grasso believe the words of this murderous narcoterrorist, whose organization murdered three Americans in 1999, in addition to thousands of Colombians? What a farce.

At the June 29 press conference, Grasso described his meeting as follows:

"He [Reyes] was very interested in the model here in the United States, because, to his surprise, we spent a bit of time talking about the breadth of share ownership in America. How stockholders were not simply those in the financial community, but those who are on assembly lines, those who are teaching school, driving buses. And I think the leadership of FARC is sophisticated enough to understand that there will be a next chapter in Colombia. [Indeed—but who will control it?]

"FARC currently has, by the government's grant, [under duress—ed.], a piece of real estate that is the size of Switzerland, that they control. That is where we met with the guerrillas at Machaca, which is somewhere to the south of San Vicente—I think.

"But it was an *extraordinary* experience, in the sense that the Comandante was trained as an engineer in the former Soviet Union, *Very* sophisticated, despite what the surface appearance may have been, in terms of his jungle fatigues and his M-16. And he knew a *lot* about investment and capital markets, and the need to stimulate outside capital coming to Colombia. Very interested in how Colombian companies could come to the U.S., and raise capital to be invested in the country.

"So, it was extraordinary . . . .

"I invited Comandante Reyes and the Supreme Commander [Manuel 'Tirofijo' Marulanda, head of the FARC] to walk the trading floor with me, and I hope that—and to do that together with President Pastrana. And I hope that when they do accept that invitation, they'll have the firsthand experience of what we talked about on Saturday. They will take the academic, and turn it into the real-life experience. It is very important to recognize that—as President Pastrana has—that FARC has got to take a much broader view of Colombia, of Latin America, and of the world stage that Colombia hopes to compete on. And I think extending and permitting differing factors the opportunity to come here, and to walk the trading floor, and to understand capitalism firsthand, will be very valuable in a post-settlement Colombian economy.

"I'm not so naive as to think that the Comandante will be here next week, but he certainly recognized the value of coming to America, and experiencing, not just the financial markets, but the technology of agriculture, which will become very important in redeveloping the Colombian economy; where and how to stimulate foreign investment in Colombia; how to raise capital, both in the region and outside of the region.

"And again, to underscore: This was a very, I believe, sophisticated leader. I think that Raúl Reyes—Comandante Reyes—is quite knowledgeable, and very much interested in coming and seeing this firsthand. Perhaps meeting many of you."

The IMF: Drug Money Is Money

"Sophistication" is also the word IMF spokesman Francisco Baker used to describe the methods which that agency has devised to measure illegal activity like growing dope, when he was interviewed by *EIR's* Spanish-language magazine, *Resumen Ejecutivo*, back in late June of 1999. Baker is the press officer of the IMF's Western Hemisphere division. "Sophistication" seems to imply the suspension of any moral judgment on where money comes from: Money is money.

According to Baker, there has been an official effort by the United Nations Statistical Committee, along with the IMF, the World Bank, the European Commission, and the Organization for Economic Cooperation and Development, to pull together a "methodology for compilations of data having to do with the national accounts of countries." This resulted in the creation of a manual called the "System of National Statistics, 1993." And, Baker said, "the part where it said that illegal crops—illegal activity, no illegal crops, particularly, but illegal activity, — should be measured, has been there since 1993."

EIR's Record: Financial Oligarchy Pushes Drugs

For more than two decades, EIR has exposed the role of the global financial oligarchy in forcing the drug trade on Third World nations, and in laundering the proceeds from drug sales. The following are some highlights of our past coverage.

"Why the World Bank Pushes Drugs," EIR, Sept. 18-23, 1978:
The threatened tidal wave of drugs is the first phase of a deliberate and operational plan by the World Bank, International Monetary Fund, and allied London, Amsterdam, and turncoat American financiers. They are engaged in forcing major portions of the Third World to abandon "expensive, wasteful" development hopes and become profitable, starving narcotics plantations. The minds and bodies of America's youth are to be sacrificed to this debtand-austerity imperative along with the lives of millions in the Third World, even as these bankers extoll the economic benefits of expanding the drug trade. . . .

John Holdson, the senior official for Latin America in the World Bank's International Trade and Monetary Flows department:
"I haven't looked at Colombia's drug industry, although I've just returned from Bolivia, and I know that the coca industry there is highly advantageous to producers. In fact, from their point of view, they simply couldn't find a better product. Its advantages are that no elaborate technology is required, no hybrid seeds, and land and climate are perfect. . . . "

From an interview with a Colombian specialist at the International Monetary Fund:
Q: ". . .To simply ignore the parallel economy means to let it grow to the point at which it would just swallow up and destroy the national economy."
A: "But there I must absolutely disagree with you, with the last thing you said. It would not destroy the national economy. From an economic viewpoint, the marijuana is just a crop, like any other. It brings in foreign exchange, and provides income for the peasants. . . . Well, you know, legality is a relative concept. In a few years, marijuana may become legal anyway."

From a conversation with a top international banker in New York City:
"Coffee prices are simply too unstable, always fluctuating on the world market, you know . . . . Drugs, on the other hand, provide a stable source of income at all times. With coffee prices like they are, Colombia will never get its development going, can't make plans like the oil producers can. . . . I happen to know that the World Bank has been pressuring some Latin American countries—not Colombia as far as I know—to find some way of statistically accounting for their contraband flows."

" 'International Monetary Fund Forces the Third World into the Drug Trade,' "interview with Frederick Wills, former Foreign Minister of Guyana, EIR, Nov. 29, 1983:

EIR: . . . One of the things the IMF pushes is what they call 'non-traditional exports.' Are they aware of the fact that these actually include illicit drugs?

Wills: Oh yes, they are aware. But there is a certain conspiracy of silence. Nobody puts down on a government balance sheet or an IMF balance sheet "Export of Dope." You put down" Agricultural Exports"! This is to cover up a multitude of sins. You may know that 90% of it is dope, but nobody puts down the word. The banks advance money, because the return on investment is very large; it is not 'risk capital.' "

Bush's Surrender to Dope, Inc.: U.S. Policy Is Destroying Colombia, EIR Special Report, April 1, 1991.
EIR quoted leading advocates of drug legalization, including:

The Economist, June 1989: "It is obvious . . . that drug dealers use banks . . . The business . . . has become part of the financial system."

U.S. Secretary of State George Shultz, Oct. 7, 1989: "We're not going to get anywhere until we can take the criminality out of the drug business . . . . We need at least to consider and examine forms of controlled legalization of drugs."

Milton Friedman, in his 1983 book Tyranny of the Status Quo: "The belief that it is desirable to legalize marijuana and all other drugs does not depend on whether marijuana or other drugs are harmful or harmless."

Inter-American Dialogue, report issued April 1986: "If selective legislation could reduce the enormous profits derived from drug trafficking, it would decrease vice and corruption.

Dennis Small, "How the Economy of Bolivia Became Addicted to Cocaine," EIR, Jan. 10, 1992:
The nations of Eurasia which have recently freed themselves from communism, are today threatened by a new, more perverse form of enslavement. They are being told by the Anglo-American establishment that if they want to solve their economic problems, they have to become part of the West's "free" economic system, and this means adopting the austerity conditionalities of the International Monetary Fund, and the "free-market reforms" associated with Harvard University's enfant terrible, Jeffrey Sachs. . . .

The promotional "sales pitch" on Jeffrey Sachs is that he proved his genius by wiping out inflation in Bolivia between 1985 and 1987—his first "success story." Inflation there dropped from an annual rate of over 20,000% in 1985, to about 11% in 1987. . . .

But the way Sachs stopped inflation, was by destroying what little existed of Bolivia's productive economy, and opening the doors wide for the international drug trade to come in and fill the vacuum he had helped create, and consolidate its death grip on the economy . . . .

The number of workers employed in coca leaf growing and processing leapt from about 350,000 (or 17% of the labor force) before Sachs worked his magic, to over 700,000 after—a third of the entire labor force.

Was all this an unfortunate mistake, a miscalculation on the part of the well-intentioned Harvard wonder boy and his establishment sponsors? Absolutely not. The destruction of Bolivia's productive economy and the skyrocketing of the drug trade were the deliberate, conscious, and intended result of Sachs's policies.

It is best to listen to Sachs himself on this subject, as he stated it bluntly in his 1988 study, Bolivia: 1952-1986:

"To preserve fiscal balance, the government had to launch a brutal battle to reduce payrolls in Comibol [the state tin company] and YPFB [the state oil company]. Although fiscally necessary, the results are stunning, and indeed reflect a social tragedy. Comibol has reduced its employment from about 30,000 workers in 1985, to just 7,000, as of 1987. Many of these workers are still unemployed, or only marginally employed, or have gone to the coca-growing region to find work. The mining towns themselves have been decimated."

Resumen's reporter grilled Baker on the IMF adoption of such a "value-free" system, but Baker stuck to his guns.

"Your question about why not include heroin: There is nothing against—I mean, ideally, it *should* include it. The problem is, that, in the particular case of Colombia, they don't know how to measure that kind of data. Crops, somehow, are easier to measure, that's why they include crops. But for you to have an idea, in the case of the Netherlands, for instance, they include prostitution as part of what the statistics measure.

"We don't have a very clear idea—I am still waiting to talk to someone who would let me know which countries are doing this. But, *in principle, countries all over the world should be measuring illegal activity as part of the exercise of assessing the size of the respective economies.* We've made recommendations to Bolivia along the same lines, and to Colombia. By the way, that recommendation to Colombia to do that, was made back in 1997 . . . . " [emphasis added]

Asked by the *Resumen* reporter about the IMF's estimates of the size of the drug trade, Baker responded:

"What I was told, is that this kind of measurement requires a lot of statistical sophistication."

In fact, as President Clinton's White House anti-drug policy adviser Gen. (ret.) Barry McCaffrey said in the summer of 1999, "It must be made very clear publicly that this is blood money: It is the blood of Colombian policemen and soldiers. It is an illegal activity . . . ."

Appendix II
French Attack London's 'City' Money Laundry

This article, by a reporter for the French newspaper Nouvelle Solidarité, *is drawn from a version which appeared in* EIR *magazine.*

As Britain's Tony Blair parades as the leader of the fight against "Islamic terror," French authorities have launched a flanking operation against Britain in the form of a Parliamentary report denouncing the City of London—as well as other Crown dependencies—as a "fiscal, banking, and financial paradise for criminals."

Attached to that report is a full study on the "economic environment of bin Laden." The French are still waiting for the extradition of Rashid Ramda, the terrorist arrested in Britain in 1996 for having orchestrated the 1995 wave of terror in France.

Entitled "The City Of London, Gibraltar And The Crown Dependencies: Offshore Centers And Havens For Dirty Money," the report, which was released to the public on Oct. 10, 2001, denounces London's great vulnerability to money-laundering, but also the British authorities' total lack of political will to engage in the fight against financial crime. "The government of Her Gracious Majesty claims to be leading the fight against terrorism, but it should first clean its own house," stated Arnaud Montebourg, special rapporteur of the Parliamentary Commission which issued the report. To the question of why the British government is not willing to impose transparency in its financial transactions, Montebourg replied that the City of London is the very heart of world finances and that Britain's own power derives from that financial power. In the year 2000, the Gross Domestic Product of the City was close to $37.7 billion—13% of Greater London' GDP, and 3% of that of the United Kingdom.

The French report was issued by a Parliamentary Commission against money-laundering, created in 1999. The Commission has already published three reports focussing on Liechtenstein, Monaco, and Switzerland.

City of London Attracts Money-Launderers

The study focusses first on the susceptibilities of the City of London due to its role as "premier financial market in the world."

Beyond its long historical experience, what makes the City of London so attractive to money-launderers is the process of financial deregulation which has occurred over the last 30 years. The City "recovered its financial importance after World War II, in particular in 1958, with the relaxing of exchange controls and the development of a Euro-bond market [dollar-denominated bonds issued in Europea] in the 1960s. The abolition of exchange controls in 1979 further boosted the City, a process amplified in 1986 by a series of deregulation measures (the Big Bang)." Deregulation and banking secrecy attract banking establishments from throughout the world. Its 481 foreign banks (twice the number of New York or Tokyo) manage nearly half of the banking assets deposited in Britain, for a total of $2.4 trillion.

On the international level, with $3.5 trillion in banking assets, the City is the strongest financial market, closely followed by New York ($3.4 trillion). The City is the world's leading center for currency trading, and with stock from some 500 companies representing 60 different countries traded at the London Stock Exchange, it is the most international of the stock exchanges. London is also number one in the specialized markets (oil, precious metals, etc.).

The City's Code of Silence

To this difficulty the report adds another one: the fact that the City of London is a state within a state. Sometimes called "the square mile," it has its own local authorities as well as justice and police representatives. The City is run by the "Corporation of London," whose powers are important. One of its main tasks is to promote the financial center. The head of the Corporation is also its ambassador to foreign countries and has a mandate to defend the interests of British finance internationally.

The City possesses its own police force under the authority of the Corporation of London, which collaborates in principle with the London police. In reality, says the Parliamentary report, "as certain French magistrates were able to confirm directly, the City police is the best guardian of banking secrecy." French Judge Van Ruymbeke reported to the Parliamentary Commission that an Italian judge, who had received no response to his investigative requests for six months, decided to go to Britain and question the head of the suspect bank directly. "He was taken into an office where there were seven or eight people and where the following sequence unfolded: He asked a question to the London policeman, who asked the same question to the City of London policeman, who then asked the same question to the bank's lawyer, who then turned to the bank official. The latter responded through the same circuit. "

The City of London has been identified in a recent French Parliamentary report as a major center of drug-money-laundering.

The report concludes, "The City thus clearly constitutes an impenetrable fortress with its particular statutes, its rituals, and its habits. A closed universe in which each financier, banker, or businessman has first of all chosen to remain silent."

Following a certain amount of scandal—the Lloyds Names, the bankruptcy of Barings, the Bank of Commerce and Credit International (BCCI), the Robert Maxwell affair, and others—Tony Blair was forced in 1997 to create more instruments of regulation. The Financial Services Authority (FSA) was created to be the sole organ of control and regulation of financial services, specifically, to lead the fight against money-laundering and endowed with reinforced disciplinary powers. One should note that prior to the creation of this agency, the City of London relied practically entirely on self-regulation. A 1992 wire from Agence France Presse (AFP) going back to 1992 reports on the Lloyds scandal. David Coleridge, the president of Lloyds, merely denied all the accusations, claiming "that an investigation was not necessary, and that the market . . . had always self-regulated among people of good company"!

Following the creation of the FSA and other measures taken in the 1990s, Great Britain adopted on paper, legislation quite similar to that of other Group of Eight countries. There is no political will, however, to enforce that legislation, some-thing which is confirmed by the small number of people deployed to this effect. The National Criminal Intelligence Service (NCIS), which centralizes this, only deploys some 30 people to check over 15,000 cases yearly of suspected laundering by financial institutions. In 10 years, between 1986 and 1996, only 100 cases for laundering were tried. During the same time frame, Italy prosecuted 538 cases and the United States, 2,034. In the year 2000 in France, 154 dossiers were transmitted to the judiciary, 80 leading to prosecutions that very same year.

The report concludes that the "modesty of the British results is all the more scandalous when compared to the power of London. The premier financial market in the world, which every day registers several tens of millions of financial and stock transactions, has not seen more than 10 convictions per year for money-laundering. The policy of liberating capital movements and of deregulating financial markets went along with a deliberate absence of all control and all sanctions."

Interior Ministry Blocks All Demands

The French Parliamentary Commission met with nothing but complaints against Britain's complete lack of cooperation with law enforcement officials worldwide. French Judge Van Ruymbeke is categorical: "Great Britain is a flagrant case of non-cooperation [in the fight against laundering] . . . and without a word of explanation! I don't mind somebody explaining to me that one cannot execute a request for information because it creates a major problem with national interests, or because it is badly formulated or because there is a juridical problem. But these things should be said! That total silence after one, two, even three years, in spite of reminders, is unacceptable."

The Interior Ministry's central service in charge of judiciary aid is accused of blocking all requests. "This service is identified by many operatives, including the British, of being the essential element blocking the system. [The] Ministry is unavoidably more sensitive to issues of internal security of the United Kingdom than to the success of collaboration with foreign countries." This explains its "reticence to extradite certain Islamic activists" in order to "preserve the British territory from that type of terrorism."

French prosecutor Jean Pierre Dintillhac describes the "constant demands for precision and more information on dossiers, which end up by tying up the magistrates, through endless demands to present the requests in a different manner, to translate, to add texts of law." Jean Claude Marin, chief of the economic and financial division of the Paris prosecutor's office, states that the British procedure is "imperialist: Everything must be done by details. Thus, one must justify that the signature in the requests in indeed that of the judge, and one practically need an affidavit to certify that so-and-so, a first judge or an instructing magistrate, are indeed judges."

As a result, of the 392 international requests transmitted by France between January 1996 and June 1999, the British had not responded to 53% of the cases concerning financial delinquency, nor to 83% of the cases of money-laundering!

The Queen's Crown Dependencies

The French report includes a whole section on the offshore Crown dependencies, targetting the direct authority of the Queen over these territories which the United Kingdom uses as back-offices for money-laundering.

The report first goes one by one through the juridical status of those dependencies. Gibraltar: Since 1713, Gibraltar has been "a dependency of the United Kingdom of which the Queen of England is the head of state." The Isle of Man: "As in the case of Gibraltar, the head of state is the Queen of England." The Isle of Jersey "is also an autonomous territory whose head of state is the Queen of England, but which is not part of the United Kingdom"; Guernsey has the same status. These territories have been engaged since the 1960s in a rapid strategy of "development," offering a complete array of banking and financial services to a clientele of multinationals or top fortunes.

The Parliamentarians target specifically the creation of offshore companies created and managed by lawyers, or by firms specialized in creating those types of companies in offshore havens, operating totally outside the boundaries of law both in Britain and in the offshore havens. They provide a screen between the real money-launderers, for which they create and manage the company, and law-enforcement authorities. Total confidentiality is offered to the real owners of the companies.

The report quotes a former money-launderer in Gibraltar: He had set up seven companies which had been all created and were managed by a very well-known law firm of Gibraltar. These companies allowed him to "open up accounts, make transfers, make payments . . . . There is a lot to pay with checks and wires; you cannot pay everything in cash . . . . Those companies were registered with my lawyer's firm with whom I entertained excellent relations . . . . In a sense, it was my office in Gibraltar!"

If the bureaucratic blocking in Britain against any investigation is outrageous, that in the Crown dependencies is even worse. The report stresses, however, that the fight against those offshore centers is the responsibility of Britain. "The multiplication and the dynamism of those offshore centers lead one to question the real political will of the United Kingdom to use all its weight vis-à-vis those territories."

The report concludes by noting that the progress made by Britain since 1997 is flimsy, and that "the British government manifests no real political will to regulate professions such as those of agents creating companies which today totally escape the authority of the FSA." It calls for a determination to close down the offshore territories altogether.

Appendix III
The Colombia of Europe—
The KLA in the Balkans

The following profile of the KLA, the Taliban of the Balkans, is *adapted from a much longer article that appeared in* EIR *June 22, 2001.*

A large black spot, like ink on a piece of blotting paper, is spreading across the map of Europe. Kosovo, Albania, and a large part of the Balkans have been swallowed up; the Black Sea, through the Caucasus, is threatened—and the spot is spreading to merge with another such spot centered around Afghanistan. The "spot" does not respect national borders or ideological, ethnic, or religious differences, it just keeps spreading, bringing misery and destruction—on which it thrives. The "spot" is what was, until recently, labelled as the "black economy," or "illegal economy," or organized crime. In fact, it is a much more pervasive and totalitarian phenomenon. It represents the creation of a new perverse form of society: a modern form of feudal anarchy.

'National Security' Drug-Running
In Afghanistan, the production of opium under the Taliban regime continues to expand, to the point that, by June 2001, the main axis controlling more than 80% of the heroin market in Europe (plus a growing slice of the heroin market in other areas, including the United States) is the Afghanistan-Kosovo axis. Or better, a Taliban-Kosovo Liberation Army axis.

One of the targets of the Taliban machine in Asia is the Russian province of Chechnya. Here, a fundamentalist "freedom fighter" organization, heavily financed and armed, has been trying to repeat the Afghan enterprise of the 1980s. The model is the same: Until recently, "Western" support; terrorism, use of organized crime and drug trafficking, forced recruitment; and violent imposition of feudal loyalty on the population on behalf of a cult-like fundamentalism.

Besides Chechnya, basically all of the southern region of Russia and almost all of the former Soviet states have been affected by growing terrorist movements with an Islamic fundamentalist façade, all traceable to the Taliban and their puppet-masters.

On May 8, 2001, commemorating the Allies' victory in World War II, Russian President Vladimir Putin compared the danger of this growing terrorist machine feeding on drug trafficking, to Fascism and Nazism: "fascism is only one example of extreme radicalism. At the end of the 1930s, Europe and the U.S. could not unite to prevent the Hitlerian aggression, and they paid a heavy price."

The Taliban-KLA Axis
On March 18, while his country was in the middle of fending off a ferocious and well-organized assault by the Kosovo Liberation Army aimed at provoking a bloody ethnic confrontation between Macedonians and ethnic Albanians, Macedonia's Prime Minister Ljubco Georgievski launched a dramatic appeal to the nation. "It is obvious that the international community cannot run away from the fact that this time we are dealing with the creation of a new Taliban by the

Western democracies within Europe," he said. He indicated in clear terms what was behind the well-armed, well-trained, and well-financed gangs that had invaded his country, using as their base a Kosovo province solidly under the control of NATO's Kosovo Forces (KFOR).

"It's the same old story. Ten [twenty—ed.] years ago we were arming and equipping the worst elements of the mujahideen in Afghanistan—drug traffickers, arms smugglers, anti-American terrorists," said Michael Levine, former U.S. counter-narcotic agent and one of the most decorated agents of the U.S. Drug Enforcement Administration (DEA), in May 1999. "We later paid the price when the World Trade Center was bombed [in 1993—ed.], and we learned that some of those responsible had been trained by us. Now we're doing the same thing with the KLA, which is tied in with every known Middle and Far Eastern drug cartel. Interpol, Europol, and nearly every European intelligence and counter-narcotics agency has files open on drug syndicates that lead right to the KLA, and right to Albanian gangs in this country."

Levine explained that "my contacts within the DEA are, quite frankly, terrified, but there's not much they can say without risking their job. The Albanian mob is a scary operation. In fact, the Mafia relied on Albanian hit-men to carry out a lot of their contracts. . . . And now, according to my sources in drug enforcement, they are politically protected."

A good method to track down the cancerous growth of the "black spot" is to look at the traffic of illegal drugs, heroin in particular. Almost all of the heroin circulating in Europe comes through the Balkans. It is mostly produced from opium cultivated in the Taliban-dominated Afghanistan and refined in Turkey. It is distributed mostly by the so-called "Kosovo mafia," whose military excrescence is known as the Kosovo Liberation Army (KLA) or the Ushtria Clirimtare e Kosoves (UCK), operating inside Serbia as the Liberation Army of Presevo, Medvedja, and Bujanovac (UCPMB), and in Macedonia as the National Liberation Army (UCK).

Opium War on Russia and West Europe

In 1988, when the Soviet troops withdrew, Afghanistan and bordering areas in Pakistan were producing about 955 tons of opium per year, one-third of the world's production. A tremendous financial resource was placed in the hands of the Taliban. The opium, refined mostly in Turkey, was smuggled into Europe by the Turkish mafia, which dominated the so-called Balkan Route, previously given the misleading name of the "Bulgarian Connection." Heroin was coming into Europe through Yugoslavia, and part of it was consistently shipped into Italy from Albania and Montenegro.

But suddenly, a new organized-crime cartel emerged, the Albanian mafia, or better, the Kosovo mafia.

In 1996, the DEA, in a report prepared for the National Narcotics Intelligence Consumers Committee, stressed: "Drug-trafficking organizations composed of ethnic Albanians from Serbia's Kosovo Province were considered to be second only to Turkish groups as the predominant heroin smugglers along the Balkan Route. These groups were particularly active in Bulgaria, the former Yugoslav Republic of Macedonia, and Serbia. Kosovan traffickers were noted for their use of violence and for their involvement in international weapons trafficking. There is increasing evidence that ethnic criminals from the Balkans are engaged in criminal activities in the United States and some of that activity involves theft of licit pharmaceutical products for illicit street distribution."

In the section on Southwest Asia, the report noted: "Despite the country's political shift to Islamic fundamentalism, Afghanistan maintained its position as the second largest producer of opium in the world." The report pointed out that Afghanistan's opium production went through "six straight years of increases during which the crop more than tripled." It also admitted, that "according to the United Nations Drug Control Program (UNDCP), total opium production is much higher [than the DEA's figures]. Relying on an in country survey of Afghan opium poppy farmers, the UNDCP estimates a potential opium yield of 2,336 metric tons from 56,824 hectares of opium poppies."

In a euphemistic passage, the DEA's report noticed with disappointment that "despite early pronouncements on their aversion to drug cultivation and production, the Taliban appears to have reached an accommodation with opium poppy farmers." It was much more than an "accommodation," of course. From then on, the Taliban's opium invasion of Europe increased, and with it, the power and the criminal machine of the Kosovo mafia and the KLA skyrocketted as well.

Several intelligence reports have stated that bin Laden and his organization, al-Qaeda, have both trained and financially supported the KLA. Bin Laden has been connected to one of the most prominent "staging areas" for the KLA, before the terrorist organization took over Kosovo with the help of 78 days of air bombing and war by NATO in 1999. The "staging area" is the Albanian town of Tropoje.

KLA: From Hoxha to Albright

Though the KLA emerged in the international media only at the end of the 1990s, the organization goes back at least to 1982, when the Albanian dictator Enver

Hoxha—who controlled Albania with an iron fist and a cult-like radicalism from World War II to the early 1980s—was pushing with every means the Greater Albania project. The first modern sponsor of Greater Albania was Hoxha, who called for the union of all Albanians-including Albania, Kosovo, the southern part of Serbia, the northwestern part of Macedonia, the northern part of Greece—especially after the death of Yugoslavia's President Josip Broz Tito in 1980.

The Kosovo radical hard-core created international centers in Switzerland, Germany, and other European cities, in addition to Hoxha's Albania. The KLA's original core went through a large number of elaborated Marxist-Leninist party names, mixing up the idea of Greater Albania with radical Hoxha thought.

They were kept in a state of political suspended animation, with minor spurts of activity, until Bosnia's Dayton Peace Agreement in 1995. Then they were activated to take advantage of the wave of resentment which spread through the Kosovars for having been "left out" of the Dayton agreement (the province had lost its autonomy in 1989, in a Serbian decision pushed through by then emerging leader Slobodan Milosevic).

Of course, there were a lot of political activities in Kosovo itself among the ethnic Albanians, but these had nothing to do with the KLA. The Kosovars formed a sort of self-declared autonomy under the leadership of Ibrahim Rugova and his Democratic League of Kosovo (LDK); Rugova advocates nonviolence and was known as the "Gandhi of the Balkans." Still now in Kosovo, despite the KLA terror regime, Rugova has the support of the ethnic Albanians. However, the KLA usurped Rugova's leadership thanks to two elements: first, the support of U.S. and British leaders, in particular Clinton Administration Secretary of State Madeleine Albright and British Prime Minister Tony Blair; and second, the support of the Kosovo mafia.

At the moment of the so-called peace negotiations in Rambouillet, a NATO assault on Serbia, Montenegro, and Kosovo had already been decided. The use of the KLA gangs inside Kosovo, especially to "triangulate" and guide the air bombings from the ground, had also been decided. The training of the KLA had been going on for a long time.

The Colombia of Europe

The NATO air campaign increased the power of the Kosovo mafia dramatically, in terms of its criminal activities and its control over the population, by eliminating every obstacle, even the vestige of a narcotics police. The bombing campaign also fed the KLA's predisposition to broaden its area of control, starting with Serbia and Macedonia.

Under the ceasefire agreement of June 1999, the KLA was supposed to disarm and disband. The 5,000 KLA guerrillas were to join the unarmed, civil protection Kosovo Protection Corps (KPC) under the leadership of the KLA military commander, Agim Cequ. Cequ is a former general in the Croatian army, reportedly trained by Military Professional Resources, Inc. (MPRI), a U.S. firm based in Alexandria, Virginia. MPRI includes on its board some of the highest-level retired U.S. military officers and is specialized in "privately" arming, training, and "advising" foreign governments and foreign groups, including the KLA.

The KLA is better armed than ever, according to observers, and based on the findings of secret weapons caches in Kosovo, Serbia, and Macedonia. Evidence is also piling up that the structure of the KLA-KPC coincides with that of the Kosovo mafia. The Albright-sponsored Thaci continues to be the political leader of Kosovo, despite the fact that his political adversary, Ibrahim Rugova, can still count on the large majority of the Kosovo-Albanian votes. "Kosovo is set to become the cancer center of Europe, as Western Europe will soon discover," stated Marko Nikovic, vice-president of the New York-based International Narcotic Enforcement Officers Association, speaking to the London *Guardian* March 13, 2000, one year after the NATO bombing campaign had officially installed the KLA in power in Kosovo.

"It is the hardest narcotics ring to crack, because it is all run by families," said Nikovic, who estimated that as of March 2000, the Kosovo mafia was handling between four and a half and five tons of heroin a month, and growing fast, compared with two tons per month before NATO and the KLA took over the province. "It's coming through easier and cheaper, and there is much more of it. The price is going down, and if this goes on, we are predicting a heroin boom in Western Europe, as there was in the early '80s"—i.e., the boom due to the increase in opium production in Afghanistan and Pakistan during the Afghanistan war. Sources in the Balkans have confirmed that the Kosovo mafia bosses, divided into four major families, are concentrating even more on Western European and U.S. markets. A high-level informant admitted, "There is nobody to stop them."

"Kosovo is the Colombia of Europe," Nikovic explained. "When Serb police [during the ruthless retaliation for the KLA assassination of Yugoslav police officers, which led to the NATO intervention] were burning houses in Kosovo, they were finding heroin stuffed in the roof. As far as I know there has not been a single report in the last year of KFOR seizing heroin. You have an entire country without a police force that knows what is going on. Everything is worked out on the basis of the family or clan structure—their diaspora have been in Turkey and Germany since Tito's purges, so the whole route is set up. Now they have found the one country between Asia and Europe that is not a member of Interpol."

"The KLA is indebted to Balkan drug organizations that helped funnel both cash and arms to the guerrillas before and after the conflict," according to a report published by the U.S.-based *Stratfor Global Intelligence* on March 3, 2000, entitled "Kosovo: One Year Later." "Kosovo is the heart of a heroin trafficking route that runs from Afghanistan through Turkey and the Balkans and into Western Europe . . . . The KLA must now pay back the organized crime elements. This would in turn create a surge in heroin traffic in the coming months, just as it did following the NATO occupation of Bosnia in the mid-1990s . . . . The route connecting the Taliban-run opium fields of Afghanistan to Western Europe's heroin market is dominated by the Kosovo Albanians; this 'Balkan Route' supplied 80% of Europe's heroin. The U.S. government has been—and likely continues to be—well aware of the heroin trade coming through Kosovo, as well as the KLA connection . . . . For the KLA, the Balkan route is not only a way to ship heroin to Europe, but it has also acted as a conduit for weapons filtering into the war-torn Balkans."

According to a NATO report which surfaced in June 1999, after the end of the bombings, "the smugglers" either trade drugs directly for weapons or buy weapons with drug earnings in Albania, Bosnia, Croatia, Cyprus, Italy, Montenegro, Switzerland, or Turkey. The arsenal of weapons smuggled into Kosovo has included: anti-aircraft missiles, assault rifles, sniper rifles, mortars, grenade launchers, anti-personnel mines, and infrared night vision gear.

As long ago as Feb. 1,1995, the British *Jane's Intelligence Review,* considered very close to intelligence circles, wrote an analysis called "The Balkan Medellín," which described a scenario in which Macedonia would become the target of "Albanian narco-terrorism," especially using the "Albaniandominated region of western Macedonia," an area dominated by drug trafficking that makes it much "richer" than the rest of Macedonia.

"The Albanian-dominated region of Western Macedonia accounts for a disproportionate share of Macedonia's shrinking GDP," reads the 1995 *Jane's* report. "This situation has strengthened Albanophobic sentiments among the ethnic Macedonian majority, especially as a great deal of revenue is thought to derive from Albanian narco-terrorism as well as associated gun-running and cross-border smuggling to and from Albania, Bulgaria and the Kosovo province of Serbia. This rising Albanian economic power is helping to turn the Balkans into a hub of criminality . . . . [The Albanian mafia is] closely associated to the powerful Sicilian mafia. If left unchecked, this growing Albanian narco-terrorism could lead to a Colombian syndrome in the Southern Balkans, or the emergence of a situation in which the Albanian mafia becomes powerful enough to control one or more states in the region."

Appendix IV
Financier George Soros—Drug-Legalizer Extraordinaire

George Soros is 71 years old, travels on an American passport, and presents himself as a philosopher-businessman philanthropist. He is, in reality, an operative for certain international financial/political interests, involved in drugs, dirty money, and irregular warfare (ranging from stockjobbing to media control) to subvert nations, and cause destruction. As of the 1990s, he had become *persona non grata* in many parts of the world. He is under criminal investigation in several nations— particularly Italy. In 1993, the chairman of the U.S. House of Representatives Banking Committee called for an investigation, after the blatant episode of Soros's having made $1-2 billion in September 1992, off European currency manipulation. But Soros is still at large, and presented in the United States as just a "public figure."

Investigating Soros and those whom he serves, will directly expose networks capable of the kind of assault operations now underway against the United States. To aid such an investigation, in April 1997, *EIR News Service* issued a 70-page Special Report, "The True Story of Soros the Golem; A Profile of Megaspeculator George Soros." We here summarize a few key points.

Drug Legalization, Narco-Money

As "philanthropist," George Soros is both the primary financier of the international drug legalization lobby, and is also a leading financier of the drug cartel's narcoterrorist machine—a connection particularly well documented in Colombia. Soros is deploying hundreds of millions of dollars a year for a narcotics-decriminalization "propaganda machine" that is now operating in about 18 countries in North and South America, the Caribbean, Europe, and Australia.

In South America, the Soros group, Human Rights Watch/Americas (formerly Americas Watch) functions as an integral part of the drug cartel's drug production and terror apparatus in at least the three major drug-producing countries— Colombia, Peru, and Bolivia.

Human Rights Watch/Americas in 1995 set up a new Drug Program, with its first year's sole objective of hampering *anti-drug* programs around the world, through alleging "human rights abuses." HRW stated at that time, that because, "national and international counter-narcotics programs . . . by and large have escaped close human rights scrutiny, in early 1995 HRW began a multi-year effort to document and challenge human rights violations caused or exacerbated by efforts to curtail drug trafficking internationally as well as in the United States."

Inside the United States, Soros has created and financed a phalanx of agencies for propaganda, pressure, money conduits, etc. for legalizing dope. On July 8, 1994, when Human Rights Watch/Americas head Aryeh Neier moved over to become president of Soros' Open Society Institute-New York, Soros ponied up $10.5 million in matching funds to be spent over a three-year period to fund an allied group, the Drug Policy Foundation (DPF), which is America's leading lobby for drug legalization. Soros had already given the DPF over $500,000 since 1992. The $10.5-million grant from Soros broke down as a $6-million pledge—$3 million for operational support and $3 million for grant support—and the remainder matched by other donors.

Kevin Zeese, formerly the national director of the National Organization for the Reform of Marijuana Laws (NORML), who at the time of Soros's DPF donation served as the DPF's vice-president and counsel, bragged that the money would allow for massive expansion on the part of DPF.

This came to be, with a priority on state-level referenda to legalize drugs for "medical use." This is seen as the wedge into all out dope decriminalization.

Soros effectively "bought" passage of drug legalization measures on Nov. 5, 1996, in California (Proposition 215) and in Arizona (Proposition 200), both for permitting "medical use" of Schedule 1 narcotics. Since then, there have been other states and referenda.

In Arizona, $440,000 of the $440,490 raised by proponents of Prop 200 came from Soros' pocket. An additional $25,000 was spent on polling by the pro-drug-legalization Drug Policy Foundation (DPF), which had received a $3-million operating program and a $3-million grant program from Soros.

For Prop 215 in California, Soros directly contributed some $550,000, and the Drug Policy Foundation, backed by him, gave another $200,000, amounting together to over one-third the cost of the referendum drive.

In his book, *Soros on Soros,* Soros writes, "I think that to treat the drug problem primarily as a criminal problem is a misconception . . . . I just think the whole idea of eradicating the drug problem is a false idea."

Soros' dope decriminalization drive is the leading part of a general set of foundations and frontgroups Soros is backing, in the name of "Open Society" and "free markets" globally, in particular throughout Eastern Europe. They function as a channels for institutional control, secret operations, money flows, pro-dope legalization, etc. A focal point for this is the Soros-created and patronized Central European University, based primarily in Budapest, but with important branches in Warsaw and Prague.

The first Soros foundation was the Open Society Fund, founded in 1979, and since December 1993, the Open Society Institute-New York. As of 1997, there were 24 national foundations in this Soros web, from the Soros Foundation-Moldova (1992), to the Open Society Foundation for South Africa (1993), and Open Society-Moscow (1995). In 1994, the expenditures for all Soros foundations were approximately $300 million; Soros is chairman of them all.

On Dec. 7, 1996, Soros' activities in Croatia were denounced by President Franjo Tudjman, in a speech to the ruling party, "In a nutshell, they created a state within the state to destabilize Croatia." On Dec. 23 that month, Croatia's Ministry of Internal Affairs announced criminal proceedings against Soros' Open Society Institute, for financial crimes—tax-dodging, forgery, falsification of currency records, etc.

Financial Warfare

In his nominal occupation—financial speculation, Soros has specialized in hit-and-run attacks on whole nations. His main business address has been his Quantum Fund NY, which is registered in Curacao, Netherlands Antilles, the Caribbean tax haven. This way he has avoided paying taxes, and also had hidden the nature of his investors, and he what does with their money. He thus operates as merely the visible face of a vast and very nasty network of private financial interests, including interconnections with leading aristocratic and royal ramilies of Europe, centered in the British House of Windsor. (This secret private network is called by its members, the "Club of the Isles.")

1992. At the time of the September 1992, crisis of the European Exchange Rate Mechanism, Soros was among the leading speculators against the British and Italian currencies which wrecked the European Exchange Rate Mechanism (ERM). But the target was not Britain as victim (though millions were hurt when the pound sank); the target—which was hit, was to knock apart the monetary cohesion of the European countries, and prevent movement toward any Eurasian economic recovery strong enough to resist British free-trade looting.

More particularly, the speculative attacks at this time led to a devastating devaluation of the Italian lira by about 30%, and to a complete dry-out of the reserves of the Italian Central Bank. Some $48 billion went out to defend the lira—and lost. Soros made an estimated $282 million from the lira devaluation, besides the $1-2 billion off the devaluation of the pound sterling.

In Italy, the impact of the lira devaluation was to cheapen the cost of purchase of Italian industry and other assets forced to be "privatized" by sell-off to global purchasers. Contingency plans for this were discussed by representatives of Soros earlier in 1992, in Italy, on June 2, at an infamous meeting on the *Britannia,* the yacht of Her Majesty Queen Elizabeth II, off the coast, with Italian government officials.

A judicial investigation of this was prompted by the filing of a legal brief—an *esposto*—in October 1995, by Paolo Raimondi, president of the International Civil Rights Solidarity Movement, with prosecutors in Milan, Rome, Naples and Florence. By December, 1996, follow-up had proceeded to the point that the Rome

Magistrate had posted George Soros' name on a list of persons subject to arrest, if they visit Italy, with intent to "obstruct justice" in terms of the investigation.

1997. In spring and summer 1997, George Soros and his Quantum Fund, were at the forefront of the hit-and-run speculative attacks on currencies and stock values in Southeast Asian nations, which forced 30-70% currency devaluations, destabilizations and impoverishment. The International Monetary Fund backed Soros in the name of "global capital flows." Malaysian President Mahathir Mohamad said in an interview with Fortune, Soros "has wiped out billions of dollars from our economy." Mahathir charged, "We have definite information that he is involved . . . . Of course, he is not the only one . . . but he started it."

Books from Progressive Press, 2002-2019

9/11 on Trial
9/11 Synthetic Terror: Made in USA
A Century of War
Barack H. Obama: The Unauthorized Biography
Battling Wall Street: The Kennedy Presidency
Before Our Very Eyes, Fake Wars and Big Lies
Conspiracies, Conspiracy Theories, and the Secrets of 9/11
Corporatism: The Secret Government of the New World Order
Dope, Inc: Britain's Opium War against the United States
Ecology, Ideology and Power
Enemies by Design
Facts and Fascism
Fall of the Arab Spring: From Revolution to Destruction
Final Warning: A History of the New World Order
Full Spectrum Dominance
George Bush: The Unauthorized Biography
Gladio: NATO's Dagger at the Heart of Europe
Global Predator
Gods of Money
How the World Really Works
ISIS IS US: The Shocking Truth
JFK - 9/11: 50 Years of Deep State
Just Too Weird
Killing Us Softly: the Global Depopulation Policy
Numbers of the Gods
Obama - The Postmodern Coup
One Thousand Americans: The Real Rulers of the USA
Presstitutes Embedded in the Pay of the CIA
Propaganda for War
Subverting Syria
Sunk: The Story of the Japanese Submarine Fleet
Surviving the Cataclysm
Target China
Terror on the Tube
Terrorism and the Illuminati
The Iraq Lie
The Kennedy Assassination Cover-up
The Money Power
The Nazi Hydra in America
The New World Order in Action
The Rape of the Mind
The Telescreen
The War on Freedom
Truth Jihad
Unmasking ISIS

www.ingramcontent.com/pod-product-compliance
Ingram Content Group UK Ltd.
Pitfield, Milton Keynes, MK11 3LW, UK
UKHW021308191224
3776UKWH00045B/524